THE
FOOD LOVER'S
TIPTIONARY

THE
FOOD LOVER'S
TIPTIONARY

AN A TO Z CULINARY GUIDE WITH MORE THAN 4,500
FOOD AND DRINK TIPS, SECRETS, SHORTCUTS, AND
OTHER THINGS COOKBOOKS NEVER TELL YOU

Sharon Tyler Herbst

Hearst Books

New York

It is the policy of William Morrow and Company, Inc., and its imprints and affiliates, recognizing the importance of preserving what has been written, to print the books we publish on acid-free paper, and we exert our best efforts to that end.

Library of Congress Cataloging-in-Publication Data

Herbst, Sharon Tyler.
    The food lover's tiptionary / Sharon Tyler Herbst.
        p.   cm.
    Includes index.
    ISBN 0-688-12146-2
    1. Cookery—Dictionaries.   I. Title.
TX349.H534   1993
641.3'03—dc20   93-14280
                                                    CIP

Printed in the United States of America

    3   4   5   6   7   8   9   10

BOOK DESIGN BY MICHAEL MENDELSOHN OF MM DESIGN 2000, INC.

Dedicated with love to Tia Tyler Leslie,
my beautiful and talented sister,
for inspiring me to write this book
and for always being there for me
with her wholehearted love and support

Acknowledgments

With each book I write (this is the sixth), it becomes ever more clear that creating a tome like *The Food Lover's Tiptionary* would be difficult at best without the behind-the-scenes support from family, friends and colleagues. This, then, is a heartfelt hug-in-print for all those dear people including:

Ron Herbst—my hero, husband, and best friend—for making me laugh and for being my anchor, business and creative consultant, computer expert, number one taster, hand-holder . . . in short, my everything;

Kay and Wayne Tyler (Mom and Dad), two of my biggest fans, for their unstinting love, support, encouragement and belief that I can accomplish anything I set my mind to;

Harriet Bell, my extraordinary editor, whose talent, wisdom, sense of humor and enthusiastic support for me and the *Tiptionary* made writing this book *pure pleasure*;

Fred Hill, my brilliant literary agent for whom I have great respect and affection, for his sagacity, wise counsel, invaluable guidance and urbane wit;

Lisa and Lou Ekus, for their incredible enthusiasm, friendship and support, both personally and through the auspices of their unsurpassed company— Lisa Ekus Public Relations;

The many branches on my support-system tree including: John, Johnny and Mildred Arwood; Sue and Gene Bain; Tommie Bloemer; Leslie Bloom; Walt and Carol Boice; Irena Chalmers; Phillip Cooke; Roni Durie; Rick Fox; Don and Donna France; Joan Gage; Joyce, Lew, Barry, Julie and Brian Herbst; Bob and Angie Irvine; Susan and Lee Janvrin; Sue and Wayne Jones; Jeanette, Tex, Kevin and John Kinney; Daniel Maye; Donna and Steve Michaud; Mary and Terry Miller; Glenn, Laura, Yei and Ken Miwa; David Nussbaum and the Ekus gang; and Kimberley and Dan Young

And all the talented people at Morrow/Hearst Books, who worked long and hard without fanfare on the design, layout, proofing and the dozens of other tasks it took to create this book in its final form

INTRODUCTION

"A host is like a general: it takes a mishap to reveal his genius."

—Horace

One day when my sister Tia and I were lunching at her house she said, "Sometimes I feel like my kitchen's a field of land mines. There are so many ways to ruin a good meal, and I've managed most of them."

Tia proceeded to recount a dinner party she'd given the previous weekend when almost everything went wrong. Her puff-pastry appetizers burned (black!) on the bottom; the flank steak (which she'd lovingly marinated forty-eight hours to tenderize) became flank "leather" on the grill; the cooked broccoli turned an unappetizing khaki green; the hollandaise for the broccoli separated into curdled clumps; and the homemade banana-rum ice cream didn't freeze. The tossed green salad and store-bought cookies, I was relieved to hear, turned out fine.

My heart went out to her—that many culinary mishaps are enough to bring any cook to her knees. But as we discussed it further, I could see that each and every one of Tia's "land mines" could have been avoided—or at least defused.

To start with, we used an oven thermometer and discovered that Tia's oven was almost fifty degrees hotter than the dial setting. That in itself was enough to overbrown her puff pastries, but she also used a dark baking sheet (which absorbs more heat) and baked the pastries on the bottom shelf of her electric oven—right above the heating element. *We're talking trouble here!*

The grilled-meat problem was simple to diagnose—it was overcooked, and even slightly overdone flank steak is unpalatably tough. I'd assumed the discolored broccoli was also the result of overcooking, but Tia insisted it was crisp-tender. "The only thing I did different," she said, "was add a little lemon juice during cooking to bring out the flavor." *Bingo!* I told her how acids like lemon juice or vinegar in the cooking water will turn broc-coli's lively green color to a sickly yellow-green.

I suggested that the hollandaise might have curdled because the heat was too high. My sister grinned sheepishly, "Well, everything else was getting done too fast so I tried to hurry things along by turning up the heat." She ended up throwing out the hollandaise. Too bad—she could have easily saved it by whisking in a little boiling water, or by turning the sauce into a blender and processing until smooth.

The ice cream disaster was traced to a bit of ad-libbing on Tia's part. "Well," she said, "I thought it would taste better with just a little more rum." *Oh-oh.* Evidentally *too* much rum because her ice cream was the con-sistency of soft pudding—probably the result of the extra alcohol, which freezes at a lower temperature than cream.

As Tia and I discussed her ill-fated evening, she was amazed at how easily her culinary traumas could have been avoided. "Do me a favor," she said, "write it all down so I don't have to relive that nightmare." She should have known better than to make such a suggestion to a writer. But, then, book ideas are born from such words.

And so I began to think about writing a kitchen-tip dictionary. My sister's cooking dilemmas, I realized, were not at all uncommon. I'd certainly en-countered my share—everything from rice burning on the bottom of a pot, to eggs sticking to the carton, to a cake that won't come out of the pan. Unfortunately, most cookbooks just don't explain how to solve life's little cooking quandaries. But I knew from experience that there's generally a way out, and usually more than one approach to solving a cooking problem.

Well, it didn't take long for me to decide to write what I had already dubbed the "tiptionary," and I was excited about it. But first I had to estab-lish the book's framework. From the start, I knew the tiptionary had to be imminently user-friendly and bursting with more helpful information than any other kitchen-tip book. I wanted it to increase the reader's cooking skills, confidence and enjoyment—to make life easier in the kitchen—to show them how to cook *smarter,* not harder. I wanted to help the reader disarm those "culinary land mines" with what I hoped would be a "gold mine" of culinary wisdom. But this book had to have something for every-one—from the accomplished cook, to the sometimes cook, to the beginner, to the noncook (someone who simply wants to know how to open a bottle of champagne or set the table for guests). In short, I wanted it to be an all-around good read for *every* food lover.

Once the parameters for *The Food Lover's Tiptionary* were drawn the real fun began—months of research and testing. Luckily, I had a great start, having gathered countless tips over the years—many of which I discovered through trial and error during a decade of professional cooking, and many that were passed along by friends, family, readers, students and fellow food pros. The process was pure pleasure, not to mention educational. The following pages are the end result of almost two years of work—more than four thousand five hundred tips, hints and shortcuts on hundreds of subjects including foods, beverages, cooking techniques, preparations, kitchen equipment, table settings and cleaning up.

The Food Lover's Tiptionary includes information on everything from bok choy to braising, from maple syrup to MSG, and from thermometers to tortillas. You'll discover a panoply of helpful hints including: how to deglaze a pan; how to make high-altitude adjustments; how to tell if an egg is fresh; how to store, pour and cook with wine; ways to cut fat and cholesterol; how to speed-chill beverages; techniques for accurate measuring; how to use chopsticks; how to properly set a table; serving secrets; how to read and understand a label; and whether or not alcohol burns off during cooking.

The tips in this book are arranged by subject, from A to Z. Where appropriate, information on buying, storing, preparing, cooking and serving is included. I tried to avoid what I call "esoteric information"—tips requiring something special that's not readily available in most kitchens. Throughout *The Food Lover's Tiptionary* you'll find pronunciations for many of the more uncommon words (and those commonly mispronounced), quick and easy reference charts, a handy system of cross-referencing and hundreds of shorthand-style recipes.

One of the things I find so fascinating about the realm of food and drink is that it's in a constant state of evolution. Discoveries are made, old truths are dispelled and new facts are uncovered constantly. That being said, I welcome your input on any of your favorite kitchen tips that aren't in this book (send them to me in care of Morrow). Who knows, we might just use them in *The Food Lover's Tiptionary II* one day.

In closing, I humbly pass these tasty bits of kitchen wisdom on, confident that they'll better equip you for everything from daily cooking to entertaining. I hope you'll use *The Food Lover's Tiptionary* often, that it serves you well, and that you find as much satisfaction in using it as I did in writing it.

THE
FOOD LOVER'S
TIPTIONARY

ABALONE [a-buh-LOH-nee]

▶ Like all fresh shellfish, abalone should be alive when purchased (the exposed muscle should move when touched) and smell sweet, not fishy. Choose those that are relatively small.

▶ Fresh abalone should be refrigerated immediately and cooked within a day.

▶ Abalone is also sold canned (once opened, refrigerate, covered with water in a sealed container, for up to 5 days), dried (store tightly wrapped in a cool, dry place indefinitely) and frozen (store for up to 3 months).

▶ Since the edible portion of abalone is a muscle, it must be pounded to make it tender. Use a mallet to flatten the meat to a ⅛- to ¼-inch thickness.

▶ Overcooking abalone toughens it. Sauté it briefly for no more than 20 to 30 seconds per side.

▶ Prevent abalone from curling during cooking by slashing the meat at ½-inch intervals with a sharp knife.

▶ Mince overcooked, tough abalone and make soup or chowder with it.

▶ *See also* SHELLFISH

ACIDULATED WATER [a-SIHD-yoo-lay-ted]

▶ Some recipes call for dipping certain peeled or cut fruits and vegetables (such as apples, artichokes and pears) in acidulated water to prevent their flesh from turning brown. To acidulate water simply add an acid such as vinegar, lemon juice or wine to it. For each quart of cold water, add 1½ tablespoons vinegar, or 3 tablespoons lemon juice, or ½ cup white wine.

ADDITIVES

▶ The word "additive" has a negative connotation for many people, but it's important that we be educated regarding what we're eating. According to the Food and Drug Administration (FDA), food additives are substances intentionally added to food either directly or indirectly with one or more of the following purposes: 1. To maintain or improve nutritional quality; 2. To maintain product quality and/or freshness; 3. To aid in the processing or preparation of food; and 4. To make food more appealing.

▶ Additives are strictly regulated—manufacturers must prove that those to be added to food are safe, a process that can take several years. The results of such studies are presented to the FDA, who then determines how the additive can be used in food.

- Some 2,800 substances are added to foods for one or more of the four listed purposes.
- In the United States, about 98 percent (by weight) of all food additives used are in the form of baking soda, citric acid, corn syrup, mustard, pepper, salt, sugar and vegetable colorings.
- The following chart (preceeded by an explanatory key) lists substances commonly added to foods and the reasons for their use.

SUBSTANCES COMMONLY ADDED TO SOME FOODS:

Acetic acid	■ pH control agent
Acetone peroxide	■ maturing and bleaching agent, dough conditioner
Ammonium alginate	■ pH control agent
Annatto extract	▲ color
Arabingalactan	■ stabilizer, thickening texturizer
Benzoic acid	● preservative
Beta carotene	▲ nutrient
	● color
BHA (butylated hydroxyanisole)	● antioxidant
BHT (butylated hydroxytoluene)	● antioxidant
Butyparaben	● preservative
Calcium bromate	■ maturing and bleaching agent, dough conditioner
Calcium phosphate	■ leavening agent
Calcium propionate	● preservative
Canthaxanthin	▲ color
Carob bean gum	■ stabilizer, thickening texturizer
Cellulose	■ stabilizer, thickening texturizer
Dextrose	▲ sweetener
Diglycerides	■ emulsifier
Disodium guanylate	▲ flavor enhancer
Dried algae meal	▲ color
EDTA (ethylene-diaminetetra-acetic acid)	● antioxidant
FD & C Colors	
Blue No. 1	▲ color
Red No. 2	▲ color

Red No. 40	▲ color
Yellow No. 5	▲ color
Fructose	▲ sweetener
Glycerine	■ humectant
Grape-skin extract	▲ color
Guar gum	■ stabilizer, thickening texturizer
Gum arabic	■ stabilizer, thickening texturizer
Heptylparaben	● preservative
Hydrogen peroxide	■ maturing and bleaching agent, dough conditioner
Invert sugar	▲ sweetener
Iodine	◆ nutrient
Iron-ammonium citrate	■ anticaking agent
Iron oxide	▲ color
Lactic acid	■ pH control agent
	● preservative
Locust bean gum	■ stabilizer, thickening texturizer
Mannitol	▲ sweetener
	■ anticaking agent; stabilizer, thickening texturizer
Methylparaben	● preservative
Modified food starch	■ stabilizer, thickening texturizer
Niacinamide	◆ nutrient
Phosphoric acid	■ pH control agent
Polysorbates	■ emulsifier
Potassium bromate	■ maturing and bleaching agent, dough conditioner
Potassium propionate	● preservative
Propylene glycol	■ stabilizer, thickening texturizer; humectant
Riboflavin	◆ nutrient
	▲ color
Saffron	▲ color
Silicon dioxide	■ anticaking agent
Sodium benzoate	● preservative
Sodium citrate	■ pH control agent
Sodium nitrate	● preservative
Sodium propionate	● preservative

Sodium stearyl fumarate	■ maturing and bleaching agent, dough conditioner
Sorbitan monostearate	■ emulsifier
Tagetes (Aztec Marigold)	▲ color
Tartaric acid	■ pH control agent
TBHQ (tertiary butyl hydroquinone)	● antioxidant
Titanium dioxide	▲ color
Tocopherols (vit. E)	◆ nutrient
	● antioxidant
Tragacanth gum	■ stabilizer, thickening texturizer
Ultramarine blue	▲ color
Vanilla	▲ flavor
Vitamin A	◆ nutrient
Vitamin C	◆ nutrient
	● preservative
	● antioxidant

KEY TO DEFINITIONS:
◆ **MAINTAIN OR IMPROVE NUTRITIONAL QUALITY**
 Nutrients: enrich (replace vitamins and minerals lost in processing) or fortify (add nutrients that may be lacking in the diet)
● **MAINTAIN PRODUCT QUALITY AND/OR FRESHNESS**
 Preservatives (Antimicrobials): prevent food spoilage from bacteria, molds, fungi and yeast; extend shelf life; or protect natural color or flavor
■ **AID IN PROCESSING OR PREPARATION**
 Emulsifiers: help to distribute evenly tiny particles of one liquid into another; improve homogeneity, consistency, stability or texture
 Stabilizers, Thickening Texturizers: impart body; improve consistency or texture; stabilize emulsions; affect "mouthful" of food
 Leavening Agents: affect cooking results—texture and volume
 pH Control Agents: change/maintain acidity or alkalinity
 Humectants: cause moisture retention
 Maturing and Bleaching Agents, Dough Conditioners: accelerate the aging process; improve baking qualities
 Anticaking Agents: prevent caking, lumping or clustering of a finely powdered or crystalline substance
▲ **AFFECT FOOD SO IT'S MORE APPEALING**
 Flavor Enhancers: supplement, magnify or modify the original taste and/or aroma of food without imparting a characteristic flavor of their own
 Flavors: heighten natural flavor; restore flavors lost in processing
 Colors: give desired, appetizing or characteristic color of food
 Sweeteners: make the aroma or taste of food more agreeable or pleasurable
▶ *See also* LABELS

Reprinted from *FDA Consumer* by permission of U.S. Department of Health, Education and Welfare Publication No. (FDA) 79-2115.

ALCOHOL

▶ Confused about what statements like "Two drinks per day is considered moderate alcohol consumption" really mean? What's considered a "drink"—a beer, a glass of wine, a jigger of whiskey? Well, 1 drink has been standardized as ½ ounce of pure (100 percent) alcohol, meaning moderate drinkers can consume 1 ounce of *pure* alcohol a day. This makes a difference in the volume consumed per serving, since the percentage of alcohol in beer is much lower than that in whiskey. In general, two "drinks" a day breaks down as follows: 1 ounce of 100-proof (50 percent alcohol) liquor; 1¼ ounces of 80-proof (40 percent alcohol) liquor; 3 ounces of fortified wine (16½ percent alcohol) like sherry or port; 4 ounces of (12½ percent alcohol) wine; or 12 ounces of (4 percent alcohol) beer.

▶ In the United States, the average amount of alcohol in distilled spirits is about 40 percent, or 80 proof.

▶ In the United States, "proof" is exactly twice the percentage of alcohol.

▶ Pure alcohol boils at 173°F, water at 212°F. A mixture of the two will boil somewhere between these two temperatures.

▶ Though it has long been thought that alcohol evaporates when heated, a USDA study has disproved that theory. In fact, from 5 to 85 percent alcohol may remain in a cooked dish, depending on various factors including how the food was heated, the cooking time, and the source of the alcohol. Even the smallest trace of alcohol may be ill-advised for alcoholics and those with alcohol-related illnesses.

▶ Because alcohol freezes at a much lower temperature than other liquids like water and milk, a frozen dessert (such as ice cream) that contains too much alcohol won't freeze properly.

▶ *See also* BEER; CHAMPAGNE; FLAMBÉING; LIQUOR, LIQUEURS AND MIXED DRINKS; WINE; WINE IN FOOD

ALMOND PASTE

▶ Almond paste is made with blanched ground almonds, sugar, glycerine or other liquid, and sometimes almond extract.

▶ The difference between almond paste and marzipan is that the latter contains more sugar, and sometimes egg whites.

▶ Almond paste is available in cans and plastic tubes, marzipan is generally found in plastic tubes. Both are commonly available in supermarkets.

▶ Once opened, almond paste and marzipan should be wrapped airtight and refrigerated.

▶ Though almond paste is the basis of marzipan, the two cannot successfully be interchanged in recipes.

▶ If almond paste or marzipan becomes hard, resoften by heating on HIGH in the microwave oven for 2 to 3 seconds.

A

ALMONDS

▸ *Almond yields:* 1 pound = 3 cups halves; 4 cups slivered.

▸ Blanch whole almonds by covering with boiling water and setting aside for 3 minutes. Strain off water, then slip off skins by squeezing almonds between your fingers and thumb. Blot with paper towels; spread the almonds in a single layer on a baking sheet and bake at 325°F for about 10 minutes.

▸ Before blanching almonds, taste them—the skin adds flavor to many dishes and baked goods, so if it isn't bitter, leave it on.

▸ Adding ¼ to ½ teaspoon pure almond extract to baked goods containing almonds will produce an even deeper almond flavor.

▸ *See also* NUTS, GENERAL *for general purchase, storage and usage information*

ALUMINUM FOIL [ah-LOO-mihn-uhm]

▸ Foods containing acidic ingredients (such as tomatoes, lemon or onions) should not come in direct contact with foil. Natural acids create a chemical reaction that can eat through the foil and/or affect the food's flavor.

▸ Aluminum foil shouldn't be reused to wrap foods for the freezer because tiny holes, created when the foil is crinkled, increase permeability.

▸ When baking food in foil, keep it from overbrowning by wrapping it shiny side out.

▸ Breadstuffs will stay warm longer if the bread basket is lined with foil, then a napkin.

▸ *See also* PLASTIC WRAP; WAXED PAPER

ANCHOVIES [AN-choh-vee; an-CHOH-vee]

▸ In the United States, anchovies are most often marketed canned in oil; choose those packed in olive oil.

▸ Canned anchovies will keep at room temperature for at least 1 year. Once opened, anchovies can be refrigerated for at least 2 months, provided they're covered with oil and the storage container is tightly sealed.

▸ Like the flavor of anchovies but find them too salty? Try soaking them in cool water for 10 to 20 minutes (the longer they're soaked, the less salty they'll be). Drain and pat dry with paper towels before using.

▸ Cover those you're not going to use right away with olive or vegetable oil and refrigerate.

▸ One half teaspoon anchovy paste (packaged in a tube and found in a supermarket's gourmet or canned fish section) is equivalent to 1 anchovy fillet.

▸ Make your own anchovy paste by pulverizing anchovy fillets with a mortar and pestle, or in a bowl with a fork.

▸ Use the oil from canned anchovies to flavor sauces, salad dressings or marinades.

▸ Whenever you add anchovies or their oil to a dish, always taste the dish before salting. Anchovies are so high in sodium that you may not need extra salt.

▸ *See also* FISH, GENERAL

APPLES

▸ Buy firm, well-colored apples with a fresh, not musty, fragrance. The skins should be tight, smooth and free of bruises and punctures.

▸ Choose the variety by how it'll be used—fresh (for eating out-of-hand, in salads, etc.), or cooked (as for applesauce and pies), or for baking whole. **All-purpose apples,** good for both cooking or eating raw, include Cortland, Crispin, Criterion, Empire, Fuji, Granny Smith, Gravenstein, Jonagold, Jonathan, Lady apple, Macoun, McIntosh, Newtown Pippin, Northern Spy, Stayman and Winesap. **Apples best for eating raw:** Gala, Golden Delicious and Red Delicious. **Apples good for cooking:** Gravenstein, Rhode Island Greening and York Imperial; **firmer varieties particularly good for baking**—Cortland, Northern Spy, Rome Beauty, Winesap and York Imperial.

▸ Store apples in a cool, dark place, or refrigerated in a plastic bag. If possible, don't let the apples touch each other during storage—they'll keep longer.

▸ *Apple yields:* 1 pound fresh = 2 large, 3 medium or 4 small; 2 to 2½ cups chopped or sliced. *Dried apples:* 1 pound = 4⅓ cups; 8 cups cooked.

▸ A dry, tan- or brown-colored area (called "scald") on an apple's skin is slightly tough, but doesn't usually affect flavor.

▸ To keep cut apples from browning, toss with lemon, orange or grapefruit juice, or dip them in 1 quart cold water mixed with 3 tablespoons lemon juice. Or, dip the apple pieces in lightly salted water. There's also a "color keeper" product made with ascorbic acid that's commonly available in supermarkets.

▸ If you're using apples in a salad with a vinaigrette, the acid in the dressing will keep the fruit from turning brown.

▸ Provide more support for baked apples by setting them in lightly greased muffin tins before baking.

▸ The skins of baked apples won't crack or burst if you cut several shallow slits around the sides of the fruit from which the steam can escape during baking.

▸ Reduce baked apple shrinkage by removing a ½-inch horizontal strip of peel from around the middle.

▸ For a wonderful breakfast dish, make sausage-stuffed baked apples. Core the apples and scoop out all but about a ¾-inch thick shell. Chop the scooped-out apple, combine it with 1 to 2 tablespoons crumbled, crisply cooked sausage, 2 teaspoons raisins and a dash of nutmeg. Return the mixture to the apple cavities and bake for about 45 minutes.

▸ Don't forget that cooked apples go nicely with meats like chicken, pork or veal, and vegetables like cabbage, onions or potatoes. They also compliment many soups and stews.

▸ If you want cooked apples to hold their shape, add any sugar called for in the recipe at the beginning of the cooking time.

▸ Apples that are past their prime lose moisture and flavor. Revive them by chopping coarsely, then covering with cold apple juice, and refrigerating for 30 minutes.

▸ Dried apples can be stored indefinitely if refrigerated tightly sealed in a plastic bag.

▸ *See also* APPLESAUCE; FRUIT, GENERAL

APPLESAUCE

▸ Any tart, cooking or all-purpose apple can be used to make applesauce.

▸ Sugar added at the beginning of the cooking time will help retain the apple's shape. So, for chunky applesauce, add the sugar before beginning to cook. For a softer applesauce, cook the apples first, then stir in the sugar.

▸ Combine 2 or more apple varieties to add interest to applesauce.

▸ Add color to homemade applesauce by leaving the peel on the fruit.

▸ A teaspoon or two of lemon juice can brighten the taste of oversweet applesauce.

▸ Honey and maple syrup make wonderful sweeteners for applesauce.

▸ Cranberry or cranapple juice adds color and flavor to applesauce.

▸ Just before serving applesauce, stir in a few tiny cinnamon candies—it'll please kids, young and old.

▸ Make fresh applesauce by combining chunks of apple (peeled or not) with a little orange juice, cinnamon and nutmeg in a blender or food processor fitted with the metal blade. Process to desired texture. Be sure to use either all-purpose apples or those meant for eating raw.

▸ *See also* APPLES

APRICOTS

▸ Buy plump, reasonably firm apricots with a uniform-colored skin. Depending on the variety, that color can range anywhere from pale yellow to deep burnt orange. Avoid fruit that's hard, green-tinged or noticeably bruised.

▸ Store unripe apricots at room temperature until ripe. Once ripe, apricots should be wrapped in a plastic bag and stored in the refrigerator for up to 3 days. They're very perishable, however, and lose their flavor rapidly.

▸ *Apricot yields:* 1 pound fresh = 8 to 12 whole; 2½ cups sliced or halved. *Dried apricots:* 1 pound = 2¾ cups; 5 cups cooked.

▶ Always handle fresh apricots gently—they bruise easily and the bruised flesh turns soft and flavorless.

▶ *See also* FRUIT, DRIED; FRUIT, GENERAL

ARROWROOT

▶ Arrowroot is a fine powder used for thickening. It comes from the dried rootstalks of a tropical tuber.

▶ Arrowroot's thickening power is about 1½ times that of all-purpose flour.

▶ Like cornstarch, arrowroot should be mixed with enough cold liquid to make a paste before being stirred into hot mixtures.

▶ Unlike cornstarch, arrowroot doesn't impart a chalky taste when undercooked.

▶ Arrowroot thickens mixtures at a lower temperature than either cornstarch or flour.

▶ Overstirring an arrowroot-thickened mixture can cause it to become thin again.

▶ Some British and early American recipes call for arrowroot flour, which is the same thing as arrowroot.

▶ *Substitutions for 1 tablespoon arrowroot:* 2¼ teaspoons cornstarch; or 1½ tablespoons all-purpose flour.

ARTICHOKES [AHR-tih-chohk]

▶ Purchase deep green artichokes that are heavy for their size and have a compact leaf formation. The leaves should "squeak" when pressed together. Avoid those that are shriveled, lightweight, mottled or have a loose-leaf formation. A slight browning of the leaf edges (called "winter's kiss"), which is caused by frost damage, doesn't usually affect the artichoke's quality. An artichoke with generous browning, however, is usually beyond its prime. In general, the smaller the artichoke the more tender it will be; the rounder it is, the larger a heart it will have.

▶ Store unwashed artichokes in a plastic bag in the refrigerator for up to 4 days. They're best, however, if used within a day or two of purchase.

▶ Wash artichokes just before using, making sure to flush out all the dirt hiding between the leaves. The easiest method is by vigorously plunging the artichoke up and down in cold water.

▶ Wearing rubber gloves will protect your hands from pricks while working with artichokes.

▶ Always use stainless steel knives and scissors to cut artichokes. Carbon blades will darken and discolor the flesh.

▶ To prepare whole artichokes for cooking: Slice off the stem to form a flat base. Snap off the tough outer leaves closest to the stem. If desired, trim about ½ inch off the pointed top. Use scissors to snip off the prickly tips of the outer leaves. Rub all cut edges with lemon to prevent discoloration.

- Soaking artichokes in acidulated water (3 tablespoons lemon juice to 1 quart cold water) for an hour before preparing will improve both the color and tenderness of the artichoke.
- There are several methods by which you can cook whole artichokes: Steaming or boiling (30 to 45 minutes), baking—a method usually reserved for stuffed artichokes (at least 45 minutes), in a pressure cooker (8 to 10 minutes) or in a microwave oven—also good for stuffed artichokes (12 to 14 minutes, plus 5 minutes standing time). Whatever method you choose, the artichokes should be positioned upright, stem side down.
- Tiny **baby artichokes** (about the size of a small egg and usually only available in the springtime) are so tender when cooked that they can be eaten whole.
- Cook artichokes in a stainless steel, Teflon-lined or enamel-coated pan—aluminum or iron will turn them an unattractive gray-green color. For the microwave oven, a microwave-safe ceramic or glass dish should be used.
- Add 1 teaspoon lemon juice per artichoke to the cooking water to retain the vegetable's color.
- The cooking water for artichokes can be seasoned with various ingredients including minced garlic, chopped shallots or peppercorns.
- One tablespoon olive or vegetable oil in the cooking water will give artichokes a slight sheen.
- One teaspoon each sugar and salt per quart of cooking water will help revive the color and flavor of over-the-hill artichokes.
- An artichoke is done when the leaves pull off easily and the base can be readily pierced with a knife tip.
- Use tongs to remove artichokes from their cooking water. Turn upside down on a rack or colander to drain for several minutes before serving.
- Eating an artichoke: First-timers need not be intimidated when this globelike vegetable is set before them. The first thing to remember is that the base of each leaf is the edible portion—the rest of the leaf is too tough to eat. Begin by pulling the leaves off one at a time with your fingers. If there's a sauce (often simply melted lemon butter), dip the leaf's base into it, then draw the leaf through your teeth, scraping off the tender portion at the base. Discard the leaf (it's nice to have a "discard" plate) and pull off another one. When all the leaves have been removed, use a spoon to scoop out and discard the small, pale, purple-tinged leaves at the bottom and the fuzzy portion called the "choke." The remaining piece is the succulent, meaty artichoke bottom, which should be eaten with a fork.
- Dipping sauces for artichokes don't have to be the usual caloric lemon- or herb-butters, flavored mayonnaise-based dips, or oil-rich viniagrettes.

You can cut calories by dipping the leaves in various salsas, or yogurt-based sauces, or even your favorite commercial low-calorie salad dressing.

▶ To make artichoke soup from leftovers, simmer all but the choke in chicken broth until very tender, puree in a blender or food processor, then strain, add milk, cream or buttermilk, and season to taste. Serve artichoke soup hot or cold.

▶ Most experts agree that artichokes ruin the flavor of wine. Certainly, wine shouldn't accompany artichokes served with any kind of viniagrette sauce because the acid would kill the wine's flavor. If you do serve wine with artichokes, choose one with high acidity, such as a Chenin Blanc.

▶ *See also* JERUSALEM ARTICHOKES; VEGETABLES, GENERAL

ASPARAGUS

▶ There are two general types of asparagus—green and white. White asparagus is grown underground and harvested just when the tips break through the soil. Choose firm, bright green (or pale ivory, for the white variety) stalks with tight tips. Avoid limp, dry-looking spears. In general, the thinner the spear, the more tender it will be.

▶ Choose asparagus stalks that are all approximately the same size and thickness—they'll cook more evenly.

▶ Store asparagus upright, standing in about an inch of water; cover the container with a plastic bag. Or, wrap the stem ends in wet paper towel, then seal the asparagus in a plastic bag. Wash just before using. Asparagus is best cooked the day it's purchased but will keep for up to 3 days.

▶ If you find that your asparagus has become limp during storage, cut a ¼ inch off the tips and stand vertically in about 2 inches of ice water. Refrigerate, covered with a plastic bag, for 2 hours and it should regain much of its crispness.

▶ *Fresh asparagus yields:* 1 pound = 16 to 20 spears; about 2 cups chopped pieces.

▶ Asparagus spears will snap off naturally where they become tough if you hold both ends and bend the spear.

▶ Don't throw out the fibrous base that snaps off of the spears. Save and cook until very tender, then puree, strain, and use in sauces and soups. The puree can be frozen for up to 3 months.

▶ If your asparagus is a little old and the entire length of the stalk is tough, remove the skin with a vegetable peeler.

▶ Thin, fresh asparagus is wonderful thinly sliced and served raw in salads. Or, serve whole spears as crudités, with a dip.

▶ Ideally, asparagus should be cooked standing up in water with the tender tips above the water level. Use kitchen string to tie the stalks together so they'll stand up easily.

- If your asparagus cooking pot isn't tall enough for the asparagus to stand up in and still be covered, invert a deep saucepan over the spears to use as a cover.
- A clean glass or ceramic coffee pot makes a good asparagus cooking pot.
- Only cook asparagus until the stalks are crisp-tender. The residual heat will continue to cook the spears for 30 to 60 seconds after they're removed from the heat.
- Thoroughly drain cooked asparagus so there's no excess moisture in the spear tips that could dilute a sauce.
- Asparagus can also be cooked in a microwave oven. For 1 pound asparagus, arrange spoke-fashion, tips toward the center, in a round baking dish with 2 tablespoons water. Cover and cook at HIGH (100 percent power) for 7 to 10 minutes, or until crisp-tender. Rotate dish a half turn after 4 minutes.
- Chop and use leftover cooked asparagus in omelets, soups or stir-frys, adding it at the last minute just so it warms through but doesn't overcook.
- Overcooked leftover asparagus can be pureed and used for soups or sauces.
- *See also* VEGETABLES, GENERAL

AVOCADOS [a-voh-CAH-doh]

- The two most widely marketed avocado varieties are the pebbly textured, almost black **Haas** and the green, smooth- and thin-skinned **Fuerte**. The Haas has a smaller pit and a more buttery texture than the Fuerte. When buying avocados, choose those that yield slightly to gentle palm pressure. They should be heavy for their size and unblemished. Avoid any that have dark, sunken spots.
- Store unripe avocados at room temperature, ripe ones in the refrigerator for up to a week.
- *Avocado yields:* 1 pound = 2 medium; about 2½ cups sliced, diced or chopped.
- Many supermarket avocados are hard and underripe. To speed the ripening process at home, place several avocados in a paper bag with an apple, pierce the bag in several places, then set aside at room temperature for 1 to 3 days.
- You can soften underripe, hard avocados in the microwave oven at MEDIUM (50 percent power) for about 30 to 45 seconds, rotating halfway through. They won't be ripe, but they will be softer.
- Perfectly ripe avocados are the easiest to peel. The skin is hard to remove from underripe fruit, whereas the flesh of those that are overripe often gets mashed and bruised during peeling.
- Make quick work of seeding an avocado by cutting it lengthwise all the

way around, then gently twisting the halves in opposite directions to separate them. Firmly smack the seed with the blade of a sharp, heavy knife; twist the knife slightly and lift the seed, still attached to the blade, right out.

▸ To peel an avocado half, use the point of a very sharp paring knife to make a lengthwise cut down the middle of the skin. If you want unblemished avocado halves, be careful to cut only through the skin and not into the flesh. At the stem end, grasp one piece of the skin between your thumb and the knife edge; pull the skin down and off the fruit. Repeat with the other strip of skin.

▸ To retard the browning of avocados, brush any cut surface with lemon juice or ascorbic acid color keeper, or leave the pit in one half, wrap well in plastic wrap and refrigerate.

▸ If the surface of an avocado turns brown, simply scrape off the discoloration and use the brightly colored avocado underneath.

▸ You can hold peeled chunks of avocado (to be used in salad, for instance) by placing them in a bowl of iced acidulated water (3 tablespoons lemon juice in 1 quart of water); cover and refrigerate. Stored this way, they'll keep their flavor, texture and color for about 3 hours.

▸ For guacamole or other dips, choose slightly overripe avocados—they'll mash more easily.

▸ Always add lemon or lime juice to guacamole—the acid not only helps keep the avocado from browning, it also brightens the flavor of this rich fruit.

▸ To help keep guacamole from browning when you make it ahead of time, place a piece of plastic wrap directly on the surface of the dip. It's oxygen that browns avocado, so the less air that gets to the surface, the better. Store guacamole in the refrigerator until ready to serve.

▸ Use avocado halves (brushed with a little lemon juice to prevent browning) as containers for seafood, chicken or pasta salad.

▸ You can also create a container for salads or dips by scooping out all the avocado flesh, then filling the shell. The Haas avocado is best for this type of container because it's thicker and firmer.

▸ Make a quick avocado dressing by combining half an avocado with ½ cup of your favorite vinaigrette dressing in a blender and processing until smooth.

▸ Frozen avocado pulp (also called avocado dip) is available in some supermarkets. It's not great, but will do in a pinch for guacamole and other highly seasoned mixtures. There's also frozen guacamole.

▸ Though avocados are high in unsaturated fat, the California Avocado Advisory Board reports that half an 8-ounce avocado contains only 138 calories.

A

▶ Want to try your hand at growing an avocado tree? Start by using a sharp knife to trim a scant ⅛-inch sliver off both ends of an avocado pit. Plant it, large end down, in damp potting soil so that the dirt covers about ⅔ of the pit. Water well, then invert a drinking glass over the pit to retain moisture. Once the pit splits (be patient), cover it with soil. When the plant is about 6 inches tall, cut off the top 2 inches. This will force lower growth and prevent the plant from becoming spindly.

BACON

▶ Look for bacon that's firm and well-colored; avoid any that looks slimy or dull. Always check the date stamp on packages of vacuum-packed bacon to make sure the bacon you buy is fresh. The stamp reflects the last date of sale.

▶ Store an unopened package of bacon in the refrigerator for no longer than a week past the date stamp. Once opened, sliced bacon can be refrigerated for up to a week. Vacuum-sealed bacon can be double-wrapped and frozen for up to a month; slab and loose slices of bacon don't freeze as well. Always defrost frozen bacon in the refrigerator overnight to prevent excessive spattering and shrinkage when cooking.

▶ Slab bacon is usually cheaper than presliced bacon. It's generally sold with the rind, which should be removed before slicing. Slab bacon can be tightly wrapped and refrigerated for several weeks.

▶ Make cracklings by dicing and frying the rind of slab bacon.

▶ Per pound, thin-sliced bacon has about 30 to 35 strips, regular has 16 to 20, and thick-sliced bacon about 12 to 16.

▶ If you roll a package of bacon into a tube and secure it with a rubber band before refrigerating, the slices will come apart more easily.

▶ Slices will be easier to separate if you remove the bacon from the refrigerator at least 30 minutes before cooking.

▶ Microwaving the bacon at HIGH for 30 seconds will also loosen the slices.

▶ Separate cold bacon by using the dull edge of a dinner knife.

▶ Semifrozen bacon is much easier to dice.

▶ The thinner the bacon, the crisper it becomes after frying.

▶ Pricking bacon with a fork reduces excess curling and helps it lie flat in the pan.

▶ Starting bacon in a cold skillet and cooking it over medium heat will minimize shrinkage.

▶ Pouring off fat as bacon cooks reduces spatter and produces crisper bacon.

▶ A bulb baster is perfect for removing excess fat from the skillet while frying bacon.

▶ Bacon grease adds a delicious flavor to myriad foods. Many cooks—particularly in the South—use bacon grease in cornbreads, to fry foods like hushpuppies and catfish, and as a flavoring for vegetables, etc.

▶ Pouring bacon grease down the drain invites a visit from the plumber. Instead pour it into a can, refrigerate until solid, then toss into the trash.

▶ Don't like curly or ruffled bacon strips? Place bacon rashers in a single layer on a baking sheet with sides and bake in a preheated 400°F oven for

10 to 15 minutes. No need to turn baked bacon. Thoroughly blot your "flat" bacon on paper towels before serving.

▸ To microwave bacon, line a microwave-safe rack or paper plate with a double layer of microwavable paper towel. Place bacon strips side by side on the rack or plate and cover with another sheet of paper towel. Six slices cooked at HIGH (100 percent power) will take 5 to 6 minutes. You can add a second and third layer of bacon strips crosswise to each other and the first layer. Put a double thickness of paper towels between bacon layers.

▸ Leftover cooked bacon strips can be wrapped airtight and refrigerated for up to 5 days, double-wrapped and frozen for up to 6 weeks. Cushion layers of bacon strips with paper towel.

▸ Recrisp leftover bacon in a skillet over medium-high heat, or in a 350°F oven for 5 to 10 minutes, or in a microwave oven on HIGH for 60 to 90 seconds.

▸ Use crumbled leftover bacon in salads or as a garnish for baked potatoes or other vegetables. It's also great in muffins, biscuits and cornbread.

▸ **Bacon bits** are preserved, dried, precooked pieces of real bacon that must be refrigerated. **Bacon-flavored bits** are an imitation-flavored, vegetable-based product that can be stored at room temperature. Be particularly careful when using the imitation bits in recipes—their strong, ersatz flavor can ruin a dish. Minced smoked sausage or ham is an infinitely better bacon substitute than artificial bits.

▸ *See also* HAM; MEATS, GENERAL; PORK

BAGELS

▸ Make your own bagel chips by cutting bagels into ⅛-inch slices, placing them in a single layer on a baking sheet, and toasting in a 350°F oven for 5 minutes a side, or until golden brown. If desired, the bagel slices can be brushed lightly with olive oil and sprinkled with salt, herbs, sesame seeds or other topping of your choice before baking.

▸ *See also* BREADS, GENERAL

BAKING, GENERAL

▸ An oven thermometer, ruler and thermometer for reading liquid temperatures should be in every baker's *batterie de cuisine.*

▸ Unless a recipe indicates otherwise, always preheat an oven for 10 to 15 minutes before beginning to bake.

▸ Always place the oven rack(s) in the desired position before heating the oven.

▸ Have your utensils and ingredients ready, your pans greased (*see* GREASING PANS) and the oven turned on before beginning to mix a cake or quick-bread batter or cookie dough.

▶ Glass bakeware conducts and retains heat better than metal, so oven temperatures should be reduced by 25°F whenever glass containers are used.

▶ Whipped butter contains 30 to 45 percent air, so should never be used in baked goods.

B

▶ When baking more than one item at a time (for instance, two loaves of bread or two baking sheets of cookies), always be sure to leave plenty of airspace between the pans, as well as between the pans and the oven walls. If using both oven racks simultaneously, position baking pans so they're not directly above one another.

▶ For more even baking, rotate baking sheets or pans front to back and top to bottom halfway through the baking time. If you're using two shelves at once, make sure they're at least 6 inches apart. Always leave plenty of space between pans on the same shelf for proper air circulation.

▶ *See also* BREADS; HIGH-ALTITUDE ADJUSTMENTS; CAKES; COOKIES; GREASING PANS; OVENS; PAN SIZES; THERMOMETERS; PIES

BAKING POWDER

▶ Baking powder is a leavener that's a combination of baking soda, an acid (such as cream of tartar) and a moisture-absorber (like cornstarch). The most common type of baking powder is **double acting**, which releases some of its gas when it becomes wet and the rest when exposed to heat.

▶ Before purchasing baking powder, check the date on the bottom of the can to be sure it isn't over the hill.

▶ Store baking powder in a cool, dry place. Once opened, baking powder should keep its punch for up to 6 months. Be sure and keep it tightly sealed after opening. It's very perishable so, unless you use if often, buy it in small cans.

▶ If you've had baking powder for more than 6 months, or are unsure of its potency for some other reason, test it by combining 1 teaspoon of it with ⅓ cup hot water. If it bubbles energetically, it's fine.

▶ Never dip a wet measuring spoon into a baking powder can, as moisture helps deteriorate this leavener.

▶ As a general rule of thumb per baked goods, per 1 cup flour use 1 teaspoon baking powder.

▶ Since some of baking powder's gas (leavening power) begins releasing the minute it's moistened, it's important in most baked goods to combine the wet and dry ingredients separately, then mix them together just before baking.

▶ Adding ½ teaspoon baking powder per ½ cup flour in batters for fried foods will produce a lighter coating.

▶ *Substitutions for 1 teaspoon baking powder:* ¼ teaspoon baking soda plus ⅝ teaspoon cream of tartar; or ¼ teaspoon baking soda plus ½ cup buttermilk or sour milk as a substitute for ½ cup other liquid in the recipe.

▸ *See also* BAKING, GENERAL; BAKING SODA; BREADS, QUICK; HIGH-ALTITUDE AD-JUSTMENTS

BAKING SODA

▸ Baking soda, also known as **bicarbonate of soda** and **sodium bicarbonate,** produces carbon dioxide gas when combined with a liquid acid ingredient such as buttermilk, yogurt or molasses.

▸ Store baking soda in a cool, dry place for up to 6 months. Because it's so perishable, it'll keep better once it's opened if transferred to an airtight container.

▸ Unsure of your baking soda's integrity? Combine ¼ teaspoon of it with 2 teaspoons vinegar—if the mixture bubbles, the soda's still active.

▸ As a general rule, use ½ teaspoon baking soda for every cup of liquid, such as buttermilk or sour milk.

▸ Baked goods that contain molasses (which is naturally acidic) will be more tender if you add ¼ teaspoon baking soda for each ⅓ cup of molasses used.

▸ The immediate rising action of baking soda and baking powder breads makes it important to have the oven preheated and pans greased before combining ingredients.

▸ Because baking soda begins releasing its gas the instant it's moistened, it should always be mixed with the other dry ingredients before any liquid is added. Once the wet and dry ingredients are combined, the batter should be placed in the oven immediately.

▸ Don't try to preserve the color of green vegetables by putting baking soda in the cooking water. The veggies will stay green, but the soda will destroy their vitamin C.

▸ Place an opened box of baking soda in your refrigerator to keep it smelling fresh. Replace it with a new box every 3 months.

▸ Sweeten the garbage disposal and kitchen drain by pouring in ½ cup baking soda and letting stand for an hour before flushing with water.

▸ *See also* BAKING, GENERAL; BAKING POWDER; BREADS, QUICK; HIGH-ALTITUDE ADJUSTMENTS

BANANAS

▸ Bananas are picked green because, contrary to nature's norm, they're one fruit that develops better flavor when ripened off the plant. By the time they reach the market, most bananas are ripe or almost ripe. Choose plump, evenly colored, yellow bananas. A flecking of tiny brown spots is an indicator of ripeness. Bananas with greening at the tips are slightly underripe.

B

▶ To ripen bananas, keep them uncovered at room temperature (about 70°F). To speed the process, place bananas in a perforated brown paper bag with a ripe apple.

▶ Store ripe bananas in a tightly sealed plastic bag in the refrigerator. The peel will turn brown but the flesh will remain unchanged.

▶ *Banana yields:* 1 pound = 3 medium or 4 small; 2 cups sliced; 1⅓ cups mashed. *Dried bananas:* 1 pound = 4½ cups slices.

▶ Toss sliced bananas with lemon or orange juice to keep them from browning.

▶ Because refrigeration discolors peeled bananas, always add them to fruit salads and desserts just before serving.

▶ When cooking with bananas choose those that are slightly underripe. They'll hold their shape better than ripe bananas.

▶ For a delicious accompaniment to grilled meats, grill slightly underripe bananas (in their peels) right alongside the meat. Cook 6 to 8 minutes, turning the bananas once during that time.

▶ For a quick low-fat dessert, horizontally cut a peeled banana and place it, cut side up, on a baking sheet that's been sprayed with nonstick vegetable spray. Sprinkle with brown sugar, cinnamon and nutmeg, and broil until sugar is bubbly.

▶ Don't throw out those overripe bananas. Peel and mash them (speedy in the blender), stir in 1 teaspoon lemon juice for each banana, and freeze in an airtight container for up to 6 months. Defrost the banana puree overnight in the refrigerator and use in breads, cakes, daiquiris and other drinks, puddings, etc.

▶ You can also freeze whole bananas (in their peels), wrapped airtight, for up to 6 months. If the banana wasn't overripe when you froze it, it can be peeled and sliced into a salad while still slightly frozen. Add it at the last minute so it won't have time to discolor. Or eat the whole banana frozen, like a popsicle. Or mash and use it in baked goods or drinks.

▶ Freeze banana (dip in orange juice first to preserve their color) slices on a baking sheet until hard, then store in a freezer-proof plastic bag to have on hand for snacks. For an extra treat, dip the banana slices in melted chocolate after freezing and let harden before transferring them to the plastic bag.

▶ *See also* FRUIT, GENERAL

BARBECUE SAUCE

▶ Bottled barbecue sauce can become "homemade" in just a few minutes by customizing it with any of the following additions: 1. Minced garlic, green pepper and onion; 2. Lemon, orange or lime juice and/or zest; 3. Port, sherry or full-bodied beer; 4. Chopped fresh chile peppers, dried red pepper flakes, cayenne or Tabasco; 5. Worcestershire or soy sauce; 6. Ma-

B

ple syrup, honey, molasses or brown sugar; 6. Chopped fresh herbs such as basil, cilantro, oregano or parsley; 7. Ground peanuts; 8. Sesame or olive oil; 9. Minced fresh ginger root; 10. Horseradish or spicy brown mustard; 11. Cracked black pepper; 12. Minced, fresh, seeded red or green tomatoes.

▸ *See also* GRILLING

BARBECUING *see* GRILLING

BARDING

▸ Barding is covering meat or fowl with a layer of fat to keep the flesh from drying out during roasting. This technique is used for lean cuts where natural fat is absent. The layer of fat bastes the meat while it cooks, keeping it moist and adding flavor.

▸ Fat used for barding can be either that which has been cut off the meat or fat from another source, such as pork fat.

▸ If you use a salted fat like bacon, first boil it for 5 minutes to remove some of the salt.

▸ To bard meat, simply lay strips of fat over the surface, or use kitchen string to tie on the fat.

▸ Remove the barding fat about 15 minutes before the meat is done to let the meat brown.

▸ *See also* LARDING

BASIL [BAY-zihl; BA-zihl]

▸ Fresh basil is plentiful during summer months and is usually sold in small bunches. Look for evenly colored, bright green leaves with no sign of wilting or dark spots. **Opal basil** is a variety with beautiful purple leaves— look for a deep color with no browning edges. **Lemon basil** and **cinnamon basil** have green leaves and a fragrance that matches their respective names.

▸ Store fresh basil in the refrigerator, wrapped in barely damp paper towels and then in a plastic bag, for up to 4 days. Or store a bunch of basil, stems down, in a glass of water with a plastic bag over the leaves and secured to the glass with a rubber band at the bottom. Refrigerate this way for up to a week, changing the water every other day.

▸ Use fresh basil in salads, in the inimitable pesto (a puree of basil, olive oil, pine nuts and Parmesan), or minced as a garnish.

▸ Basil loses much of its flavor in long-cooking dishes, so always stir in 1 or 2 tablespoons minced fresh basil just before serving.

▸ Freeze basil in the summer for use all year long. Finely chop cleaned basil leaves, then combine with enough olive oil to make a paste. Spoon tablespoonful of the paste into ice cube trays or onto a plastic-wrap-lined baking sheet and freeze until solid. Then transfer to a plastic bag and use as needed to flavor sauces, soups, salad dressings, etc.

▶ To dry-preserve fresh basil, wash the leaves then blot them dry with paper towels. Let the leaves air-dry for about 15 minutes, place alternate layers of the basil and coarse salt in a container that can be tightly sealed. Store at room temperature for up to 6 months.

▶ *See also* HERBS

BAY LEAVES

▶ Fresh bay leaves are rarely available in markets, except occasionally in specialty produce markets, primarily in California, where it grows rampantly. Dried bay leaves are available in any supermarket. The short, oval Turkish bay leaves have a more subtle flavor than the long, narrow California variety. Don't use any that are mottled with brown spots.

▶ Bay leaves are used to add pungent, woodsy flavor to long-cooking dishes like soups, stews and meats. Leaving them in food too long can turn a dish bitter.

▶ Always remove bay leaves from food before serving—they never soften and make an unpleasant mouthful. For easy retrieval, spear the leaf with a toothpick before adding it to the dish, or put it in a tea infuser.

▶ Never crumble a bay leaf before adding it to a dish—retrieving the pieces will be impossible.

▶ *See also* HERBS

BEAN CURD *see* TOFU

BEANS, CANNED

▶ *Canned beans yields:* 1 15-ounce can = about 1¾ cups drained.

▶ Always drain and rinse canned beans to remove excess salt.

▶ For almost-instant soup: puree a can of your favorite beans, add broth and a drained can of whole beans, plus seasoning of your choice.

BEANS, DRIED

▶ Among the most popular dried beans on the U.S. market today are black beans, black-eyed peas, chickpeas (garbanzos), kidney beans, lima beans, pink beans and pinto beans.

▶ Choose plump dried beans; discard any that are discolored or shriveled. Tiny holes in dried beans signal bug invaders.

▶ Dried beans can be stored in an airtight container for up to a year in a cool, dry place. They can be frozen indefinitely.

▶ *Dried bean yields:* 1 pound = about 2½ cups uncooked; 5½ to 6½ cups cooked.

B

▶ Before preparing dried beans, check them thoroughly for tiny pebbles or other debris.

▶ Most dried beans need to be soaked in water for several hours or overnight to rehydrate them before cooking. Use a large bowl or pot (to allow for beans to increase in size as they soak) and cover the beans with at least 3 inches of cold water. (If flatulence is a problem, change the water at least twice during the soaking process.) Always drain off the soaking water and add fresh water in which to cook the beans.

▶ Quick-soak method: If you can't soak the beans overnight, put them in a large pan, cover with water and bring to a boil. Remove from heat, cover and let stand for 1 to 2 hours. Then cook according to the recipe directions.

▶ Beans labeled "quick-cooking" have been presoaked and redried before packaging. They don't require presoaking and take considerably less time to prepare. However, after cooking, the texture of these "quick" beans isn't as firm to the bite as regular dried beans.

▶ If you're preparing a dish that contains two different types of beans (black beans and great Northern beans, for example), cook them separately, then combine when they're done. Every variety requires a slightly different cooking time and, if cooked together, one's bound to be over- or underdone.

▶ Prevent foaming and boilovers by adding 2 to 3 teaspoons vegetable oil to the cooking water.

▶ Salting the cooking liquid for dried beans tends to slow the cooking and toughen the beans. Salt the beans after they're cooked.

▶ Acidic ingredients, such as tomatoes or wine, also slow down the cooking time so either make allowances or add the acidic food when the beans are almost done.

▶ Always simmer dried beans. Boiling can cause the cooking liquid to overflow, as well as the beans to break apart and the skins to separate.

▶ If you want beans with a firm texture, cook them uncovered. Covering the pot produces softer beans.

▶ Further reduce the risk of flatulence by draining off the cooking liquid after the beans have simmered for 30 minutes and replacing it with fresh boiling or other liquid. Continue to cook until beans are done.

▶ Since the cooking time for dried beans varies greatly, always test their doneness by tasting them. They should feel smooth yet firm and not mushy on the tongue. Or, gently squeeze a bean between your thumb and index finger—if the core is still hard, cook the beans longer.

▶ As soon as the beans are done, drain off the hot cooking liquid or they'll continue to cook.

▶ Refrigerate leftover beans and use within 5 days in salads, stir-frys, soups, etc.

▶ *See also* LENTILS; PEAS, DRIED

BEANS, FRESH GREEN *or* WAX

B

▶ Green beans are also called **string beans** and **snap beans;** a pale yellow variety is known as **wax bean.** Select fresh beans that have firm, smooth, brightly colored pods. They should be crisp enough to snap when bent in half. Avoid those that are discolored, spotted or leathery-looking.

▶ Store unwashed fresh green beans in an airtight plastic bag in the refrigerator for up to 4 days. Wash just before using; remove strings and ends, if necessary.

▶ Most fresh beans available today don't require stringing, as the fibrous string has been bred out of the species. If you have beans that do need stringing, simply snap off the stem end and use it to pull the string down and off the pod.

▶ *Fresh bean yields:* 1 pound = 3½ cups whole; 2¾ cups trimmed and cut.

▶ Don't overcrowd green beans while cooking. Use a pot large enough for the beans to move around in freely.

▶ Don't add baking soda to the cooking water for green beans. It may keep them green, but will leach out valuable nutrients in the process, not to mention affect their flavor.

▶ A pinch of sugar in the cooking water will bring out the flavor of fresh beans. It'll also reenergize the flavor of over-the-hill beans.

▶ Green beans will lose some of their gorgeous bright green color if cooked in a covered pot with acidic ingredients like lemon juice or tomatoes.

▶ Be careful not to overcook fresh beans—they should be crisp-tender when done. Overdone beans will loose some of their bright green color as well as their fresh flavor.

▶ A garnish of toasted slivered or sliced almonds is a wonderful complement for cooked beans.

▶ Young, thin green beans are perfectly wonderful raw in salads. Accentuate their bright green color by blanching them in boiling water for 10 seconds, then plunging into ice water to stop the cooking process. Thoroughly blot dry with paper towels before using.

▶ Quickly defrost frozen green beans by letting them stand in cold water for 5 to 10 minutes; work the beans apart with your fingers as they thaw.

▶ *See also* BEANS, DRIED; LIMA BEANS; VEGETABLES, GENERAL

BEAN SPROUT *see* SPROUTS

BEAN THREADS

▶ Also called **cellophane noodles, Chinese vermicelli** and **glass noodles,** these translucent threads are made from the starch of green mung beans. Dried bean threads are available in oriental markets and the ethnic section of many supermarkets.

B

- Store bean threads, wrapped airtight, in a cool, dry place for up to 6 months.
- Bean threads are an almost-instant food. In order to use them in stir-frys or other cooked dishes, all you need do is soak them in very hot water for about 30 seconds. Drain well before adding to a dish.
- No need to presoak when these noodles are used in soups. Just add at the last minute and cook only until soft, about 30 seconds.
- When dry bean threads are deep-fried, they explode into puffy, gossamer strands in a mere 2 or 3 seconds. These crispy threads are used in many Chinese chicken salad recipes.
- Store leftover deep-fried bean threads in an airtight plastic bag at room temperature for no more than 3 days.

BEEF

- The United States Department of Agriculture (USDA) grades beef on three factors: 1. conformation (proportion of meat to bone), 2. finish (proportion of fat to lean), and 3. overall quality. The three top grades—Prime, Choice and Select—are those commonly available to consumers. Prime cuts are usually found only in upscale meat shops and fine restaurants. The meat's grade is stamped within a purple shield at regular intervals on the outside of each carcass, so consumers rarely see the imprint. As with all of nature, the older the animal the tougher the meat.
- When purchasing beef, look for brightly colored, red to deep red cuts. Marbeling (flecks or streaks of fat in the meat) should be moderate.
- To store fresh beef: If the meat will be cooked within 6 to 8 hours of purchase, it may be left in its plastic-wrapped package. Otherwise, remove the packaging and wrap loosely with waxed paper (leave ground beef in its shrink-wrap packaging). Store in the coldest part of the refrigerator for up to 2 days for ground beef, 3 days for other cuts. The object is to let the air circulate and keep the meat's surface somewhat dry, thereby inhibiting rapid bacterial growth. To freeze: Ground beef can be frozen, wrapped airtight, for up to 3 months, solid cuts for up to 6 months.
- When choosing beef cuts, remember that those most tender (**rib, short loin** and **sirloin**) will come from the animal's most lightly exercised muscles, namely along the upper back. Heavily used muscles produce less tender cuts such as **chuck** (near the animal's front end) and **round** (from the rear).
- As a general rule, the less tender the cut, the cheaper it is and the longer it takes to cook. Choose moist-heat cooking methods (such as braising or stewing) for inexpensive cuts.
- Tender cuts of meat should be prepared with a dry-heat cooking method like broiling, frying or roasting.
- *See also* GROUND BEEF; MEATS, GENERAL; ROASTS; STEAKS; VEAL

BEER

- Confused by the myriad beers on the market? Here's a quick synopsis: **lager**—America's most popular beer, lager is pale-colored and light-bodied with a mellow flavor; **ale**—ranging in color from light to dark amber, the flavor slightly bitter and stronger than lager; **bock**—a dark brown German brew that's full-bodied, slightly sweet and almost twice as strong as lager; **malt liquor**—a robust, dark beer with a bitter flavor and relatively high alcohol content; **porter**—a strong, full-bodied beer with a slightly bittersweet flavor and dark brown color; **stout**—dark-roasted barley gives this brew an intensely dark color, bitter flavor and extremely dense body; **wheat beer**—made with malted wheat, this beer has a pale color and subtle, lagerlike flavor; **fruit beer**—mild ales flavored with fruit concentrates.

- The term "light beer" in the United States refers to beer with reduced calories and, usually, less alcohol. In Europe, the term distinguishes between pale and dark lagers.

- Unlike wine, beer should not be aged. It's best when consumed as fresh as possible.

- Unpasteurized beer should be refrigerated and consumed within 1 or 2 weeks.

- Always store beer standing upright. Laying it on its side exposes more of the liquid to the air in the bottle, which will diminish the beer's flavor.

- For maximum aroma and flavor, the ideal serving temperature for light (lager-style) beers is 45° to 50°F; ales, porters and stouts are best in the 50° to 60°F range.

- Beer can begin to lose its flavor with temperature fluctuations so don't move it in and out of the refrigerator excessively.

- The thinnest film of soap or oil on a beer mug will cause beer to loose its sparkle and collapse the foam. After washing, thoroughly rinse beer glasses and, if possible, air-dry them. To completely avoid any soap residue, wash the glasses in hot, salted water.

- If you drink a lot of beer, keep beer mugs in the freezer. There's nothing like a cold beer served in a frosty mug on a sweltering summer day.

- If you like a lot of foam on your beer, pour it straight down into the center of the glass. This method also releases more of the beer's aroma. Light-foam enthusiasts will get the desired result by slowly pouring the beer onto the side of the glass.

- The amount of foam beer produces also depends on its temperature. Ice-cold beer will produce light foam, whereas room-temperature beer promotes a thicker froth.

- Beer makes a great addition to many dishes including soups, sauces, stews and breads. Substitute beer for an equal amount of the liquid called for in the recipe.

▶ Beer's also great for steaming clams and mussels. Or use it as the cooking liquid when boiling shrimp.

▶ A full-flavored brew like ale or bock beer will contribute more flavor to a dish than a light lager.

▶ Beer's a particularly compatible beverage with spicy cuisines such as Chinese, Indian, Mexican and Thai. Spicy or smoked sausages are great paired with dark beer. As a general rule, the more highly seasoned the food, the more full-bodied the beer should be.

▶ *See also* ALCOHOL; CHAMPAGNE; LIQUORS, LIQUEURS AND MIXED DRINKS; WINE

BEETS

▶ Choose firm beets with smooth, unblemished skins. In general, small or medium beets are more tender than large ones. If the beet greens are attached they should be crisp and brightly colored.

▶ Because they leach moisture from the bulb, beet greens should be removed as soon as you get home. Leave 1 to 2 inches of the stem attached to prevent loss of nutrients during cooking. Store beets in a plastic bag in the refrigerator for up to 3 weeks.

▶ *Beet yields:* 1 pound, trimmed = 2 cups chopped.

▶ Just before cooking, wash beets gently so as not to pierce the thin skin. Don't peel beets or trim their stems until after cooking or they'll lose both nutrients and color.

▶ Beets can be boiled, baked or cooked in a microwave oven. However you cook them, remove the skin (which slips off easily) after cooking. Unless, of course, you're making beet soup, the only instance in which you peel the beets before cooking.

▶ Add ½ teaspoon each sugar and salt to the cooking water when boiling over-the-hill beets.

▶ Beet greens are flavorful and shouldn't be wasted. After removing them from the beet, wash, blot dry with paper towels, and refrigerate in a plastic bag for up to 3 days. Cook them as you would spinach.

▶ Or wash and shred young, tender beet greens to use in salad.

▶ Boiled beets will keep more of their intense color if you add 2 tablespoons lemon juice or vinegar to the cooking water.

▶ To peel cooked beets, cut off both ends, then hold them under cold, running water and slip off the skins.

▶ When combining beets with other vegetables, always add them last or they'll discolor the other food.

▶ Use raw, finely grated beets in salads.

▶ Be forewarned that beet stains are almost impossible to remove from plastic or wood. Generously rubbing a storage container or chopping block with oil helps, but isn't failsafe.

► Keep your fingers from becoming stained with difficult-to-remove beet juice by wearing disposable plastic gloves (available at drugstores).

► *See also* VEGETABLES, GENERAL

BELL PEPPERS; SWEET BELL PEPPERS; SWEET PEPPERS

► Choose sweet bell peppers (green or red) that have a richly colored, shiny skin, and are firm and heavy for their size. Avoid those that are limp, shriveled, or which have soft or bruised spots. Red bells are simply vine-ripened green bell peppers; because they've ripened longer, they're very sweet. There are also yellow, orange, purple and brown bell peppers.

► Store bell peppers in a plastic bag in the refrigerator for up to a week. Seeded, chopped bell peppers can be frozen for up to 6 months.

► Wash bell peppers thoroughly before seeding. Cut peppers in half by slicing vertically from one side of the stem all the way around to the other side of the stem. Break halves apart and the seed core should pop right out. Cut away the membranes, which can be bitter.

► Another way to seed a bell pepper is to hold it firmly in you palm and smack the stem end firmly against the countertop or other flat surface. The jolt will loosen the seed core, which you can pull right out.

► Do bell peppers "repeat" on you? Next time, get rid of the offending agent by using a vegetable peeler to remove the skin.

► Peppers are much easier to cut if you cut from the flesh (not the skin) side. Place halved, seeded peppers, skin side down, on the cutting board and slice or chop away.

► Roast your own whole peppers by using tongs to hold them over a gas flame, turning as the skin blackens. Or roast a lot of peppers by cutting them in half, seeding, and placing on a baking sheet, skin side up. Place 3 to 4 inches from a broiling unit and char until the skins are black. When the peppers are charred, put them in a plastic or paper bag, then seal and let stand for at least 15 minutes. This steaming process will help loosen the skin. Remove from the bag and, when the peppers are cool enough to handle, use your fingers or a knife to peel off the skin. Tiny bits of char remaining on the peppers are acceptable.

► Place roasted, peeled peppers in a large screw-top jar, cover with olive oil and refrigerate for up to 1 week.

► Rubbing vegetable oil over the skins of peppers to be stuffed will keep them supple.

► To give added support to stuffed peppers while baking: cut them crosswise (rather than lengthwise), stuff, then place in lightly greased muffin tins and bake as usual.

► Adding some of the pepper seeds to the filling for stuffed peppers contributes flavor and texture.

B

- If you love the look of red bell peppers in a dish but find that they're either unavailable or too pricey, substitute roasted red peppers or pimientos, both of which are commonly available in jars. The flavor will be slightly different, but the visual effect the same.
- Make an edible container for salads or dips by cutting off the top inch of large bell peppers, then removing the core and seeds. If the peppers are huge, cut them in half crosswise and use as containers.
- *See also* VEGETABLES, GENERAL

BERRIES, GENERAL

- Always check the bottom of a berry container at the market. If it's a see-through basket, look for unripe, bruised or moldy berries. If it's a cardboard basket, be sure it's not stained with berry juice, which indicates that some berries are at least crushed, if not rotten. Follow selection suggestions (see individual berry listings) to make sure the ones you buy are ripe.
- To retard bruising and spoilage in berries, store them in a single layer on a paper-towel-lined jelly-roll pan or other large pan with shallow sides. Discard any bruised or moldy berries. Cover the berries lightly with paper towels and refrigerate (see information on individual berries for storage time).
- Don't wash berries until just before using them. Some berries—like strawberries—can become waterlogged if exposed too long to water, so wash them quickly, but gently. Refrigerated berries aren't as likely to bruise while washing as room-temperature berries.
- To freeze washed (and blotted very dry) blackberries, blueberries, boysenberries, etc., arrange them in a single layer on a jelly-roll pan (or other baking sheet with sides), freeze until hard, then transfer to a plastic bag. Or place a large plastic bag on a baking sheet and place a single layer of berries in the bag. When the berries are solid, seal the bag and return to the freezer. Berries may be frozen for up to 9 months.
- Defrost frozen berries by placing the sealed plastic bag of them in a large bowl of cold water for about 10 minutes. After defrosting, the berries won't be as firm or as fresh, but the flavor will be wonderful.
- Frozen berries exude much more juice than fresh, so always reduce the liquid and increase the thickener when using them in pies or cobblers.
- Berries—particularly the larger, heavier ones like blackberries, will sink if added to a thin cake batter. Make sure the batter is thick enough to hold the berries in suspension. Add the berries at the last minute to avoid bruising that might be caused by excessive stirring.
- If berries aren't sweet enough, combine them with 1 tablespoon granulated sugar per cup of berries and let stand at room temperature for 30 to 60 minutes, stirring once or twice.

- Sugar softens berries—particularly those that are usually cut, such as strawberries—so don't add it too far in advance of serving.
- Add a sophisticated touch to berries by drizzling them with a little liqueur. Frangelico (hazelnut-flavored), Grand Marnier (orange) or Amaretto (almond) all complement berries nicely.
- For a delicious dessert, crush ½ cup berries (strain out the seeds, if necessary) and fold into 1 cup whipping cream that's been beaten until stiff (sweetening is optional). Either spoon over or fold into whole or sliced berries.
- To make your own delicious fresh berry syrup to top everything from pancakes and waffles to ice cream: Combine 1½ cups water, 3 cups sugar and ½ teaspoon salt in a medium saucepan. Cook, without stirring, over high heat until syrup reaches 200°F on a candy thermometer. Stir in 2 cups berries (chopped, if large); cook for 2 more minutes. Cool, then refrigerate in an airtight container for up to 2 months.
- Remove berry stains from your hands by rubbing them well with lemon wedges.
- *See also* BLACKBERRIES; BLUEBERRIES; CRANBERRIES; RASPBERRIES; STRAWBERRIES

BEVERAGE CONTAINERS

- Glass mugs make a great presentation for hot drinks. To prevent the glass from cracking, place a dinner tablespoon in the mug and slowly pour the hot liquid onto the spoon. The spoon will disperse and absorb some of the heat, preventing damage to the mugs.
- Cleaning thermos bottles and thermal carafes can be a problem. Sometimes it seems almost impossible to remove telltale stains or odor, particularly those from coffee. The old standby method is to put about ¼ cup baking soda in the container, then fill with hot water and let stand overnight. Wash and rinse *thoroughly* before using. Or you might want to try filling the container with hot water, then dropping in a denture-cleansing tablet. Let stand for 1 hour. If problem persists, repeat procedure.

BISCUITS

- For the tenderest, flakiest biscuits: Make sure the fat (butter, margarine, etc.) is cold. Cut it into the dry ingredients *only* until the mixture resembles coarse (about ¼-inch) crumbs. The distribution of tiny lumps of fat creates flaky, tender biscuits; overmixing produces crumbly biscuits.
- For yeastlike biscuits in a fraction of the time, substitute 1 teaspoon each baking soda and ascorbic acid powder (vitamin C) for the baking powder (or yeast, if it's a yeast biscuit recipe). Mix and bake as usual—no rising time necessary.

B

▸ Once the flour's been added, don't overwork the dough or you'll produce tough biscuits. Press the dough together gently only until it holds together.

▸ To roll out the dough so the biscuits are uniform in height, roll out the dough between two ½-inch-high sticks.

▸ Excess handling causes tough biscuits, so once you roll out the dough, cut as many biscuits as possible from that first rolling.

▸ Rerolling toughens the dough. So does excess flour so use as little as possible when rolling out the dough.

▸ If you don't have a rolling pin, use your lightly floured fingers to quickly pat the dough out to the desired thickness.

▸ Biscuits don't have to be round. Form the dough into a large square, then cut into smaller squares, rectangles or triangles with a sharp knife. Or use the divided insert from an old-fashioned metal ice cube tray to make small biscuit squares. Flour the cutting instrument so the dough won't stick. A bonus from making square biscuits: no leftover scraps to roll out and cut.

▸ Dip a biscuit cutter in flour to keep the dough from sticking.

▸ If you don't have a biscuit cutter, use a thin-lipped glass or an empty, clean 14- to 16-ounce can.

▸ Use a rolling cookie cutter to cut out several biscuits in one motion.

▸ For biscuits that split open easily, roll out the dough to about ¼ inch thick, then fold it over before cutting. Make butter biscuits by brushing melted butter over the dough before folding and cutting.

▸ For biscuits that are crisp on the outside, brush them with water and arrange 1½ inches apart on a baking sheet.

▸ For soft biscuits, brush with milk or melted butter and arrange on a baking sheet so they're touching.

▸ If you don't like the way drop biscuits spread, drop the batter into greased muffin tins and bake as usual.

▸ Burned bottoms on your biscuits? Rub the burned part over a grater to remove the scorched area.

▸ To store leftover biscuits, wrap in foil and store at room temperature for up to 3 days.

▸ Biscuits can be frozen, wrapped airtight in heavy-duty foil, for up to 3 months.

▸ To reheat biscuits, put the foil packet in a 300°F oven for about 10 minutes. Thaw frozen biscuits at room temperature before heating, or heat frozen biscuits at 300°F for about 25 minutes. Or microwave at HIGH (100 percent power) for 10 to 30 seconds.

▸ *See also* BAKING, GENERAL; BAKING POWDER; BAKING SODA; BREADS, GENERAL; BREADS, QUICK; GREASING PANS; HIGH-ALTITUDE ADJUSTMENTS; MUFFINS; POPOVERS

BLACKBERRIES

► Choose plump, glossy, deep-colored berries without hulls. If the hulls are still attached, the berries are immature and were picked too early—the flavor will be tart.

► Fresh blackberries can be refrigerated for up to 2 days.

► *Blackberry yields:* 1 pint = 1½ to 2 cups berries.

► Blackberries are delicious for both cooking and out-of-hand eating.

► Blackberries have lots of seeds, which you may want to strain out of sauces.

► *See* BERRIES, GENERAL *for complete storage and cleaning information*

BLANCHING

► Blanching is used to firm the flesh, to loosen skin (as with peaches or tomatoes) and to heighten and set color and flavor (as with vegetables before freezing).

► The technique for blanching food is to plunge it into boiling water briefly, then into cold water to stop the cooking process.

► Make sure the water is boiling rapidly and begin timing the second the food hits the water.

► Have a bowl filled with ice water standing at the ready in which to plunge the blanched food in order to stop the cooking.

► *See also* PARBOILING

BLENDERS

► Nothing can beat the blender for making silky-smooth purees, soups and sauces, or for whipping up frothy drinks from breakfast shakes to frozen daiquiris.

► Use the blender for chopping small amounts of foods like nuts, bread-crumbs and whole spices that would get lost in a food processor work-bowl.

► The blender's tall, narrow, leakproof container makes it better for liquid mixtures than the food processor. The container's shape, however, means that not much air can get to the ingredients, making it impossible to whip air into foods like egg whites and whipping cream.

► Some manufacturers offer 1-cup blender jars that can be attached to the blade housing. These small containers usually have screw-on tops and are good for chopping small amounts of food and blending salad dressings.

► Before turning on the motor, always cover the blender, placing your hand on the lid to prevent it from popping off in case it's not firmly seated.

► If pieces of food become lodged in the blades, stop the machine and use a narrow rubber spatula or the handle of a wooden spoon to move the food. Make sure the blades have come to a complete stop before doing so.

► If a mixture is so thick that it won't move, adding a little liquid will help.

► Be careful not to tax your blender's motor with heavy ingredients or too much volume. If the machine begins to labor, increase the speed. If that doesn't help, stop the machine and remove half the ingredients, blending the food in two batches.

► When blending hot mixtures, always begin at low speed and gradually increase to high. Starting at high speed can force the hot liquid up and out of the blender and scald your hands or face.

► Always make sure the blades have stopped completely before removing the blender jar from the motor base.

► Frozen juice concentrate can be quickly liquified by whirling it in a blender for a few seconds. Add the required water and process until juice is frothy.

► Turn any oil-based salad dressing into a creamy-style dressing by blending it until slightly thickened.

► A brief whirl in the blender will rescue a gravy with lumps or an egg-based sauce that's separated.

► Don't let the blender blades stand so long that food dries on them. If you can't clean the blender right away, pour some hot water in it to soak.

► Quickly clean a blender jar by filling it halfway with hot water, adding a drop of dishwashing detergent, and whirling the mixture for 30 seconds. Rinse thoroughly.

► *See also* FOOD PROCESSORS; IMMERSION BLENDERS

BLUEBERRIES

► Always choose berries that are plump, firm, uniform in size and a silver-frosted indigo blue color.

► Refrigerate blueberries, tightly covered, for up to 10 days. Before using, discard shriveled or moldy berries, and remove any stems.

► *Blueberry yields:* 1 pint = 2 cups; 1 10-ounce package frozen = 1½ cups.

► When blueberries "bleed" in baked goods, it's usually because they were frozen, then defrosted before being added to the batter. Always add frozen berries to the batter in their solid state, and stir them in at the last minute. Fresh blueberries won't bleed out their juice unless the skins are broken. If using canned blueberries, be sure to drain them well, then blot thoroughly on several layers of paper towels.

► Have you ever made a blueberry cake, muffins or other baked goods only to find when you cut into it that the berries have turned an ugly greenish brown color? The culprit is likely baking soda, which creates an alkaline condition that affects the color of blueberries. (Baking soda is generally used in baking to counteract an acid ingredient, such as buttermilk or yogurt.) So, if possible, substitute milk for buttermilk (or other acidic ingredient) and baking powder for the baking soda. The leavening result will be close and at least the berries won't be discolored.

▶ For blueberry heaven, toss 1 pint blueberries with 2 to 3 tablespoons pure maple syrup and 2 teaspoons freshly grated orange zest. Crown the maple-kissed berries with a drizzle of heavy cream. Or fold ½ cup vanilla-flavored yogurt into the maple berries.

▶ *See* BERRIES, GENERAL *for complete storage and cleaning information*

BOK CHOY [bahk CHOY]

▶ Also called **pak choy** and **Chinese white cabbage,** bok choy is a mild, versatile vegetable that resembles a bunch of wide-stalked celery with long, full leaves.

▶ Choose bok choy that has firm, white stalks topped with crisp, green leaves. Avoid any bunches with wilted leaves or soft stalks.

▶ Store it in an airtight plastic bag in the refrigerator for up to 4 days. Wash and trim off the base just before using.

▶ Bok choy is great raw in salads. Chop the crunchy stalks as you would celery; shred the leaves.

▶ Use a light touch when cooking bok choy. Sauté or stir-fry the chopped stalks for just a minute or two before adding the chopped or shredded leaves, which only take about 30 seconds.

▶ *See also* VEGETABLES, GENERAL

BRAISING

▶ A method of cooking used for less tender cuts of meat and other foods. The food is first browned, then covered airtight and cooked in a small amount of liquid at a low temperature for a lengthy period of time.

▶ The pot you choose for braising should be heavy and just slightly larger than the ingredients (plus liquid) it will hold. This allows the food (rather than the space around it) to absorb the heat.

▶ Meat will brown better if you use a paper towel to blot any moisture off the surface. Dusting the meat with flour will also contribute to browning.

▶ Make sure the pot or pan and the fat are hot (not smoking) before adding the meat to brown.

▶ Only a small amount of liquid is needed for braising. Too much, and the food will end up being poached.

▶ Once the meat or other food is browned, add the liquid called for in the recipe and immediately cover the pot and reduce the heat.

▶ If braising on the stovetop, reduce the heat to low or medium-low, just so the liquid is simmering.

▶ Oven-braising should be done at 300° to 325°F. Because the oven heat surrounds the pot, this form of braising cooks more evenly.

▶ *See also* COOKING, GENERAL

BRAZIL NUTS

▶ Actually the seed of a giant tree that grows in the Amazon, Brazil nuts come in clusters of 8 to 24 inside a hard pod that resembles a small coconut.

▶ A brazil nut shell is extraordinarily hard. To temper the shells so they're easier to crack, you can bake the nuts at 400°F for 15 minutes, then cool; or freeze them for 6 hours, then crack.

▶ Another method for relaxing the shells is to cover the nuts with water in a saucepan, bring to a boil, then boil for 3 minutes. Drain off hot water, then cover with ice water and let stand for 2 minutes before draining and cracking.

▶ If you don't have a heavy-duty nutcracker, use a hammer or mallet to crack the brazil nut's armorlike shell.

▶ *See also* NUTS, GENERAL *for general purchase, storage and usage information*

BREADCRUMBS

▶ Make your own fresh breadcrumbs in a food processor with the metal blade by tearing *lightly* toasted bread slices into pieces, then processing to the desired texture. Use quick on/off pulses until the crumbs are evenly chopped. You can do the same thing in a blender but, because of the narrow blender jar, work with only 2 slices of bread at a time.

▶ Dry breadcrumbs—plain or seasoned—can be found in supermarkets. Or you can make your own by placing a single layer of bread slices on a baking sheet and baking at 300°F until completely dry and lightly browned. (Using stale bread isn't recommended because it usually tastes like what it is—old.) Cool completely before breaking into pieces and processing until fine in a blender or a food processor with a metal blade. If using a blender, only process 1½ to 2 slices at a time. If you don't have either of these appliances, put the dry bread slices in a heavyweight plastic bag, seal, then crush the slices with a rolling pin.

▶ *Breadcrumb yields:* 1 untrimmed regular slice of bread = about ½ cup fresh breadcrumbs; 1 slice dried bread = about ⅓ cup crumbs.

▶ Breadcrumbs can be refrigerated, tightly sealed, for a week, frozen for at least 6 months.

▶ You can season your own breadcrumbs at a fraction of the cost of store-bought seasoned crumbs. Simply add crumbled dried herbs, finely grated cheese and salt and pepper, if desired.

▶ Buttered, sautéed breadcrumbs make a delicious topping for vegetables, casseroles and even some salads. Melt 1 tablespoon butter for each cup of soft crumbs (2 tablespoons for dry crumbs) in a large skillet over medium-high heat. When the butter is hot and bubbly, add the breadcrumbs, tossing until evenly coated. Sauté, stirring often, until crumbs are golden brown. Cool at least partway before using. The longer the crumbs cool, the crisper they'll become.

▶ Breadcrumbs are a quick, nutritious thickener for soup. Try whole-wheat or rye crumbs for hearty meat soups or stews. They can also be used to thicken sauces, or in sauced dishes or casseroles.

▶ Many cereals can be crushed and used as a substitute for breadcrumbs. Try corn, wheat or rice flakes, staying away from those that are sweetened. Three cups flakes will yield about 1 cup crumbs.

▶ If substituting cracker crumbs, use only ¾ cup for each cup of bread-crumbs called for in a recipe.

▶ *See also* CRUMBS, GENERAL

BREADING

▶ For fail-safe breading, first dry the food by blotting it with paper towels, then dip it in flour, shaking off any excess. Dunk floured food in well-beaten egg, letting the excess liquid drain before dipping food into a bowl or plate filled with fine bread or cracker crumbs. Coat both sides of food with crumbs, using your fingers to pat crumbs over any bare spots.

▶ Milk can be used instead of egg for a dipping mixture, but doesn't provide as much "glue."

▶ Save on cleanup by tossing egg- or milk-dipped food in a plastic or paper bag filled with crumbs and shaking until it's well coated.

▶ Breading will stick better if you refrigerate the breaded food for 30 to 60 minutes before cooking.

▶ Besides bread and cracker crumbs, there are many unsweetened cereals (like corn, wheat or rice flakes) that can be crushed and used. Three cups flakes will yield about 1 cup crumbs.

BREAD MACHINES

▶ Bread machines are computer-driven wonders that mix, knead, rise, punch down, bake and sometimes cool bread—all in a single compart-ment. You simply measure and add the ingredients, press a button to specify the cycle, and let the machine do its thing while you're busy doing something else. An added bonus is the one-compartment mixing bowl–baking pan, which saves time on cleanup.

▶ All bread machines are about the size of an old-fashioned bread box. Each contains a nonstick canister that serves as a mixing bowl and baking pan. A motor-driven blade at the bottom of this compartment mixes and kneads the dough. A heating coil handles the baking. Each function—mixing, rising and baking—is controlled by a sophisticated microcom-puter that regulates timing, temperature and the motor.

▶ Among the bread machines currently on the market are the Panasonic

B

(which is also marketed under the name of National), Zojirushi, Seiko and Magic Mill. There's also the Hitachi, Regal and Sanyo, which are basically the same machine, as are the Dak and Welbilt.

▶ There are three basic loaf shapes—vertical rectangle, horizontal rectangle and cylindrical—depending on the brand and model of bread machine.

▶ Though the vertical rectangle is the shape most manufacturers use, it can be problematic. The top sometimes collapses, forming a slight hollow in the bread's top crust.

▶ Besides their unconventional shapes, bread-machine loaves have a singularly distinctive characteristic—a bottom hole created by the mixing blade. In addition to the blade, some machines have a kneading pin, which pulls at the dough and maximizes kneading. This removable pin creates a small hole in the side of the bread.

▶ Most bread machines have a capacity to make either 1- or 1½-pound loaves; however, the sizes range from ½ to 2 pounds.

▶ Machines that yield 1-pound loaves (about 8 slices) use around 2 cups of dry ingredients and ½ cup liquid. Those that produce 1½-pound loaves (about 12 slices) can hold 3 to 4 cups of dry ingredients and 1 to 1½ cups of liquid. This means that an average 2-pound-loaf yeast bread recipe would have to be divided in half to fit in a machine with a 1½-pound capacity. The same recipe would have to be altered drastically—reduced by about two-thirds—to fit a 1-pound machine.

▶ Dry ingredients include everything from flour to oats to bran; liquids include foods like milk, water and eggs.

▶ Always follow the manufacturer's instructions for how to add and layer ingredients. The way ingredients are added depends on the model of bread machine. The directions for some machines say to put the yeast in first, whereas others start with the liquid, followed by the dry ingredients and topped with the yeast. Some bread machines have a separate yeast dispenser, which automatically adds the leavener according to the machine's software program.

▶ The timing for most bread machines is programmed for the use of active dry yeast. Some machine manuals give directions for using quick-rising yeast. Compressed fresh yeast shouldn't be used for machine-baked breads.

▶ Substituting ¼ cup gluten flour for whole-wheat flour in whole-grain loaves will give them a better texture.

▶ Unless the recipe calls for melted butter, always cut butter into pieces and soften it before adding to the mixture. This makes it easier for the butter to combine with the other ingredients.

▶ Substituting honey or other liquid sweeteners for sugar can cause over-browning, so make allowances when choosing the crust selection.

▶ Timing for the various cycles differs from machine to machine. For instance, the basic bread setting takes 4¼ hours on one machine and only 3 hours and 10 minutes on another—with almost identical results. Some machines have a rapid-bake setting, which produces a loaf of bread in about 2¾ hours. Check the owner's manual for your particular machine to see how long each cycle is programmed to take.

▶ A programmable timer is available on most machines. This allows you to delay the machine's starting time up to 9 hours. That means you can get up in the morning to the fragrance of freshly baked bread—or walk into the house after a hard day's work to a well-deserved treat. Remember to calculate the time according to how long your machine takes to produce a finished loaf.

▶ When using the timer for delayed starting, it's vital that the yeast doesn't touch the liquid. Don't use ingredients like eggs or fresh milk products that might spoil during the wait.

▶ When setting the timer for delayed baking, don't forget to allow for the bread to finish baking about an hour before you want to serve it. This gives the bread a chance to cool and set, making it easier to slice.

▶ Bread machines with containers shaped like a horizontal rectangle sometimes have trouble blending in ingredients in the corners. If that's the case, simply use a rubber spatula to move the ingredients from the corners toward the center during the mixing process.

▶ All machines have a dough setting, which mixes the ingredients, kneads the dough and takes it through its first rising. The dough can then be removed from the machine, shaped into loaves, rolls, coffee cakes, bread sticks or whatever, and set to rise the second time outside the bread machine. Some machines have a timer that can be used with the dough setting, which means that when you get home from work the dough will be ready and waiting to be shaped into pizza, rolls, etc.

▶ Some bread machines have a raisin-bread setting that sounds an alarm indicating the kneading will end in 5 minutes. This allows raisins, nuts, chopped dried fruit, etc. to be added to the dough with just enough time to be kneaded into it without being pulverized.

▶ If your machine doesn't have a raisin feature, simply check the user's manual to see how long mixing/kneading takes in your machine. Then set a timer to go off 5 minutes before the kneading is to be finished and add the ingredients. They should be evenly distributed by the time the dough is ready for the first rising.

▶ At least one manufacturer offers a whole-wheat setting, engineered for use with heavy, whole-grain doughs.

▶ Some machines have a French bread mode, which is specially programmed for this sometimes difficult bread.

B

▶ Some bread machines have a viewing window through which you can see how the bread's developing. If your machine doesn't have a window, it won't hurt to lift the lid and check the dough's progress during the kneading cycle. (Don't lift the lid of a machine with a yeast dispenser until the yeast has been added.) Though bread-machine manuals warn against peeking, doing so could prevent a failed loaf of bread. However, never open the lid during the rising or baking cycles.

▶ Dough that's the proper consistency should form a soft, pliable mass around the blade. If the dough is lumpy or in chunks, it's too dry. Add a tablespoon of liquid and let it mix into the dough. Check after a minute or so and add a little more liquid if the dough isn't the right texture. An overly moist dough can be brought to the right consistency by adding flour, a tablespoon at a time, until the dough is soft but not sticky.

▶ Dough that's too dry won't rise properly and the resulting bread will be dense and heavy with a cracked top.

▶ A dough that's too soft because of excess liquid can mushroom out of the pan, causing the baked loaf to fall. It can also create bread that is dense, moist or with an uneven crumb.

▶ Many bread machines have a cooling feature—a fan that circulates air, cooling the bread and crisping the crust while it's still in the machine. Such a cycle is mandatory if the bread finishes baking while you're at work or before you get up in the morning. Otherwise, the hot bread would sit in the machine and steam in its own heat, creating a soggy crust and overly moist interior.

▶ If your machine doesn't have a cooling cycle, immediately remove the bread from the machine when it's finished baking.

▶ If a cooled bread is hard to remove from the container, gently rap the pan on the side of the counter. Or use a rubber mallet to tap lightly on the sides of the pan.

▶ If the mixing blade comes loose and gets stuck in the bottom of the baked loaf, simply wait for the loaf to cool, then pull the blade out with your fingers. Be careful not to scratch the blade's nonstick finish.

▶ Bread-machine success will come with experience, so don't give up if you have a few failures. Every time a loaf doesn't turn out right, make a note to adjust the recipe the next time you use it. Before long, your bread machine will be turning out a successful loaf every time you use it.

▶ Bread-machine drawbacks include nonremovable containers, which increases the hazard of spilling ingredients onto the heating element—a mess to clean. All of the machines are extremely noisy, and they can become very hot during the baking cycle. Some breads have a tendency to overrise in a bread machine, which causes the top to collapse slightly.

▶ *See also* BREADS, GENERAL; BREADS, YEAST

BREADS, GENERAL

▶ Bread can be divided into one of four basic categories: **yeast breads,** which are leavened with yeast and require kneading to stretch the flour's gluten; **batter breads,** yeast-leavened breads which are beaten instead of kneaded; **quick breads,** which use baking powder, baking soda or eggs for leaveners, and require gentle mixing; and **unleavened breads,** like matzo, which are quite flat because they contain no leavening at all.

▶ A flour's protein content has a definite affect on bread—the more protein, the more gluten (desirable in yeast breads). Check the flour package label under Nutritional Information to select one that has a protein level appropriate for what you're baking. Flours with 12 to 14 grams protein per cup are best for yeast breads; those with 9 to 11 grams are better for quick breads.

▶ Add nutrition to any bread with the Cornell Enrichment Formula. Before measuring flour into measuring cup, add 1 tablespoon each soy flour and nonfat milk powder, and 1 teaspoon wheat germ. Spoon in flour and level off. Repeat for each cup of flour used in the recipe.

▶ Using room-temperature ingredients in both yeast- and quick-bread mixtures speeds rising and baking times. Bring milk, juice, beer, etc., to room temperature before adding to the other ingredients. Dry ingredients that have been refrigerated should also be brought to room temperature.

▶ The liquids used to make bread bring their own characteristics to bread. *Water* creates a crisp crust and brings out the flour's wheat flavor. *Potato water* (that in which peeled potatoes have been boiled) adds flavor and gives bread a smooth crumb; the added starch makes the dough rise slightly faster. *Milk products* (including milk, buttermilk, yogurt and sour cream) give the bread a creamy beige color and produce a fine texture and a soft, brown crust. *Eggs* give bread a rich, moist crumb, a creamy yellow color and brown crust. *Fruit and vegetable juices* add flavor and body. Baking soda is added to quick breads made with fruit juice to neutralize its natural acid. *Liquid sweeteners* such as molasses, honey and maple syrup give bread a moist crumb and dark crust. *Vegetable and meat broths* add flavor and create a lightly crisp crust. If the broth is salted, reduce the salt in the recipe. *Beer, wine, cider and liquors* give bread a smooth grain and distinctive flavor. *Coffee and tea* provide a rich color and dark, crisp crust.

▶ The only time it's necessary to scald milk is when you use the raw, unpasteurized variety, which contains an organism that breaks down flour's gluten structure.

▶ One beaten large egg has a leavening power equal to ½ teaspoon baking powder.

B

- For extra leavening in loaves that contain a lot of heavy ingredients, substitute 1 beaten large egg for ¼ cup of the liquid called for in the recipe.
- Bread made without fat—like French bread—has a shorter shelf life than those with fat because fat holds moisture in baked goods.
- Breads that contain moist ingredients such as carrots, dried fruit or potatoes will stay soft longer than plain breads.
- When using a glass baking pan instead of metal, reduce the oven heat by 25°F.
- Don't think you have to always use loaf pans for bread baking. A round, 1½-quart casserole or soufflé dish can be substituted for an 8- by 4-inch loaf pan; a 2-quart dish can replace a 9- by 5-inch loaf pan.
- Baking breads at lower temperatures creates thicker, chewier crusts; higher temperatures give thinner, crisper crusts.
- To allow for oven discrepancies, check bread 10 to 15 minutes before the end of the recipe's designated baking time.
- If bread is browning too fast, cover it lightly with a "tent" of aluminum foil. Make sure the bread is on the middle rack of the oven.
- Cool bread completely, sitting right side up on a rack, before cutting or wrapping for storage. Any residual warmth will cause moisture to condense on the inside of the wrapping.
- If there are burned spots on the crust of a homebaked loaf, rub them off with the fine side of a grater.
- Don't ruin a loaf of freshly baked bread by using the wrong knife. A good serrated bread knife is worth its weight in gold. A serrated electric knife also works well.
- Round loaves require a slightly different slicing technique than the standard loaf shape. Cut the bread vertically in half, then place the cut side down and cut vertical slices. Or, if you're not using the bread for sandwiches, simply cut a round loaf into wedges.
- Most breads will stay fresh for 5 to 7 days at room temperature if wrapped airtight. The exception is a bread made without fat, such as French or Italian, which will stay fresh only for a day or two.
- Make crostini (Italian for "little crusts") with second-day French or Italian bread. Cut the bread into ¼-inch-thick slices, brush one side with olive oil, and broil about 30 seconds on each side, or until crisp and golden brown. The olive oil can be seasoned with herbs, garlic or other flavorings.
- Crostini make great soup or salad accompaniments. Or top with pâté or cheese, or olive or other spread to serve as hors d'oeuvre.
- If you don't store bread at room temperature, then freeze it. Bread turns stale fastest when stored in the refrigerator.
- To freeze bread, double wrap it airtight. Freeze yeast breads for up to 3 months; quick breads up to 6 months.

‣ If you freeze an unsliced loaf, it's a simple process with most breads to simply slice off what you want as you need it. Exceptions to this rule are very dense loaves such as rye and some quick breads like banana bread. Frozen bread slices will defrost in 10 to 15 minutes at room temperature. Or place in a microwave oven at HIGH (100 percent power) for about 10 seconds.

‣ If you place a piece of waxed paper or plastic wrap between bread slices before freezing, it'll be much easier to separate them while frozen.

‣ It's much easier to cut bread into very thin slices if it's frozen.

‣ Thaw frozen breads at room temperature and eat as soon as possible— bread that's been frozen dries out more quickly than fresh.

‣ A pizza cutter makes quick work of trimming bread crusts.

‣ Double wrap and freeze leftover bread slices and trimmings (adding to the bag as you have them) and use them to make breadcrumbs, stuffing, croutons, bread pudding, etc.

‣ Revive a loaf of less-than-fresh bread by slicing it thickly, and spreading with softened butter mixed with grated Parmesan or other cheese, minced herbs or crushed garlic. Wrap in foil and heat in a 325°F oven for about 15 minutes or until warmed through.

‣ Another way to restore dried-out bread or rolls is to sprinkle lightly with water, wrap loosely in foil or a sealed paper bag, and heat until warm in a 300°F oven. For crusty rolls, brush with water and heat, uncovered, at 350°F.

‣ To moisten and warm dried-out bread, place it in a colander set over a pot of simmering water. Cover and steam just until the bread is warmed through.

‣ *See also* BAGELS; BAKING POWDER; BAKING SODA; BISCUITS; BREADCRUMBS; BREADS, QUICK; BREADS, YEAST; FLOUR; GREASING PANS; HIGH-ALTITUDE ADJUSTMENTS; MUFFINS; PITA BREAD; POPOVERS; YEAST

BREADS, QUICK

‣ Quick breads are those leavened by baking soda, baking powder or eggs. Biscuits, cornbread, muffins and banana (or other fruit/nut) breads are among the most popular quick breads.

‣ Before beginning to mix a quick-bread batter, prepare the pans (*see* GREASING PANS) and turn on the oven.

‣ Too much baking powder or baking soda gives bread a crumbly, dry texture and bitter undertaste. It can also make the batter overrise, causing the bread to fall.

‣ Too little baking powder or baking soda produces a bread with a heavy, gummy texture.

B

- Because baking soda and baking powder begin releasing gas the instant they're moistened, they should always be mixed with the other dry ingredients before any liquid is added. Once the wet and dry ingredients are combined, the batter should be placed in the oven immediately.
- The immediate rising speed of baking soda and baking powder breads makes it important to have the oven preheated and pans greased before combining ingredients.
- Self-rising flour produces lighter quick breads because it contains less gluten. It can be substituted for all-purpose flour in quick breads by omitting both salt and baking powder.
- Use a light touch when mixing the dry and wet ingredients together. They should be stirred just until the dry ingredients are moistened—don't worry about small lumps, they'll disappear during baking. If you beat or otherwise overmix a quick-bread batter, you'll wind up with dense, tough bread.
- After turning a quick-bread batter into a baking pan, sprinkle the top with seeds, coconut, chopped nuts, etc., for a decorative touch. The topping should be an ingredient integral to the bread.
- Check a quick bread for doneness by inserting a toothpick or wooden skewer near the loaf's center. It should come out clean.
- It's normal for quick breads to have a cracked top, the result of a natural expansion of leavening gases during baking.
- Cooling quick breads in the pan for 10 minutes before transferring them to a rack to cool allows the bread to "set," making it easier to handle.
- Muffins and quick loaf breads that have dried out can be rehydrated by using a skewer to poke holes in them, then drizzling with fruit juice, rum, brandy or liqueur, or other complementary flavored liquid. Seal the bread tightly in foil or a plastic bag and refrigerate for a day or two.
- Quick breads past their prime can be thinly sliced (slice muffins crosswise), placed on a baking sheet, and toasted on both sides under the oven broiler. Or place the slices in a toaster oven and toast until golden brown. If desired, the slices can be brushed lightly with melted butter before toasting.
- For a delicious, triflelike dessert, cut overly dry, sweet quick bread into 1-inch chunks, drizzle with liqueur or fruit juice, and layer with fresh berries or other fruit and pudding or whipped cream. Cover and refrigerate for 4 to 6 hours.
- Make an instant bread pudding by coarsely crumbling leftover sweet quick bread and folding it into custard or pudding. Cover and refrigerate for 4 hours before serving.
- To make crumbs from leftover quick bread, arrange thin slices in a single layer on a baking sheet, and bake at 350°F until crisp and golden brown.

When cool, crumble and use as a topping for cobbler, ice cream or pudding.

▶ Use leftover breadcrumbs in pork or poultry stuffings.

▶ *See also* BAKING POWDER; BAKING SODA; BISCUITS; BREADCRUMBS; BREADS, GENERAL; BREADS, YEAST; FLOUR; GREASING PANS; HIGH-ALTITUDE ADJUSTMENTS; MUFFINS; POPOVERS; YEAST

BREADS, YEAST

▶ There are two basic kinds of yeast breads—those that are kneaded and those that are beaten, called "batter breads."

▶ **Batter breads** require extra yeast and vigorous beating but no kneading. Because the gluten isn't completely developed by a long kneading process, the texture of a batter bread is more open and coarse, the flavor slightly more yeasty due to additional leavening. The batter, which should be thick enough to stand a wooden spoon up in, rises once in the bowl in which it was mixed. It's then stirred down and turned into the baking pan, where it rises a second time before baking. In theory, almost any yeast bread recipe can be converted to a batter bread by simply adding less flour and doubling the yeast.

▶ The most commonly used flour in breadmaking today is derived from wheat, which contains a protein called gluten. When dough is kneaded or beaten, gluten forms the elastic network that holds in the carbon dioxide gas created by the leavener. The gas bubbles cause the gluten to stretch and expand, forming the bread's framework. The less gluten (protein) in the flour, the weaker the elasticity. And without a strong elastic network, the gas bubbles escape into the air rather than leavening the bread.

▶ Dense, low-gluten doughs like those made with rye flour will rise better and faster if you double the amount of yeast. The bread will taste slightly yeastier, but not to its detriment.

▶ Flour absorbs less liquid during hot, humid months than in dry weather because it will have already absorbed some of the moisture from the atmosphere. That's why many yeast-bread recipes give a range of flour amounts. Your best guideline is to start with the lower amount, adding only enough flour to keep the dough from being too sticky to work with.

▶ A dough that is slightly tacky to the touch will yield a lighter loaf; too much flour creates bread that's dry and dense.

▶ Yeast needs "food" in order to grow and expand, and that nourishment usually comes from some type of sugar. If you want to make a sugar-free loaf, omit the sweeteners and add 1 teaspoon malt (available in natural food stores) for each package of yeast used.

▶ In general, sweet yeast doughs take longer to rise than those that are sa-

B

vory. This is because, though sugar is "food" for yeast and encourages its growth, a lot of sugar overpowers the leavening action and slows rising.

▸ On the plus side, sugar adds flavor and tenderness to bread, helps brown the crust and creates a nicely textured loaf.

▸ Kneading is a technique used to mix and work a dough in order to form it into a cohesive, pliable mass. During kneading, the gluten in the flour forms a network of strands that stretches and expands. It's this gluten framework that enables the dough to hold in the gas bubbles formed by a leavener, thereby making the bread rise. Kneading can be done either manually or by machine.

▸ *Kneading by hand* is done with a pressing-folding-turning action performed by pressing down into the dough with the heels of both hands (throw your weight into it) then pushing away from the body. The dough is folded in half, given a quarter turn and the process repeated. Depending on the dough and the method used, kneading time can range anywhere from 5 to 20 minutes. Well-kneaded dough is smooth and elastic.

▸ If you're working with a particularly sticky dough, such as one made with rye flour, oil your hands slightly and the dough won't cling to them.

▸ If you want to keep your hands clean while kneading, wear the thin plastic gloves found in pharmacies, or slip plastic bags over your hands.

▸ *Mechanical kneading* can be done in a large mixer equipped with a dough hook (some machines have two hooks) or a food processor with a plastic or metal blade (consult your owner's guide for specific directions). There are also special breadmaking machines that mix, knead, rise and bake bread all in a single container.

▸ Spraying an electric mixer's dough hook(s) or food processor's blade with nonstick vegetable spray (or coating with a thin layer of vegetable oil) keeps the dough from climbing up the hook or blade during kneading. It also speeds cleanup.

▸ A damp dish towel placed under the pastry board on which you knead bread will keep the board from sliding around the countertop.

▸ Keep your work surface *lightly* dusted with flour to keep the dough from sticking.

▸ If you mistakenly knead too much flour into dough, lightly sprinkle it with warm water. Gradually knead in enough water to make the dough pliable.

▸ If layers of flour and dough build up on your palms, rub your hands together over a sink or wastebasket. Don't knead these dry dough particles back into the dough.

▸ Don't dirty another bowl for the dough to rise in. Use the bowl in which the ingredients were mixed, wiping it out with paper towel before oiling it lightly. Or oil the baking pan you'll be using and let the bread rise in that.

▶ If you want to give the dough a boost, pour boiling water into a heatproof bowl and let it stand while you're kneading the dough. Discard the water, dry the bowl, and put the dough in the warm bowl.

▶ Yeast doughs need a warm place in which to rise. Begin by covering the dough's container with a slightly damp towel to retain natural moisture. Ideally, dough should rise in an 80°F environment, but will rise at temperatures up to 100°F without killing the yeast.

▶ Warm places where dough can rise: Inside a gas oven warmed only by the pilot light (tape a note to the oven door to remind yourself that bread is rising inside); in an electric oven heated at 200°F for 1 minute, then turned off; set over a pan of water placed on the bottom shelf of a closed oven; if you're doing laundry, put the dough (in its bowl or pan) near (not on top if the machine vibrates) of the washer or dryer; or, run the clothes dryer on the heat cycle for 1 minute, then turn off the machine and put the dough inside; bring 2 cups of water to a boil in your microwave oven to create a warm, moist atmosphere, then turn off the power, set the dough inside and close the door. You'll find all kinds of creative places in your house where your bread dough can incubate.

▶ *Micro-rising bread dough:* Dough can rise in a microwave oven in about a third the regular time of conventional methods. However, any form of quick rising means the dough won't have as much time to develop its full flavor. *You must have a microwave oven with 10 percent power.* Any higher than that and your dough could turn into a half-baked lump. To micro-rise enough dough for 2 standard-size loaves, set 1 cup hot water at the back corner of your microwave oven. Place the dough in a large, greased, microwave-proof bowl. Cover with plastic wrap, then a damp towel. Set the power level at 10 percent power; cook for 8 minutes. Let the dough rest for 5 minutes. Repeat at 10 percent power for 5 to 8 minutes longer, or until the dough has doubled in bulk. The second rising—after the dough is shaped into loaves—will take about 10 minutes, but the loaves must be in glass baking dishes. Refer to your microwave owner's guide for specific information on rising bread in your microwave oven.

▶ Wherever you choose to let bread dough rise, be sure the rising location is draft-free. Drafts are enemies of yeast and will cause dough to rise unevenly and slowly.

▶ If your dough just isn't rising (and you've proofed the yeast to make sure it's alive), it could be because the environment is too cold. If that's not the case, dissolve another package of yeast in ¼ cup warm water and ½ teaspoon sugar (*see* YEAST). Add this mixture to the dough slowly, kneading it in well. Cover the dough, set it in a warm place and it should rise.

▶ Yeast dough should rise to double its original bulk. To test it after the first

B

rise, poke two fingers into the dough; don't be timid—jab them in a good ½ inch. If the indentations stay, the dough's ready. The finger-poke method is only good for the first rise.

▸ Once the dough has doubled, give it a good sock in the middle with your fist. This is called punching down the dough. Knead it for about 30 seconds to remove any air bubbles before shaping it into loaves.

▸ Though two risings are traditional, bread will be lighter and finer textured if you have time for three risings (twice in a bowl, the last in the pan).

▸ Or, after punching down the dough you can return it to the bowl, cover tightly and refrigerate for up to 2 days. It will continue to rise in the refrigerator and should be punched down once a day. Remove the dough from the refrigerator at least 3 hours before shaping into loaves.

▸ It's not necessary for the dough to rise to the top of the pan for the final rising. On the contrary, if you allow the shaped loaves to increase by more than double, you run the risk of the bread collapsing during baking. Have your oven preheated and ready to go so the bread can begin baking as soon as it's doubled.

▸ The tops of many yeast breads are slashed just before baking; some are slashed before the second rising. Such slashes not only give bread a professional look, but allow excess gas to escape during baking, preventing ragged splitting of the loaf's top. Use a very sharp knife or a serrated knife (a tomato knife works well), razor blade or metal food-processor blade to do the slashing. Pointed scissors can also be used to snip the top of the dough. Make slashes ¼ to ½ inch deep.

▸ Glazes add shine, color and flavor to the top crust. Use a pastry brush to coat the dough with glaze before it goes into the oven. You can slash the tops of unbaked loaves before or after brushing them with a glaze and sprinkling with seeds or nuts.

▸ *Water* produces a crisp crust. Brush the dough with water before it goes into the oven, then again 10 minutes before baking time is complete. Placing a pan of hot water on the oven shelf below the bread will also create steam for a crisper crust. Remove the water from the oven 10 minutes before the bread is done to let the crust dry out.

▸ *Egg glazes* add color, shine and hold seeds in place. Egg yolks give a dark-brown crust; egg whites a shiny crust; whole eggs give shine and color. Mix 1 whole egg with 1 tablespoon water; 1 egg yolk or white with 2 teaspoons water.

▸ *Milk* or *melted butter* creates a soft, tender crust.

▸ *Syrupy sweeteners* like honey, molasses or maple syrup create a soft, shiny, slightly sweet crust. Mix 1 teaspoon syrup with 2 teaspoons water or melted butter.

▸ You can make your own crackly, flour-crunchy *Dutch-crunch topping* for breads. For 2 loaves, dissolve 3 ¼-ounce packages active dry yeast and 1 teaspoon sugar in ¾ cup warm (110°F) water. Let stand until foamy, about 5 minutes. Add 1 tablespoon sugar, 1 teaspoon salt, 1 tablespoon vegetable oil and 1 cup rice flour (*not* oriental sweet rice flour). Beat until smooth, then cover and let rise until doubled, about 30 minutes. Spread over the tops of dough just before the second rising.

B

▶ Yeast dough can be easily frozen before baking. Let the dough rise once, then punch it down and form into a loaf. Lightly oil a large piece of plastic wrap (with enough overlap to cover bread). Place plastic wrap, oiled side up, in a loaf pan, Add shaped dough and seal plastic wrap; freeze until dough is solid. Remove frozen dough from pan and double wrap in freezer-weight foil or a plastic bag; return to freezer for up to 2 months. Before thawing, remove plastic wrap and put frozen dough into a greased pan. Cover and thaw overnight in refrigerator. The next day, cover dough lightly with a kitchen towel and let bread rise in a warm, draft-free place until doubled in size. Bake as usual.

▶ To cut rolled dough (as for cinnamon rolls) or delicate baked breads into slices, wrap a long piece of thread or unflavored dental floss around the area to be cut and pull ends together slowly. The thread (or floss) will "slice" cleanly through the dough or bread.

▶ Almost any kneaded yeast dough can be made into breadsticks. Pinch off walnut-sized pieces of dough and use your palm to roll them into pencil-thin ropes. Place, ½ inch apart, on a lightly greased baking sheet; cover and let rise in a warm place for 20 minutes. Brush with a glaze and sprinkle with sesame or other seeds, salt, cracked pepper, grated Parmesan, chili powder—whatever you like. Bake at 350°F for 20 to 30 minutes, or until crisp and golden brown.

▶ For a crisper crust on any bread, place a shallow pan (9- by 13-inch is perfect) filled halfway with hot water on the bottom shelf. The water creates steam, which in turn promotes a crisp crust.

▶ Baking breads on a special baking tile (found in gourmet stores) or an unglazed terra-cotta tile (found in a tile store or masonry supply) produces a wonderfully crisp bottom crust.

▶ Place bread baking pans about 4 inches apart near the center of the middle shelf of a preheated oven.

▶ Resist opening the oven door to peek during the important first 15 to 20 minutes of baking time. It's not unusual for a loaf to increase in size by one third during the first 15 minutes of baking. This dramatic rise—known as "oven-spring"—could be diminished by a sudden draft.

▶ Bread can also be started in a cold oven if you're in a hurry and trying to speed the last few minutes of rising time. When a dough has almost doubled, place the loaves in a cold oven and set the temperature 25°F higher

B

than called for in the recipe. Bake 5 minutes less than the time called for in the recipe before checking for doneness.

▶ For an even, golden-brown side and bottom crust, remove bread from its pan 5 or 10 minutes before it's due to be done and place directly on the oven rack.

▶ Test yeast breads for doneness by removing them from the pan (use oven mitts) and lightly tapping the bottom of the loaf. If it sounds hollow, it's done. If it's not done, return the loaf directly to the oven rack and bake 5 minutes longer.

▶ Another way to test a yeast bread for doneness is with a quick-read thermometer. Insert it into the bottom middle of the loaf—a reading of 180° to 185°F tells you it's done.

▶ For quick, oven-fresh bread at the last minute: Bake bread for 10 minutes less than the recipe suggests. Remove from oven, let cool in pan for 10 minutes, then transfer to a rack to cool completely. Freeze for up to 3 months. When ready to use, remove from freezer and thaw in wrapping at room temperature. Remove wrapping and bake on middle shelf at 350°F for about 20 minutes, or until golden brown.

▶ Always cool bread right side up on a rack. For the best texture, cool for 2 to 3 hours before slicing.

▶ If you're disappointed with a dense, dry loaf of bread, simply slice it thinly (cut the slices in half, if they're large) and toast until dry in a 275°F oven. Serve these crisp "crackers" with spreads as a soup or salad accompaniment, or with cocktails.

▶ Leftover croissants make great accompaniments for soups and salads if you cut them crosswise into ¼-inch-thick slices and toast on both sides under the broiler just until golden brown.

▶ *See also* BREADCRUMBS; BREAD MACHINES; BREADS, GENERAL; BREADS, QUICK; FLOUR; GREASING PANS; HIGH-ALTITUDE ADJUSTMENTS; YEAST

BREAKFAST / BRUNCH

▶ For a speedily assembled company breakfast or brunch without having to get up at the crack of dawn, gather recipe ingredients the night before. For instance, you can combine biscuit or muffin ingredients (keeping the dry ingredients separate from the moist ingredients), and even grease the muffin tins so they'll be ready to go. Or chop the vegetables for a special omelet or scramble, and mix and refrigerate the egg mixture for it.

▶ The night before, you can also set the table, put out serving dishes and utensils that will be used, and line roll baskets with napkins. Put condiments like syrups, honey and jam in small pitchers or dishes, cover with plastic wrap, and leave at room temperature. Do the same with butter, cream cheese, crème fraîche, etc., only store in the refrigerator.

▶ The one piece of cookware that can make life easier for morning cooks is a good, heavy skillet—preferably with a nonstick coating, which makes cooking eggs a breeze.

▶ *See also* BACON; BISCUITS; EGGS; MUFFINS

B

BROCCOFLOWER [BROK-uh-flow-er]

▶ Broccoflower is a relatively new vegetable that's a cross between broccoli and cauliflower. It looks like a cauliflower, only its color is a bright light green. Broccoflower's flavor is milder than that of either of its parents.

▶ Look for a firm broccoflower with compact florets; the leaves should be crisp and green. The size of the head doesn't affect the quality, but avoid any specimens with brown spots.

▶ Store unwashed broccoflower, tightly wrapped, in the refrigerator for up to 5 days.

▶ Before using, wash thoroughly and remove the leaves at the base and trim the stem.

▶ *Broccoflower yields:* 1 pound fresh = about 1½ cups chopped or sliced.

▶ Broccoflower can be cooked in any way suitable for cauliflower (*see listing*).

▶ *See also* VEGETABLES, GENERAL

BROCCOLI [BROK-uh-lee]

▶ Buy broccoli with a deep, strong color—green, or green tinged with purple. The buds should be tightly closed and the leaves crisp.

▶ Store broccoli, unwashed, in an airtight plastic bag in the refrigerator for up to 4 days.

▶ Wash and trim broccoli before using. If the stalks are tough, peel before cooking.

▶ *Broccoli yields:* 1 pound fresh = 2 cups chopped; 1 10-ounce package frozen = 1½ cups chopped.

▶ The quicker you cook broccoli the greener it will remain.

▶ Don't add an acid like lemon juice or vinegar to the cooking water or you'll end up with gray-green broccoli.

▶ Broccoli heads cook more quickly than the stems. To insure more even cooking, cut the stems in 2 or 3 places, slicing all the way through the floret.

▶ The heads will cook more quickly if you cut them into 3 or 4 pieces.

▶ When a recipe calls for broccoli heads and you don't plan to use the stems within a few days, blanch the stems in boiling water for 2 minutes. Cool, then freeze in an airtight plastic bag for up to 3 months. The stems are great for stir-frys, soups, etc.

▶ When using broccoli in stir-frys, casseroles or other dishes with mixed foods, boil it (*see* PARBOILING) for a few minutes, cooling immediately in ice water to stop the cooking.

B

▸ When serving broccoli as crudités, brighten its color by blanching it for 1 minute in boiling water. Plunge into a bowl of ice water to stop the cooking.

▸ If you don't like the smell of cooking broccoli, throw a couple of thick chunks of bread into the cooking water. Bread slices work, too, though they sometimes dissolve and are hard to remove. Or toss a couple of red bell pepper pieces into the pot. Use a slotted spoon to retrieve the pot sweeteners before serving the broccoli.

▸ Turn leftover or overcooked broccoli into a delicious broccoli bisque. Put the broccoli into a blender (you may have to do it in batches if there's a lot), add milk, broth or cream and a shot of sherry; process until smooth. Strain, if desired, and heat gently or serve cold.

▸ *See also* BLANCHING; VEGETABLES, GENERAL

BROILING

▸ Make cleanup a breeze by spraying the broiler pan with nonstick vegetable spray (or coating lightly with vegetable oil) before beginning to cook.

▸ Or you can line the broiler pan with foil, discarding the foil after it cools.

▸ Always preheat the broiler and broiling pan.

▸ A piece or two of bread in the bottom of the broiler pan will soak up the grease and prevent a possible fire.

▸ You can also reduce fire risk by pouring a little water in the bottom of a broiler pan. The drawback with this method is that it produces steam, which isn't desirable for most broiled foods.

▸ Broiled meat, fish or poultry will brown more evenly if brought to room temperature before cooking.

▸ Blot the surface of food to be broiled to remove excess moisture.

▸ Reduce the risk of flare-ups by trimming excess fat from meats, and removing poultry skin.

▸ When a recipe says to "broil 4 inches from the heating element," it's referring to the food's surface, not the bottom of the pan. If you measure from the rack on which the pan sits, the food will be too close to the heat and could burn before it cooks through. Use a ruler for accuracy when measuring the distance between the food's surface and the heat source.

▸ In general, the thinner the food you're broiling (such as thin pork chops, chicken breasts or fish fillets), the closer to the heat source it should be. Rare-cooked steaks and other such foods should also be close to the heat. Food that is thick or that should be cooked through (such as chicken halves) should be positioned further from the heat source.

▸ Drain off the fat as it's rendered out of the meat. Letting it accumulate could cause a fire.

B

- If excess fat does cause a fire, smother it by covering with a large pan lid or sheet of heavy-duty foil.
- Most broiled food requires basting. Always warm the basting liquid so it doesn't slow down the cooking or browning.
- If you're watching calories, baste broiled food with low-calorie salad dressings.
- If you haven't oiled the broiler pan or lined it with foil for easy cleanup, sprinkle it liberally with powdered soap or salt, then cover with wet newspaper or paper towels as soon as you're done cooking.
- *See also* COOKING, GENERAL

BROTH, CANNED

- There are two basic styles of canned broth: ready-to-serve (which is already diluted) and condensed (which requires added liquid). Check the label—using undiluted condensed broth in a recipe could produce an unpalatably salty dish.
- Boost the flavor of canned chicken or beef broth by adding 2 chopped medium celery stalks, 1 chopped small onion, 1 chopped medium carrot, 3 parsley sprigs, 1 bay leaf and ½ cup water to each can (of about 14 ounces) broth. Bring to a boil, then cover and simmer for 30 minutes. Strain before using.
- Adding dried mushrooms to canned beef broth gives it a rich complexity that belies its commercial beginnings. Bring the broth to a boil, then remove from heat and add 4 to 5 dried mushrooms. Cover and let stand for 1 hour. Process in a blender until pureed; strain, if desired. Add water or red wine to dilute if the flavor's too strong. This fortified broth makes a great base for soups, stews and sauces.
- Put canned broth in the refrigerator overnight before using. That way, the fat will congeal and can be removed easily before using the broth.
- Use a muffin tin to freeze ½-cup portions of leftover broth, then turn the broth "cubes" out into a freezer-proof plastic bag, seal tightly, and freeze for up to a year.

BROWN SUGAR *see* SUGAR

BRUSSELS SPROUTS

- Buy small bright green Brussels sprouts with compact heads. Loose-leaved, dull sprouts are over the hill.
- Try to buy sprouts the same size so they'll all cook in the same amount of time.
- Store sprouts, unwashed, in an airtight plastic bag in the refrigerator for up to 3 days. Long storage for Brussels sprouts gives them a strong flavor.

▸ *Brussels sprouts yields:* 1 pound fresh = 4 cups; 1 10-ounce package frozen = 18 to 24 sprouts.

▸ Before cooking sprouts, wash and blot them dry. Cut off a thin slice and cut an X in the stem end of each Brussels sprout; pull off any loose or pale leaves. The X-cut allows the heat to more easily penetrate to the sprout's center, thereby cooking it more quickly and evenly.

▸ Don't add an acid like lemon juice to the cooking water or you'll end up with gray-green sprouts.

▸ Brussels sprouts should be cooked only until crisp-tender, usually about 10 minutes. Their color should be bright, intense green. Overcooking will turn sprouts an ugly olive-drab.

▸ To check Brussels sprouts for doneness, pierce the stem end with a fork. It should penetrate easily.

▸ If you don't like the smell of Brussels sprouts cooking, toss a couple of thick chunks of bread into the cooking water (bread slices sometimes dissolve and are hard to remove). Or toss a couple of red bell pepper pieces into the pot. Use a slotted spoon to retrieve the pot sweeteners before serving the sprouts.

▸ Brussels sprouts' nutty flavor is enchanced by toasted almonds.

▸ After cooking and cooling, sprouts can be cut into ¼-inch slices and sautéed with scallions, garlic and minced ginger for a wonderful change of pace.

▸ Brussels sprouts can also be cooked, cooled, quartered and made into a cold salad, mixed with diced tomatoes and tossed with a vinaigrette.

▸ *See also* VEGETABLES, GENERAL

BUTTER

▸ There are two main types of butter on the market—**regular butter** and **unsalted butter.** Products labeled "sweet cream butter" (a term for any butter made with fresh cream) actually contain salt. Unsalted butter is labeled as such.

▸ **Whipped butter** has air beaten into it, therby increasing its volume and creating a softer, more spreadable consistency when cold. It comes in salted and unsalted forms. Most whipped butters contain 30 to 45 percent air, so should never be used in baked goods.

▸ Storing butter: Store regular butter, wrapped airtight, in the refrigerator for up to 1 month. Butter absorbs flavors like a sponge, so be sure it's wrapped airtight. Since salt acts as a preservative, unsalted butter is more perishable than regular butter and should be refrigerated for no more than 2 weeks. Both regular and unsalted butter can be frozen, wrapped airtight in a plastic bag, for up to 6 months.

▸ *Butter yields:* 1 pound = 4 sticks; 2 cups. One stick = ½ cup; 8 tablespoons.

▸ Salted and unsalted butter can be used interchangeably in cooking or baking. However, if a recipe calls for unsalted butter and you use salted butter, reduce the salt called for in the dish or baked good. There's about ⅜ teaspoon of salt in every stick of butter.

B

▶ Using unsalted butter gives the cook more control over the final flavor of a dish.

▶ Use unsalted butter to grease pans. Salted butter may cause baked goods to stick to pans.

▶ Use a butter wrapper to grease a pan with remnants of the clinging butter.

▶ To cleanly cut cold butter, cover the knife blade with plastic wrap.

▶ Butter scorches easily when used for techniques like sautéing. Avoid the problem by substituting vegetable oil for one quarter of the butter.

▶ If you do burn butter while melting it for sautéing, you might as well throw it out because its bitter flavor will transfer to the food you're cooking.

▶ The microwave oven is great for melting butter. In a 600- to 700-watt oven at HIGH (100 percent power), 2 tablespoons cold butter will melt in about 45 seconds, ¼ cup in about 50 seconds, and ½ cup in about 1½ minutes. Residual heat will continue to melt the butter even after it's removed from the oven. Cover the container in which the butter is melting with a piece of waxed paper to protect oven walls against spatters.

▶ Soften butter for spreading on bread or toast by placing a stick in the microwave oven at MEDIUM-LOW (30 percent power) for about 20 seconds.

▶ To quickly soften a stick of hard butter to use in a recipe, cut it into ½-inch-thick slices and place on a microwave-safe plate. Microwave at MEDIUM-LOW (30 percent power) until soft, about 30 seconds.

▶ If you don't have a microwave oven, butter will soften more quickly if you grate or thinly slice it. Either use a grater or vegetable peeler, or put it in a food processor fitted with a slicing disk. Let it stand for about 10 minutes (set it over—not in—a bowl of hot water to speed things up), then mix or beat as desired.

▶ Company-pretty butter can easily be created in several ways: use a butter curler for butter curls; create butter balls with a melon baller; press butter into decorative butter or candy molds; or use a pastry bag with a large star tip to pipe softened butter into small glass bowls. Butter curlers and molds, pastry bags and melon ballers can all be found in gourmet shops and often in department-store housewares sections.

▶ Homemade butter is fun and easy to make in the food processor. Put the processor bowl and metal blade in the freezer for 15 minutes. Pour 2 cups cold, heavy whipping cream (not ultra-pasteurized) into the workbowl fitted with the metal blade. Process for 2 minutes; scrape down sides of bowl. Continue to process until the solids separate from the liquid, about 4 minutes. Pour off the liquid (whey), cover and refrigerate, and use for

B

sauces and soups within 3 days. Turn butter out onto a square of cheese-cloth or heavy-duty paper towel; twist to extract as much liquid as possible. Cover butter and refrigerate for up to 2 weeks. Let stand at room temperature for 30 minutes before serving. Makes about 6 ounces butter and 1 cup liquid.

▸ Make your own whipped butter by using electric beaters to whip softened butter until very light and fluffy.

▸ Add pizzazz to plain butter by adding flavorful ingredients like minced herbs, grated cheese, sesame seeds (ground and toasted), spices, mustard, honey or maple syrup, chopped chutney, citrus juice (such as orange or lemon)—let your imagination lead the way. Simply soften the butter, and blend or beat in the added ingredient. A word of caution when adding a liquid or semiliquid such as honey, juice or liqueur: Add the liquid *very* gradually, beating constantly, or the mixture will separate.

▸ Make a great spread for breads, waffles and pancakes by mixing 2 to 4 tablespoons of your favorite preserves with a stick of softened butter.

▸ *Substitutions for 1 cup butter in cooking or baking:* 1 cup margarine; or ⅞ cup vegetable oil, lard or vegetable shortening; or ⅘ cup strained bacon fat; or ¾ cup strained chicken fat.

▸ *See also* FATS AND OILS; MARGARINE

BUTTERMILK

▸ You can substitute buttermilk for regular milk in most baking recipes if you add ½ teaspoon baking soda for each cup of buttermilk to the dry ingredients.

▸ In most recipes, buttermilk can be substituted for yogurt or sour milk.

▸ Buttermilk adds its delicious tang to baked goods, salad dressing, soups and sauces.

▸ Buttermilk powder is a boon for those who don't have a carton of buttermilk sitting in the fridge. For baking recipes that call for buttermilk or sour milk, simply substitute ¼ cup buttermilk powder plus 1 cup water for each cup of fresh buttermilk needed. Mix the buttermilk powder in with the dry ingredients, the water with the other moist ingredients.

▸ Store unopened buttermilk powder in a cool, dry place for up to 3 years. Once opened, refrigerate for up to 1 year. The powder will stay fresher if you first cover open can with foil, then the lid.

▸ *Substitutions for 1 cup buttermilk (for baking):* 1 cup plain yogurt; or 1 tablespoon vinegar or lemon juice plus enough milk to equal 1 cup (stir, then let stand for 5 minutes); or 1¾ teaspoons cream of tartar plus 1 cup milk.

▸ *See also* MILK

CABBAGE

▶ Choose a green or red cabbage with fresh, crisp-looking leaves that are firmly packed; the head should be heavy for its size. Avoid any cabbage with dull, withering leaves or brown spots.

▶ Store cabbage in the refrigerator, tightly wrapped in a plastic bag, for up to 2 weeks. Before using, remove the core; rinse and blot dry.

▶ *Cabbage yields:* 1 pound = about 4 cups shredded; 2 cups cooked.

▶ Adding ½ tablespoon lemon juice or vinegar for each cup of cooking water for red cabbage will preserve its color and keep it from turning purple.

▶ Cabbage should be boiled just until tender, about 5 minutes for coarsely shredded cabbage, longer for cabbage chunks. Overcooking will turn it limp and produce an awful odor.

▶ Cabbage will produce less flatulence if you boil it for 5 minutes, drain well, then continue to cook in fresh boiling water. This technique, of course, is only possible when cooking whole or large chunks of cabbage; it would overcook shredded cabbage.

▶ You can cook shredded cabbage ahead of time, then plunge it into a bowl of cold water to stop the cooking. Drain well and blot dry, then wrap in a plastic bag and refrigerate. The next day, it can be added at the last minute to stir-frys or other sautéed food.

▶ If you're cooking cabbage wedges, try steaming them. The wedges will hold together better than if they were boiled.

▶ The odor of cooking cabbage can permeate the house. To reduce the smell, toss a couple of thick chunks of bread into the cooking water. (Bread slices sometimes dissolve and are hard to remove.) Use a slotted spoon to retrieve the pot sweeteners before serving the cabbage.

▶ The easiest way to remove whole cabbage leaves for stuffing is to core the cabbage, then immerse in a pot of boiling water. Reduce to a simmer, and heat the cabbage for 1 minute. Remove the cabbage from the water, drain well and blot dry with paper towels. Carefully remove the softened outer leaves and, when they'll no longer peel with ease, return the cabbage head to the simmering water. Repeat as necessary until you have enough cabbage leaves.

▶ For the crispest slaw, shred the cabbage, then immerse in ice water for an hour. Drain well and blot dry before refrigerating in a plastic bag until ready to use.

▶ *See also* VEGETABLES, GENERAL

CAKES

▶ Ovens are notoriously temperamental and can be off by as much as 75°F (sometimes more). That's why an oven thermometer (*see* THERMOMETERS) is a good investment, particularly for something as delicate as cake.

▶ You'll get better volume from cakes if the ingredients are at room temperature before you begin mixing. To take the chill off refrigerated milk and other liquids, heat in a microwave oven for 30 seconds or so, just until body temperature. Refrigerated dry ingredients like flour or nuts should sit out at room temperature for about 30 minutes.

▶ Before beginning to mix the batter, prepare the pans (*see* GREASING PANS) and turn on the oven, positioning the rack in the center of the oven.

▶ Shiny pans are best for cakemaking because they reflect the heat, thereby producing cakes with tender crusts.

▶ Whenever using a glass baking pan instead of metal, reduce the oven heat by 25°F.

▶ Be generous when greasing cake pans (about 1 tablespoon per layer-cake pan) and your cakes won't stick.

▶ Tube pans used for chiffon, sponge or angel food cakes are never greased. The ungreased sides of the pan allow enough traction for the delicate batter to cling to as it bakes and cools.

▶ Whenever a chocolate cake recipe calls for greasing and flouring the pan, grease it, then dust with unsweetened cocoa (or carob) powder instead.

▶ You don't always have to use round pans for layer cakes. Try substituting 8-inch square baking pans, or 2 to 3 8- by 4-inch loaf pans. Reduce the baking time slightly, checking for doneness about 15 minutes before the time suggested.

▶ Cake flour produces lighter cakes because it contains less gluten. If a recipe calls for cake flour and you don't have any, substitute 1 cup stirred all-purpose flour, minus 2 tablespoons, for each cup cake flour.

▶ In general, count on using about 1½ teaspoons baking powder for every cup flour in layer, bundt or pound cake batters.

▶ Before measuring syrupy sweeteners such as honey and corn syrup, lightly coat the measuring cup or spoon with vegetable oil. Every drop of the syrup will easily slip out. The same result can be obtained if you measure the fat called for in a recipe and then use the same (unwashed) utensil as the measure for the sweetener.

▶ Cold butter can be softened in preparation for beating in a couple of ways. Cut a stick into ½-inch-thick slices, place on a microwave-safe plate and heat at MEDIUM-LOW (30 percent power) for about 30 seconds. Or, grate or thinly slice it using a grater, vegetable peeler, or a food processor fitted with a 2mm slicing blade. Let it stand for about 10 minutes (set it over— not in—a bowl of hot water to speed things up), then mix or beat as desired.

► When creaming butter and sugar together, add salt and any spices called for in the recipe. Beating them into the butter will better disperse them throughout the batter later on.

► Be sure and beat the butter (or other fat) with the sugar as long as the recipe directs. Not beating thoroughly can create a coarse-textured or heavy, compact cake.

C

► Don't worry if a whipped butter-sugar mixture looks "curdled" after the eggs are beaten in. The problem will correct itself once the flour is added.

► Eggs for cakes should be at room temperature. To quickly warm refrigerated eggs, place them in a bowl of very warm (but not hot!) water for 5 to 10 minutes. If using the eggs separated, place the yolks in one bowl, the whites in another, and then place the separate bowls in a pan of warm water. Don't fill the pan so full that the water gets into the eggs.

► Add richness to cakes by substituting 2 egg yolks for 1 whole egg.

► For lighter cakes, separate the eggs. Add the yolks to the butter mixture; beat the whites, then fold them into the final batter.

► Buttermilk can be substituted for regular milk in most layer-cake recipes. Add ½ teaspoon baking soda for each cup buttermilk to the dry ingredients when buttermilk is used. The result will be a light, tender cake.

► Use an electric mixer for heavy batters (such as those for pound cakes) in order to incorporate as much air as possible.

► Raisins, chocolate chips and nut pieces will settle to the bottom unless the cake batter is thick enough to suspend them. If the batter is thin and you're determined to add such items, chop them very finely (they still might sink).

► Tossing nuts, raisins and other chopped dried fruit in flour will help keep them suspended in cake batters.

► To allow room for the cake to rise during baking, don't fill the pan more than half to three-quarters full with batter, depending on the cake.

► After pouring a layer-cake batter into a pan, rap the bottom of the pan against the countertop several times to release any large air bubbles. (Don't do this with batters laden with chopped nuts, chocolate chips, etc., or these could end up at the bottom.)

► Dispel air from the more delicate chiffon, sponge or angel food cake batters by running a knife in a zigzag pattern through the batter.

► For the best results, oven heat must circulate freely and evenly between pans. Arrange cake pans so they have at least 2 inches between each other and the sides of the oven. If cakes are baked on two shelves, position them so that one doesn't sit directly beneath another. Don't bake more than three cake layers at a time in one oven.

► Don't open the oven door during the first 15 minutes of baking time. After this time, open the door gently; sudden movement or temperature changes can cause a cake to fall.

C

- To compensate for hot spots in ovens, reverse the position of a cake pan or pans from side to side after 20 minutes of baking time. Don't move the cake during the first 20 minutes or it could fall.
- If you're baking a cake that always "domes" slightly in the middle, try covering it lightly with foil. Remove the foil during the final 15 minutes of baking so the top turns a nice golden color.
- If cake is browning too fast, cover it lightly with a "tent" of aluminum foil.
- To allow for oven variances, test a cake for doneness 5 to 10 minutes before the end of the baking time.
- Test deep cakes (like Bundt or pound cakes) for doneness with a long wooden skewer, commonly found in supermarkets. If it comes out clean, the cake's done. Some recipes say the skewer should be "almost clean," meaning a few crumbs clinging to the pick are fine.
- A chiffon, sponge or angel food cake is done when it springs back when lightly touched in the center with your finger. Layer cakes can also be tested this way.
- A foam-type cake like chiffon, sponge or angel food that hasn't risen enough is probably due to one of three things: The egg whites were over-beaten—stiff but dry, rather than moist and glossy; or underbeaten—the whites weren't stiff enough; or the batter was overmixed, rather than gently folded, as the flour was added.
- If a foam-type cake falls after it's baked, it could also be because the whites were overbeaten, or that the cake was cooled right side up. Overmixing can also cause these types of cake to be tough.
- Layer cakes should be cooled in the pan for 10 minutes before turning out onto a rack to cool completely. If your cakes have a tendency to stick, set the pan on a wet towel during that first 10 minutes. Spray the rack with nonstick vegetable spray if you have trouble with cake sticking to it.
- Run a dinner knife around the edge of a layer cake to loosen it from the pan. Be sure to press the knife against the pan so as not to dig into the cake.
- If a cake cools in a waxed-paper-lined pan so long that the paper sticks, use a hair dryer to blow hot air over the pan's bottom for a minute or so. Or, return the cake to a 350°F oven for 3 to 5 minutes. Then invert the pan and remove the cake.
- If parchment or waxed paper sticks to the bottom of a cake, lightly brush the paper with warm water. Let stand 1 minute, then remove the paper.
- To speed the cooling of layer cakes, place them in the freezer for 10 to 15 minutes while you make the frosting. Keep in mind that the warm cake will slightly lower the freezer's temperature.

▶ Cool a jelly-roll cake by immediately inverting it onto a dish towel that's been dusted with powdered sugar. Roll the warm cake up in the towel, let stand until cool, then unroll and fill as desired.

▶ Chiffon, sponge and angel food cakes are cooled by inverting the pan, which keeps the cake from falling. Many tube pans have legs on which the pan can stand so air can circulate underneath. If yours doesn't have built-in legs, invert the pan and position the tube over a narrow-necked bottle.

▶ You can leave a cooled angel food cake in the pan, covered tightly with foil for up to a day, until you're ready to frost it.

▶ To loosen an angel food cake from its pan, use a long knife with a thin blade or a metal spatula. Press the instrument firmly against the side of the pan and slowly rotate the pan until you're back to your starting point. It's important to keep the knife or spatula pressed against the pan so the cake won't get torn in the process. Angel food cakes must be *thoroughly* cool before you try to remove them from the pan or they could fall in the process.

▶ Angel food cakes "set" and are easier to slice if you freeze them, wrapped airtight, for 24 hours. Bring to room temperature before frosting.

▶ You run the risk of the cake sticking to the plate if it's not thoroughly cooled before being transferred.

▶ Unfrosted layer cakes and sponge-type cakes like chiffon and angel food can be frozen in a heavyweight plastic bag for up to 6 months. To thaw, remove from bag and let stand at room temperature for 1 to 2 hours.

▶ If there are burned or overbrowned places on a cake, simply cut them off and put frosting on the cake that's thick enough to fill and cover the gouges.

▶ To split cake layers, loop a long piece of unflavored dental floss tightly around the center of the cake horizontally. Cross the ends, then slowly but firmly pull on each end. The floss will cut cleanly through the cake.

▶ Another splitting method is to stick toothpicks at 1½-inch intervals at the level you want to cut the cake. Let the toothpicks guide you as you use a long, thin (preferably serrated) knife to cut the cake in half.

▶ Almost any single-layer (8- to 9-inch) cake can be turned into an upside-down cake. Start by generously greasing the pan, then drizzle the bottom with ⅓ cup melted butter, sprinkle evenly with ½ cup packed brown sugar and ½ teaspoon each ground cinnamon and nutmeg. Top with ½ to 1 cup chopped nuts, then sliced fruit such as apples, peaches, plums or even canned pineapple or other sliced fruit. Pour cake batter over fruit and bake as usual. When the cake tests done, invert it onto a serving plate. Let stand for 5 minutes before removing cake pan.

▶ For a quick and pretty decoraton, place a paper doily on top of an unfrosted cake and sprinkle it liberally with sifted confectioners' sugar or cocoa powder (or sift the sugar and cocoa together for a third color). Carefully remove the doily from the cake to reveal the lacy design. To reserve the sugar or cocoa, place the used doily over a piece of waxed paper, shake the powder off, then transfer it back into its container. For special designs, make your own stencil, or choose one from a crafts or fabric store. You can stencil a name, or numbers, or even a decorative border. Or, use several stencils together with contrasting colors.

▶ A serrated knife is good for cutting cakes; or one with a long, thin blade. Either will cut easier if you soak the blade in very hot water for a couple of minutes, then dry it off just before cutting the cake.

▶ If you serve a lot of cakes, invest in a cake cutter—long, thin metal tines with a handle.

▶ Keep cakes fresh by investing in a cake cover, or a covered cake carrier.

▶ The more airtight a cake storage container, the longer the cake will stay moist and fresh.

▶ Cut an apple in half and put it in the storage container with a cake to help keep it moist.

▶ If you don't have a cake cover and need to cover a cake with a soft frosting, stick toothpicks at 4-inch intervals in the top and sides of the cake; lightly drape a large sheet of plastic wrap over the picks. Foil can also be used, but isn't as flexible.

▶ If a cake's too dry to be usable as is, make a triflelike dessert by cutting it into chunks and placing in a large bowl. Sprinkle with liqueur or fruit juice, cover with plastic wrap, and let sit at room temperature for an hour or so. Then combine the cake chunks with custard or whipped cream (or a mixture of the two) and maybe some chopped fresh fruit. Spoon into stemmed glasses, cover and refrigerate for at least 3 hours before serving.

▶ If you think a cake's beyond repair (too dry, or fallen and too moist), make crumbs out of it in a food processor with a metal blade. Do it in batches so as not to overfill the processor. If the crumbs are too moist, spread them in a single layer on a baking sheet and bake at 300°F until dry. Store dried cake crumbs, tightly wrapped, in the freezer for up to 6 months and use as a topping for desserts like fresh fruit, ice cream or puddings. Or, fold the cake crumbs into a custard or pudding, then cover and refrigerate for at least 3 hours before serving.

▶ Instead of frosting your next summertime cake, make an easy ice-cream cake by removing the cake from the pan and splitting it horizontally. Return the bottom half to the pan; spread with softened ice cream. Replace the top half of the cake and finish with more ice cream. Place the cake in the freezer for about 2 hours, or until the ice cream is firm. If an ice-cream cake has been frozen so long that it's hard, remove it from the freezer 20 to 30 minutes before serving. Cut into squares or wedges and top with fresh berries or a chocolate or caramel sauce.

▶ For your child's next birthday, try this idea instead of a traditional cake. Fill flat-bottomed ice-cream cones half full with cake batter, set on a baking sheet and bake until done. The baking time will have to be reduced— about the same as for cupcakes. Cool cake cones on a rack. When ready to serve, top with a scoop of ice cream.

▶ *See also* BAKING, GENERAL; DESSERTS, GENERAL; FROSTING; FLOUR; FRUITCAKE; GREASING PANS; PASTRY BAGS

CANDLES

▶ Storing candles in the refrigerator or freezer will help them burn slower and drip less.

▶ Beeswax candles that have been stored in the refrigerator or freezer will get a dull film on the surface. Simply let them come to room temperature, then run them over your palm and the film will disappear.

▶ Soaking candles in a concentrated solution of saltwater will make them almost drip-proof. Mix 2 tablespoons salt per candle with just enough water to cover. Let candles soak for 2 to 3 hours; rinse well and dry. Wait at least a day before using so the wicks can dry.

▶ A long wooden skewer or a piece of dry spaghetti makes it easy to light several candles at one time without burning your fingers.

▶ Lighted candles help dispel the odor of cigarette smoke.

▶ Clean soot marks off candles by wiping them with rubbing alcohol.

▶ If candles have burned unevenly, heat a sharp knife blade (use an old knife) for 2 minutes in boiling-hot water. The hot blade will slice cleanly through the candle, making it like new. Carve a little hollow around the wick with the tip of the knife. Remove the wax residue from the blade by dipping the knife back into the hot water, then wash with hot, soapy water.

CANDY

▶ Before beginning the candymaking process, gather and measure out all the ingredients and assemble the equipment you'll be using.

▶ The right equipment can spell the difference between success and failure when making candy. Use heavy saucepans (preferably aluminum because of their superior heat conductivity) that are the size called for in the recipe. Too small, and the candy mixture could boil over; too large, and it may not cover the candy thermometer's bulb. A thermometer (*see listing*) is indispensable for candymaking and an inexpensive investment for what it delivers—taking the guesswork out of candy temperatures.

▶ If you absolutely don't want to buy a candy thermometer, test candy syrups using the cold water method (*see next listing*).

▸ Candy recipes are based on an exacting balance between ingredients so follow them precisely. Unless you're an experienced candymaker, don't substitute ingredients; be sure to measure everything accurately.

▸ Never try to rush a candy mixture by cooking it at a higher temperature than the recipe directs, or slow it down by reducing the heat.

▸ Never double a candy recipe—it'll affect the cooking time, which will alter the candy's final quality.

▸ The final temperature of a candy syrup affects how moist the finished candy will be; the lower the temperature, the softer the candy.

▸ High humidity (over 60 percent) in the room in which you're cooking will affect the finished candy. On rainy days, cook the candy mixture a degree or two higher than indicated in the recipe to help compensate. Some candies—like divinity—absolutely cannot be made on a humid day so either wait until it's dry or make something else.

▸ One of the most common problems in candymaking is sugar crystallization. This can happen when even a single sugar grain clinging to the side of the pan is stirred back down into the syrup. To prevent this, heat the sugar over low heat, *without stirring,* until it's completely dissolved. To dissolve any sugar crystals on the side of the pan, tightly cover the pan and let the mixture cook for about 3 minutes. This causes steam, thereby melting the sugar crystals, which trickle down into the syrup. Or dip a natural-bristle pastry brush in hot water and wash down the sides of the pan to dissolve any clinging sugar crystals.

▸ The microwave oven has a major advantage in candymaking and that's the lack of direct heat. That means overcooking or scorching is minimalized. Avoid boilovers when making candy in a microwave by using a container that holds at least twice as much as the volume being cooked. Read your microwave instruction manual for full directions.

▸ Before beginning to make fudge, line the pan with buttered foil or plastic wrap, letting enough excess hang over the edges to use as "handles." Doing so will allow you to lift out the block of cooled fudge and cut it on a cutting board. That way, you can make firm, downward cuts and not scratch the pan. It also eliminates cleanup.

▸ The secret to successful fudge is the beating technique. Use a wooden spoon to beat fudge from the thin, glossy stage to the point where it becomes slightly thick. At that point, add nuts or other ingredients, then continue to beat just until the fudge begins to lose its gloss. Immediately turn the fudge into the pan and cool until firm enough to cut.

▸ If you've overbeaten fudge so that it's too thick to pour into the pan, use your hands to shape it into logs. Wrap the logs in plastic wrap, cool until firm, then unwrap and slice as desired.

▶ Store candy in an airtight container in a cool, dry place. Stored properly, most candy will keep for 2 to 3 weeks.

▶ Store hard candies and soft candies separately or you're liable to end up with sticky hard candy.

▶ Place a sheet of waxed paper or plastic wrap between layers of stored candy.

▶ Candies like fudge and caramels can be wrapped airtight and frozen for up to a year. To thaw, let candy stand at room temperature, unopened, for about 3 hours.

▶ *See also* CANDYMAKING TEMPERATURES; SUGAR SYRUPS; THERMOMETERS

CANDYMAKING TEMPERATURES AND COLD-WATER TESTS

▶ If you don't have a candy thermometer, here are the tests for telling the temperature of a candy syrup. A cold-water test is performed by letting a drop or two of candy syrup fall into a glass measuring cup of very cold water.

Stage of Hardness	Temperature	When a small amount of sugar syrup is dropped into very cold water it:
Thread	230° to 234°F (110° to 112°C)	Forms a soft 2-inch thread.
Soft ball	234° to 240°F (112° to 116°C)	Forms a soft ball that flattens of its own accord when removed.
Firm ball	244° to 248°F (118° to 120°C)	Forms a firm but pliable ball.
Hard ball	250° to 265°F (121° to 129°C)	Forms a rigid ball that is still somewhat pliable.
Soft crack	270° to 290°F (132° to 143°C)	Separates into hard, though pliable, threads.
Hard crack	300° to 310°F (149° to 154°C)	Separates into hard, brittle threads.

CANDY THERMOMETERS *see* THERMOMETERS

CAPERS

▶ Capers are the sun-dried flower buds of a native Mediterranean bush. They're most commonly pickled in a vinegar brine, but can also be found salted and sold in bulk. Capers range in size from the tiny nonpareil variety from southern France, to the giant buds from Italy and Spain, which can be as large as the tip of your finger.

▸ Store brine-packed capers, tightly sealed, in the refrigerator for up to 9 months (the buds must be covered with brine). Salt-packed capers should also be in an airtight container and can be stored at room temperature for about 6 months.

▸ Before using capers (no matter how they're packed) turn them into a sieve or fine-mesh collander and flush well with cold running water to remove excess salt or brine. Blot well with paper towels before using.

▸ Capers add piquancy to all manner of foods including eggs, fish, meat, pizza, poultry, salads, sauces and vegetables. They may be sprinkled over the top of the food, as a garnish, or chopped (if they're large) and incorporated into the dish.

CARROTS

▸ The best carrots are young and slender. Look for those that are firm and smooth; avoid any with cracks or that have begun to soften and wither. If buying carrots with their greenery, make sure the leaves are moist and bright green. Carrot greens rob the roots of moisture and vitamins, so remove them as soon as you get home.

▸ Store carrots in a plastic bag in the refrigerator for up to 2 weeks. As they age, they'll lose flavor and firmness. A light rinsing is all that's necessary for young carrots; older carrots may need peeling to remove a bitter skin. Trim the ends before using.

▸ Don't store carrots near apples, which emit ethylene gas that can give them a bitter taste.

▸ *Carrot yields:* 1 pound = 3 cups chopped or sliced; 2½ cups shredded.

▸ Limp carrots will regain much of their vigor if soaked for about 30 minutes in ice water.

▸ The core of older carrots can turn woody and bitter and therefore should be removed. To do so, cut the carrot lengthwise in quarters, then slice out the midsection, which is usually a little darker than the rest of the carrot.

▸ Besides using a vegetable peeler, you can peel whole carrots by dropping them into boiling water for 2 to 3 minutes, then plunging them into a bowl of ice water. When the carrots are cool, use your fingers to rub off the skin. This technique is particularly useful when you find yourself with lots of carrots to peel.

▸ Some of a carrot's flavor and nutrients go down the drain when it's peeled. Unless carrots are very old or the peel is discolored, simply scrub them well and leave the peel on.

▸ You can substitute an equal amount of cooked, pureed carrots for mashed pumpkin.

▸ When using carrots in stir-frys and other dishes containing several foods mixed together, boil them first (*see* PARBOILING) for a few minutes, cooling immediately in cold water to stop the cooking. They can be dried and stored in a plastic bag in the refrigerator until you're ready to toss them in with the other foods to finish cooking.

► *See also* VEGETABLES, GENERAL

CASSEROLE DISHES; CASSEROLES

► Casserole dishes are measured by volume. If you're unsure of how large a dish is, fill it with water, then measure the liquid. Casserole dishes are most commonly found in the following sizes: 1, 1½, 2 and 3 quarts.

► If you want a crisp topping, don't cover a casserole dish during baking.

► Freeze a cooked or uncooked casserole by lining a casserole dish with heavy-duty aluminum foil, leaving enough overhang on all sides to cover and seal the food. Add the casserole ingredients and either freeze until solid, or bake, cool to room temperature and then freeze (it's not necessary to seal the dish during the relatively short time it takes to freeze). Once the food is frozen, use the excess foil overhang to lift it from the dish; cover the food with the foil overhang and seal airtight. Double wrap in freezer-proof plastic bag, label and freeze until ready to use. Meanwhile, your casserole dish can be used for other purposes. To thaw, remove the wrapping and place the frozen food back in the dish in which it was baked or formed.

► When reheating frozen casseroles, it's best to defrost them in the refrigerator overnight. If that isn't possible, cover and reheat in a 350°F oven, allowing almost double the baking time. To test for doneness, insert a dinner knife into the center of the food, leave for 10 seconds, then check the knife with your fingertips for heat.

► Turn any casserole into an au gratin dish by sprinkling the contents with a topping of bread crumbs and grated cheese; butter may also be dotted over the top. After the dish is baked, the topping will be crisp and golden brown.

► *See also* PAN SIZES

CATSUP *see* KETCHUP

CAULIFLOWER [KAWL-ih-flow-uhr]

► Though the most common cauliflower found in the markets today is white or ivory-colored, there are also pale purple and green varieties. Choose a firm cauliflower with compact florets; the leaves should be crisp and green with no sign of discoloration or withering. Avoid cauliflower with any sign of yellowing or brown spots. The size of the head doesn't affect the quality.

► Store unwashed fresh cauliflower, tightly wrapped, in the refrigerator for up to 5 days. Before using, wash thoroughly, remove the leaves at the base and trim the stem.

- *Cauliflower yields:* 1 pound fresh = 1½ cups chopped or sliced; 1 10-ounce package frozen = 2 cups chopped or sliced.
- The green leaves at the base of a cauliflower head are edible. They take longer to cook and have a stronger flavor than the florets.
- Cauliflower can be cooked whole. Since the stem is denser than the florets, either remove it by cutting into and removing some of the core, or trim it and slash a ½-inch-deep X in the base. Cook a whole head in 3 quarts boiling water for 20 to 30 minutes.
- Separate the cauliflower into florets, and cut the florets into several pieces to shorten cooking time.
- Once the florets are cut off, the cauliflower stems can be chopped or sliced and cooked or used raw in salads.
- Adding 2 tablespoons lemon juice, 1 tablespoon vinegar or 1 cup milk to the cooking water will keep cauliflower white. Do this whether cooking the cauliflower until done, or simply blanching the vegetable for use as crudités.
- Cooking cauliflower florets in milk will not only turn them as white as possible, but will also sweeten their flavor. The flavored milk can be used for soups or sauces.
- Only cook cauliflower until crisp-tender. Overcooking will turn the texture mushy and the flavor strong; it'll also stink up the house.
- If you mistakenly overcook cauliflower, use a blender or food processor to turn it into a puree. Add butter and plenty of freshly ground pepper and you've created a delicious dish.
- Dispel cauliflower's smell during cooking by tossing a couple of thick chunks of bread into the cooking water. Bread slices work, too, though they sometimes dissolve and are hard to remove. Or toss a couple of red bell pepper pieces into the pot. Use a slotted spoon to retrieve the pot sweeteners before serving the cauliflower.
- When serving cauliflower raw (without blanching), soak it in salted ice water for about 15 minutes to expel any bugs.
- *See also* VEGETABLES, GENERAL

CAVIAR [KA-vee-ahr; KAH-vee-ahr]

- The most prized (and costliest) caviar sold in the United States is **beluga**, from the beluga sturgeon that swim in the Caspian Sea. Its soft, extremely large (pea-sized) eggs can range in color from pale silver-gray to black. Next in quality is the medium-sized, gray to brownish gray **osetra** caviar, and the smaller, gray **sevruga**. Other popular (and much less expensive) types of caviar include **whitefish**, **lumpfish** and **salmon** (also called **red caviar**).

- The label term *malossol* (Russian for "little salt") indicates that minimum salt was used to process the roe. The less salt used in the processing, the more perishable the caviar.
- *Fresh caviar* is extremely perishable. Buy only as much as you need and keep it cool in an insulated bag on the way home from the market. Fish eggs should have a fresh, briny smell and be firm, shiny and separate.
- Store fresh caviar, unopened, in the refrigerator for up to a month. Ideally, it should be stored at about 28°F, which is much cooler than a home refrigerator. Compromise by packing the container of caviar in a plastic bag filled with ice; seal and store in the coldest part of the refrigerator. Drain the melted water and replenish the ice as necessary. Once opened, cover and refrigerate the caviar for no more than 2 to 3 days.
- *Pressed caviar* (damaged or fragile eggs that can be a combination of several different roes) should be handled the same way as fresh caviar.
- *Pasteurized caviar* (roe that's been partially cooked) can be stored at room temperature until opened, but should also be consumed within 3 days.
- Caviar should be served very cold, preferably in a bowl surrounded by ice. Present it with toast points and lemon wedges. Minced onion, sour cream and hard-cooked egg whites and yolks are customary, but purists think unnecessary, garnishes.
- Champagne and iced vodka are the traditional potables served with caviar.
- Caviar's flavor and texture are greatly diminished by cooking, so stir it into a hot dish just before serving. A gentle touch is necessary to keep the eggs from breaking and turning mushy.
- Caviar has long been touted as a hangover cure due to its inherent acetylcholine content, which is linked to increased alcohol tolerance.

CAYENNE [KI-yen; KAY-yen] *see* PEPPER

CELERIAC [seh-LEH-ree-ak]
- Also called **celery root**, celeriac is a knobby, brown root vegetable with an ivory-white interior. It tastes like a cross between parsley and strong celery.
- Choose a relatively small, firm celeriac with a minimum of rootlets and knobs. Avoid those with soft spots, which signal decay. Any green leaves still attached to the root are inedible.
- Store celeriac in a plastic bag in the refrigerator for up to a week. Trim and peel just before using.
- *Celeriac yields:* 1 pound, trimmed and peeled = about 2½ cups chopped.
- Right after peeling, soak celeriac for about 15 minutes in cold water mixed with 3 tablespoons lemon juice to prevent discoloration.
- Raw celeriac is wonderful grated or shredded and used in salads.

▶ This vegetable can be boiled, braised, sautéed, baked or cooked in soups. It's also great boiled and pureed.

▶ *See also* VEGETABLES, GENERAL

CELERY

▶ Choose a firm bunch of celery that is tightly formed. The leaves should be green and crisp, not yellowing or wilted.

▶ Store celery in a plastic bag in the refrigerator for up to 10 days. Leave the ribs attached to the stalks until ready to use.

▶ Wash celery and trim the base and leaves just before using.

▶ *Celery yields:* 1 medium stalk, trimmed = about ½ cup chopped or sliced.

▶ Don't throw out celery leaves—they're wonderful in soups, salads and stuffings; they also make an attractive garnish.

▶ It's easy to "string" tough ribs—snap a ½-inch length at the top so it's still hanging on, then pull the piece down the length of the rib. The strings will pull right off.

▶ Wilted raw celery can be revived by soaking trimmed ribs in a bowl of ice water for at least 1 hour. Add 2 tablespoons fresh lemon juice to perk up the flavor.

▶ Celery can be braised, steamed or boiled, and doesn't take long with any of these methods. Cook celery just until crisp-tender or it will become unappealingly limp.

▶ If you add chopped celery to soup, do so in the last 10 minutes or so— that way this vegetable will retain some of its wonderful texture.

▶ Make celery-brush garnishes by cutting ribs in 2- to 5-inch lengths (depending on how large you want the brush). Slit each piece lengthwise at about ¼-inch intervals to within 1 inch of the other end. Place cut celery in a large bowl of ice water; cover and refrigerate for 1 hour, or until they curl.

▶ *See also* VEGETABLES, GENERAL

CELERY ROOT *see* CELERIAC

CELLOPHANE NOODLES [SEHL-uh-fayn] *see* BEAN THREADS

CHAMPAGNE [sham-PAYN]

▶ Dom Perignon, a seventeenth-century French monk and cellarmaster, is credited for the discoveries that led to modern champagne-making techniques. It's said that when he first tasted this celebrated wine, he shouted out to his fellow monks, "Oh, come quickly, I am drinking stars!"

▶ The only *true* champagne comes from the Champagne region in northeast France. Other countries call their effervescent wines by other names, such as Italy's *spumante*. In the United States, such wines are generally referred to simply as "sparkling wines." The term "champagne," however, is commonly used by consumers.

- ▶ The notation *"méthode champenoise"* on the label indicates the wine has undergone a second fermentation in the bottle, and usually indicates a superior sparkling wine.
- ▶ The label on a champagne bottle indicates the level of sweetness as follows: *brut* (bone dry—less than 2 percent sugar); *extra sec* or *extra dry* (dry—up to 2.5 percent sugar); *sec* or *dry* (slightly sweet—up to 4 percent sugar); *demi-sec* (sweet—up to 6 percent sugar); and *doux* (very sweet— over 6 percent sugar). The last two are considered dessert wines.
- ▶ Champagne and other sparkling wines should be served quite chilled, between 40° to 50°F, depending on the quality. Since cold mutes flavors, the cheaper the champagne, the colder you want it. On the other hand, the complexity and subtle flavors of vintage champagnes are better showcased at about 50°F.
- ▶ Champagne should be refrigerated for only about 2 hours before serving. Refrigerating champagne or other white wines for more than a few hours can dull both flavor and bouquet.
- ▶ You can "speed-chill" champagne in about 20 minutes by completely submerging the bottle in a bucket filled with half ice and half water. This will chill the wine much faster than ice alone. If the bucket is shallow, invert the bottle for the last 5 minutes to make sure all the wine is chilled.
- ▶ If champagne's properly chilled and handled, the cork should release from the bottle with a muted "poof," rather than a loud "pop." If properly opened, the wine shouldn't burst out of the bottle when the cork's removed. It's a good idea, however, to have a glass standing by just in case.
- ▶ To open champagne, begin by removing the foil, which often has a "zipper" or perforation to facilitate removal. Untwist the wire cage that encloses the cork. Hold the bottle at a 45-degree angle, making sure the cork isn't pointed at anyone. With your fingers over the cork to keep it from ejecting prematurely, gently rotate the bottle (not the cork) with your other hand. As you feel the cork begin to loosen and lift, use your thumb to gently ease it from the bottle.
- ▶ Always serve sparkling wines in the slender champagne glasses called "flutes," which provide less surface from which the bubbles can escape. You'll also get more of the wine's bouquet from a flute. The old-fashioned shallow, wide-brimmed champagne glass allows both bubbles and bouquet to disperse twice as fast.
- ▶ Soap film or dust on a glass will destroy champagne's effervescence.
- ▶ It's cheating, but if you want maximum bubbles in your champagne, use a sharp, pointed knife to etch an X in the bottom of the flute.
- ▶ *Save the sparkle!* Special metal champagne stoppers—available in some

wine stores and gourmet specialty shops—are the perfect way to preserve the bubbles in leftover champagne. If you can't find one of these three-dollar wonders, drop a stainless-steel trussing needle or pin into the bottle and use a rubber band to fasten a balloon over the bottle's neck. Either method will retain the wine's effervescence for about 2 days.

▶ If the bubbles dissipate in sparkling wine, revive them by dropping a raisin into the bottle.

▶ *See also* ALCOHOL; BEER; LIQUORS, LIQUEURS AND MIXED DRINKS; WINE

CHEESE

▶ There are two broad categories of natural (versus processed) cheese—ripened (such as cheddar and Swiss) and fresh (such as cottage cheese and cream cheese).

Ripened cheeses—firm, semifirm and semisoft:

▶ Ripened cheeses may be cured by various processes including heat or (friendly) bacteria. Some are flavored and others, like many cheddars, are colored with natural dye. After curing, natural cheese begins a ripening process at a controlled temperature and humidity until the desired result is obtained.

▶ Ripened cheeses are classified according to texture: *Firm* (also called *hard*)—like Parmesan and pecorino; *semifirm*—like cheddar, Edam and Swiss; *semisoft*—like Gouda, Monterey Jack and Tilsit; and *soft-ripened*—like blue cheese, Brie and Roquefort.

▶ When buying semifirm or semisoft packaged cheese, check the wrapping to be sure it's not torn. Turn the package over, inspecting all sides, to be sure there's no mold on the cheese and that the edges aren't cracked or dry. Check the package for a "sell by" date to make sure you're not getting a product that should have been pulled from the shelves.

▶ When buying firm or hard cheeses like Parmesan and Romano, check that there are no cracks and that the color is even from the outer edge to the center. Such signs indicate the cheese is beginning to dry out.

▶ Store firm, semifirm or semisoft cheeses, wrapped airtight in a plastic bag or foil, in your refrigerator's cheese compartment (or the warmest location of the fridge). Most will keep for several weeks. If a cheese comes with a rind, leave it on until you're ready to use it.

▶ To keep cheese longer, dampen a sheet of paper towel with cider vinegar and wrap it around the cheese, then put inside a plastic bag and seal. Recheck the paper towel every couple of days and remoisten, if necessary. The vinegar will inhibit the growth of mold.

▶ Rubbing cheese with vegetable oil before wrapping and refrigerating will keep it from drying out if the wrapping isn't airtight.

▶ Most firm, semifirm and semisoft cheeses can be frozen, but most will

C

undergo a change in texture during the process. The harder cheeses will turn crumbly, while softer ones might separate slightly. These textural changes won't be noticeable if you use the cheese in cooked dishes.

▶ To freeze cheese, double wrap it and freeze firm and semifirm cheeses for up to 6 months, soft and semisoft for up to 4 months. Thaw in the refrigerator and use within a few days of defrosting.

▶ *Cheese yields:* Four ounces (¼ pound) firm, semifirm or semisoft cheese = about 1 cup grated cheese.

▶ Don't worry if a little mold appears on the surface of a firm or semifirm cheese—just use a sharp knife to carve away the bad spots, plus a little for insurance.

▶ For maximum flavor, let cheese (except the soft varieties like cottage cheese) sit out at room temperature for 30 to 60 minutes (depending on how warm the room is) before serving.

▶ Cheeses like cheddar, Swiss, and Jack are easier to grate—either by hand or in the food processor—if they're cold. On the other hand, hard cheeses like Parmesan and Romano are easier to handle if they're at room temperature.

▶ Food-processor cleanup after grating cheese will be a breeze if you first spray the metal blade or grating disk with nonstick vegetable spray before using.

▶ When using a food processor for softer cheeses (like Muenster) that get messy when grated, spray the inside of the workbowl and cover, as well.

▶ When using the food processor's metal blade to chop cheese, first cut the cheese into 1-inch chunks; larger pieces could jam the blade.

▶ A hand grater with large holes does a good job of grating semisoft cheeses like Monterey Jack.

▶ Firm and semifirm cheeses can be grated ahead of time and refrigerated in a plastic bag until ready to use. If grated cheese sticks together, simply break up the pieces with your fingers.

▶ Use a vegetable peeler to shave off thin strips or slivers of cheese for salads and garnishes.

▶ Use Edam's red wax rind as a decorative container for dips or spreads. Simply cut off the top inch, then use a spoon to scoop out most of the cheese, leaving a ¼-inch shell. Room-temperature cheese will be easier to remove from the shell; it will also blend more readily with other ingredients for a dip or spread.

Soft-ripened cheeses:

▶ Soft-ripened cheeses such as Brie and Camembert have a soft, creamy texture throughout when fully ripe. Look for rounds no more than 1 inch thick; thicker than that and they can get overripe on the edges before ripening in the center.

- Soft-ripened cheeses can be brought to perfect creamy-thick ripeness if stored, tightly wrapped, at room temperature for a day or two.
- Store ripe cheese in the refrigerator; bring to room temperature before serving.
- The natural, downy-white rind of soft-ripened cheeses is edible, so don't discard it when serving it as an appetizer.
- Chunks of room-temperature Brie or Camembert (rind removed) are wonderful tossed with pasta. The cheese melts quickly and deliciously coats the pasta.
- To remove the white rind of soft-ripened cheese, chill the cheese and use a sharp knife to cut off the rind. Or bring the cheese to room temperature to soften it, then use a spoon to scoop it out of the rind.
- Use a fork to crumble blue cheeses like Roquefort into large or small chunks.

Fresh cheeses:
- Among the more popular fresh cheeses on the market today are cottage cheese, cream cheese, pot cheese and ricotta.
- Fresh cheese is highly perishable so it's best to buy it at a market with a rapid turnover. Check the date on the package to make sure you're buying the freshest cheese available.
- *Cottage cheese* comes in several forms: *Creamed* cottage cheese contains 4 to 8 percent milkfat; *low-fat* cottage cheese can contain from 1 to 2 percent fat (check the label); and *nonfat* is just that—zero fat.
- Store cottage cheese in its container in the coldest part of the refrigerator for up to a week. It'll stay fresh longer if you store it in its original container turned upside down.
- *Cream cheese* also comes in several forms: *regular*—about 33 percent milk fat; *whipped* cream cheese—spreadable regular cream cheese made soft and fluffy by the manufacturer's whipping; *Neufchâtel* and *light* cream cheese—both softer and lower in calories and fat than regular cream cheese; and *nonfat* cream cheese, which is made with skim milk.
- Store cream cheese in its original wrapping in the coldest part of the refrigerator. After opening, rewrap airtight and use within a week.
- The advertisements are true when they say that cream cheese has about half the calories of an equal amount of butter or margarine. Just don't forget to spread the cream cheese almost as thinly as you do butter or you'll wind up with more calories than you want.
- To speed-soften cream cheese in the microwave oven, remove it from the foil package and place, uncovered, on a microwave-safe plate. For 8 ounces, cook at MEDIUM (50 percent power) for about 1 minute, 3 ounces for about 30 seconds. Let stand for 1 minute before using.

▸ If mold shows up on soft cheeses like cream cheese or cottage cheese, throw them out! There's no way they can be safely salvaged.

Processed cheese:

▸ Processed cheese lacks the distinctive flavor and texture of natural cheese. It's been pasteurized for added storage life and combined with emulsifiers for smoothness. Many processed cheeses also contain colorings and preservatives.

▸ According to U.S. government standards, only 51 percent of a processed cheese's final weight actually needs to be cheese.

▸ Processed products labeled "cheese spread" or "cheese food" contain added liquid for a softer, more spreadable mixture.

Cooking with cheese:

▸ Cheese can turn stringy, rubbery, or grainy when exposed to high heat. To avoid this problem, shred or cut cheese into small pieces; stir it into a sauce or other mixture toward the end of the cooking process and cook over low heat only until the cheese melts.

▸ To avoid overheating a cheese sauce and turning it grainy, cook it in the top of a double boiler over simmering water. Make sure that the bottom of the top pan doesn't touch the water.

▸ To rescue overcooked cheese that has become a rubbery mass, cut it into medium pieces and process in a blender until smooth, adding a little cream, if necessary. If the rubbery cheese is part of a sauce, include some of the sauce liquid in the blender. Return the cheese to the pan and cook, stirring constantly, over very low heat until it's melted and smooth.

▸ Because low-calorie cheeses contain less fat, they don't melt as well as regular cheese.

▸ Though not nearly as flavorful as natural cheeses, processed cheeses melt more easily and with fewer problems because they contain emulsifiers.

CHEESECAKE

▸ Cheesecakes require a delicate balance of ingredients, particularly eggs, cheese and liquid. Don't make any major substitutions or the finished product will be drastically altered.

▸ It's essential to use the size pan specified in a cheesecake recipe.

▸ Add and blend cheesecake ingredients in the precise order given in the recipe.

▸ Before beginning to mix the cheesecake, position the oven rack in the middle of the oven; preheat oven 15 minutes. Use an oven thermometer for accurate oven temperature.

▸ Cracks are a common problem for which there are several reasons. One is that, as a cheesecake bakes, its moisture evaporates. If too much moisture is lost, or if it evaporates too quickly, cracking will occur on the cheesecake's surface. This problem can be alleviated by increasing the oven's humidity. To do so, place a shallow pan of hot water on the bottom shelf before beginning to preheat.

C

▶ To help prevent a pastry crust from becoming soggy, brush it lightly with well-beaten egg white to seal the surface. Refrigerate for 15 minutes before filling and baking.

▶ When making a crumb crust for cheesecake, form a "skirt" of aluminum foil around the outside bottom of the springform pan to prevent any butter in the crust from leaking out onto the oven floor.

▶ Prebaking a crumb crust for 10 minutes at 350°F will help keep it crisp. Completely cool a prebaked crust before filling.

▶ Seal a prebaked crumb or pastry crust by using the back of a dinner teaspoon to spread 2 to 3 ounces of melted, semisweet chocolate over the crust, to within ¼ inch of the outside edge. Put the coated crust in the refrigerator for about 10 minutes to set the chocolate before filling with the cheesecake mixture.

▶ The cheese being used *must* be at room temperature. This makes it easier to blend with other ingredients, creating a smooth, homogeneous mixture.

▶ Always beat cream cheese until light and fluffy before blending in other ingredients such as eggs.

▶ Ricotta and cottage-cheese-style cheeses should be beaten or processed in a blender until *completely* smooth before adding remaining ingredients. Otherwise, your cheesecake could have a grainy texture.

▶ Once the cheese is beaten until smooth and fluffy, add the other ingredients slowly, beating or stirring gently. If you beat too much air into the mixture at this stage, the cheesecake might puff up beautifully during baking, then fall drastically. This creates cracking and a dense cheesecake.

▶ Egg whites must be room temperature in order to insure full volume when beaten.

▶ Beat all ingredients together until very smooth before gently folding in whipped cream (for unbaked cheesecakes) or stiffly beaten egg whites (for baked).

▶ Convert a plain dessert cheesecake to a savory cheesecake by omitting the sugar and adding various herbs or spices like ground cumin, chili powder or minced fresh herbs. For the crust, use cracker instead of cookie crumbs.

▶ Some delicate, custard-style cheesecakes are baked in a "water bath," which simply means that the cheesecake pan is immersed halfway in hot water. The water acts as insulation and diffuses the oven heat so the mixture will set without separating. Although solid pans are suggested for use with water baths, springform pans may be used if heavy-duty foil is firmly pressed over the outside of the pan to prevent leakage.

► Cheesecakes baked in a very slow oven for a longer period of time will shrink less when cooled.

► Cheesecakes require even heat in order to rise properly. For this reason, it's important not to open the oven door during the first 30 minutes of baking time. Drafts can cause a cheesecake to fall or crack.

► To allow for variations in ovens, test a baked cheesecake 5 to 10 minutes before minimum time indicated in a recipe.

► Don't worry if your cheesecake's center is slightly jiggly or soft—it will firm as the cheesecake cools.

► Partially cooling a cheesecake in the oven, with the oven door ajar, helps prevent cracks in the top of the cheesecake.

► Concentric cracking and/or an overbrowned top indicate either the oven heat was too high or the cheesecake was baked too long.

► Set a baked cheesecake on a rack to cool. After 30 minutes, run a thin-bladed knife between cheesecake and pan to loosen. Continue cooling until room temperature.

► Leave the cooled cheesecake in its pan, cover tightly and refrigerate overnight or at least 6 hours before serving. This allows the cheesecake to set and will make it easier to cut; it also makes the texture creamier.

► Cracks do not ruin a cheesecake! Disguise any scars with a topping such as slightly sweetened sour cream or whipped cream, fresh berries, your favorite jam (stir until easily spreadable, or stir in 1 tablespoon liqueur). Let any filling sink into the cracks for a few minutes, then add more if necessary so the surface is even.

► *See also* CHEESE; CRUMBS, GENERAL; DESSERTS, GENERAL; PIE CRUSTS

CHEESECLOTH

► Cheesecloth is a lightweight natural cotton cloth that won't fall apart when wet or flavor the food it touches. It comes in both fine and coarse weaves, the latter commonly available in supermarkets; fine-weave cheesecloth will more likely be found in gourmet shops.

► Look for cheesecloth bags in supermarkets and kitchenware stores. They're perfect for poaching large foods like whole fish.

► Cheesecloth has many uses including bundling herbs and spices (tie with string) to season soups and stews; forming a self-basting cover for chicken and poultry (*see* POULTRY); wrapping baked goods like fruitcakes and soaking with alcohol; wrapping whole fish so they don't fall apart during poaching; lining molds (such as for *coeur à la crème*); wrapping around a lemon half to squeeze out seedless juice; and straining soups or sauces.

▶ Out of cheesecloth? Use a clean piece of nylon stocking as a strainer for soups and other liquid mixtures.

CHERRIES

▶ There are two main groups of cherries—sweet and tart. The larger of the two are the firm, heart-shaped sweet cherries that can range from the dark red to purplish black Bing, Lambert and *Tartarian* to the golden, red-blushed Royal Ann cherries. The smaller, softer sour cherry varieties include Early Richmond, Montmorency and English Morello. Sour cherries are usually too tart to be eaten fresh, but make excellent pies and other baked goods. They're not found in markets as often as the sweet varieties but are widely available canned.

▶ Choose brightly colored, shiny, plump fruit. Sweet cherries should be quite firm, but not hard. Sour varieties should be medium-firm. Stemmed cherries are a better buy, but those with stems last longer.

▶ Store unwashed cherries in a plastic bag in the refrigerator for up to 5 days. Wash them just before using.

▶ *Cherry yields:* 1 pound = 2½ to 3 cups pitted.

▶ The tip of a vegetable peeler or a pointed knife can be substituted for a cherry pitter. You can even use a paper clip. Just pull one end out straight and use the opposite end as a hook.

▶ Cherries can be frozen—pitted or not—for up to a year. Rinse and dry them before storing in zip-closure freezer bags. Seal all but about ½ inch of the bag, then insert a straw into the opening and suck out as much air as possible; remove the straw and quickly zip up the opening. The less air in the bag, the better the cherries will keep. Thaw overnight in the fridge or for 30 minutes at room temperature.

▶ Canned pie cherries are usually not as red as nature intended due to their processing. Add a drop or two of red food coloring to a cherry pie or cobbler mixture to help bring back nature's blush.

▶ Pure almond extract makes magic in baked cherry desserts. Just a little bit—⅛ to ¼ teaspoon—makes cherries taste more like cherries.

▶ Cherries have a natural affinity for chocolate. For a summertime treat, buy big, sweet cherries with stems. Wash and dry *thoroughly* (the slightest bit of moisture will sieze up the chocolate), then dip in melted chocolate and set on a waxed-paper-lined baking sheet and pop in the fridge until the chocolate is set.

▶ For a quick summer dessert, combine pitted, halved or whole sweet cherries with a little brandy and sugar in a saucepan and warm over low heat for about 5 minutes, or until the cherries begin to soften. Spoon hot cherries and sauce over vanilla ice cream.

▶ Dried sour cherries—available in specialty gourmet shops and many supermarkets—can be used as you would raisins in cookies, cakes, breads, sauces, desserts, etc. If desired, you can rehydrate the cherries by covering them with boiling-hot water or liqueur and letting stand for about 30 minutes.

▶ *See also* FRUIT, GENERAL

CHESTNUTS

▶ Fresh, unshelled chestnuts are in season from September through February. Choose firm, plump nuts without shell blemishes. Chestnuts can also be found canned—either whole, in pieces, or as a puree. Prepared chestnuts are sold unsweetened, or sweetened, as in marrons glacés. Dried chestnuts can be found in ethnic markets.

▶ Store fresh chestnuts in a plastic bag in the refrigerator for up to 2 weeks. They can be frozen for 4 months.

▶ *Chestnuts yields:* 1 pound shelled, peeled and cooked = about 1 cup puree; dried chestnuts: 3 ounces = 1 cup fresh.

▶ Chestnuts have a dark, leathery shell and a brown skin—both of which must be removed before eating (the skin usually comes off with the shell).

▶ Heating chestnuts greatly facilitates shelling and peeling. The nuts can either be heated, then peeled and cooked as directed in a recipe, or they can be cooked until tender and then peeled.

▶ Before doing either, use the point of a paring knife to slash an X on the flat side of each nut, being sure to cut through the skin.

▶ *Stovetop method for peeling chestnuts:* Place nuts in a saucepan, cover with cold water and bring to a boil. If you just want to peel the nuts, cook for 4 minutes, then remove from heat and peel. To cook chestnuts until tender, cover and simmer for 20 to 30 minutes (depending on the size of the nuts). Chestnuts are done when they're tender when pierced with the tip of a knife.

▶ *Oven-roasting method for peeling:* Bake in a single layer at 425°F for 10 to 15 minutes (for peeling only), or for 15 to 25 minutes to cook the chestnuts until tender. Stir nuts occasionally during the roasting time.

▶ Always peel chestnuts while they're still warm. If they cool so much that the shell won't easily come off, reheat them briefly.

▶ Dried chestnuts can be rehydrated by covering them with boiling water, then simmering for about 1½ hours, or until tender.

▶ *See also* NUTS, GENERAL

CHICKEN

▶ See POULTRY for general data including information on buying, storing and testing for doneness.

▶ *Chicken yields:* Allow about ½ pound bone-in or ¼ to ⅓ pound boneless chicken per serving. A general rule of thumb is that a chicken will yield about 1 cup cooked meat per pound of whole chicken. For example, a 3-

to 4-pound broiler-fryer will yield about 3 to 4 cups cooked chicken after boning. You'll get about 2 cups cooked chicken from ¾ pound skinned, boned chicken breasts.

▶ As with any poultry, the younger the chicken, the more tender it is. Older birds, however, have more flavor.

▶ Younger chickens (broilers, capons, fryers, roasters and Rock Cornish game hens) can be cooked with dry-heat methods such as baking, frying, grilling, roasting and sautéing. For older birds—like hens and baking and stewing chickens—use moist-heat methods such as braising and stewing.

▶ Reduce shrinkage in boneless chicken breasts by removing the clearly visible white tendon.

▶ If you're watching calories, fat and/or cholesterol, remove the skin and any pockets of fat you find on the chicken.

▶ Dieters take note: 3 ounces cooked, skinless white meat contains 147 calories, 4 grams fat and 72 milligrams cholesterol; the same amount of dark meat has 174 calories, 8 grams fat and 79 milligrams cholesterol.

▶ Help tenderize an older chicken by marinating it overnight in the refrigerator.

▶ Add flavor by rubbing chicken all over with a paste of minced, fresh herbs (tarragon is a classic), garlic and olive oil. If you don't have fresh herbs, soak 1 to 2 teaspoons dried herbs in twice as much wine or water for 30 minutes. Add a little oil, then rub the mixture all over the chicken.

▶ When stuffing a chicken, count on about ¾ cup dressing per pound.

▶ Rubbing mayonnaise all over the skin produces a crisp, deep golden brown roasted chicken. One caveat: It won't work with low- or nonfat mayo.

▶ Get a head start on grilling whole chickens by partially cooking them in the microwave while the coals preheat.

▶ Dipping chicken pieces into evaporated milk mixed with a little beaten egg will help a fried-chicken coating stick.

▶ Toss the milk-coated chicken pieces in a plastic or paper bag filled with crumbs or flour and shake until they're well coated.

▶ For super-crispy fried chicken, use half flour and half cornstarch instead of flour only. Season as usual and add ½ teaspoon baking powder.

▶ Sneak a little fiber into the coating of fried or oven-fried chicken by using oat bran mixed with your favorite seasonings.

▶ Cracker or unsweetened cereal (like bran, corn or wheat flakes) crumbs also make a nice coating for fried chicken.

▶ The coating will stick better if you refrigerate the coated chicken, uncovered, for 30 to 60 minutes before cooking.

▶ For a dry, crispy coating, fry chicken pieces only until nicely browned, then finish in a 350°F oven.

▶ When broiling chicken, blot the surface with paper towel to remove excess moisture. Trim all excess fat and remove skin to reduce flare-ups.

▶ Chicken halves should be placed farther away from the broiler's heat source to prevent burning the top before the insides are done.

▶ If boiling chicken specifically to use in a casserole, salad or other dish, cook it three quarters through, then turn off the heat and cover the pan. Let the chicken rest in its cooking liquid for 1 hour before cooling and cutting into pieces. This rest period produces a juicier bird with an incredibly tender texture.

▶ Brown chicken over medium heat. High heat can cause the outside meat to turn stringy.

▶ Both under- and overcooking result in a tough chicken. For the tenderest results, cook boneless chicken to an internal temperature of 170°F, bone-in chicken to 180°F.

▶ To render chicken fat for use in cooking, place the pieces of fat in the top of a double boiler over simmering water. Cook until the fat liquefies; strain into an airtight jar and refrigerate.

▶ *See also* POULTRY; ROCK CORNISH GAME HENS

CHILE PEPPERS; CHILES

▶ When buying fresh chiles, choose those with deep, vivid colors. Avoid any that show signs of shriveling or soft spots.

▶ Store chiles in a plastic bag in the refrigerator vegetable drawer for up to 2 weeks, depending on how fresh they were when purchased.

▶ A chile's seeds and membranes can contain up to 80 percent of its capsaicin, the potent compound that gives some chiles their fiery nature. Since neither cooking nor freezing diminishes capsaicin's intensity, removing a chile's seeds and veins is the only way to reduce its heat.

▶ As a general rule, the larger the chile the milder it is. Small chiles are much hotter because, proportionally, they contain more seeds and veins than larger types.

▶ Caution is the byword when working with chiles because the seeds and membranes contain oils that can severely irritate skin and eyes. Once the chile is cut open, don't touch your mouth, nose, or eyes. Wash your hands with soap and water as soon as you're finished handling the chiles—and still don't touch your eyes. Most soaps just don't remove all the oil from your hands. The surest way to keep the irritating oil off your hands is to wear rubber gloves. If rubber gloves don't give you enough flexibility, use the disposable, paper-thin plastic gloves commonly found in most drugstores.

▶ To remove the seeds from dried chiles, cut off the stem, split the chile lengthwise, then use a spoon to scrape out the seeds.

▶ When cooking chiles over high heat in a skillet or wok, avoid breathing in the harsh fumes, which can irritate your throat, nose and eyes.

► If your mouth is on fire from the heat of chile peppers, the best remedies are dairy products or starchy foods. Drinking milk or eating ice cream, bread, rice or potatoes will diminish the pain. Alcohol increases the absorption of capsaicin, so don't try to quench the fire with a cold beer or margarita.

C

CHILI

► Always make a double batch, freezing half for a quick meal another week.
► Leftover chili is great when spooned over spaghetti, in tacos and burritos, as an omelet filling, as a topping for burgers or frankfurters, or spooned into a split baked potato and topped with cheese.
► *See also* SOUPS AND STEWS

CHIVES

► For the freshest chives, buy them potted and keep them on a well-lit windowsill. Snip off whole chives close to the base, rather than lopping off the tops of the entire bunch.
► When buying bundles of chives found in the supermarket, look for those with a uniform green color and no signs of wilting or browning.
► Store fresh chives by wrapping them in paper towel, then in a plastic bag; refrigerate for up to 1 week.
► Fresh chives can be frozen by first washing and patting dry with paper towel then sealing airtight in a plastic bag. If desired, snip them before freezing. Freeze for up to 6 months, and don't defrost before using.
► The easiest way to cut fresh chives is to snip them with scissors. Snip the tops of the entire bunch, rather than snipping each chive individually.
► If fresh chives aren't available, finely chopped scallions are a better substitute than dried chives. If you must use dried chives, add them directly to a hot dish without reconstituting.
► Chives are one of those herbs that lose almost all flavor when dried. Because of their appearance (even when reconstituted), dried chives don't work well as a garnish. Dried chives should be stored in a cool, dark place and used within 3 months.
► The frozen, snipped chives found in supermarkets aren't as flavorful as fresh, but they're much better than dried. Insure maximum freshness by putting the tub of frozen chives in a freezer-weight plastic bag. They can be frozen for up to 6 months. Simply remove what you need and quickly return the chives to the freezer.
► Add frozen chives directly to a dish without thawing.
► When substituting frozen or dried chives for fresh, use the same amount as called for in the recipe.
► Stir chives into cooked or cold preparations at the last minute to preserve their delicate, fresh flavor. Added to a dish too soon, and the flavor of chives becomes harsh and slightly sour.

▶ Use long, uncut chives to create a variety of interesting garnishes. Tie them into bows, form them into circles or triangles—securing the shape by sticking the tip into the cut end, fan out 3 to 5 chives atop a dish, use chives to tie bundles of julienned vegetables, and so on. If the chives are too stiff to manipulate, blanch them for 10 seconds in boiling water.

▶ *See also* SCALLIONS

C

CHOCOLATE

▶ Chocolate should be stored, tightly wrapped, in a cool (60° to 70°F), dry place. Under ideal conditions, dark chocolate can be stored for years. However, because of the milk solids in both milk chocolate and white chocolate, they shouldn't be stored for longer than 9 months.

▶ When chocolate is stored at warm temperatures, it develops a pale gray "bloom" (surface streaks and blotches), caused when the cocoa butter rises to the surface.

▶ Chocolate that's been stored in damp or cold conditions can form tiny gray sugar crystals on the surface.

▶ Even when chocolate has been poorly stored, it can still be used, with flavor and texture affected only slightly.

▶ *Chocolate yields:* 1 6-ounce package chocolate chips = 1 cup.

▶ **White chocolate** isn't truly chocolate because it doesn't contain chocolate liquor—the thick, dark paste left after the cocoa butter is extracted from the nibs. Instead, white chocolate is usually made of a mixture of sugar, cocoa butter, milk solids, lecithin, and vanilla. Because white chocolate has a tendency to scorch and clump when overheated, it must be melted over very low heat.

▶ Beware of products labeled "artificial chocolate" or "chocolate-flavored." Just as the label states, they aren't the real thing, as both flavor and texture confirm.

▶ Spray whatever container you use to melt chocolate in with nonstick vegetable spray and the melted chocolate will slip right out.

▶ Because all chocolate scorches easily—which completely ruins its flavor—it should be melted slowly over low heat. Chocolate chips melt faster than squares. Various chocolates have different consistencies when melted. Unsweetened chocolate becomes runny; semisweet, sweet and white chocolate hold their shape until stirred.

▶ One melting method is to place coarsely chopped chocolate in the top of a double boiler over simmering water. Remove the top of the pan from the heat when the chocolate is a little more than halfway melted and stir until it's completely smooth.

▶ Chocolate can also be melted in a microwave oven. Put the chocolate in a microwave-safe bowl and heat at MEDIUM (50 percent power). Four ounces of chocolate will take about 3 minutes in a 650- to 700-watt oven, but the timing will vary depending on the oven and the type and amount of chocolate. White chocolate has a tendency to scorch easily, so should be handled with extra care.

▸ One-ounce, paper-wrapped squares of chocolate can be melted—right in the paper to save on cleanup—in the microwave oven at MEDIUM (50 percent power). One 1-ounce square will take 1½ to 2 minutes, 2 squares about 3 minutes and 3 squares about 4 minutes.

▸ Semisweet chocolate chips and squares hold their shape when melted, so don't wait for them to "look" melted or you're liable to singe the chocolate.

▸ To melt chocolate for decorating, put finely chopped chocolate or chocolate chips in a small, heavy-duty plastic bag (if the bag's not heavy-duty, it could melt). Set the unsealed bag upright in a small bowl and microwave at MEDIUM (50 percent power) until *almost* melted; let stand 5 minutes until completely melted. Or *seal* the bag and set in a bowl of very hot water until chocolate is melted (make sure that no water gets into the chocolate). Thoroughly dry the bag with a paper towel before snipping a tiny hole in a corner of the bag. Pipe a decorative design directly onto the dessert, or onto a sheet of waxed paper.

▸ Though chocolate can be melted with liquid (at least ¼ cup liquid per 6 ounces chocolate), a single drop of moisture in melted chocolate will cause it to seize (clump and harden).

▸ Seizing can sometimes be corrected if vegetable oil is immediately stirred into the chocolate at a ratio of about 1 tablespoon oil per 6 ounces chocolate. Slowly remelt the mixture and stir until smooth.

▸ Cool melted chocolate to room temperature before adding to cookie doughs or cake batters. Otherwise, you're liable to melt the fat in the mixture, which will cause a textural change in the baked product.

▸ Room-temperature chocolate is easier to grate than chocolate that's too warm or too cold.

▸ To grate chocolate by hand, start with a large, thick piece—it's easier to handle. Place a box grater over a piece of waxed paper. Hold one end of the chocolate in a piece of paper towel to prevent the heat of your hands from melting it. Firmly rub chocolate over the coarse side of grater. Or, use a Mouli rotary grater for fast and easy results.

▸ Chocolate can be grated in a food processor in several ways. Using either the thin slicing blade or the grating disk, gently press chocolate into blade with the plunger. Or break chocolate into small chunks and chop with the metal blade, using on/off pulses.

▸ Run a vegetable peeler across a chilled bar of chocolate to create chocolate flakes.

▸ Once grated, chocolate should be refrigerated until ready to use.

- Grated or flaked chocolate can be used to decorate or garnish all kinds of desserts from cakes to ice cream.
- Chocolate leaves make an extraordinary garnish and they're surprisingly easy to make. Begin by choosing 6 to 8 nonpoisonous, firm leaves (such as camellia) with stems attached; wash and thoroughly dry the leaves. Melt about 2 ounces chocolate. Using a small metal spatula or the back of a dinner teaspoon, thickly spread melted chocolate over the underside of the leaves. Be careful not to let chocolate run over the edges of the leaves; use your fingertip to remove any excess chocolate from the edges. Place the leaves, chocolate side up, on a waxed-paper-lined baking sheet; chill until chocolate is set. Hold leaves up to light to look for bare spots. Patch with additional chocolate, then chill again to set. Remove leaf from chocolate by grasping the stem and pulling the leaf gently away from chocolate. Refrigerate the chocolate leaves until ready to use.
- *Substitutions (for use in cooking or baking):* For 1 ounce unsweetened chocolate, substitute 3 tablespoons unsweetened cocoa plus 1 tablespoon butter; or 3 tablespoons carob powder plus 2 tablespoons water. For 1 ounce semisweet chocolate, substitute ½ ounce unsweetened chocolate plus 1 tablespoon granulated sugar. For 6 ounces semisweet chocolate chips, substitute ½ cup plus 1 tablespoon unsweetened cocoa, plus ¼ cup plus 3 tablespoons granulated sugar, plus 3 tablespoons butter.
- *See also* COCOA POWDER

CHOPPING BLOCKS *see* CUTTING BOARDS

CHOPSTICKS
- Japanese chopsticks are pointed at the eating end and Chinese chopsticks are blunt. Shorter, kid-sized chopsticks are also available.
- Having trouble getting those chopsticks to work? Try this: Position one chopstick, narrow end down and about two thirds from the tip, in the crook of your thumb. Let the other end of the stick rest on your ring finger, with your middle finger on top of it. Slightly squeeze the stick with the base of your thumb to hold it in place. This bottom chopstick will remain stationary while you're eating. Hold the other chopstick between your index finger and the tip of your thumb, much as you would a pencil. Move this stick in an up-and-down, pincerlike motion to pick up food between it and the bottom chopstick, always keeping the tips of the chopsticks even. Practice at home with two long wooden skewers and you'll look like a pro the next time you eat at an Asian restaurant.

CHUTNEY [CHUHT-nee]
- Use chutney as an instant glaze for grilled or broiled meat, poultry or fish. Finely chop any large fruit pieces, then thin chopped chutney with a little

vegetable oil and brush over the food before and during cooking.

- Chutney is a wonderful flavor enhancer for dozens of dishes. Just be sure to finely chop any large pieces of fruit in the chutney before using in any of the following ways.

- Combine 2 tablespoons chutney with olive oil, mayonnaise or sour cream for an exotic salad dressing.

- Puree chutney with a little cream, chicken or vegetable broth, oil or melted butter and drizzle over hot vegetables or meats.

- Whip chopped chutney with softened butter or cream cheese for a delicious spread for bread.

CINNAMON

- Cinnamon is the inner bark of a tropical evergreen tree. Ceylon (or true) cinnamon has a tan color and mildly sweet flavor. *Cassia*—a close relative of true cinnamon—is what's commonly sold in the United States as ground cinnamon. It has a darker, reddish-brown color and a more pungent, slightly bittersweet flavor.

- As with any whole spice, the flavor of stick cinnamon is more intense than that of commercially ground cinnamon. It can also be stored longer.

- Cinnamon sticks make great swizzle sticks for all kinds of hot drinks including cider, cocoa, coffee, hot buttered rum, mulled wine, etc.

- You can buy the relatively expensive cinnamon sugar in your supermarket's spice section or you can make your own for a third the cost by combining ½ cup granulated sugar with 1 to 1½ tablespoons ground cinnamon. Store it in an airtight container. A clean, used herb or spice jar with a shaker top works perfectly.

- Make your own cinnamon-flavored sugar by burying 3 cinnamon sticks in a pound of granulated or confectioners' sugar. Store at room temperature in an airtight container for 2 weeks, stirring once a week. This type of cinnamon sugar differs from the one mentioned in the previous tip because it stays white.

- Cinnamon sugar can be used to sweeten coffee, as an ingredient in desserts, for decorating cookies, cakes and other baked goods, or for sweetening fruit and other desserts.

- A pinch of cinnamon makes magic in many savory dishes like soups, stews and meat marinades.

- Cinnamon toast is instant comfort food. Lightly toast slices of bread in the toaster while you heat your oven's broiling unit. Butter one side of the toast and place slices, buttered side up, on a baking sheet. Sprinkle liberally with cinnamon-sugar; avoid getting any on the baking sheet or it will burn. Broil until the sugar is melted and bubbly.

- Want to give your house that homey, fresh-baked feeling? Combine 1 teaspoon ground cinnamon, or 1 cinnamon stick (broken into several pieces), with 6 cups water and bring to a boil. Then reduce to a simmer, and let it fill your house with the scent of nostalgia.

▶ *See also* SPICES *for storage information*

CITRUS FRUITS

▶ Fruit that's heavy for its size will be much juicier than its lightweight counterparts.

▶ Room-temperature fruit will yield more juice than refrigerated fruit.

▶ Use your palm to roll citrus fruits around on the countertop a few times before squeezing to maximize juice yield.

▶ Get more juice by pricking the skin of citrus fruit in several places with a fork, being careful not to go all the way to the flesh. Microwave on HIGH (100 percent power), uncovered, for 10 to 20 seconds, depending on the size of the fruit. Let stand 2 minutes before rolling the fruit between your palm and the countertop. Cut open and squeeze out the juice.

▶ If you don't have a microwave oven to encourage the juice, place citrus fruit in a preheated 300°F oven for 5 minutes. Cool before juicing.

▶ If you plan on using lemon or other citrus juice to flavor several dishes over a period of days, squeeze enough at one time and refrigerate what you don't use immediately in an airtight screwtop jar. It will keep that way for about 5 days.

▶ Whenever using juice for baked goods like breads or cakes, pick out the seeds, but leave any pulp, which will add a nice flavor bonus.

▶ The word "zest" refers to the outer colored portion of the citrus peel. The white pith is bitter and should be avoided.

▶ Freshly grated orange or lemon zest packs a flavor wallop no bottled dried zest can match.

▶ Always thoroughly wash citrus fruits before using their peel (zest) for anything.

▶ It's always easier to grate a whole citrus fruit.

▶ If you need both the zest and juice of a citrus fruit, remove the zest before juicing the fruit.

▶ Even if you aren't planning on using the zest right away remove it (either in grated form or cut into strips) and freeze for up to 6 months. That way you'll have citrus zest on hand to flavor everything from baked goods to beverages.

▶ It's easier to grate a citrus fruit if you run it diagonally across a grater, rather than up and down.

▶ By far the easiest way to remove the peel from a citrus fruit is to use a citrus zester or stripper (*see next listing*).

▶ To peel an orange or grapefruit to use the sections in a salad, immerse the whole fruit in a pot of boiling-hot water and let stand 4 minutes. Remove fruit from the water and cool until it's easy to handle. When you peel away the skin, the pith should come right off with it. Any remnants can be pulled off with a grapefruit knife.

► Place an orange or lemon strip in each compartment of an ice cube tray, fill with water and freeze. These citrus cubes not only look good, but they flavor the beverage as they melt.

► Store citrus zest (most often lemon or orange) covered with vodka in a small screw-top jar in the refrigerator. The zest will keep for months, and the citrus-flavored vodka can be used in beverages, sauces, etc.

► Remove the flesh and segments from orange or small grapefruit halves and use as ''bowls'' for fruit salad or a dessert fruit compote.

► Hollowed-out orange or lemon halves make great individual serving dishes for sherbet.

► *See also* CITRUS STRIPPER; FRUIT, GENERAL; GRAPEFRUIT; LEMONS; LIMES; ORANGES

CITRUS STRIPPER; CITRUS ZESTER

► A **citrus stripper** is a tool with a notched, stainless-steel edge that cuts ¼-inch-wide strips of citrus peel.

► Citrus zesters have 5 tiny cutting holes that create threadlike strips of peel. A good-quality **citrus zester** (available in gourmet specialty shops and many supermarkets) is an easy way to get long thin strands of citrus zest. Press *firmly* as you draw the zester down along the skin of the fruit.

► For long, continuous strips of zest, use a citrus stripper to begin at one end, spiraling around and down the fruit. Don't press so hard that you cut into the bitter, white part (pith) of the skin.

CLAMS

► When buying hard-shelled clams (like littleneck, cherrystone, chowder, pismo or butter clams) in the shell, make sure the shells are tightly closed. If a shell is slightly open, tap it lightly. If it doesn't snap shut, the clam is dead and should be discarded. The shells should be whole, not broken or cracked. To test a soft-shell clam (like the razor or geoduck), lightly touch its neck; if it moves, it's alive.

► Store live clams in an open container covered with a moist cloth for up to 2 days in a 40°F refrigerator.

► Shucked clams should be plump and the liquor (liquid) surrounding them clear.

► Store shucked clams in their liquor in the refrigerator for up to 3 days, in the freezer for up to 3 months.

► If there's not enough liquor to cover the shucked clams, make your own by dissolving ½ teaspoon salt in 1 cup water.

► *Clam yields:* 1 pint = about 18 shucked clams; 2 7½-ounce cans minced clams = about 18 shucked clams.

▶ Get rid of sand by soaking live clams in cold, salted water (use ⅓ cup salt per gallon water) for an hour.

▶ Sand can also be removed by covering the clams with water, then sprinkling liberally with cornmeal. Let stand about 3 hours.

▶ Clams found floating after either of these procedures should be discarded.

▶ Always scrub live clams well under cold, running water.

▶ Clams are much easier to open if you put them in the freezer (in a single layer) for 30 to 45 minutes.

▶ A quicker method for relaxing clams so they're easier to open is to drop a few at a time into boiling water. Retrieve with a slotted spoon after 15 seconds and open.

▶ If you don't have a clam knife for opening clams, a beer-can opener works well.

▶ All clams should be cooked at low heat to prevent toughening.

▶ Clams cooked in their shells are done just when their shells open.

▶ Use only fresh or frozen clams for soups and stews. The texture of canned clams is too soft for long-cooking dishes.

▶ Add minced clams to soups and stews at the last minute so they don't lose their texture.

▶ *See also* SHELLFISH

CLAY-POT COOKING; CLAY COOKERS

▶ Always immerse both the top and bottom of a clay cooker in tepid water for 15 minutes before using.

▶ Clay-pot cooking should always begin in a cold oven; set the heat after the dish is in position. Adjust cooking times for recipes not specifically designed to start in a cold oven.

▶ Sudden changes in temperature can crack clay cookers. When removing the dish from a hot oven, always set it on a rack, or triple-folded towel, or wooden chopping block—never directly on a cold countertop.

▶ Clay cookers are not designed for stovetop cooking and will most likely crack if exposed to direct heat.

CLEANING

▶ Cleaning as you go makes life a lot simpler at the end of the meal. While a dish is cooking on stovetop or in the oven, wash the utensils, cutting boards or other cookware you used to prepare the food. Pop whatever dirty dishes there are into the dishwasher and set the pans to soak just before sitting down to eat. The only things that shouldn't be soaked are utensils or servingware made of wood, or those that are glued.

▶ Reduce cleanup time by using cookware designed to go from freezer to microwave, or from freezer to oven.

C

- Place a saucer adjacent to the stove on which to rest spoons and spatulas you're cooking with to keep the stovetop clean.
- Store leftovers that will be used within a few days in the pot or casserole dish in which the food was cooked, then reheat in that same container.
- Make scrubbing pans easier and prevent grease and debris from going down the drain by wiping out greasy pots with used paper napkins or paper towels before washing.
- Never scour iron pots and pans—simply wash them with soap and hot water. Dry *thoroughly* to prevent rusting.
- Pans with burned residue on the bottom will be easier to clean if you fill them with 2 inches of water. Add 1 tablespoon baking soda and bring to a boil. Cover and boil for 5 minutes, then remove from heat and let stand for 30 minutes before scrubbing.
- Burned-on food will come off of pans easier if you scrape the area well, then cover it with water and add ½ to 1 cup salt (depending on the pan's size). Bring to a boil, then boil for 20 minutes. Remove the pan from the heat, cover and let stand overnight. Use a metal spatula the next morning to loosen as much of the burned area as possible and finish the job with a scouring pad.
- Remove stains from aluminum pans by filling with water and adding 2 tablespoons vinegar or lemon juice per quart of water. Bring to a boil, then continue to boil gently for 15 minutes. Let water cool in pan.
- If you can't get stains out of Corningware or Pyrex, spray them with oven cleaner, following manufacturer's directions.
- Rub coffee or tea stains on chinaware with a paste of water and baking soda.
- If your kitchen sponge is getting smelly, soak it overnight in a mixture of 2 cups warm water and 2 tablespoons baking soda. Rinse thoroughly before using.
- Toss your kitchen sponge on the top rack of the dishwasher when it needs cleaning. Rinse out by hand after the cycle is finished.
- An old toothbrush is great for cleaning small places in garlic presses, electric can openers, strainers, grinder parts, or along the edges of a sink molding—you name it. Clean the toothbrush first by running it through a dishwasher cycle in the silverware holder.
- Protect your good china and crystal during washing by lining the sink with a dishtowel.
- Silver serving pieces can be returned to their original glory by using a soft cloth and rubbing with a paste of baking soda and water.
- Remove stubborn waterlines on vases by rubbing them with a vinegar-soaked cloth or paper towel.
- To remove soap film from countertops, rinse with a mixture of 1 quart water and 1 teaspoon white vinegar.

▶ Use a generously salted lemon half to clean stainless steel kitchen sinks. A plain lemon half will work on smooth aluminum pans.

▶ Use foil to line your stove's burner pans, as well as the bottom of an electric oven. Don't cover oven racks with foil—it prevents air from circulating and causes uneven baking.

▶ Clean an electric can opener by running a damp piece of heavyweight paper towel through the cutting mechanism.

▶ To clear a grease-clogged sink, pour in 1 cup each baking soda and salt, followed by 1½ to 2 quarts boiling water.

▶ Use nail polish or paint remover to get rid of sticky label residue from bottles or jars you want to keep. Keep in mind that these removers can mar the surface of some plastic containers.

▶ *See also* OVENS, CONVENTIONAL

CLOVES

▶ The reddish brown, nail-shaped clove is the dried, unopened flower bud of the tropical evergreen clove tree. Cloves are sold whole and ground.

▶ Cloves are very pungent and should be used in moderation.

▶ Make your own pomander balls by inserting whole cloves into apples, lemons or oranges. So you don't snap off the end of the cloves, use a skewer or toothpick to pierce a small hole in the fruit, then insert the clove. A bowlful of these fragrant pomanders can be used as a centerpiece, or use one at each place setting for a favor.

▶ *See also* SPICES *for storage information*

COCOA POWDER, UNSWEETENED

▶ After cocoa beans are processed, about 75 percent of the cocoa butter is extracted, leaving a dark brown paste (chocolate liquor), which is subsequently dried, then ground into a powder known as unsweetened cocoa.

▶ For *Dutch-process cocoa* the beans (or resulting paste) are treated with an alkaline solution, which helps neutralize cocoa's natural acidity. This process create a darker, more mellow-flavored powder.

▶ Store cocoa, sealed airtight, in a cool, dark place for up to 2 years.

▶ In an emergency, you can substitute 3 tablespoons unsweetened cocoa powder plus 1 tablespoon butter or margarine for 1 ounce unsweetened chocolate.

▶ If you add cocoa powder to a brownie or cake recipe, decrease the flour by 1 tablespoon for every 2 tablespoons cocoa you use. To compensate for the cocoa's added bitterness, add 2 teaspoons sugar for each tablespoon cocoa used.

▶ Add 1 or 2 tablespoons unsweetened cocoa powder to chili or meat stews to give them a rich, husky flavor.

▶ *See also* CHOCOLATE

COCONUT

▸ Fresh coconuts are available year-round, with a peak season from October through December. Choose one that's heavy for its size and that sounds full of liquid when shaken; avoid those with damp "eyes."

▸ Store whole, unopened coconuts at room temperature for up to 6 months, depending on the degree of ripeness. Once the coconut is opened, refrigerate chunks of the meat (submerged in the juice drained from the coconut) in a tightly sealed container for up to 5 days. Grated fresh coconut should be sealed airtight in a plastic bag and refrigerated for up to 1 week, frozen for up to 6 months.

▸ *Coconut yields:* 1 medium coconut = 3 to 4 cups grated coconut.

▸ To open a coconut, first drain the liquid by piercing 2 of the 3 eyes with an ice pick. This thin juice can be used as a beverage, though it shouldn't be confused with coconut "milk." Crack the shell with a hammer and break the meat away, using a knife to peel or scrape off the dark inner skin.

▸ Chunks of coconut meat can be grated or chopped either by hand or in a food processor with the metal blade.

▸ Packaged coconut is available in cans or plastic bags, sweetened or unsweetened, shredded or flaked, and dried, moist or frozen. Unsweetened, dried coconut is most often available at natural food stores and Asian markets.

▸ Unopened canned coconut can be stored at room temperature for up to 18 months; coconut in plastic bags for up to 6 months. Refrigerate both after opening.

▸ If shredded commercial coconut has become dry, soak it in milk for 30 minutes before using. Drain well, then blot dry on paper towels. Save the coconut-flavored milk for baking and use within 5 days. Or combine the milk with chunks of fresh fruit in the blender for an exotically flavored beverage.

▸ Canned, unsweetened coconut milk—not to be confused with the sweetened coconut "cream" commonly found in supermarkets—can be found in Asian markets and some supermarkets. Coconut milk adds a subtle flavor and silky texture to many soups, sauces and desserts. It can also be used to cook rice and pasta.

▸ Make your own coconut milk at home by combining equal parts water and shredded fresh or dried unsweetened coconut and simmering until foamy. Cover and remove from heat; let stand 15 minutes. Pour mixture into a blender or a food processor with a metal blade; process for 1 minute. Strain the liquid through a very fine sieve or a sieve lined with a double thickness of cheesecloth. Cover and refrigerate for up to 5 days. You can repeat the process for a second, diluted batch of coconut milk. Discard the coconut meat afterward.

- Make coconut "cream" in the same manner as coconut milk but use 1 part water to 4 parts coconut. For an even richer result, substitute milk for water.
- Toasted unsweetened coconut makes a wonderful garnish for many Asian dishes, fruit salads and some vegetables. Toasted sweetened coconut is great on desserts. Spread coconut in a single layer on a baking sheet with shallow sides. Bake at 325°F, tossing occasionally, for about 10 minutes, or until golden brown.
- Create colored coconut by combining 1 cup coconut with 3 to 5 drops food coloring in a bowl; toss until evenly colored.

C

COFFEE

- Ever wonder what all those coffees on some restaurant menus are? Here's a brief summary: *espresso*—a very strong brew made with dark-roasted coffee under pressure, served in a tiny espresso cup; *caffè macchiato*—espresso with a dollop of steamed-milk foam, served in an espresso cup; *cappuccino*—espresso topped with foamy steamed milk, served in a regular-size cup or glass mug; *caffè latte*—espresso plus a liberal amount of foamy steamed milk, usually served in a tall glass mug; *caffè mocha*—caffè latte with chocolate added; *caffè au lait*—equal portions of hot milk and coffee; *café brûlot*—coffee blended with spices, orange and lemon peel and brandy, then flamed; *Irish coffee*—strong coffee, Irish whiskey and sugar, usually served in a glass mug with a dollop of whipped cream; *Thai coffee*—coffee mixed with sweetened condensed milk; *Turkish coffee*—very strong coffee made by boiling finely ground coffee, sugar and water together; *Viennese coffee*—strong, usually sweetened coffee served in a tall glass and topped with whipped cream.
- If possible, purchase coffee (whole bean or freshly ground) from specialty coffee shops. The flavor is greatly superior to the preground canned coffee found in markets.
- Generally, a blend of two or more types of coffee beans produces a richer, more complex brew than a single-bean coffee.
- If you're watching your caffeine intake but love coffee with a robust flavor, try the dark-roast decaffeinated coffee beans found in coffee shops. The flavor is surprisingly rich.
- Decrease caffeine by using a half-and-half mixture of regular and decaffeinated coffee.
- Keep ground coffee fresh by storing it, double wrapped in an airtight container, in the freezer.
- For maximum freshness, refrigerate coffee beans in an airtight container for up to 1 month. Air is one of coffee beans' worst enemies, so make sure the container has little airspace between the lid and the surface of the

beans. For longer storage, double wrap coffee beans in airtight freezer bags or containers and freeze for up to 6 months.

▶ For maximum flavor, grind only as many beans as needed to brew each pot of coffee.

▶ Generally, the finer the grind, the fuller the flavor.

▶ Whether you grind coffee beans in a coffee grinder or in a special unit of your coffee maker, it's important to remove all of the ground residue after each use. Otherwise, the natural oils in the coffee-bean particles will turn rancid, giving an off-flavor to subsequent batches of coffee beans. A narrow rubber spatula does a great job of removing ground-coffee residue, as does a small brush or a slightly dampened piece of paper towel.

▶ For perfect coffee, first make sure your equipment is scupulously clean. Residual oils are left inside the pot each and every time you brew coffee. If that residue is not removed completely, it will affect each fresh pot of coffee, giving it a bitter, rancid flavor.

▶ Always make coffee with freshly drawn cold water, and make sure the water tastes good. If your tap water's highly chlorinated or has a distinctive mineral taste, the resulting coffee can be bitter and off-tasting. In that case, it's better to use bottled water. Make sure you're using the correct amount, grind and brewing time for your coffee maker.

▶ For a full-flavored cup of coffee, use 2 level tablespoons (1 coffee measure or ⅛ cup) for each 6 ounces (¾ cup) water. (Remember that a standard coffee cup holds 6 ounces, whereas a mug often holds 10 to 12 ounces.) For stronger coffee, use 2 level tablespoons for each 4 ounces (½ cup) water.

▶ For a last-minute coffee-filter replacement, cut a piece of paper towel to fit your coffee-maker basket.

▶ To save a weak pot of coffee at the last minute, stir in a teaspoon or two of good-quality instant coffee. Let stand 3 minutes before serving.

▶ If you find coffee too acid for your system, try adding a pinch of salt to the grounds before brewing begins.

▶ The flavor of coffee begins to deteriorate within 15 minutes after it's brewed. Leaving the coffee on a heating element accelerates this problem, which starts as the aromatic oils evaporate and ends with the coffee tasting bitter and flat. To retain first-cup freshness, transfer the brew to a vacuum-insulated carafe that's been preheated with hot water. These thermos carafes are available in a wide variety of attractive colors and styles.

▶ Never reheat coffee—it just makes it bitter.

▶ Instant coffee is more palatable if you combine the water and coffee granules in a pan, bring to a boil, then remove from the heat, cover and let stand for 3 minutes.

- Make your own "instant" coffee by putting 2 tablespoons ground coffee in a tiny strainer (or tea infuser) lined with paper towel. Place the strainer or infuser in a coffee cup, then pour 6 ounces boiling water over the grounds. Cover and steep for 3 minutes, or until coffee is desired strength. Remove strainer and drink. For larger mugs, increase the coffee and water ratio accordingly.
- Spice up your coffee by sprinkling a dash or two of cinnamon, cloves or nutmeg over the grounds before brewing. Orange or lemon peel can also be added in this way. Just before serving, a drop (not too much) of vanilla can be stirred into the brew.
- Pass sticks of cinnamon to use as coffee stirrers.
- For iced coffee, make coffee cubes by pouring cooled coffee into ice-cube trays and freezing until solid. Fill a glass with coffee ice cubes, and top with chilled coffee, and if desired, milk. If you don't have time to make coffee ice cubes, make the coffee stronger than you normally would, so the flavor will still be rich even after being diluted by melting regular ice.
- Whenever pouring hot coffee into a glass cup or mug (as for Irish coffee), put a spoon in the cup first, then pour the coffee onto the spoon. This little trick will diffuse the heat and keep the glass from cracking.
- Dish soap and detergent will leave an infinitesimal soap film on your coffeepot that will distort the flavor of coffee. For the truest flavor, use a little baking soda and hot water to clean your coffeepot. Be sure to rinse thoroughly!
- Never use anything abrasive to clean a coffeepot. Brushes, cleansers, and the like, will scratch the container's interior surface, and every scratch captures coffee oils (which quickly turn rancid) and mineral deposits. Metal coffeepots are more susceptible to scratches than those made of glass or porcelain.
- Freshen a stale-smelling coffeepot by filling it with a mixture of boiling water and 2 teaspoons baking soda. Cover and let stand until cool. Rinse thoroughly.
- A paste of salt and vinegar will remove coffee or tea stains from china cups.

COLANDERS [KAWL-an-der; KUHL-an-der] *see* SIEVES

COLE SLAW
- Personalize store-bought cole slaw by stirring in shredded cheddar cheese, apple, carrots or green or red bell pepper, caraway or celery seeds, toasted almonds, sour cream, or a dash of balsamic vinegar.

CONDENSED MILK *see* SWEETENED CONDENSED MILK

CONDIMENTS *see* CHUTNEY; HORSERADISH; HOT PEPPER SAUCES; KETCHUP; MAYONNAISE; MUSTARD; SALSA

CONFECTIONERS' SUGAR *see* SUGAR

CONVECTION OVEN COOKING

▸ Convection ovens have a fan that provides continuous circulation of hot air, which cooks food more evenly and up to a third faster (even when the oven's crowded). The hot-air circulation makes convection ovens particularly suited for foods like baked goods and roasted and broiled meats and fish.

▸ When converting a recipe from a conventional to a convection oven, reduce the temperature by 25° to 75°F (follow manufacurer's instructions).

▸ Because they heat up so fast, convection ovens usually require little or no preheating.

▸ Unlike microwave ovens, convection ovens require no special cookware or major adjustments in cooking time or technique.

▸ For meats and fish, the convection-oven temperature can be lowered 25°F, and the roasting time decreased by 25 to 30 percent.

▸ Convection ovens can easily overbrown baked goods, so be on the safe side and lower the oven temperature by 50° to 75°F, but keep the baking time about the same.

▸ *See also* COOKING, GENERAL; MICROWAVE COOKING; OVENS, CONVENTIONAL

COOKIES

▸ There are six basic cookie styles. **Drop cookies** are made by dropping spoonfuls of dough onto baking sheets; **bar cookies** are created when a batter or soft dough is spooned into a shallow pan, then cut into bars after baking; **hand-formed (or molded) cookies** are made by shaping dough by hand into balls, logs, crescents and other shapes; **pressed cookies** are formed by pressing dough through a cookie press (or pastry bag with a decorative tip) to form fancy shapes and designs; **refrigerator cookies** are made by shaping the dough into logs that are refrigerated until firm, then sliced and baked; **rolled cookies** begin with dough that's been rolled out into a thin layer, then cut out with cookie cutters.

Mixing and forming cookie dough:

▸ Never use diet or whipped margarine, or anything labeled "spread," to make cookies. Their low fat and high water content will produce unsatisfactory results.

▶ Unless the recipe so directs, sifting the flour is usually unnecessary. Simply stir the flour, spoon it lightly into the measuring cup, and level off the top with the back of a dinner knife.

▶ Once the flour has been added, take care not to overmix the dough. Too much handling develops the gluten and can produce tough cookies.

▶ Most unbaked cookie doughs can be refrigerated for at least a week.

▶ Most unbaked cookie doughs can be frozen for up to a year if wrapped airtight, in freezer-weight plastic bags or foil. When ready to bake, remove the dough from the freezer and, if formed into a log, slice and bake. If dough is too hard to slice immediately, let stand at room temperature for 15 to 30 minutes.

▶ To freeze drop-cookie dough, drop it onto a baking sheet and freeze until solid. Then transfer the dough drops to freezer-proof wrapping. Place frozen dough drops on baking sheets, cover lightly with waxed paper and let thaw 30 to 45 minutes at room temperature before baking.

▶ Forming cookies the same size and shape will promote even baking and browning.

▶ When rolling out cookie dough, work with a small amount at a time, covering the rest with plastic wrap to keep moist.

▶ Make cleanup a breeze by rolling out cookie dough on a waxed-paper-covered countertop. Keep the waxed paper from slipping by sprinkling a few drops of water on the countertop before arranging the paper.

▶ Or you can roll out cookie dough on a smooth countertop without sticking if you spray the surface beforehand with nonstick vegetable spray. All you need for cleanup is a soapy sponge or cloth.

▶ When rolling out dough, always start at the center and roll outward.

▶ To save time and cleanup, roll out and cut cookies right on the baking sheet.

▶ A pizza cutter works well for cutting rolled-out cookie dough.

▶ Cookie dough won't stick to cookie cutters if you spritz them first with nonstick vegetable spray. Or dip them in flour or confectioners' sugar whenever the dough begins to stick.

▶ Drop-cookie recipes call for scooping up cookie dough with a spoon, then dropping it onto a baking sheet. The "teaspoon" or "tablespoon" called for in most recipes generally refers to regular tableware, not measuring spoons.

▶ When cutting a log of chilled refrigerator-cookie dough, give the log a quarter turn every 4 to 6 slices to keep it round.

Baking sheets and pans:

▶ Shiny heavy-gauge aluminum baking sheets are good heat conductors and will produce the most evenly baked and browned cookies.

▶ Dark sheets absorb more oven heat and can cause cookies to overbrown or burn. Lining dark sheets with heavy-duty aluminum foil will alleviate the overbrowning problem.

▶ Insulated baking sheets—two sheets of aluminum with an air pocket sealed between them—are fine for soft cookies, but cookies won't get crisp when baked on them. Cookies may also take 1 to 2 minutes longer to bake on insulated sheets.

▶ If all you have are thin, lightweight baking sheets, place one on top of the other to prevent cookies from burning.

▶ In a pinch, invert a jelly-roll pan and use the bottom for a baking sheet.

▶ Always use the pan size called for in a bar-cookie recipe. A smaller pan, and the cookies will be too thick and gummy in the middle. A larger pan will produce thin, dry results.

▶ If using a glass pan instead of one made of metal for bar cookies, reduce the oven temperature by 25°F.

▶ When making bar cookies, line the pan (usually 8- by 8-inch or 9- by 13-inch) with foil, leaving at least 3 inches of overhang on each end. Grease foil if the recipe calls for a greased pan. Once the cookies are baked and cooled, use the overhang to lift the cookie slab out of the pan, then cut into bars or squares. The foil not only saves on cleanup, but cutting the cookies outside the pan keeps the pan from getting marred.

▶ Use vegetable shortening, nonstick vegetable spray or *unsalted* butter or margarine to grease baking sheets and pans. Salted butter or margarine may cause cookies to stick and overbrown on the bottom.

▶ Too much grease on baking sheets can cause cookies to spread and over-brown on the bottom.

▶ Unless the cookie dough requires refrigeration, grease baking sheets before you begin mixing the dough.

▶ Greasing baking sheets is usually unnecessary with cookies—such as shortbread—that have a high ratio of fat.

▶ To flour greased baking sheets, sprinkle the surface with about ½ tablespoon flour; tap and rotate the sheet until the entire surface is coated with flour. Invert sheet over the sink and shake it gently to remove excess flour.

▶ Speed cleanup by covering baking sheets with foil, greasing the foil if the recipe indicates. When you're through baking, simply remove the foil—*voilà,* clean baking sheet!

Baking and cooling cookies:

▶ Always preheat the oven for 10 to 15 minutes before beginning to bake. When using glass baking pans (as for bar cookies), reduce the oven temperature by 25°F.

▶ Always use an oven thermometer for accurate temperatures. Invest in a good mercury thermometer, available in gourmet or kitchen-supply shops. The all-metal, spring-style thermometers found in supermarkets can become unreliable after a small jolt or fall.

► All ovens have hot spots, so if you're baking more than one sheet of cookies at a time, insure even browning by rotating the sheets from top to bottom and front to back halfway through the baking time.

► To allow for oven variances, prevent overbaking by checking cookies a couple of minutes before the minimum baking time.

► If you're baking successive batches of cookies and using the same baking sheet, always let it cool to room temperature before putting more dough on it. Otherwise, the cookie dough can begin to melt and spread, which will affect the cookies' final shape and texture. It can also cause the cookie bottoms to brown before the inside is done.

► If you're baking several batches of cookies, speed your turnaround time by dropping cookie dough (or placing cookie-dough cutouts) onto sheets of foil or parchment paper. That way they'll be ready to slide right onto the cooled baking sheets.

► In general, bar cookies are done when a toothpick inserted in the center comes out clean.

► Cool individual cookies on a rack.

► If cookies fall apart as you're removing them from the baking sheet with a spatula, wait a minute or so until they firm up before transferring them to a cooling rack.

► Bar cookies are usually cooled and stored right in the baking pan. Most are cut *after* they've cooled. The exception are crisp-style bars, which must be cut while warm—before they crisp—to prevent unsightly crumbling.

► Make sure cookies are *completely* cool before storing or they'll "sweat" and get soggy.

► Dress up plain or store-bought cookies by dipping half of each cookie into melted chocolate. The chocolate-dipped cookie can then be dipped into toasted coconut, chopped nuts, chocolate jimmies or colored sprinkles. Place on a waxed-paper-lined baking sheet and refrigerate until chocolate sets.

► Make an almost-instant glaze for bar cookies by sprinkling the surface with chocolate chips as soon as you remove the cookies from the oven. Cover with foil or a baking sheet and let stand for 3 to 5 minutes, or until the chocolate melts (chocolate chips look whole, even when they're melted). Use a rubber spatula or the back of a spoon to gently spread the chocolate evenly over the surface of the cookies. Cool completely before cutting into squares or bars.

► Make cookie sandwiches by spreading the bottom of one cookie with about a teaspoon of jam or frosting, or a mixture of peanut butter and honey or jelly. Place a second cookie, bottom side down, on top of the filling.

Storing cookies:

▸ Never store crisp and soft cookies in the same container, or the crisp ones will soon soften.

▸ If crisp cookies become soft during storing, recrisp them by reheating about 5 minutes in a 300°F oven.

▸ Keep soft cookies moist by adding 1 or 2 apple quarters to the storage container. Cover tightly and let stand for 1 to 2 days before removing the fruit. This same technique works with soft cookies that are dry because of overbaking or age.

▸ Store cookies in airtight containers such as screw-top jars or sealed plastic bags. This prevents humidity from softening crisp cookies and air from drying soft cookies.

▸ Separate layers of decorated, moist or sticky cookies with waxed paper to prevent their sticking together.

▸ Bar cookies may be stored, tightly covered, in the pan in which they were baked.

▸ Cookies that require refrigeration should be covered tightly so they don't absorb other food odors.

▸ Cookies in the freezer are culinary security! Make sure cookies to be frozen are wrapped airtight, either in freezer-weight plastic bags or foil; expel as much air as possible. Rigid, plastic freezer containers may also be used and are especially good for delicate cookies.

▸ Cookies can be frozen from 4 to 6 months, depending on the temperature and conditions in the freezer. Place a sheet of waxed paper or plastic wrap between cookie layers.

▸ If you're going to freeze cookies, it's best to frost them after freezing and thawing. However, frosted cookies can be frozen for up to 6 months if you first freeze them individually. To do so, place a tray of uncovered cookies in freezer; freeze until hard. Immediately transfer frozen cookies to a labeled, airtight storage container and return to freezer as quickly as possible.

▸ Always label your storage containers with a piece of tape indicating name of cookie, quantity and date stored.

▸ Most baked cookies defrost at room temperature in 10 to 15 minutes.

▸ Don't throw out those cookie crumbs! Use them over ice cream and pud-dings, or freeze until you have enough to make a cookie-crumb crust for a pie or cheesecake.

Giving or mailing cookies:

▸ Bar cookies or other soft cookies are best for mailing. Choose those that won't dry out or crumble during the journey. Avoid those with frostings or pointed edges; fragile, thin cookies run the risk of becoming cookie crumbs by the time they reach their destination.

▶ Always wrap soft and crisp cookies separately to preserve their textures.

▶ Use foil to wrap cookies in pairs (flat sides together) or in small stacks.

▶ Rigid containers such as cookie tins, plastic or cardboard boxes, coffee or shortening cans with plastic lids, or cardboard half-gallon milk cartons make good mailing or giving containers.

C

▶ Pack cookies close together so they won't have room to move around and break during transit.

▶ Separate layers of cookies with waxed paper or plastic wrap.

▶ If packing a variety of cookies in one container, place several of one kind of cookie in separate paper or foil cupcake liners.

▶ Shrink-wrapping large individual cookies or small stacks of cookies pre-serves their freshness, makes them sturdy for mailing, and adds a profes-sional look for gift-giving. Here's how: Preheat the oven to 325°F, then line a baking sheet with 2 layers of heavy-duty paper towel; set aside. Wrap cookie stacks or large single cookies firmly in a good-quality plastic wrap (bargain brands will melt!), overlapping the edges at the bottom middle of the cookie. Cut away any excess plastic wrap that bunches up at the overlap. Place the paper-towel-lined baking sheet in the oven for 5 minutes. Remove from oven and arrange wrapped cookies, 1 inch apart, on hot baking sheet. Return sheet to oven, leaving the door ajar so you can watch the cookies closely. The plastic wrap will shrink tightly around the cookie packages in just a few seconds. Cool the wrapped cookies on racks.

▶ Pack the container of cookies to be mailed in a sturdy, corrugated box with plenty of room for a cushion of filler (crumpled newspaper or other paper, Styrofoam pellets, popcorn, or plastic bubble-wrap). Pad the bot-tom of the box with several inches of filler, add the container of cookies, then more filler around the sides and on top.

▶ Don't skimp on postage when mailing cookies. You don't want all your hard work to become tasteless and dry by mailing cookie packages third class.

COOKING, GENERAL

▶ Your tongue is like a flavor road map. Sweetness is tasted on the tip of the tongue, sourness on the forward edges, salt on the tip and sides, and bitterness at the far back.

▶ Tape a notepad to the inside of one of your kitchen cabinet doors and create a running grocery list by jotting down items as you think of them or run out.

▶ Turn on the oven the second you walk through the door so it can be preheating while you begin meal preparations.

▶ Read a recipe all the way through to be sure you have the necessary in-gredients and cooking utensils.

C

▶ Always chop, measure and otherwise prepare all the ingredients for a recipe *before* beginning to cook.

▶ Start preparing each meal by beginning with the dish that takes longest. That way, it can be cooking while you prepare the other items.

▶ If you're preparing several dishes, scan the recipes to see if there are any of the same ingredients called for. If so, chopping them at the same time saves on time and cleanup. Otherwise, if one recipe calls for ¼ cup onions and another for ¾ cup, chop 1 cup to begin with.

▶ Have several kitchen timers on hand, setting them for each dish that's cooking. When you're busy, it's easy to forget, which means you could wind up with a ruined dish.

▶ Room-temperature foods cook and bake faster than refrigerated food.

▶ If you're beating or whisking a mixture in a bowl on the countertop and the bowl keeps moving around, set it on a slightly dampened dish towel and it'll stay put.

▶ When working with foods that can stain your hands (like beets), or that can leave a volatile residue on them (like chiles), wear disposable plastic gloves (available at drugstores) to protect your hands. If you don't have gloves, generously coat your hands with vegetable oil, then wash off when you're through working with the troublesome ingredient.

▶ Before stirring a sticky mixture, or one that stains, spray the spoon, rubber spatula, etc., with nonstick vegetable spray or coat it lightly with vegetable oil. Be sure and spray the utensil over the sink so you don't get an oily film on your kitchen floor

▶ Instead of using a pastry brush to coat foods (like meat, bread, etc.) with oil, fill a small, clean spray bottle (from hairspray, glass cleaner, etc.) with oil and lightly spritz it over the food. You'll get fewer calories that way.

▶ The cooking term "reduce" refers to the process of boiling a liquid until much of the moisture evaporates. The resulting liquid is thicker and more intensely flavored. Never season a liquid that's to be reduced until after the reduction or you could wind up with an overseasoned mixture.

▶ If you put raw meat, poultry or fish on a dish during preparation, or use it to transfer the food from kitchen to grill, don't put the cooked food on that same dish without first washing it thoroughly. Otherwise, bacteria from the raw food can be transferred to the cooked dish.

▶ If a dish lacks pizzazz and tastes "flat," try stirring in 1 or 2 teaspoons full-flavored vinegar such as balsalmic.

▶ If you somehow oversweeten a savory dish (vegetables, dressings, salad dressings, etc.), try stirring in ½ to 1 teaspoon vinegar to balance the sweet.

▶ Add flair to food by using a variety of ethnic ingredients intrinsic to various cuisines: Caribbean—hot chiles, cilantro, cinnamon, cloves, coconut, ginger, lime juice, nutmeg and turmeric; Chinese—black bean sauce, garlic, fresh ginger, oyster sauce, sesame oil (dark) and soy sauce; Greek—allspice, cinnamon, cloves, dill, fennel, garlic, mint, nutmeg and oregano; Italian—basil, fennel, garlic, onion, oregano and tomato; Japanese—garlic, ginger, miso, scallions, soy sauce, plum or rice vinegar and wasabi; Mexican—cayenne, chile pepper, cilantro, onion, oregano and unsweetened cocoa powder; Thai—basil, bean sauce, chili paste, curry, fish sauce, lemon grass and mint.

▶ To keep a pot from boiling over, give the steam a tiny outlet by placing a toothpick between the pot and cover. The toothpick trick also works well with a covered casserole dish in the oven.

▶ Rubbing vegetable oil around the inside of the top of the pot will prevent boilovers in custards, milk, pasta, etc.

▶ When using a double boiler, put a few marbles or a jar lid in the bottom pan—they'll warn you by rattling when the water gets too low and save the pan from scorching.

▶ When you're cooking particularly odoriferous foods like broccoli, Brussels sprouts or cauliflower, toss a couple of thick chunks of bread into the cooking water (rye bread works best). Bread slices work, too, though they sometimes dissolve and are hard to remove. Or, toss a couple of red bell pepper pieces into the pot. Use a slotted spoon to retrieve the pot sweeteners before serving the food.

▶ You can also keep odors at bay by draping a cloth (dampened with a half-and-half solution of water and vinegar, then wrung out) over the cooking pot, making sure the edges are well away from the heat source so as not to cause a fire.

▶ Stovetop reheating of frozen foods such as sauces, soups and stews should be done over low heat. Add just enough water to cover the bottom of the pan, cover and cook, stirring often to break up the food as it defrosts. Once defrosted, increase the heat to medium and cook until heated through.

▶ Always taste as you cook, and taste all the components of the dish—filling, sauce, etc. How else will you know what the finished product will taste like?

▶ Before removing a pan from the stove, turn off the burner.

▶ Make sure oven mitts or pads are dry before handling a hot pan or dish. Wet material lets the heat through and could result in a burned hand.

▶ Remember that chilling food mutes its flavor, so when serving cold salads, soups, etc., be sure to taste just before serving and adjust the seasoning if necessary.

▶ Kitchen panache: Never point out kitchen mishaps when they can be handled with style and flair. If your corn soufflé flops into a puddle, simply call it corn "pudding" and act like that's just how it's supposed to look. It will still be delicious!

▶ To help diminish lingering, unpleasant cooking odors, bring a pot of water and two lemon halves (squeeze the juice into the water before dropping in the halves) to a boil; cook for 10 minutes. Adding cloves to the water also helps.

▶ A paste of baking soda and water makes a good odor-eater for hands. Lemon juice works well, too.

▶ Always quickly cool leftovers at room temperature, then refrigerate or freeze promptly after serving. Food will cool more quickly if divided into small portions.

▶ Use refrigerated leftovers within 2 to 3 days.

▶ *See also* BARDING; BRAISING; BROILING; CLAY-POT COOKING; CONVECTION OVEN COOKING; COOKING LIGHT; DEEP-FRYING; GRILLING; HIGH-ALTITUDE ADJUSTMENTS; LARDING; MICROWAVE COOKING; POACHING; PRESSURE COOKING; ROASTING; SAUTÉING; SLOW COOKERS; STEAMING; STIR-FRYING

COOKING LIGHT *(Ways to reduce calories, fat, salt and cholesterol)*

▶ One gram fat—whatever the form (butter, oil, etc.) equals 9 calories.

▶ One gram alcohol contains 7 calories, so watch those alcoholic beverages (*see* ALCOHOL).

▶ One gram carbohydrate or protein equals 4 calories.

▶ Most experts advise that no more than 30 percent of daily calories should come from fat. To calculate the percentage of calories from fat that a food contains, find the "fat grams per serving" on the label and multiply by 9. This gives you the total calories from fat. Now divide that number by the total calories per serving. The result is the percentage of calories that come from fat.

▶ Eating more slowly is one way to eat less—it takes about 20 minutes for the signal to go from the stomach to brain to tell it you're not hungry. One age-old method to slow eating is to cut food into tiny pieces and chew each piece 20 times.

▶ Make it a habit to put your fork down between bites.

▶ Try eating with your other hand—if you're right-handed, use your left hand.

▶ Unless you're proficient with them, eating with chopsticks will help slow down your eating pace.

▶ The term "no sugar added" on the label simply means that the ingredients don't include table sugar. To get the *real* story, check a label for the words corn syrup, dextrose, fructose, glucose, maltose or sucrose—all of which are sugar.

▶ The word "sodium" on food labels can be interpreted as follows: Per serving, a product labeled "sodium free" has less than 5 milligrams, "very low sodium" less than 35 milligrams and "reduced sodium" less than 140 milligrams.

▶ If you're watching your salt, avoid high-sodium prepared condiments such as ketchup and barbecue sauce. There are many reduced-sodium condiments (such as soy sauce and ketchup) in markets today.

▶ If you're a salt-free cook, offer guests freshly ground pepper and tiny bowls of flavorings like minced fresh herbs, garlic or ginger root with which to season their food. It wouldn't hurt to have a salt shaker on the table, either. Unsalted food tastes terribly bland to those who aren't used to doing without.

▶ Use ⅜ cup salt-free tomato paste mixed with ½ cup water as a substitute for sodium-laden tomato sauce.

▶ To avoid saturated fats, cut out butter, lard, coconut or palm oil, suet and hydrogenated oils such as margarine or vegetable shortening.

▶ Many products like *refritos* (refried beans) and tortillas contain lard. Look for those made with vegetable oils to reduce saturated fat. Some refritos are fat free.

▶ Using low-fat substitutions in dairy products can make a big caloric difference. For example, a cup of regular sour cream contains about 493 calories, whereas the same amount of low-fat sour cream averages about 280 calories. Plain low-fat yogurt weighs in around 143 calories. An 8-ounce glass of whole milk contains about 157 calories, while 2 percent low-fat milk equals 121, 1 percent is 102, and nonfat a scant 86 calories.

▶ Choose cheeses that are made from low- or nonfat milk. If salt in the diet is a concern, look for low-sodium cheeses.

▶ Nonfat or low-fat evaporated milk will add texture to sauces and other dishes without excess calories.

▶ Remember that fat adds texture and body to dishes. So, whenever substituting reduced-calorie dairy products, it's best not to go down more than one step. If a recipe calls for whipping cream, you can use half-and-half or rich milk and come close to the end result. Using nonfat milk, however, would produce less than satisfactory results—it would be better to chose a recipe with no dairy products.

▶ Create your own sour cream substitute by combining ½ cup low-fat cottage cheese, ¼ cup nonfat milk and 2 teaspoons lemon juice in a blender, processing until smooth and creamy. Cover and refrigerate for up to 4 days. Blend with fresh herbs and seasonings for an easy low-calorie dip. Makes about ¾ cup.

▶ For a low-calorie sour cream substitute, try Quark—a soft, unripened cheese with the texture and flavor of sour cream. Quark comes in two versions—low-fat and nonfat. It isn't as tart as yogurt and its texture is richer than either low-fat sour cream or yogurt. Do not use as a substitute when baking.

C

- Reduce the oil called for in a salad dressing and substitute vegetable juice, defatted chicken broth, wine, etc.
- Make a creamy low-calorie dressing by combining ½ cup nonfat yogurt, 1 cup fresh herbs and 1 to 2 tablespoons fresh lemon, lime or orange juice in a blender jar. Puree until smooth; salt and pepper to taste. If dressing is too thick, thin it with a little non- or low-fat milk.
- Select lean cuts of meat and trim all excess fat before cooking.
- Remember this general rule: The younger the animal, the lower the fat content—veal has less fat than beef.
- In marinades for meat or other food, substitute wine, citrus juice or tomato juice for the oil.
- Use nonstick vegetable sprays instead of oils or fats.
- Nonstick cookware cuts way down on the necessity for fat when sautéing foods. If necessary, you can always spritz the skillet with nonstick vegetable spray.
- If using oil or fat for sautéing, don't just pour it from the bottle into the pan—you'd be surprised how much more you use that way. Get into the habit of measuring it, starting with 1 or 2 teaspoons of oil, and only adding more if necessary.
- Remove the skin from chicken before cooking with moist-heat methods like braising or stewing. Because the skin holds in moisture, remove it *after* cooking when using dry-heat methods like grilling and broiling.
- Turkey is even lower in fat than chicken. Ground turkey and turkey cutlets are commonly found in most supermarkets today. The cutlets cook in minutes, and ground turkey can be used to substitute part or all of the beef called for in burgers, chili or meatloaf.
- Buy turkey pastrami, sausage and other usually high-fat meat products and save calories in a big way.
- For moist, low-fat chicken or fish, cook it *en papillote*. Simply place an individual serving of chicken or fish on a piece of parchment (the classic way) or foil large enough to enclose it. Top with minced vegetables or herbs or tomato sauce; seal packet and bake.
- The next time you want a hamburger (but not all the calories), substitute shredded carrots for a third to half the meat. The result will be juicy and flavorful. Or you can substitute cooked and mashed beans or potatoes.
- Substitute cooked, fiber- and protein-rich dried legumes like beans or lentils for meat in casseroles.
- Grilling or broiling meats on a rack allows excess fat to drip away.
- Put cooked ground meat in a colander, set on plate and press down on the meat with a spoon to drain off as much grease as possible.
- Make a small portion of cooked meat seem larger by thinly slicing it, then fanning the slices over one side of the plate.
- For a delicious, low-calorie sauce for meat or fish, combine pureed roasted

peppers (fresh or those in a jar) with a little stock or evaporated skim milk and heat until warmed through.

► Make soups a day in advance and refrigerate them. Doing so will solidify any fat, which you can lift off before reheating.

► Enrich sauces the low-fat way by using vegetable purees to thicken them.

► Substituting 2 egg whites for 1 whole egg will reduce a recipe's cholesterol. One teaspoon of vegetable oil can be added, if desired.

► Use all-fruit, no-sugar jams instead of butter or regular spreads.

► If you love fruit juice but are watching calories, dilute it with sparkling water.

► For a quick, naturally sweet sauce, puree berries or fruit, thinning with a little fruit juice, if necessary. Combine the puree with a little nonfat mayonnaise or yogurt for a wonderful fruit-salad dressing.

► In many dishes (such as fruit compotes, puddings and mousses) thawed frozen-juice concentrate can be used as a substitute for sugar. Such substitutions are not recommended for baked goods unless you're an experienced baker and understand the delicate balance between flour and liquids and sugars.

► Substitute angel food cake for pound cake—it's lower in cholesterol, fat and calories.

► For a rich-tasting, low-fat dessert topping fold 1 stiffly beaten egg white into 1 pureed ripe banana mixed with ½ teaspoon pure vanilla extract. Spoon over puddings, cakes or fruit.

► Another relatively low-calorie dessert topping is whipped low- or nonfat evaporated milk. Pour the evaporated milk into a shallow metal cake or pie pan, then freeze until ice crystals form around the edges. Using a chilled bowl and beaters, whip the milk until fluffy. Flavor with ½ to 1 teaspoon pure vanilla extract, if desired. To sweeten, gently beat 1 to 2 tablespoons confectioners' sugar into the whipped milk.

► *See also* COOKING, GENERAL

CORN

► Choose ears with bright green, snugly fitting husks, and fresh-looking, pale golden to golden brown silk; the silk should be dry, not soggy. The kernels should be plump and milky, and come all the way to the ear's tip; the rows should be tightly spaced. Don't buy corn that's been husked—the husk was probably removed by the market because it was discolored or wilted, a sign the corn is old. Even if the husks were removed with the greengrocer's best intentions, husked corn deteriorates faster. Because corn's sugar immediately begins its gradual conversion to starch (which lessens its natural sweetness), it's important to buy it as soon as possible after it's picked. Try to buy fresh corn from a produce market with high volume to be sure it's the freshest possible.

- Store fresh corn in a plastic bag in the refrigerator for no more than a day after purchase. It's best used the day you buy it.
- Strip off the husks and silk, and rinse off the corn just before cooking.
- Rub a damp paper towel over an ear of husked corn to remove that pesky silk. A clean, damp, soft-bristle toothbrush also works well.
- *Corn yields:* 2 medium ears = 1 cup kernels; 1 10-ounce package frozen corn = 1¾ cup kernels.
- To remove corn kernels from the cob, begin by cutting a small piece off the tip so that it's flat. Holding the stem end, stand the cob upright on its flat end. Set it on a plate and use a firm-bladed, very sharp knife to cut downward, removing the corn 3 or 4 rows at a time. To get the "milk" of the corn, use the back of the blade to scrape what's left of the juice from the cobs.
- Adding salt to the boiling water will toughen the corn.
- Corn will be sweeter if you add 1 teaspoon sugar for each quart of water.
- Cooking corn in equal amounts of milk and water will produce a tender, sweet result.
- Unlike many vegetables, corn gets tougher—not softer—when over-cooked. Depending on the size of the ear and the age of the corn (older corn takes longer), corn on the cob can take anywhere from 3 to 10 minutes to cook in boiling water.
- Corn on the cob doesn't have to be shucked to be cooked in boiling water. On the contrary, it's even sweeter when cooked *in* the husk. Gently pull back the husks, remove the silk, then replace the husks, tying them together at the top with string. Cook as you would husked corn on the cob.
- Always cover the pot when cooking corn on the cob so the steam cooks the portions not submerged in water.
- Corn on the cob is a good candidate for microwave cooking. Rinse off each ear and immediately wrap in waxed paper. Cook at HIGH (100 per-cent power) as follows: 1 ear—3 to 5 minutes; 2 ears—5 to 7 minutes; 4 ears—9 to 12 minutes.
- To grill corn, remove the silk, but leave the husks; use a metal twist tie to close the husk at the top. Soak the corn in cold water for 15 minutes so the husks don't burn while grilling. Grill for 15 to 30 minutes, depending on the size of the ear.
- When sautéing shucked corn, stir frequently and cook quickly. It'll only take about 3 minutes for it to be perfectly crisp-tender.
- Remove the kernels from leftover cooked corn on the cob and use the next day in soups, salads, succotash, hash, muffins, pancakes—you name it!
- Don't discard those leftover cobs (either fresh or cooked)! Throw them in a pot, cover with milk, or a mixture of milk and water, and bring to a boil. Reduce to simmer, cover, and cook for 30 minutes. Remove the cobs

and use the delicious liquid as a base for soups or sauces.
▶ *See also* VEGETABLES, GENERAL

CORNBREAD

▶ Give homemade cornbread a crispy crust by preheating the pan. Put 1 to 2 tablespoons vegetable oil or bacon drippings in a 8- or 9-inch square pan (swirl the oil so it coats the sides of the pan) before placing the pan in a preheated 400° oven for 10 minutes. Quickly turn the cornbread batter into the preheated pan (it will sizzle) and bake according to the recipe.
▶ Add flavor to cornbread by mixing ½ to 1 cup grated cheese, chopped scallion greens or crisply cooked bacon into the batter.
▶ For slightly sweet cornbread, add 2 tablespoons brown sugar and ¼ teaspoon ground nutmeg to the dry ingredients.
▶ For an intriguing taste, melt 3 tablespoons peanut butter (don't overheat or it will turn to glue) and stir into the wet ingredients of a cornbread batter.
▶ *See also* BREADS, QUICK

CORNISH GAME HENS *see* ROCK CORNISH GAME HENS

CORNMEAL

▶ There are two main styles of cornmeal—steel-ground and stone- or water-ground. Most cornmeal in supermarkets is steel-ground, which means the husk and germ have been almost completely removed. Stone-ground cornmeal retains some of the corn's hull and germ, making it more nutritious. It's commonly available in natural food stores.
▶ Steel-ground cornmeal can be stored almost indefinitely in an airtight container in a cool, dark place. Because of the fat in the germ, stone-ground meal is also more perishable. Store it in an airtight container in the refrigerator for up to 4 months.
▶ Cornmeal comes in three textures—fine (often called *corn flour*), medium (the texture most commonly available commercially) and coarse (also known as *polenta*). *Masa Harina* is a special corn flour used to make corn tortillas and tamales.
▶ Add a toasty nuance to polenta, cornbread and other cornmeal dishes by first sautéing the cornmeal in a small amount of oil, stirring occasionally, until golden brown. Then add liquid (for polenta or mush), or cool the cornmeal to room temperature and use for cornbread or other baked goods.
▶ Cornmeal can be dry-roasted by placing a single layer of it in a shallow baking pan and roasting at 300°F for about 10 minutes; or toast it in a dry skillet, stirring often, until golden brown.

▸ If you absolutely cannot seem to make polenta without lumps, whisk the cornmeal into cold water before heating and cooking.

CORNSTARCH

▸ Cornstarch is a dense, powdery "flour" made from a corn kernel's endosperm.

▸ Cornstarch-thickened sauces are clear, whereas those thickened with flour are opaque.

▸ To thicken a mixture you need half as much cornstarch as you do flour. Therefore, for each tablespoon flour called for in a recipe, substitute ½ tablespoon cornstarch.

▸ Flour is more heat stable than cornstarch for thickening, so when cooking a mixture that requires very high heat, use a combination of the two. Otherwise, if a recipe calls for 2 tablespoons cornstarch, use 1 tablespoon cornstarch and 2 tablespoons flour.

▸ Because cornstarch easily forms lumps when combined with liquid, mix it with a small amount of cold liquid to form a thin paste before stirring into a hot mixture.

▸ Stir constantly as you add the cornstarch paste to a hot liquid, bringing the mixture to a boil. Cook for about 2 minutes, stirring often, for the mixture to reach maximum thickness.

▸ Stirring cornstarch together with some of the granulated sugar in a recipe will also help disperse it in liquid.

▸ Mixtures thickened with cornstarch will begin to thin if cooked too long or at too high a temperature, or if stirred too vigorously.

▸ Some old-fashioned or European baking recipes call for using all or part cornstarch instead of all flour. Such recipes produce a finer-textured, more compact product than flour alone. In British recipes, cornstarch is referred to as cornflour.

CORN SYRUP

▸ Corn syrup is produced when starch granules from corn are processed with acids or enzymes. This thick, sweet syrup comes in light and dark forms. Light corn syrup has been clarified to remove all color and cloudiness. The more strongly flavored dark corn syrup is a mixture of corn syrup and refiners' syrup.

▸ Light and dark corn syrups may be used interchangeably, but remember that the dark form adds color and a slightly bolder flavor.

▸ Corn syrup inhibits crystallization, which makes it particularly good for frostings, candies, jams and jellies.

▸ Baked goods made with corn syrup retain their moisture and stay fresh longer.

▸ Corn syrup gives foods a slightly dense, chewy texture.

▸ Corn syrup can be substituted for other syrups, but isn't as intensely sweet as honey or maple syrup.

▸ Substitution for 1 cup light corn syrup: 1¼ cups granulated sugar plus ¼ cup water.

▸ Substitution for 1 cup dark corn syrup: ¾ cup light corn syrup plus ¼ cup light molasses; or 1¼ cups packed brown sugar plus ¼ cup water.

▸ *See also* SYRUPS

COTTAGE CHEESE *see* CHEESE

CRABS

▸ Choose live crabs that are active, have hard shells (except for soft-shell varieties) and are heavy for their size. Cooked whole crabs and crabmeat should have a fresh, sweet smell.

▸ Refrigerate live crabs, covered by a damp towel, until just before cooking. They can also be stored on a layer of damp newspapers in an ice-filled cooler. Live crabs should be used the day they're purchased.

▸ Before cooking, check to make sure the crab is still alive. It will be sluggish because of the cold, but should still show some movement in its legs.

▸ Refrigerate leftover cooked crabmeat, tightly covered, for no more than 2 days.

▸ Canned crab is available flaked, or as lump or claw meat. Once opened, refrigerate and use canned crab within 2 days. Crab legs and claws are available cooked or frozen.

▸ Taste canned crabmeat—if it has a metallic taste, let it soak in ice water for 5 minutes. Drain and blot dry before using.

▸ Always use your fingers to pick over crabmeat—fresh or canned—to make sure there are no tiny pieces of shell.

▸ *See also* SHELLFISH

CRANBERRIES

▸ Cranberries are usually sold in see-through 12-ounce plastic bags, so you can't pick through them. Look for berries that are a bright, intense color (from light to dark red).

▸ Store cranberries in an airtight plastic bag in the refrigerator for at least a month. They can be frozen for up to a year.

▸ Before using cranberries, discard any that are soft, discolored or shriveled; pluck off any stems.

▸ *Cranberry yields:* 1 12-ounce bag = about 3 cups whole berries; about 2½ cups finely chopped berries.

▸ Make quick work of chopping fresh or frozen cranberries by using a food processor with the metal blade. Use quick on/off pulses to insure control.

C

- There's no need to defrost frozen cranberries before using them in a recipe.
- Only cook whole cranberries until they pop—longer than that and they'll turn to mush and start to get bitter.
- Cranberry mixtures won't boil over while cooking if you add 1 teaspoon of vegetable oil for each 12-ounce package to the mixture.
- Adding ¼ teaspoon baking soda to cranberries while cooking neutralizes some of the fruit's natural acidity, which means you'll need less sugar.
- If you're using a meat grinder to chop cranberries, freeze them first to make the job easier.
- Add a sophisticated touch to homemade cranberry relish by substituting red wine for all or part of the liquid called for in the recipe. The resulting color and flavor are terrific.
- Combine equal amounts of homemade cranberry sauce with your favorite chutney to create a delicious condiment for meats.
- Cranberry sauce (not the jellied type) makes a great topping for waffles and pancakes. Make cranberry syrup by combining cranberry sauce with a little light corn syrup, stirring over low heat until warmed through.
- Sweetened, dried cranberries are available in many supermarkets. Use them like raisins in baked goods or for snacks.
- To rehydrate dried cranberries, cover them with water, liqueur or other soaking liquid in a medium bowl. Cover and microwave on HIGH (100 percent power) for 30 to 60 seconds; let stand for 5 minutes before using. Or pour a very hot liquid over the berries, cover and let stand for at least 20 minutes.
- *See also* BERRIES, GENERAL

CREAM

- Cream is categorized according to the amount of milk fat it contains. **Light cream** (also called **coffee cream** and **table cream**) can contain between 18 to 30 percent milk fat. **Light whipping cream** (also simply called **whipping cream**) contains 30 to 36 percent fat; **heavy** (or **heavy whipping**) **cream** has a fat content of between 36 and 40 percent. **Half and half** is a mixture of equal parts milk and cream, and contains from 10 to 18 percent milk fat.
- *Ultra-pasteurized cream* has been briefly heated at temperatures up to 300°F to kill the microorganisms that cause milk products to sour. It has a longer shelf life than regular cream but doesn't whip as well and has a slightly "cooked" flavor.
- Refrigerate cream in the coldest part of the refrigerator as soon as you get home from the market. Most creams will keep up to a week past the pull date on the carton.

▶ Cream can be frozen as long as there's at least a ½ inch of airspace at the top of the cardboard container. Double wrap the container in a freezer-proof plastic bag; freeze for up to 6 months. Defrost in the refrigerator overnight; shake cream well before using.

▶ *Whipping cream yields:* 1 cup heavy or whipping cream = 2 cups whipped cream.

▶ *Substitutions (for use in cooking or baking) for 1 cup of:* half and half—1½ tablespoons melted butter plus enough whole milk to equal 1 cup, or ½ cup light cream plus ½ cup whole milk; light cream—3 tablespoons melted butter plus enough whole milk to equal 1 cup; heavy whipping cream—⅓ cup melted butter plus ¾ cup whole milk (not to be used for whipping).

▶ If you think cream has just begun to sour, whisk in ⅛ teaspoon baking soda. The soda will counteract the natural lactic acid in the cream. Taste the cream before using to make sure the flavor is acceptable.

▶ The bowl in which you whip cream should be deep enough so the cream can double in volume.

▶ A small amount of cream (less than 1 cup) will whip better in a deep, narrow bowl than one that's large and wide.

▶ Cream will whip faster if you chill the beaters and bowl in the freezer for 15 minutes. The cream should also be as cold as possible.

▶ If you haven't had time to chill bowl and beaters, set the bowl in which you whip cream in a larger bowl filled with ice water.

▶ Protect yourself and your kitchen from spatters when whipping cream by laying a sheet of plastic wrap or waxed paper (with a hole cut for the beater stems) on top of the bowl.

▶ Spatters will be minimal with an electric mixer if you start out at medium speed, gradually increasing the speed as the cream thickens.

▶ You'll get more volume from whipped cream if you wait until the cream forms soft peaks before adding sugar or flavorings such as vanilla or liqueurs.

▶ Use confectioners' sugar to sweeten cream—it not only dissolves quickly, but it also helps stabilize whipped cream because it contains cornstarch.

▶ Adding 1 teaspoon light corn syrup per cup of whipping cream will also help stabilize the cream after it's whipped.

▶ Depending on how sweet a dessert is, you may not want to sweeten whipped cream. Unsweetened cream has its own natural sweetness and makes a striking counterpoint to very sweet desserts.

▶ If you accidentally overbeat whipping cream so that it begins to turn buttery, gently whisk in additional cream, 1 tablespoon at a time. Don't "beat" the cream again or you'll be right back where you started.

▶ Try serving whipped cream at the soft-peak stage with some desserts.

When slightly soft, the cream makes gentle folds over fruit, cobblers, etc. This texture is often much more inviting than stiffly beaten cream standing at attention atop a dessert.

▶ To make chocolate whipped cream, stir together 2 tablespoons each unsweetened cocoa powder and confectioners' sugar. Slowly add 1 cup whipping cream, stirring constantly so the mixture stays smooth. Refrigerate for 30 minutes before beating.

▶ To make lightened whipped cream, beat 1 or 2 room-temperature egg whites with ¼ teaspoon cream of tartar until stiff but not dry. Fold into 2 cups whipped cream (1 cup before beating) until thoroughly combined.

▶ Cream can be whipped in advance for use hours later. Simply whip it until stiff, then spoon it into a sieve lined with a double layer of cheesecloth. Set over a bowl with the bottom of the sieve 2 inches above the bottom of the bowl. Cover tightly and refrigerate for up to 48 hours. If, when you get ready to use the cream, it's a little too stiff, whisk in 1 to 2 tablespoons liquid cream.

▶ Cover and refrigerate leftover whipped cream and use dollops of it atop coffee for a luxurious way to begin or end the next day.

▶ Leftover whipped cream can also be frozen. Line a baking sheet with plastic wrap onto which you spoon serving-size dollops of whipped cream. Freeze, uncovered, until firm. Transfer the solid whipped-cream mounds to a plastic bag, seal airtight and return to the freezer for up to 2 weeks. Remove and use the dollops as you need them atop desserts or coffee. The cream will be soft in 5 to 10 minutes; less time for coffee and hot desserts. If the cream isn't sweetened, you can use it to enrich soups, sauces and other dishes.

▶ When used as a frosting, whipped cream often becomes very soft and begins to be absorbed by the cake. Gelatin will prevent that problem. In a small bowl, stir 1 teaspoon unflavored gelatin into 3 tablespoons water or other liquid (using liqueur, orange juice, etc., will flavor the cream); set aside 5 minutes to soften gelatin. Place the small bowl in a pan of very hot water; stir mixture until gelatin is completely dissolved. Cool to room temperature. Beat 1 cup of whipping cream until soft peaks form. Beating constantly at medium-high speed, gradually drizzle gelatin mixture into whipped cream. Use immediately to frost cakes; mixture sets up quickly and becomes difficult to spread.

▶ Pour heavy cream over berries or other fruit a few minutes before serving. The natural acid in the fruit will begin to slightly coagulate the cream, making it extra thick and luscious.

▶ When using cream in cooking, remember that the more fat it contains the more immune it is to curdling. Heavy whipping cream can be added to a sauce and boiled over high heat and usually not have any problem.

▶ If the ingredients you're mixing cream with are highly acidic, reduce the cream first by cooking it over medium heat until the volume is decreased by half. Then add the reduced cream to the rest of the mixture.

▶ Unsweetened whipped cream can be served as a garnish for dishes such as peas, mashed potatoes and hot or cold soups. If desired, you can salt the cream slightly before whipping. You can also fold in 1 or 2 tablespoons minced chives or other herbs after the cream is whipped.

▶ Fold 1 to 2 tablespoons horseradish into whipped cream for a delicious accompaniment for roast beef.

▶ You'll save loads of calories by substituting undiluted evaporated whole or skim milk for cream in sauces. No, the texture won't be the same, but it will be close.

▶ *See also* CRÈME FRAÎCHE; MILK; SOUR CREAM

C

CREAM CHEESE *see* CHEESE

CRÈME FRAÎCHE [krehm FRESH]

▶ Crème fraîche is a matured, thickened cream with a slightly tangy, nutty flavor and velvety rich texture. It's available in some supermarkets at a premium price.

▶ Store crème fraîche in an airtight container in the refrigerator for up to 10 days.

▶ Crème fraîche is ideal for sauces or soups because it can be boiled without curdling. It's also delicious spooned over fresh fruit or other desserts like warm pies, cobblers or puddings.

▶ Make your own crème fraîche by combining 1 cup heavy whipping cream with 2 tablespoons buttermilk (or ½ cup sour cream) in a screw-top glass jar; shake well to combine. (All ingredients should be at room temperature. If they're not, combine in a saucepan and heat just to body temperature, not over 100°F.) Cover and let stand at room temperature for 8 to 24 hours, depending on how warm the cream and the room are. Stir well, then cover and refrigerate for at least 8 hours before using. The buttermilk-based crème fraîche is slightly tangier than that made with sour cream.

▶ Crème fraîche can be flavored in many ways, depending on its use. Stir in the additives after the cream has thickened but before you refrigerate it. Flavorings that can be used include 1 to 2 tablespoons minced fresh herbs, horseradish, crystallized ginger, honey or confectioners' sugar.

▶ For lighter crème fraîche, whip it until soft peaks form (it won't become stiff like whipped cream). This works only with crème fraîche made with buttermilk.

▶ For extra-thick crème fraîche, turn it into a sieve lined with a double layer of cheesecloth or into a paper-filter-lined coffee cone. Set over a bowl with the bottom of the sieve or coffee cone 2 inches above the bottom of the bowl. Cover tightly and refrigerate for 24 hours.

CROCKPOTS see SLOW COOKERS

C

CROUTONS [KROO-tawns]
- Croutons are a crunchy accompaniment for everything from soup to salad to vegetables. They're commercially available either plain or variously seasoned.
- Homemade croutons are fresher and better-tasting than store-bought, and easy to make. Combine your choice of seasonings such as minced fresh (or crumbled dried) herbs and salt and pepper with olive oil. Brush the flavored oil over both sides of bread slices, then stack as many slices as you can cut at one time (it'll depend on the thickness of the slices) and cut bread into cubes. Cut the cubes as large or small as you wish, depending on how the croutons are to be used. Croutons to be used as a vegetable garnish, for example, would be much smaller than those for soups or salads. Spread the cubes in a single layer on a large baking sheet and bake at 300°F until dry and crisp; the length of time will depend on the size of the crouton.
- For low-calorie croutons, brush your favorite low-fat salad dressing over bread slices and follow directions in previous tip.
- Cool croutons completely before using. Store in an airtight plastic bag at room temperature for up to a week. For longer storage, freeze for up to 6 months.

CRUMBS, GENERAL
- Crumbs can be used for a variety of cooking purposes. Cookie crumbs can be turned into a pie or cheesecake crust, or sprinkled atop desserts, or folded into puddings. Savory crumbs made from bread, crackers or unsweetened cereals can be used as a breading, as a thickener for soups and other liquid mixtures, or to garnish vegetables or casseroles.
- Use the following amounts to make 1 cup finely crushed crumbs: 14 graham cracker squares, 14 Oreos (including middle), 15 gingersnaps, 16 Famous chocolate wafer cookies, 22 vanilla wafers, 24 Ritz crackers, 28 saltine squares, or 3 cups corn, wheat or bran flakes.
- *See also* BREADCRUMBS

CUCUMBERS
- Choose firm cucumbers with smooth, brightly colored skins. Avoid any that have shriveled or soft spots. Smaller cucumbers are younger, which means they're not as bitter, and have thinner skins and fewer seeds. Many cucumbers found in supermarkets today are waxed to prolong shelf life.

Hothouse (or English) cucumbers—which are usually wrapped in plastic wrap—are thinner, longer (up to 1½ feet) and virtually seedless. They're not usually waxed but are comparatively more expensive than regular cucumbers.

C

▶ Store whole cucumbers, unwashed, in a plastic bag in the refrigerator for up to 10 days. Cut cucumbers can be wrapped and refrigerated for up to 5 days.

▶ Wash cucumbers just before using. If the skin is thin and unwaxed, peeling usually isn't necessary. To be sure of the skin, cut off a slice and taste it—if it's bitter, peel it.

▶ Cucumber seeds can often be bitter. To seed a cucumber, cut it lengthwise in half, then use a teaspoon to scrape out the seeds.

▶ To give cucumber slices a scalloped look run the tines of a dinner fork down the length of a whole cucumber, cutting through the skin and at least ⅛ inch into the flesh. Repeat all the way around the cucumber, then slice it crosswise.

▶ To remove excess water from the cucumbers and make them crisp for use in salads or other cold dishes, sprinkle peeled and chopped or sliced cucumbers with salt, top with a layer of ice cubes and refrigerate for 1 hour. Drain the cucumbers, pat dry with a paper towel, then cover and refrigerate until ready to use.

▶ Cucumbers can be baked, broiled, sautéed and braised. To prepare cucumbers for use in cooked dishes, first peel and seed them, then salt generously and let stand for 1 hour, cut side down, on paper towels. Wipe off excess salt and moisture with paper towels, then cook as desired.

▶ Create an edible container by cutting a cucumber in half lengthwise and using a pointed spoon to hollow it out, leaving sides ¼ to ½ inch thick. Fill with dip, sauce, salad, etc.

▶ Long, ½-inch-thick strips of cucumber make great swizzle sticks for drinks like Bloody Marys, Moscow mules, or a simple glass of tomato or vegetable juice.

▶ Cut crisp peeled cucumbers into ½-inch slices and soak in pickle juice for 4 days for "homemade" cucumber pickles.

▶ *See also* VEGETABLES, GENERAL

CURRANTS *see* RAISINS

CURRY POWDER

▶ Authentic Indian curry powder is freshly ground each day and can vary dramatically depending on the region and the cook. Such curry powder is a pulverized blend of up to twenty spices, herbs and seeds.

▶ Commercial curry powder bears little resemblance to freshly ground blends. It comes in two main styles—standard and Madras, which is hot-

C

ter. Commercial curry powders vary significantly, however, so you'll have to keep trying them to see which one you like.

▶ To eliminate curry powder's "raw" taste, sauté it in a dab of butter for a minute or so before adding to your recipe.

▶ A pinch of curry powder adds an exotic touch to all kinds of foods including baked goods, soups, vegetables, rice, dumplings and salad dressings. Be sure to start with a light touch. You can always add more, but too much can ruin a dish.

▶ Be careful when adding curry powder to foods that won't be eaten within an hour or so. Curry is one of those spices that gets hotter the longer it stands

▶ *See also* SPICES *for storage information*

CUSTARDS

▶ There are two types of custard: baked custard is firm enough to hold its shape; stirred custard is cooked on a stovetop and is creamy and pourable. Depending on the texture of stirred custard, it can be served as a dessert or as a dessert sauce.

▶ All custards require slow cooking and gentle heat in order to prevent the mixture from separating (curdling).

▶ A general rule for thickening custards is to use 2 egg yolks or 1 whole egg for each cup of milk.

▶ Stirred custards are generally made in the top of a double boiler over hot, not boiling, water, so the heat is continual but gentle. High heat can scorch the milk (which will ruin the custard's flavor) and cause the eggs to separate.

▶ Constant stirring is necessary in order for the protein in the eggs to coagulate evenly.

▶ When a stirred custard recipe calls for egg yolks only, it's important to remove as much of the white as possible. That's because egg whites coagulate at a lower temperature than egg yolks, which will make the mixture look lumpy.

▶ If a stirred custard recipe calls for whole eggs, strain the cooked mixture through a fine sieve for a perfectly smooth result.

▶ Don't try to hurry stirred custards by raising the heat—the mixture will curdle. Most stirred custards take at least 10 minutes to cook.

▶ If your custard begins to curdle, pour it into a blender jar, cover and process until smooth. (Start blender at low speed and gradually increase to high.) Clean the pan of any residue, then return the custard to the pan and begin cooking again.

▶ A stirred custard is done when it leaves a velvety coating on the back of a metal spoon. Run your finger across the custard-dipped spoon; if it leaves a definitive track, the custard's ready.

▶ Another method for testing custard is by cooking it until it registers 170°F on a candy thermometer.

▶ As soon as a custard tests done, remove it from the heat or it will continue to cook.

▶ If your custard's not as silky smooth as you'd like, pour it through a fine sieve into a bowl.

C

▶ You can quickly cool a stirred custard by placing the pan in a large bowl of ice water. Stir the custard constantly until it reaches the desired temperature.

▶ Once the custard has cooled to room temperature, immediately cover the surface with plastic wrap (put it right *on* the custard surface) and refrigerate. The custard will become slightly thicker when cold.

▶ Baked custards are generally baked in a water bath—the water acts as insulation and diffuses the oven heat so the mixture will set without separating.

▶ Don't beat the mixture for a baked custard until foamy or the surface of the final custard will be crusty and pockmarked.

▶ If you plan on unmolding a baked custard, you'll have better luck if you bake it in metal rather than glass molds.

▶ Set filled custard cups in a 13- by 9-inch baking pan, place the pan on the oven rack, then pour hot tap water into the pan almost halfway up the sides of the custard cups.

▶ To test a baked custard for doneness, insert a dinner knife halfway between the edge and the center. If the knife comes out clean, the custard's done. The center will still be jiggly, but will firm as it cools.

▶ A custard that "weeps" (oozes liquid) has been baked too long or at too high a temperature.

▶ Baked custards can be served hot, warm or chilled.

▶ All custards should be refrigerated, covered, and consumed within 3 days.

▶ *See also* DESSERTS, GENERAL

CUTTING BOARDS

▶ For years, the conventional wisdom has been that plastic cutting boards are better than their wooden counterparts for safety against food-poisoning bacteria. However, according to a study done by two microbiologists at the University of Wisconsin's Food Research Institute, the opposite is true. Tests proved that wooden cutting boards are actually so inhospitable to contaminants like poultry and meat juices that bacteria disappeared from wood surfaces within minutes. On the other hand, bacteria on the plastic boards multiplied at room temperature.

▶ If you use plastic cutting boards, it's wise to have two—one for foods that will be eaten raw (such as salad ingredients) and one for foods to be well cooked.

- Bacteria can accumulate in the knife cuts made on a plastic cutting board. If yours is very scarred, buy a new board.
- After each use, all cutting boards should be scrubbed thoroughly with hot water and detergent.
- Most plastic cutting boards can be washed in the dishwater.
- Deodorize any cutting board by rubbing with a paste of baking soda and water.
- Discolored cutting boards can be helped by rubbing them with lemon juice; let stand for 5 minutes before wiping off.
- Cutting boards can be sanitized by scrubbing them with a mixture of 1 quart hot water mixed with ⅓ cup household bleach. Wash well with hot, soapy water.

DATES

- Fresh dates are available in some specialty markets from late summer through mid-fall. Dried dates are available year-round and are sold packaged or in bulk, pitted or unpitted. Chopped, dried dates are also available in packages.
- Choose fresh dates that are plump and soft, with a smooth, shiny skin. Avoid very shriveled dates or those with mold or sugar crystals on the skin.
- Store fresh dates in a plastic bag in the refrigerator for up to 2 weeks. Dried dates can be stored, wrapped airtight, at room temperature in a cool, dry place for up to 6 months, in the refrigerator for up to 1 year.
- *Date yields:* 8 ounces of pitted dates = about 1½ cups chopped.
- If dates are stuck together in a solid mass, pop them into a microwave oven and heat at MEDIUM (50 percent power) for 30 to 60 seconds; let stand 1 minute before separating. Or put the block of dates on a baking pan and heat in a 300°F oven for about 5 minutes.
- *See also* FRUIT, DRIED

DECANTING *see* WINE

DEEP-FRYING

- Adding ½ teaspoon baking powder per ½ cup flour in batters for deep-fried foods will produce a lighter coating.
- Air-drying batter-coated food for 30 minutes before deep-frying reduces spattering when the food hits the hot oil.
- To allow for bubbling up and splattering, the pot in which you deep-fry should be filled no more than halfway with oil.
- The oil or fat you use for deep-frying should have a high smoke point—the temperature to which it can be heated without smoking. Butter and margarine have low smoke points, so aren't good for frying; shortening, lard and most oils are. The best oils for frying are canola, corn, peanut, safflower and soy.
- The temperature of the fat is all-important in deep-frying and can mean the difference between success and disaster. If the fat isn't hot enough, food will absorb fat and be greasy; too hot, and it will burn.
- The most accurate method of testing the temperature of oil for deep-frying is a deep-fat thermometer (*see* THERMOMETERS). If you don't have one, use the age-old method of dropping a cube of white bread into the oil. If it browns uniformly in 60 seconds, the temperature is 350 to 365°F;

40 seconds, the temperature is about 365 to 382°F; 20 seconds, the temperature is about 382 to 390°F.

► Make sure the bulb of your thermometer is completely immersed in the oil, but not touching the bottom of the pan. Otherwise, the reading could be affected.

► Never heat oil until it smokes, a sign that it's breaking down, which will affect the flavor.

► It's best to fry food in small batches. Large amounts of food lower the oil's temperature, which means that it's more likely to soak into the food.

► Keep deep-fried foods warm by placing them in a single layer on a paper-towel-lined baking sheet in a 275°F oven while you finish frying.

► Remove food particles from used deep-frying oil by straining it through a coffee filter, or a sieve or funnel lined with a double layer of cheesecloth. Cover, tightly seal and refrigerate strained oil; it can then be used one more time.

► Refresh used oil by frying a raw potato or a handful of parsley for about 10 minutes, then removing before beginning to fry "real" food. The potato and parsley help eliminate used-oil odors and flavors.

DEEP-FRYING THERMOMETERS *see* THERMOMETERS

DESSERTS, GENERAL

► When you're deciding on what to serve for dessert, always consider the other dishes of the meal. Otherwise, if you're serving a light meal of soup and salad, you might want to serve a rich dessert like cheesecake or chocolate mousse. On the other hand, a rich entree like stroganoff would be better followed with sorbet or fresh fruit.

► For an elegant and extraordinarily easy dessert, place strawberries in a stemmed glass and pour champagne over them.

► For an easy last-minute dessert, puree 1½ cups fruit (such as strawberries, raspberries, chopped peaches or nectarines) with 1 cup ricotta cheese. Cut a store-bought pound or sponge cake horizontally into 3 layers and spread the fruit mixture between the layers and on the top. If you like, drizzle the cake layers with rum, brandy or liqueur before spreading them with the fruit mixture. Garnish with whipped cream and whole berries or slices of fruit.

► To make an almost-instant chocolate fondue, combine 6 ounces chocolate chips and ⅓ cup whipping cream; melt and stir until smooth. Remove from heat and stir in 1 teaspoon pure vanilla extract and, if desired, 1 tablespoon brandy or liqueur. Serve with whole strawberries or chunks of fruit or cake to dip into the chocolate.

► Split large leftover biscuits or scones and use them as shortbread, layering them with berries and whipped cream. If the biscuits are dry, sprinkle lightly with almond- or orange-flavored liqueur.

▶ To unmold a frozen dessert, dampen a towel with hot water, wring it out, then wrap it around the mold for 2 to 3 minutes. Then insert a dinner knife between the pan and contents to break the suction. Cover the mold with a serving plate, invert them together and remove the mold.

▶ The eye-pleasing finishing touches you give desserts can really make a difference. A garnish doesn't have to be elaborate, but it should reflect the flavor of the dessert it adorns. It can be as simple as a perfect strawberry or as showy (but easy) as chocolate leaves (*see* CHOCOLATE).

D

▶ Nuts are one of the easiest garnishes to create. You can chop them finely, or grind and put them in a sieve to sprinkle over cakes, puddings, etc. Whole or halved nuts can be dipped halfway into chocolate, then set on waxed paper until the chocolate is set.

▶ Edible flowers (*see* FLOWERS) make a stunning garnish for desserts. Sprinkle a few around a cake, or top individual servings of parfait or mousse with a single blossom. Or pull the petals off and sprinkle them over desserts.

▶ Make cakes and other desserts company-pretty by serving them on a doily-lined plate.

▶ Add a festive glow to dessert by attaching candles in clip-on candle holders (designed for Christmas trees) to the edge of your dessert plates. Light the candles just before serving the dessert.

▶ *See also* CAKES; CHEESECAKES; COOKIES; CUSTARDS; FLOWERS, EDIBLE; ICE CREAM; PIES; SOUFFLÉS

DEVILED EGGS

▶ Deviled eggs will be more stable, and sit flat without wobbling, if you cut off a tiny piece from the bottom of each half. They'll stand without any problem while you stuff and serve them.

▶ Put the ingredients for a deviled egg stuffing in a small, zip-closure plastic bag, seal, then squish the contents together until well mixed. Snip off a corner of the bag, pipe the mixture into the hard-cooked egg whites, and throw the bag out.

▶ If you're packing deviled eggs for a picnic, place them in an airtight container, then pack in ice or surround with blue-ice packets.

▶ *See also* EGGS, COOKING METHODS (HARD-COOKED)

DOUGHNUTS; DONUTS

▶ Doughnuts can be leavened with either yeast (**raised doughnuts**) or baking powder (**cake doughnuts**).

▶ Choose doughnut recipes that have proportionately more egg yolks. The doughnuts produced won't absorb as much oil.

▶ Spice up a basic doughnut dough by adding 1 teaspoon ground cinnamon and ½ teaspoon each ground nutmeg and allspice.

▸ The traditional doughnut shape is formed by using a special doughnut cutter that cuts out the center hole in the dough. It can also be made with two biscuit cutters, one large and one small (for the hole).

▸ The softer a doughnut dough, the more tender the doughnuts will be.

▸ Chilling any doughnut dough before frying will prevent it from absorbing too much oil in the frying process.

▸ To allow for bubbling up and splattering, don't fill the frying pot more than halfway with oil.

▸ The oil temperature for frying doughnuts is vital. If the fat isn't hot enough, the doughnuts will be greasy; if it's too hot, they'll burn. Use a deep-fat thermometer (*see* THERMOMETERS) to make sure the temperature is accurate.

▸ Only fry a few doughnuts at a time. Crowding the pan will lower the oil's temperature, which translates to greasy doughnuts.

▸ For less greasy doughnuts, quickly dip them in boiling water immediately after frying. Use a slotted spoon to transfer the doughnuts directly from the hot oil to the boiling water. Drain the doughnuts on paper towels.

▸ For almost-instant doughnuts, use canned, refrigerated biscuit dough, cutting out a center hole and frying as usual.

▸ Coat doughnuts with granulated sugar while warm, or cool and dip in confectioners' sugar or glaze.

▸ To sugar-coat doughnuts, place granulated sugar in a paper bag. Add 1 or 2 doughnuts at a time; shake gently.

▸ For a basic sugar glaze, in a small saucepan, combine 2 cups sugar and 1½ cups water; bring to a boil. Cook 4 minutes without stirring. Cool 15 minutes before stirring in 1 teaspoon pure vanilla extract.

▸ For a confectioners' sugar glaze, in a small bowl, combine 1 cup confectioners' sugar with 1 to 2 tablespoons liquid (milk, orange juice, liqueur, etc.), stirring in only enough liquid to make a smooth, creamy glaze.

▸ Cool warm doughnuts on a rack at least 10 minutes before serving.

▸ Cake doughnuts don't keep well and should be served the same day made or frozen.

▸ Unglazed doughnuts may be frozen in a plastic bag for up to 6 months.

▸ To reheat frozen doughnuts, place them (still frozen) on an ungreased baking sheet, lightly cover with foil, and heat at 350°F for 10 to 15 minutes.

DRIED FRUIT *see* FRUIT, DRIED

DRY MILK

▸ Also known as **powdered milk,** dry milk comes in three forms—whole milk, nonfat milk and buttermilk.

- Because of its fat content, powdered whole milk must be refrigerated. Powdered nonfat milk and buttermilk can be stored, unopened, for up to 6 months in a cool, dry place. Once the packaging is opened, transfer to an airtight container; refrigerating will help retain the milk powder's freshness.
- After reconstituting dry milk, cover and store it in the refrigerator for up to 3 days.
- *Dry milk yields:* 1 pound = 3⅔ cups; 14 cups reconstituted.
- To measure dry milk powder, spoon lightly into a measuring cup, then level off with the flat edge of a knife.
- Reconstituted dry milk can be whipped and used as a topping for fruit, desserts, etc. Dissolve 1 cup dry milk in ⅔ cup cold water. Place in freezer until ice crystals form around edges. Using a chilled bowl and beaters, whip milk until soft peaks form; add 1 tablespoon lemon juice and beat until stiff. If desired, gently beat ½ to 1 teaspoon pure vanilla extract and 2 to 4 tablespoons confectioners' sugar into whipped milk.
- Cover and refrigerate whipped dry milk for up to an hour.
- *See also* BUTTERMILK; MILK

DUCK

- Choose a fresh duck with a broad, fairly plump breast; the skin should be elastic, not saggy. For frozen birds, make sure the packaging is tight and unbroken.
- Fresh duck can be stored, loosely covered, in the coldest section of the refrigerator for 2 to 3 days. Remove any giblets from the body cavity and store separately.
- Frozen duck should be thawed in the refrigerator. It can take from 24 to 36 hours, depending on the size of the bird. Never refreeze duck once it's been thawed.
- Farm-raised duck is much fattier than its wild counterpart. To diminish the fat and produce a crispy skin, begin by rinsing the bird; thoroughly blot dry with paper towels. Remove excess fat in the body cavity, then prick the skin all over at ½-inch intervals, being careful not to pierce the duck's flesh. These punctures will allow the fat to drain out as it melts during roasting. Generously rub the duck inside and out with salt and pepper. Place duck, breast side down, on a baking rack set over a baking pan. Refrigerate, uncovered, overnight to let the skin dry out. Roast on the middle rack in a preheated 500°F oven for 30 minutes. Reduce heat to 425°F and continue roasting the duck for 20 to 30 minutes, or until the juices run clear when a thigh is pierced (155° to 160°F on a meat thermometer).
- A duck is the least likely fowl candidate for stuffing—the bread in the stuffing absorbs so much fat that it becomes inedible.

- Farm-raised ducks are so fatty that they don't require basting.
- To diminish a wild duck's gamy flavor, rub it inside and out with lemon juice or a paste made with fresh ginger root and sherry (powdered ginger will work, too) before cooking. Fill the cavity with chunks of onion, celery, lemon and orange.
- Wild ducks are often so lean that the breast requires barding *(see listing)*. They also do better when roasted in a moderate (350°F) oven than at higher temperatures.
- Robust sauces flavored with herbs, wine, ginger, or tomato will also camouflage a duck's overt gamy flavors.
- A duck's juices shift to the center as it cooks, so always let the bird rest for about 15 minutes after it's finished cooking so the juices can redistribute throughout the flesh. Cover the duck lightly with foil during this rest period to keep it warm.

DUMPLINGS

- Any rich biscuit dough can be used for dumplings.
- To prevent heavy dumplings with soggy bottoms, make sure the liquid in which they're cooked bubbles gently but continually.
- For light, fluffy dumplings, cover the pan and leave it covered until the cooking time is almost complete. Sudden drafts affect the temperature and can deflate the dumplings. If you want to watch what's happening, use a glass pie plate as a pot cover.

EGGNOG

► Always check the date code on the carton of commercial eggnog to make sure it's as fresh as possible. It will keep for about 5 days in the refrigerator.

► Folding stiffly beaten egg whites into commercial eggnog lightens the texture and decreases the sweetness.

► Lighten the calorie and cholesterol count of homemade eggnog by making it with nonfat evaporated milk and egg whites instead of whole milk (or cream) and whole eggs. Use 2 egg whites for each whole egg called for in the recipe.

► Make homemade eggnog lighter by separating the eggs, beating the whites until stiff, and folding them into the eggnog mixture just before serving.

► Homemade eggnog leftovers should be covered tightly and refrigerated for no more than 2 days.

► For holiday brunches, make an eggnog "smoothee" by processing a cup of your favorite chopped fruit with a cup of eggnog in a blender until smooth. Or, make an eggnog fizz by putting 3 ice cubes in a tall glass, filling it halfway with eggnog, and topping off with soda water. Stir gently to combine.

► Substitute eggnog for the milk or other liquid called for in a cake or coffeecake recipe.

► Don't throw out that leftover eggnog after the winter holidays. Freeze it in 1-cup portions in small freezer bags for up to 6 months. Thaw overnight in the refrigerator and use in sauces, puddings, quick breads, cakes and pies.

► Buy quarts of your favorite eggnog after the holidays and freeze them right in the unopened carton (inside a large freezer bag), so you can have an eggnog "fix" whenever you want. Stand cartons upright until frozen solid then wrap in a freezer-proof plastic bag.

► Many eggnogs separate after defrosting. If this happens, simply pour into a blender and process until once again smooth and homogeneous.

EGGPLANT

► Choose an eggplant that's firm, smooth-skinned and heavy for its size; avoid those with soft or brown spots. Male eggplants have fewer seeds (which are often bitter) than the female of the species; they have a rounder, smoother blossom end or base. The blossom end of a female eggplant is generally indented. Eggplants become bitter with age and are very perishable.

▸ Store eggplants in a cool, dry place and use within 1 to 2 days of purchase. For longer storage (up to 5 days), place them in a plastic bag and store in a refrigerator vegetable drawer.

▸ *Eggplant yields:* 1 pound = 3 to 4 cups chopped.

▸ Young eggplants don't require peeling. Once peeled, however, the flesh discolors rapidly, so peel just before using. A vegetable peeler works well, so does an ultra-sharp paring knife.

▸ To prevent the eggplant's flesh from discoloring, brush it with lemon juice or dip it in 1 quart cold water mixed with 3 tablespoons lemon juice.

▸ To remove any bitterness from eggplant, and keep it from absorbing excess oil, use the age-old salting and weighting method. Generously salt eggplant slices, then place in a single layer on several sheets of paper towels. Cover with more paper towels, then a large baking sheet. Weight the baking sheet with something heavy, such as several 1-pound cans, a six-pack of cola, etc. Let eggplant drain for 30 minutes; rinse and blot dry before cooking.

▸ Eggplant absorbs oil like a sponge, so avoid frying it if you're watching calories.

▸ It'll absorb less oil if you either batter it, or dip first in beaten egg, then bread crumbs. Let battered or breaded eggplant dry for 30 minutes in the refrigerator before frying.

▸ To keep eggplant from turning mushy in long-cooked dishes like stews and soups, add it during the final 10 minutes or so of cooking time.

▸ *See also* VEGETABLES, GENERAL

EGGS

▸ The majority of eggs on the market are graded under federal (USDA) supervision. In descending order, egg grades are AA, A and B, the classification determined by both exterior and interior quality. Eggs are also sorted for size based on their minimum weight per dozen: jumbo (30 ounces per dozen), extra large (27 ounces), large (24 ounces), medium (21 ounces), small (18 ounces) and peewee (15 ounces). Extra large, large and medium are the sizes most commonly found in markets.

▸ USDA-graded eggs must be carefully washed and sanitized, which removes much of nature's protective coating (called *bloom*). Producers replace this coating, however, by lightly spraying the shell with a natural mineral oil. This thin film seals the shell's pores, thereby helping reduce moisture loss and preventing invasion by bacteria.

▸ Only buy eggs stored in the refrigerator case; choose AA- or A-graded eggs. Storage temperature is the major contributor to egg quality, or lack of it. Those "farm-fresh" eggs sold at roadside stands may not be as "fresh" as you think.

▸ Always check the date on the carton to be sure you're getting the freshest available eggs. Some eggs have a Julian date (1 through 365) displayed on their carton to indicate the day on which the eggs were packed. With the Julian system, January 1 is number 1, December 31 is number 365. Some producers stamp their cartons with a date 30 days past the pack date. According to the American Egg Board, fresh eggs in the shell can be stored in their carton in the refrigerator for 4 to 5 weeks beyond the pack date without significant quality loss.

▶ Open the carton at the store to check that none of the eggs are cracked. Slightly move each egg with your finger to make sure it isn't stuck to the carton because of a crack (and resulting leak) that you can't see on the bottom.

E

▶ An egg's shell color—white or brown—is determined by the breed of hen that laid it and has nothing to do with either taste or nutritive value.

▶ Fertile eggs are expensive because of high production costs, and they're no more nutritious than nonfertile eggs. They contain a small amount of male hormone and don't keep as well as other eggs.

▶ If you're buying eggs to be used in recipes, purchase large eggs. That's what most recipes use (whether or not the size is stated). Using extra-large or medium eggs in a baked-good recipe could significantly alter the outcome.

▶ Refrigerate eggs the minute you get them home. When left at room temperature, they lose more quality in a day than in a week in the refrigerator.

▶ Storing them in the carton in which they came helps keep eggs from losing moisture and absorbing odors. Tranferring them to the egg container in the refrigerator door exposes them to both odors and possible damage.

▶ Always store eggs large end up—it keeps them fresher and helps keep the yolk centered. Never place them near odoriferous foods (like onions) because they easily absorb odors right through their shells.

▶ Fresh, uncooked eggs are highest in flavor and quality if used within a week. They can, however, be refrigerated for 4 to 5 weeks (providing the shells are intact) beyond the date on the carton.

▶ *Yields for large eggs:* 1 cup = 5 whole, 7 whites, 14 yolks; 1 large yolk = about 1 tablespoon; 1 large white = about 2 tablespoons (⅛ cup). If you only need half an egg, lightly beat 1 whole egg, then measure out about 1½ tablespoons.

▶ If eggs are stuck to a carton, fill the indentations with a little cool water and let stand about 5 minutes. The eggs should loosen easily.

▶ How do you tell if an egg is fresh? Place it in a bowl of salted, cool water. If it sinks, it's fresh—if it floats, throw it out.

▶ The thick, cordlike strands of egg white that anchor the yolk to the shell membrane so that it stays centered are called chalazae [kuh-LAY-zee]. The more prominent the chalazae, the fresher the egg. These strands don't interfere with flavor or quality. However, because they will form lumps when cooked, you may want to strain them out from mixtures that should be smooth, like custards.

- ► If a recipe calls for room-temperature eggs, setting them out 30 minutes before using should do the trick (unless the room is very cold).
- ► To quickly bring refrigerated eggs to room temperature, place them in a bowl of very warm, but not hot, water for 5 to 10 minutes. If using the eggs separated, place the yolks in one bowl, the whites in another, and then place the separate bowls in a pan of warm water. Don't fill the pan so full that the water sloshes into the eggs.
- ► Eggs cook more evenly if they're at room temperature.
- ► You're less likely to break the yolk if you crack an egg on a blunt surface, like the rounded edge of a bowl
- ► When adding eggs to a mixture (such as a cake batter) break them one by one into a small bowl or cup before mixing into the main mixture. If you break eggs directly into a mixture, you run the risk of spoiling it all with one bad egg.
- ► Though it's easier to separate eggs when they're cold, egg whites will reach their fullest volume if they're at room temperature when beaten (*see following section on egg whites*).
- ► It's not a good idea to separate eggs by passing the yolk back and forth from one half of a shell to the other. That's because minute bacteria on the shell's surface might transfer to the egg.
- ► An inexpensive egg separator makes separating eggs a breeze. Or try gently cracking them into a funnel over a bowl—the yolk stays in the funnel while the white passes through.
- ► The most basic (but messiest) way to separate eggs is with your hand. Cup your hand and crack the egg into it. The white falls through your fingers while the yolk stays nestled in your palm.
- ► If a recipe calls for both the yolks and whites to be beaten, beat the whites first and transfer them to a plate; then *immediately* beat the yolks. Properly beaten whites can stand for a minute or two, and you don't have to wash the beaters, as you would if the yolks were beaten first.
- ► If you live in an area where salmonella-infected eggs are a problem (mainly in the Northeastern and Mid-Atlantic states), use eggs only in recipes that require temperatures of 160°F, which will kill almost any bacteria. Pasteurization—which kills salmonella—occurs when eggs are cooked at 140°F for 3½ minutes. Since egg whites coagulate between 144° and 149°F, and yolks between 149° and 158°F, any method of cooking eggs in which the white is thoroughly set and the yolk has begun to thicken is sufficient to kill most salmonella.
- ► There's a product on the market called pasteurized liquid whole eggs that eliminates the worry about salmonella. As with milk products, pasteuri-

zation kills bacteria, so these eggs are completely safe. They are perishable, but are fine if refrigerated and used by the date on the carton.

► Pasteurized liquid whole eggs can be used in any recipe in which you'd use shell eggs including pancakes, batters, omelets, baked goods, Casesar salads and even homemade mayonnaise. To substitute pasteurized liquid whole eggs, use ¼ cup for each large egg. For homemade mayonnaise, substitute ⅛ cup liquid eggs for each egg yolk.

► Choose heavy-gauge pans for stovetop egg cooking. Heavy skillets won't warp and will conduct heat more efficiently.

► Nonstick pans are a boon for cooking eggs—particularly for omelets. A bonus with nonstick finishes is that you'll need less fat to cook eggs.

E

► Always use vegetable oil or unsalted butter to cook eggs on the stovetop—like fried, scrambled or omelets. Salted butter can cause eggs to stick to the pan.

► Cooking eggs over gentle heat for a longer time (rather than over high heat for a brief period) allows for even heat penetration, bringing the yolk to a thickened (not hard) stage.

► Cooking eggs over high heat can cause the yolks to toughen and the whites to become rubbery. The same problems occur if eggs are over-cooked, even when the heat is low.

► To prevent bacteria from multiplying, don't leave cooked-egg dishes out at room temperature for more than 2 hours, including preparation and serving time.

► Thoroughly reheat any leftover egg dishes before serving.

► Dropping an egg on the floor can create a real mess. It'll be easier to clean up if you lightly sprinkle the egg with salt, then let it sit for 20 minutes. A damp paper towel will pick the mess right up.

► After working with raw eggs, wash your hands, utensils, countertops, etc., with hot soapy water.

► Egg-coated dishes should be soaked in warm water. Hot water "cooks" the egg right onto the dish's surface.

► *See also* DEVILED EGGS; EGGS, COOKING METHODS; EGG SUBSTITUTES

Egg whites:

► Tightly covered egg whites can be refrigerated for up to 4 days, frozen for up to 6 months.

► An easy way to freeze extra egg whites is to place one in each section of an ice-cube tray. Freeze, then pop the egg-white cubes out into a freezer-weight plastic bag. Thaw what you need overnight in the refrigerator.

► Eggs separate more easily when they're cold, but you'll get more volume when beating egg whites if you wait until they're room temperature.

► To safely separate eggs, crack one at a time, placing each white in a custard cup before transferring it to the mixing bowl. This prevents accidentally getting any broken yolk into a bowl of whites. A drop of egg yolk, which contains fat, will prevent egg whites from reaching their full volume.

▸ If a speck or two of yolk gets into the whites, use the corner tip of a paper towel to blot it up. A cotton-tipped swab works well, too.

▸ To quickly warm cold egg whites for beating, set the bowl of whites in a larger bowl of warm water. Stir occasionally until whites have reached room temperature.

▸ For beating egg whites until stiff, use a small, deep bowl with a rounded bottom for 4 to 5 egg whites; a large, deep bowl for more.

▸ The composition of the bowl in which you beat egg whites can make a big difference. Copper bowls react chemically with egg whites to form fluffy, high-rise whites. The same result can be obtained using stainless steel or glass bowls with the addition of cream of tartar. The naturally slick surface of a glass bowl doesn't give as much traction for the egg whites to climb the sides. Never use aluminum (which can cause egg whites to turn slightly gray) or plastic or wooden bowls, which are hard to clean well enough to be fat-free.

▸ Adding a small amount of acid, such as cream of tartar, lemon juice or vinegar, stabilizes egg whites and allows them to reach their full volume and stiffness. The natural acid on the surface of a copper bowl achieves the same result. Use ⅛ teaspoon of the acid ingredient per egg white, except for meringues, where ⅛ teaspoon is sufficient for 2 egg whites. Add the acid to the whites just as they begin to become frothy during beating.

▸ When beating whites with an electric mixer, start at medium-low speed and gradually increase to high.

▸ Egg whites beaten without sugar will not peak as firmly as those with sugar.

▸ It's very important to beat egg whites only until they're stiff, but not dry. Overbeaten egg whites will collapse and begin to reliquify.

▸ If you accidentally overbeat egg whites, gently stir in another egg white that's been beaten by hand just until frothy. Once the mixture is combined and the whites are again shiny and moist, remove about ¼ cup to bring the volume back into balance.

▸ To prevent loss of volume, use egg whites as soon as they are beaten.

▸ Folding stiffly beaten egg whites into another mixture must be done by hand. Using a large rubber spatula, quickly but gently cut into the middle of the mixture. Bring the bottom of the batter up and over the remaining mixture. Rotate the bowl a quarter turn with each folding motion. Fold gently to retain as much air as possible. Stop folding when no white streaks remain.

▸ If folding stiffy beaten egg whites into a very thick or heavy mixture, first stir in about a quarter of the whites. This will loosen the mixture and

enable the remainder of the beaten whites to be folded in with ease.
- *See also* MERINGUE

Egg yolks:

- The color of the yolk depends entirely on the hen's diet. Hens fed on alfalfa, grass and yellow corn lay eggs with darker yolks than wheat-fed hens.
- Blood spots on egg yolks are the result of a natural occurrence, such as a blood vessel rupturing on the surface of the yolk. They neither indicate that the egg is fertile, nor do they affect flavor or quality. If you wish, remove the blood spot with the tip of a knife, being careful not to puncture the yolk.
- When adding egg yolks to a hot mixture, always temper the yolks first by stirring some of the hot mixture into the yolks. Then slowly stir the slightly heated yolks into the hot mixture.
- If you have leftover egg yolks, fill a small container with cold water, then slide the unbroken yolks into the water. Seal the container airtight and refrigerate for up to 2 days.
- Leftover egg yolks that won't be used within a day or two can either be cooked or frozen. To cook, carefully place them in a small saucepan and cover with at least 1 inch of cold water. Bring to a boil; immediately remove from heat, cover and let stand for 15 minutes. Remove the cooked yolks from water with a slotted spoon. Cover and refrigerate for up to 5 days; or wrap airtight and freeze for up to 4 months.
- Freezing leftover yolks requires a little special treatment because yolks become so gelatinous when frozen alone that they're almost impossible to use. To inhibit gelation, add ⅛ teaspoon salt or 1½ teaspoons sugar or corn syrup to each ¼ cup of yolks (4 yolks) and beat to combine. Whether you add salt or sugar depends on how you'll be using the yolks later on. Label the container as to what you used, and freeze for up to 3 months.

EGGS, COOKING METHODS

Fried eggs:

- Fried eggs won't spatter as much if you lightly dust the pan with cornstarch.
- Make sure the butter's bubbling hot before adding eggs to be fried.
- Once the eggs are in the pan, immediately reduce the heat to low.
- Speed the cooking of fried eggs by covering the pan.

Hard-cooked and soft-cooked eggs:

- According to the American Egg Board, the terms "hard-" and "soft-boiled eggs" are really misnomers because boiling eggs makes them tough and rubbery. Instead, such eggs should be "hard-" or "soft-cooked" in hot water.

▶ To cook eggs in their shells, place a single layer of them in a saucepan and top with at least 1 inch of water. Cover and bring to a boil, then remove from heat and let stand. Large soft-cooked eggs should remain in the water for 1 to 4 minutes; large hard-cooked eggs for 15 to 17 minutes. After the eggs are cooked as desired, drain off hot water and immediately cover with cold water, add a few ice cubes and let stand until cool enough to handle for soft-cooked eggs, until completedly cooled for hard-cooked.

▶ Cooling eggs in very cold or ice water prevents a dark gray-green surface from forming on the yolk.

▶ Egg shells won't crack during cooking if you pierce the large end with a needle, thumbtack or egg piercer. The bonus with this method is that the egg will also be easier to peel.

▶ If you accidentally crack the shell as you're getting ready to hard-cook an egg, wrap it in foil, then cook as usual. Cool by plunging the whole package into the cold water.

▶ A few drops of food coloring added to water in which hard-cooked eggs will be prepared will make it easy to distinguish them from raw ones in the refrigerator. Or, after cooking and cooling, use a crayon to mark the egg.

▶ When cooking eggs that will be used sliced or halved, turn them over halfway through the cooking time to keep the yolk centered.

▶ Refrigerate hard-cooked eggs as soon as they're cooled and use within 1 week. If possible, store them in their original carton.

▶ If hard-cooked eggs are going to be out of the refrigerator for more than 3 hours (as in the case of an Easter-egg hunt), it's safest not to eat them. Either make two batches of eggs—one for hiding, another for eating, or consider hiding plastic eggs, and exchange them for the real thing later.

▶ If you can't remember whether or not a refrigerated egg is hard-cooked, give it a spin on the countertop. A cooked egg will spin easily, whereas a raw egg will wobble because the liquid is moving inside the shell.

▶ Very fresh eggs (less than a week old) are harder to peel than those that are slightly older.

▶ Hard-cooked eggs are easier to peel if you first gently roll them between your palm and the countertop, creating dozens of hairline cracks in the shell. Starting at the large end, peel the egg under cold running water, or dip it into a bowl filled with cold water.

▶ If you find after peeling a hard-cooked egg that it's not done, do this: pierce once or twice with a fork, then microwave at MEDIUM (50 percent power) for 10 to 20 seconds. Let stand 20 seconds before checking for doneness.

▶ Hard-cooked eggs are much easier to slice if they're cold.

▶ If you use a lot of sliced, hard-cooked eggs, invest in an egg slicer, available at many supermarkets, hardware stores and gourmet shops.

▶ If you don't have an egg slicer, use a sharp, thin-bladed knife, dipping it into cold water every few slices.

▶ A wire cheese slicer also works well for slicing eggs.

▶ Make a lacy hard-cooked egg garnish by rubbing the white, then the yolk through a fine sieve onto a sheet of waxed paper. Sprinkle the egg filigree over salads, vegetables or other dishes as a garnish.

▶ Extra hard-cooked egg yolks can be frozen successfully (*see preceding listing, Egg yolks*), but cooked whites become watery and tough if frozen.

▶ *See also* DEVILED EGGS

E

Microwaving eggs:

▶ Though a microwave oven can cook eggs in many ways, it isn't good for preparations like omelets or soufflés, both of which need a dry heat to puff properly.

▶ Egg yolks cook faster than egg whites because they contain fat, which attracts the microwaves.

▶ To cook unbeaten eggs, always pierce the yolk with a toothpick or the tines of a fork to prevent steam building up pressure and causing the yolk to explode.

▶ Cook unbeaten eggs at 30 to 40 percent power.

▶ Beaten egg mixtures cook well at HIGH (100 percent power).

▶ Covering eggs with waxed paper, plastic wrap or a lid will help them cook more evenly.

Omelets:

▶ Omelets cook quickly so always have your filling ingredients chopped and cooked, if necessary, before you begin cooking the eggs.

▶ Heat the omelet pan over medium-high heat. The butter should be sizzling before the omelet mixture is added.

▶ Unlike other egg dishes, omelets should be cooked quickly.

▶ Topping an omelet with sauce dresses it up. The sauce should be reflective of the omelet's ingredients. For example, if the omelet is filled with Italian ingredients like green peppers, Italian sausage and mozzarella cheese, then it's appropriate to top it with marinara sauce.

▶ Omelets aren't just for breakfast or brunch. They make great dinner entrees, accompanied by rolls and a salad or potatoes.

▶ *See also* SCRAMBLED EGGS

Poached eggs:

▶ For eggs to retain their shape when poached, they should be very fresh. A solid, firm white will prevent the yolk from breaking.

▶ A little vinegar (2 tablespoons per quart) in the cooking water will help coagulate egg whites and keep poached eggs from spreading as they cook.

▶ An egg ring is a round band, usually with a handle, that holds the shape of an egg while it's being poached or fried. Butter or oil the rings well before using them for either method.

▶ If you don't have egg rings, use clean tuna cans, with both the top and bottom removed. Crumpet rings also make a good form for perfectly round poached eggs.

▶ Poach eggs in part water, part broth for added flavor. Milk-poached eggs are deliciously sweet and tender (but don't add vinegar to the milk or it will curdle).

▶ Bring the poaching liquid to a boil, then reduce to a simmer before adding eggs.

▶ Crack cold eggs, one at a time, into a saucer or custard cup. Holding the dish close to the liquid's surface, gently slip each egg into the simmering liquid. If you're not using egg rings, use a spoon to corral the egg white and pull it toward the yolk.

▶ A poached egg won't spread as much if you use a spoon to form a whirl-pool in the poaching water, then slide the egg into the vortex.

▶ Test for doneness by using a slotted spoon to lift each egg from the water; press with your fingertip. The white should be firm, the yolk soft.

▶ Drain poached eggs briefly on paper towels to remove excess liquid.

▶ Poached eggs can be made in advance and stored until you're ready to use them. Have a bowl of ice water standing by; plunge the cooked eggs directly into the cold water. Cover and refrigerate for up to 2 days.

▶ To reheat poached eggs that have been made in advance, use a slotted spoon to set them in hot water for a minute, or just until warmed through.

▶ Hard-poached eggs can be cooled, then chopped for use in egg salads or sandwiches.

Scrambled eggs:

▶ For lighter eggs, add 1 tablespoon water per egg.

▶ Adding ¼ teaspoon cornstarch per egg before beating will make scrambled eggs and omelets fluffier.

▶ Adding 1 tablespoon sour cream for every 2 eggs makes rich, creamy scrambled eggs and omelets.

▶ One teaspoon sherry per egg gives omelets and scrambled eggs a fabulous flavor.

▶ The secret to successfully scrambling eggs is slow cooking over low to medium-low heat. Either start in a cool skillet, or cook them in the top of a double boiler over hot (not boiling) water.

▶ A rubber spatula does a great job of moving the eggs around the pan.

Don't worry about melting the rubber—the heat is (or should be) too low to damage it.

► Always remove scrambled eggs from the heat a minute before you think they're done—the residual heat will continue to cook them.

EGG SUBSTITUTES

► Egg substitutes are cholesterol-free and can be used in cooking and baking in many (though not all) of the same ways as regular eggs.

► The main ingredient in egg substitutes is egg white (about 80 percent). No yolks are used, but other ingredients can include nonfat milk, tofu, vegetable oils, emulsifiers, stabilizers, antioxidants, gums and artificial colors. Vitamins and minerals are added to boost nutrition.

E

► If you're MSG-sensitive, check an egg substitute's label—some contain it, others don't.

► Thaw frozen egg substitutes in the refrigerator before using.

► Egg substitutes can be used in place of raw egg in Caesar salad.

EMERGENCIES

► Baking soda will put out an electrical fire, so keep a box near your electric range.

► If fat has been overheated and catches fire, immediately cover it with a pan lid. Without oxygen, the fire will die out.

► Always keep a fire extinguisher in your kitchen for emergencies. Check the pressure gauge periodically to make sure the extinguisher is still charged.

ENTERTAINING

► Write your menu down so you can check off the dishes as they're prepared (some in advance, hopefully), and as you dish them up to serve.

► Create an instant atmosphere of "Mom-and-apple-pie" by combining 1 quart water with 1 teaspoon vanilla, 3 cinnamon sticks (break them in half) and 4 whole cloves. Bring to a boil, then reduce heat and simmer, uncovered, adding water occasionally as it cooks away.

► For a make-at-home place-card holder, bundle about 8 cinnamon sticks together, tie them with a colorful ribbon, and insert a flower or sprig of baby's breath just under the ribbon. Wedge the corner of the place card between two cinnamon sticks so that it sits at an angle.

► Make an instant napkin ring by tying a brightly colored piece of yarn or ribbon around a napkin, inserting a fresh flower, sprig of baby's breath or other seasonal decorative touch under the ribbon.

► The table setting: Forks go on the left, knives and spoons on the right; the knives positioned with the cutting side toward the plate. No more than three pieces of silverware should be placed on each side of the plate.

Arrange the silver in the order it will be used, from the outside working in. Dessert utensils should be positioned at the top of the plate—the spoon should be closest to the plate, the handle on the right; the fork above the spoon, facing in the opposite direction. Glasses go on the right, with the water glass directly above the knife, and wine or other glasses to the right of the water glass. The bread plate goes opposite the glasses, above the forks, with a butter knife sitting across the top of the plate. If a salad plate is used, place it to the left of the forks.

► The water should be poured and candles lit when the guests sit down. Pour the wine after they're seated.

► Warm dishes, serving bowls and platters in a 200°F oven. Warm dishes keep the food warm longer.

► When serving food to seated guests, serve from the left; remove plates from the right.

► Since glasses are on the right side of a table setting, it's appropriate to pour beverages while standing to the right of your guest.

► Foods like buttered artichokes, corn on the cob, ribs and fried chicken are messy to eat. Provide each guest with a finger bowl—a small bowl (such as a custard cup) of water with a lemon slice floating on top. Or buy inexpensive washcloths, soak them in lemon water, squeeze dry and fold into quarters. Place the dampened cloths in a plastic bag and set aside. Before offering them to guests, microwave for a minute or so, just until warm.

► Lining a bread basket with foil, then a napkin, will help keep bread and rolls warm. Cut the foil off at the rim of the basket so it doesn't show.

► Or heat a ceramic tile in the oven, then put it in the bottom of a bread basket. Cover with a napkin and add the rolls.

► If you've dripped sauce, meat juices, etc., on the edge of a serving platter, clean it off with a damp paper towel before serving.

► When passing food around the table, pass it in a clockwise direction (from your right to your left).

► When passing salt and pepper, protocol dictates that you put the shakers or mills down on the table, rather than hand them directly to the guest requesting the seasoning.

► Use a notebook to record the date you entertained, who the guests were, what you served, and any centerpiece or other decoration details. That way you won't repeat yourself.

► *See also* CANDLES; ICE CUBES

ESCARGOT [ehs-kahr-GOH] *see* SNAILS

EVAPORATED MILK

► Evaporated milk comes in whole, low-fat and nonfat (skimmed) versions, and has had 60 percent of the water removed. It's sold in cans and, unlike sweetened condensed milk, is not sweet.

▶ Evaporated milk has been heat-sterilized in the can, making it safe to store unopened at room temperature for up to 6 months.

▶ Once opened, transfer unused evaporated milk to an airtight container, such as a screwtop jar, and use within 5 days.

▶ *Evaporated milk yields:* 1 14½-ounce can = 1⅔ cups; 3⅓ cups reconstituted.

▶ Undiluted, evaporated milk adds richness to custards, sauces, soups, etc.

▶ When mixed with an equal amount of water, evaporated milk can be substituted for fresh milk in recipes.

▶ Slightly frozen evaporated milk can be whipped and used as a relatively low-fat dessert topping. To quickly bring the milk to the proper state, pour it into a shallow metal pan (a cake pan will do); freeze until ice crystals form around the edges. Using a chilled bowl and beaters, whip the milk until fluffy. Flavor with ½ to 1 teaspoon pure vanilla extract, if desired.

▶ Acid increases the stability of whipped evaporated milk. Stir in 1 tablespoon lemon juice (per 1 cup milk) *after* the milk is beaten.

▶ Whipped evaporated milk will hold its shape longer if you stabilize it with gelatin. Soften ½ teaspoon unflavored gelatin in ¼ cup evaporated milk for 5 minutes. Then heat over low heat, stirring constantly, just until gelatin dissolves. Stir hot milk mixture into ¾ cup cold evaporated milk, place in freezer until ice crystals form around edges, then whip.

▶ If desired, sweetened whipped evaporated milk with confectioners' sugar (2 to 4 tablespoons) *after* it's been beaten. Sprinkle the sugar over the surface and beat just until it's incorporated.

▶ Whipped evaporated milk will stay foamy for about 45 minutes in the refrigerator; gelatin-stabilized milk slightly longer.

▶ Don't try to substitute sweetened condensed milk—which is about 40 percent sugar—for evaporated milk.

▶ *See also* MILK; SWEETENED CONDENSED MILK

F

FATS AND OILS

▸ Fats and oils are used in cooking to add richness and flavor to foods, to tenderize baked goods and for frying. Choose the fat you buy according to how you'll use it. Butter, for instance, will add more flavor to baked goods like cakes and cookies; oil is a better choice for frying.

▸ Store fats like butter, lard and margarine, tightly wrapped, in the refrigerator for up to 1 month; unsalted butter (which is more perishable) for 2 weeks. They can also be frozen, wrapped airtight in a plastic bag, for up to 6 months. Shortening and most oils can be stored in a cool, dark place at room temperature for 3 months, but quality will be retained better if they're refrigerated.

▸ Oils with a high proportion of monounsaturates—such as olive and peanut oil—are more perishable and should be refrigerated if kept longer than a month.

▸ Did you know that the term *hydrogenated* refers to the process of hardening unsaturated oil into a semisolid? This transforms it into a saturated fat and research shows that hydrogenated oils may actually be more damaging than regular saturated fat for anyone limiting cholesterol.

▸ Omega-3 oils are found in the tissues of all sea creatures. These special polyunsaturated oils have been found to be particularly beneficial to coronary health. In order of importance, those fish that are good sources of Omega-3 are: sardines, herring, mackerel, Atlantic bluefish, tuna, salmon, pilchard, butterfish and pompano.

▸ If you buy oil in large jugs for the sake of economy, fill a screw-top pint bottle with it. Store the pint at room temperature for ready use and refrigerate the large container.

▸ Monounsaturated oils have been shown to be particularly effective against high cholesterol, the best being olive, canola and almond oil.

▸ Polyunsaturated fats have also been shown to reduce cholesterol. The best of these oils are safflower, sunflower, soy, sesame, corn and peanut.

▸ If you're trying to limit cholesterol intake, avoid coconut, palm and palm kernel oil. Check prepared food labels carefully to guard against these ingredients.

▸ When some oil (like olive oil) is refrigerated, it becomes cloudy and too thick to pour. It will reliquify if allowed to stand at room temperature. To reliquify more quickly, place the sealed bottle of oil in a large bowl of very warm water. Let stand for about 10 minutes, turning the bottle every couple of minutes. Or, for bottles that have no metal on them, remove the lid and microwave at HIGH (100 percent power) for 30 to 60 seconds. Let stand 3 minutes before pouring.

► Confused about all the olive-oil terms and exactly what's what? Here's a quick primer: *Extra-virgin olive oil* is considered the finest and fruitiest of the olive oils (also the most expensive). Next, in order of descending quality are *superfine, fine* and *virgin* olive oils. The lesser quality *pure olive oil* is probably the least flavorful of the lot.

► There are dozens of flavored oils on the market that can add depth and intrigue to many dishes. Among the most popular are almond, hazelnut, mustard, sesame and walnut oil. There are also oils flavored with herbs or other ingredients such as garlic or sun-dried tomatoes.

► Never use an oil—particularly if you haven't used it in a while—without smelling and tasting it. A dish can easily be ruined by the smallest amount of rancid oil.

F

► The oil or fat you use for deep-frying should have a high smoke point— the temperature to which it can be heated without smoking. Butter and margarine have low smoke points, so aren't good for frying; shortening, lard and most oils are. The best oils for frying are canola, corn, peanut, safflower and soy.

► Letting oil or fat heat until it smokes can cause it to ignite.

► Thoroughly wash and dry a dish detergent bottle and use it for cooking oil. The squirt-type spout makes quick work of measuring and pouring small amounts.

► Or, fill an atomizer with oil and use to spray pans, foods to be basted, etc. The result: fewer calories, broader coverage.

► Use a paper towel to wipe off the sides and bottom of a bottle of oil before returning it to the cupboard.

► To get every last bit of shortening out of the can, pour in about 1 or 2 cups boiling water and slosh around until all the shortening clinging to the sides melts. Put the can into the refrigerator until the fat cools and solidifies, then skim off the fat.

► To clarify the oil from deep-fat frying, or bacon or other meat drippings, pour the liquid fat into a funnel lined with a paper coffee filter, several thicknesses of fine cheesecloth or heavyweight paper towel. Cover strained oil tightly and store in the refrigerator or freezer.

► You can sprinkle bottled olive or salad oil right onto salads by poking 3 or 4 holes in the foil seal that comes on a new bottle.

► Never pour used oil or fat down the drain. Pour fats that become solid when cold into a plastic-wrap-lined bowl, refrigerate until firm, then remove the plastic and toss into the trash. Used oil should be poured into a screw-top bottle, sealed and discarded in the same manner.

► Before measuring syrupy sweeteners such as honey and corn syrup, lightly coat the measuring cup or spoon with vegetable oil. Or measure the oil called for in a recipe and then use the same (unwashed) utensil to measure a syrup. Either way, every drop of the syrup will easily slip out instead of clinging to the sides of the cup!

▶ *See also* BUTTER; DEEP-FRYING; LARD; MARGARINE

FENNEL [FEHN-uhl]

▶ Fresh fennel has a broad, bulbous, off-white base, pale green, celerylike stems and bright green foilage. All parts of this aromatic plant are edible.

▶ Fennel is often mislabeled "sweet anise," which causes people who don't like the flavor of licorice to avoid it. In truth, the flavor of fresh fennel is sweeter and more delicate than that of fresh anise. When fennel is cooked, its flavor becomes even lighter and more elusive than when raw.

▶ Choose clean, crisp bulbs with no sign of browning. Any attached greenery, which is naturally soft, should be a fresh green color.

▶ Store fennel, tightly wrapped in a plastic bag, in the refrigerator for up to 5 days.

▶ Before using, fennel should be washed, the base trimmed, and the stalks and greenery removed.

▶ *Fennel yields:* 1 pound = 2 small fennel bulbs.

▶ Fennel's fragrant, graceful greenery can be used as a garnish or snipped like dill and used in salads or other cold dishes. Stir it into hot dishes as a last-minute flavor enhancer.

▶ Both the base and stems of fennel can be eaten raw in salads. Its crispness adds a nice textural contrast.

▶ Fennel can be cooked in a variety of methods such as braising and sautéing. It can be boiled, then pureed, and makes a particularly nice addition to soups and stews.

▶ *See also* VEGETABLES, GENERAL

FILBERTS *see* HAZELNUTS

FILO *see* PHYLLO

FISH, GENERAL

▶ When categorized according to fat content, fish are divided into three general groups—lean, moderate-fat and high-fat. *Lean fish,* which have a fat content less than 2½ percent (the fat is concentrated in the liver), include black sea bass, cod, croaker, flounder, haddock, hake, halibut, perch, pollack, red snapper, rockfish, sole and tilefish. *Moderate-fat fish,* which are generally less than 6 percent fat, include barracuda, bonito, catfish, striped bass, swordfish, trout and whiting. *High-fat fish* can contain as much as 30 percent fat (as with eel) but usually average closer to 12 percent. These include Atlantic herring, bluefish, butterfish, mackerel, sablefish, shad, smelt, sturgeon and yellowtail. Salmon can range from moderate- to high-fat, depending on the species (*see* SALMON).

▶ Omega-3 oils are special polyunsaturated oils that are particularly beneficial to coronary health. In order of importance, the fish that are particularly good sources of Omega-3 are sardines, herring, mackerel, Atlantic bluefish, tuna, salmon, pilchard, butterfish and pompano.

▶ When buying *fresh, whole fish* look for bright, clear full eyes; shiny, brightly colored skin; firm flesh that springs back when pressed with your finger; a fresh, mild odor; and red to bright pink gills that are free of slime or residue. *Fish fillets and steaks* should have a fresh odor, firm texture and moist appearance.

▶ Saltwater fish (like cod and flounder) have thicker bones than freshwater fish (such as catfish and trout), which have hundreds of minuscule, filament-thin bones—a source of frustration for many diners. That's because saltwater provides more buoyancy than fresh water. So, if you don't like fighting those tiny bones be sure and choose saltwater species when buying whole fish.

▶ When buying dried salt cod, choose white, thick, supple pieces.

▶ Salt cod should be soaked for 24 hours in the refrigerator (use a glass or ceramic bowl). Change the water several times during soaking. Bone-in salt cod must be soaked a little longer.

▶ Remove the bones and skin from salt cod before using.

▶ *How much to buy per serving:* whole fish—¾ to 1 pound; fillets—4 to 5 ounces; steaks—5 to 6 ounces.

▶ Immediately refrigerate fresh fish, tightly wrapped, and use within a day or two. Never store ungutted fish, as the entrails decay much more rapidly than the flesh. Wrap fish that will be stored overnight airtight so its odor won't transfer to other foods.

▶ When buying *raw frozen fish,* make sure it's solidly frozen. Its wrapping should be undamaged; the fish should have no odor. Any white, dark, icy or dry spots indicate damage through drying or deterioration. Avoid any fish you think might have been thawed and refrozen.

▶ Store frozen fish, double wrapped, in the freezer for up to 6 months.

▶ Before handling fish, rinse your hands in cold water and they won't smell as fishy.

▶ Always double check a market fish for scales by running a serrated knife from the tail toward the head end. A grapefruit knife works well. If there are a lot of scales, plunge the fish first into boiling-hot water, then into cold water—this technique loosens the scales.

▶ It's easier to scale fresh-caught fish if the fish is wet, so run cold water over it before beginning.

▶ Double wrap and freeze fish bones to make a stock or soup in the future.

▶ Remove fish from the refrigerator 30 minutes before cooking.

▶ Frozen fish fillets and steaks are better cooked from the frozen state. If fish is thawed completely, it loses much of it's natural moisture and become dry during cooking. When cooking frozen fish, add a few minutes to the cooking time to compensate.

▶ If you need to thaw fish to separate individual pieces, only partially thaw it.

▶ Partially thawing frozen fish in milk to cover will diminish any "frozen" flavor.

▶ One pound of frozen fish will take about 24 hours to thaw completely in the refrigerator. To quick-thaw, place the wrapped, frozen fish in cold (never warm) water, allowing about 1 hour for 1 pound of fish.

▶ To micro-thaw a pound of frozen fish, place in a covered dish and microwave at MEDIUM-LOW (30 percent power) for about 6 minutes, turning and separating pieces after 4 minutes. Let stand in the microwave oven for 10 minutes.

F

▶ Always pat frozen, thawed fish dry with paper towels before preparing.

▶ Never refreeze fish once it's been thawed.

▶ To test fish for doneness, prod it with a fork at its thickest point. Properly cooked fish is opaque, has milky white juices and just begins to flake easily. Undercooked fish is still translucent and the juices are clear and watery. Overcooked fish looks dry, has little of its natural juices left and falls apart easily.

▶ If you're cooking fish ahead to serve cold, remove any skin while the fish is warm. It's much easier to remove than when it's cold.

▶ If you've overcooked fish so that it's dry, serve it with sauce or drizzle with a little melted butter.

▶ Tweezers are perfect for removing fine bones from cooked fish.

▶ Fish cools rapidly so it's a good idea to have the serving plate or individual dinner plates heated.

▶ Toasted almonds make a flavorful garnish for almost any fish.

▶ Sauces flavored with sherry, brandy or ginger disguises the "fishy" flavor of some fish.

▶ The odor of caramel does wonders for diminishing fishy smells. Simply put a ½ cup sugar in a small, heavy saucepan (lined with heavy-duty aluminum foil to save on cleanup) and cook over medium heat until the sugar is liquid and caramelized. Let cook a few minutes until the caramel odor permeates the air. After the caramel cools, simply lift out the foil and discard.

▶ Leftover fish makes a delicious salad the next day. If desired, cut the fish into chunks and marinate it overnight in salad dressing; serve over greens.

▶ Or use leftover fish to make chowder, chock-full of diced potatoes, onions and celery, and flavored with herbs and crisp bits of bacon.

- For an easy, quick fish pâté, combine leftover fish in a blender or food processor with herbs of choice and enough moistener (stock, sour cream, mayonnaise, etc.) to make it smooth. Spoon into crocks, cover and chill until set.
- If there's a fishy odor left in the pan after washing, fill the pan half full with a half-and-half mixture of vinegar and water. Bring to a boil, cook for 5 minutes, then cool in the pan. Wash again with hot, soapy water.
- Remove the fishy smell from your hands, knife and cutting board by rubbing them all thoroughly with lemon wedges.
- *See also* ANCHOVIES; FISH, COOKING METHODS; SALMON; SHELLFISH; SMOKED FISH

FISH, COOKING METHODS

- *For moist-heat cooking methods* like poaching, steaming or stewing, choose lean fish such as cod, flounder, perch, red snapper or sole.
- You can use lean fish for dry-heat methods like baking as long as you baste frequently to keep the fish from drying out.
- *For dry-heat cooking methods* like baking, broiling and grilling, choose moderate- to high-fat fish such as bluefish, butterfish, catfish, salmon, striped bass, swordfish or trout.
- *For fat-based cooking methods* like sautéing, pan-frying and deep-frying, lean to moderate-fat fish are the best choice; lean fish can also be used. High-fat fish are too rich to fry.
- If you cook a lot of fish, invest in a wide (5 to 6 inches), slotted spatula. It will make transferring the fish from pan to plate much easier.

Baking fish:

- Baking fish at 450°F will quickly seal in the fish's natural juices, making it deliciously moist and tender.
- A general rule for baking fish is to cover and bake for 10 minutes for each inch of thickness. To allow for oven variances, check the fish for doneness after about 7 minutes per pound.
- Fish needs some kind of insulation to keep moist during baking. The baking dish can be covered, or the fish itself can be coated with butter and crumbs, or topped with a sauce before being baked. Lean fish—such as flounder or halibut—can be covered with a layer of finely chopped vegetables, herbs, etc.
- The French technique of enclosing fish in parchment paper or foil (*en papillote*) is the perfect way to keep baked fish moist. Simply cut a piece of parchment paper or foil large enough to enclose the fish, butter the paper or foil, and lay the seasoned fish on top. For individual servings, use a piece of foil for each fish fillet or steak. Bring paper or foil over the top of the fish; roll or fold the edges to seal the package tightly. Bake 7 to 10 minutes per inch of thickness measured at the fish's thickest point.

To serve, place package directly on dinner plate, slash an X in the top and peel back the paper or foil.

▸ To "bake" fish in the microwave, arrange fillets in a round baking dish with the thinnest part pointing inward, cover with waxed paper, and cook at HIGH (100 percent power) for 3 minutes per pound. Turn dish at least once during baking time.

Broiling and grilling fish:

▸ For broiling and grilling, choose fillets or steaks that are about 1 inch thick. Thicker than that and the exterior can char before the inside is done.

▸ Fish fillets retain their shape better when broiled if cooked with the skin on. The skin can be removed after cooking, if desired.

▸ Position the fish so that the top surface is 3 to 6 inches from the heat source. The thicker the fish, the greater the distance.

▸ There's usually no need to turn fish that are broiled. The radiant heat will cook it through.

▸ If you *are* going to turn broiled fish, do this: Place each piece of fish along one side of a length of lightly oiled foil about 2½ times larger than the fillet or steak. When ready to turn, lift the edges of the foil on the side where the fish is, and flip the fish over so that it comes to rest on the opposite side of the foil.

▸ To keep grilled fish from sticking, first brush the grill lightly with vegetable oil, or spray with nonstick vegetable spray. Do the same thing if using a fish basket for grilling.

▸ Leave the skin on fish fillets to be grilled and they'll retain their shape better. If desired, remove the skin after cooking.

▸ Grill twice as much fish as you need for dinner, cover and refrigerate the leftovers to be used the next day in a cold fish salad.

▸ *See also* GRILLING

Frying fish:

▸ It's important that the surface of fish to be fried is thoroughly dry.

▸ Butter and margarine have a low smoke point, so use oil or a combination of butter and oil for sautéing or pan-frying fish.

▸ Coatings like flour, cornmeal or crumbs keep fish moist and give it a crisp crust.

▸ Don't bread fish too far in advance or it will become soggy (*see* BREADING).

▸ Fish to be pan- or deep-fried are wonderful when dipped in batter.

▸ The temperature of the fat is all-important—it can make the difference between fish that's crisp and moist or soggy and fat-laden (*see* DEEP-FRYING).

▶ Blot pan- or deep-fried fish on paper towels to absorb excess grease before serving.

▶ Keep fried fish warm in a 275°F oven until all of it is cooked. Lay fish on a paper-towel-lined baking sheet. Don't keep fish in the warm oven for more than 20 minutes or it could become dry.

Poaching and steaming fish:

▶ Poach fish in a wide shallow pan (such as a skillet), or a special pan called a fish poacher.

▶ Many types of steamers are available on the market today. If you don't have one, improvise by setting a rack on empty tuna cans (tops and bottoms removed). The water level should not touch the fish that sits on the rack.

▶ A couple of sprigs of celery leaves added to the poaching or steaming liquid will diminish fish odor.

▶ Adding a couple teaspoons of acid such as lemon juice or white wine to the poaching liquid for fish will whiten and firm its flesh.

▶ It'll be easier to remove whole or large pieces of poached fish from the pan if you lightly wrap the fish in cheesecloth before lowering it into the poaching liquid. Drape the ends of the cheesecloth over the top of the fish as it cooks. When it's done, simply lift out the fish by the cheesecloth ends. There are also special cheesecloth fish-poaching bags available in specialty kitchenware shops.

▶ Always poach fish fillets in a single layer. The poaching liquid should just reach the top of the fish.

▶ Once the poaching liquid comes to a boil, immediately reduce it to a simmer; letting it boil could break the fish apart.

▶ If you're poaching fish to be served cold, let it cool in the cooking liquid and it'll be moister.

▶ Don't throw out poaching liquid—save it to use for a soup or sauce. If you don't want to use it immediately, freeze and label the liquid.

FLAMBÉING [flahm-BAY-ing; flahm-BAY]

▶ Though it has long been thought that alcohol evaporates when heated, a USDA study has disproved that theory. In fact, from 5 to 85 percent of the alcohol may remain in a cooked dish, depending on various factors including how the food was heated, the cooking time, and the source of the alcohol. Even the smallest trace of alcohol may be ill-advised for alcoholics and those with alcohol-related illnesses.

▶ The best liquid for flambéing is brandy or an 80-proof liquor or liqueur. Never use spirits that are 150 proof—they're far too volatile and could explode when lighted.

▶ Always choose a spirit whose flavor complements the food to be flambéed.

▶ Heat the spirits in a small saucepan over medium heat just until bubbles begin to form around the edge of the pan. Overheating will evaporate much of the alcohol and the mixture may not ignite.

▶ Or place up to ⅓ cup liquor in a 1-cup glass measure and microwave at HIGH (100 percent power) for about 20 seconds (less time for a smaller amount).

▶ Use a long-handled match to ignite a flambéed mixture.

▶ Always ignite the fumes, not the liquid itself.

▶ Never lean over the dish as you light the fumes or you may end up with singed brows.

▶ If a flambéed dish won't ignite it's probably because it isn't hot enough.

▶ Never blow out the flames on flambéed food. Doing so doesn't let the alcohol burn off completely and your dish could end up with the flavor of raw alcohol.

▶ After flaming, stir the food to combine the flavors.

▶ If you don't want to flame food in the conventional way, take the short-cut of soaking sugar cubes in a flavored extract (brandy, lemon, orange or rum). Place the cubes around the dessert and light with a match.

▶ *See also* ALCOHOL; WINE

FLOUR

▶ **All-purpose flour** is made from a blend of high-gluten hard wheat and low-gluten soft wheat. It's a fine-textured flour milled from the inner part of the wheat kernel, and contains neither the germ (the sprouting section) or the bran (the outer husk). By U.S. law all flours not containing wheat germ must have niacin, riboflavin, and thiamin added; such flours are labeled *enriched.* All-purpose flour comes *bleached* and *unbleached,* which can be used interchangeably. All-purpose flour is suitable for most kinds of baking including quick and yeast breads, biscuits, muffins, cookies and cakes.

▶ **Bread flour** is a specially formulated flour high in protein—usually about 14 grams per cup. It's about 99.8 percent unbleached flour, with a smidgen of malted barley flour. Bread flour produces a hearty loaf with a firm crumb.

▶ **Cake or pastry flour** comes from soft wheat. It's fine-textured, high in starch and makes particularly tender cakes and pastries.

▶ **Gluten flour** is a high-protein, hard-wheat flour treated to remove most of the starch (leaving a high gluten content). It's used in doughs made with low-gluten flours like rye, and to make low-calorie "gluten" breads.

▶ **Instant flour** is a granular flour especially formulated to dissolve quickly in hot or cold liquids. It's used mainly as a thickener in sauces, gravies and other cooked mixtures.

▶ **Self-rising flour** is an all-purpose flour to which baking powder and salt have been added. One cup of self-rising flour contains about 1½ teaspoons baking powder and ½ teaspoon salt. Self-rising flour can be substituted for all-purpose flour in yeast breads by omitting the salt; in quick breads by omitting both salt and baking powder.

▶ **Semolina flour** is made from durum wheat and is usually ground more coarsely than other wheat flours. Most good pasta is made from semolina.

▶ **Whole-wheat flour** is a light brown flour that tastes of the grain. It has a higher fiber, nutritional and fat content than all-purpose or bread flour because it's milled from the whole kernel and contains the germ.

▶ Check the flour package label under *Nutritional Information* to select one that has a protein level appropriate for what you're baking. Flours with 12 to 14 grams protein per cup are best for yeast breads; those with 9 to 11 grams are better for quick breads and pie crusts.

F

▶ Store flour in airtight containers like canisters or wide-mouthed screw-top jars. All-purpose and bread flours can be kept at room temperature for up to 6 months. Temperatures above 75°F invite bugs and mold. Flours containing part of the grain's germ (such as whole-wheat flour) turn rancid quickly because of the fat in the germ. Purchase such flours in small quantities and store, tightly wrapped, in the refrigerator for 6 months, in the freezer for a year.

▶ Always bring chilled flours to room temperature before using in recipes for baked goods.

▶ Characteristics of flour vary greatly. Flour absorbs less liquid during hot, humid months than in dry weather because it will have already absorbed some of the moisture from the atmosphere. These variations can be particularly noticeable when making yeast bread. For the best results, add only enough flour to keep the dough from being too sticky to work with. A dough that is slightly tacky to the touch will yield a much nicer loaf than one that is dry.

▶ Unless a recipe specifically calls for sifted flour, there's no need to go to the trouble. Measure by stirring the flour, then gently spooning it into a measuring cup and leveling off with the flat edge of a knife. The stirring is necessary because, though most all-purpose flour is now "pre-sifted," it settles and compacts during storage.

▶ *To substitute all-purpose flour for self-rising flour:* Put 1½ teaspoons baking powder and ½ teaspoon salt in a measuring cup, spoon in all-purpose flour, and level off with a knife. Repeat for each cup of self-rising flour called for.

▶ *To substitute all-purpose flour for cake flour:* Measure out 1 cup all-purpose flour, then remove 2 tablespoons.

- *To substitute cake flour for all-purpose flour:* Use 1 cup plus 2 tablespoons cake flour.
- Whole-wheat flour can be substituted for all-purpose or bread flour in bread recipes, but the resulting loaf will be much denser. For a better bread, substitute half the all-purpose flour with whole-wheat flour and add ⅓ cup toasted wheat germ.
- Make your own oat flour by processing rolled oats in a blender or food processor until powdery. Substitute the oat flour for up to a third of the flour called for in bread recipes.
- No need to wash a flour sifter after each use. Simply rap it sharply on the edge of the sink, then store for future use.
- To eliminate flour's "raw" taste in sauces, soups, etc., put it in a shallow pan and bake at 350°F until deep golden brown.
- To substitute flour for cornstarch for thickening purposes, use 2 tablespoons flour for each tablespoon cornstarch.
- Put all-purpose flour in a large salt shaker and use it to dust pans and work surfaces.

FLOWERS, EDIBLE

- Some flowers can be used as a drink or food garnish or as an integral part of a dish, such as a salad.
- Not all flowers are edible. Be sure to buy flowers either from specialty produce markets or supermarkets that carry gourmet produce. Flowers that have been sprayed with pesticides, such as those found at a florist, should *never* be eaten.
- Before using a flower from your garden (assuming it hasn't been sprayed with pesticide), call your local poison control center to make sure it isn't poisonous.
- Some of the more popular edible flowers are chive blossoms, chrysanthemums, daisies, nasturtiums, pansies, roses and violets.
- Store edible flowers in an airtight container in the refrigerator for up to a week.
- Flowers can be used whole, or you can pull off the petals and scatter them over a dish.
- Some of the larger flowers—like squash blossoms—can be stuffed and deep-fried.
- *See also* SQUASH BLOSSOMS

FOIL *see* ALUMINUM FOIL

FOOD PROCESSORS

- A food processor can be the workhorse of a busy kitchen. Having it readily available—sitting out on the countertop—is the only way you'll get into the habit of using it for everyday cooking.

▶ Having an extra food processor workbowl on hand speeds preparation time because you don't have to stop and wash the bowl between uses. Many manufacturers sell bowl inserts that can be lifted out after using, leaving you with a clean workbowl.

▶ Make cleanup a breeze by spraying the grating or slicing disks, or the metal blade with nonstick vegetable spray before using. If you're processing a particularly sticky mixture, spray the inside of the workbowl and cover, as well.

▶ If the lid goes on with difficulty, spray nonstick vegetable spray on the inside edge that touches the bowl.

▶ Technique makes all the difference in the world when using a food processor. When working with the metal blade, for instance, using quick on/off pulses when chopping some foods keeps the pieces bouncing around in the workbowl and in the blade's path. It's the surest way to keep chopped onions from becoming onion puree or nuts from turning into nut butter.

F

▶ When using the slicing or shredding disks, the pressure you apply to the pusher should be gentle but steady. Soft foods like cucumbers require less pressure than dense foods like potatoes.

▶ When processing liquid mixtures, don't overfill the bowl or the liquid might leak out between the metal blade and the shaft, as well as at the rim of the bowl. Your owner's manual will tell you how much is too much.

▶ When there's a dish that requires many foods to be cut, always start with the driest and least odoriferous food first. For instance, you might chop mushrooms, then zucchini, then bell peppers and, finally, onions. All you need is a simple paper-towel wipe-out between vegetables. As you chop or slice them, transfer the vegetables to individual sheets of waxed paper or paper plates to save on cleanup.

▶ Foods with a similar texture, like apples and crisp pears, can be chopped together. Cut such foods into 1-inch chunks before chopping them.

▶ When slicing or shredding several vegetables for one dish, it's not necessary to remove them from the workbowl as they're sliced unless you plan to cook them separately.

▶ The small plastic blade is specifically for kneading bread. The metal blade has a tendency to cut the dough, which ruins much of its elasticity.

▶ Ever wonder why that tiny hole is in the bottom of your processor's food pusher? It's for slowly drizzling liquid (such as oil) into the workbowl— a method for making mayonnaise and other emulsions.

▶ For all its wonders, there are certain tasks the food processor just can't do. Whipping potatoes is one—the processor's high speed turns the potatoes into a sticky glob. Processors can't cut geometrical shapes like cubes or wedges, nor can they beat air into egg whites or whipping cream without special attachments.

▶ *See also* BLENDERS; IMMERSION BLENDERS

FREEZING FOOD

▶ Line the bottom of the freezer compartment (but don't cover the fan vent) with plastic wrap or foil to help keep it clean. Ice cube trays won't stick anymore, either.

▶ It's a good idea to keep a freezer thermometer in your freezer to make sure the temperature is at 0°F or a little below.

▶ Food storage life is diminished every time the temperature rises 10° above 0°F.

▶ Never open the freezer door during a power outage. Doing so lets warm air in and can hasten defrosting.

▶ Overloading a freezer slows down the freezing process, which can affect the flavor and quality of food.

▶ When adding several containers of unfrozen food to a freezer, space them well apart to hasten the freezing process. Once they're frozen solid, you may stack them as desired.

▶ Freezing food in wrappings or containers not specifically designed for the freezer can diminish both flavor and nutrients. Check the label on packages of aluminum foil or plastic bags to make sure they're suitable for freezing. Don't risk letting food get freezer burn or be otherwise damaged by storing it in the wrong material.

▶ Regular plastic wrap, foil and plastic bags are not vapor- or moistureproof. If you're unsure of the wrapping or container, double wrap food by placing it inside a zip-closure plastic bag.

▶ Oxygen is stored food's greatest enemy. For that reason, choose containers for freezing that are as close as possible to the volume of food to be frozen.

▶ Clean, thoroughly dry milk or cream cartons are good for storing foods. You can cut them down the fit the food precisely. Double wrap the carton in a freezer-weight plastic bag.

▶ You'll get more mileage from your freezer space if you use plastic freezer bags instead of rigid containers. Simply transfer the cooled food to the plastic bag, remove as much air as possible and seal. Place the bag on a plate until frozen solid, then remove the plate. The freezer bags can be washed and reused as long as they're intact.

▶ It's important to get as much air as possible out of plastic bags containing food to be frozen. To do so, place the food in a zip-closure bag and seal all but about ½ inch of the bag. Insert a straw into the opening and suck out as much air as possible; remove the straw and quickly zip up the bag.

▶ If you don't have freezer tape to label your frozen-food packages do this.

Once the food is frozen solid in freezer-safe containers, insert a small piece of paper noting the contents and date frozen. Reseal until ready to use.

▶ Putting warm food in a freezer lowers the freezer's temperature, which can affect the stability of the other frozen foods in the compartment.

▶ Always cool food at least to room temperature before freezing. Chilled food freezes faster, and therefore tastes fresher when reheated.

▶ Food, with the exception of sauced dishes, should be as dry as possible before freezing.

▶ If a recipe calls for blanching a food before freezing, be sure and do so. This step is usually for the purpose of destroying natural enzymes that would affect that particular food's quality during the freezing process.

▶ Seasonings have a way of changing flavor in some frozen foods. If you're making a dish specifically for freezing, it's best to season after it's thawed and heated.

F

▶ It's possible to freeze an entire cooked or uncooked casserole and still be able to use the dish while the food waits in the freezer. To do so, line a casserole dish with heavy-duty aluminum foil. Leave enough overhang on all sides to cover and seal the food. Add the casserole ingredients and either freeze until solid, or bake, cool to room temperature and then freeze. Use the foil overhang to lift the frozen food from the dish; cover the food with the foil overhang and seal airtight. Double wrap in a freezer-proof plastic bag, label and freeze until ready to use. Meanwhile, the dish can be used for other purposes. To thaw, remove the wrapping and place the frozen food back in the dish in which it was baked or formed.

▶ Convenient, single-serving portions can be frozen easily in individual freezer bags, microwave-safe containers, or heavy-duty foil or plastic wrap. Use the same method as described in the previous tip for large casseroles.

▶ Do not refreeze food that has been frozen and reheated. Not only will the flavor be lackluster, but the possibility of bacterial growth in such food is greatly increased.

▶ Food that's icy cold and still contains some ice crystals may be refrozen. It should, however, be used soon, as refrozen food has a short life.

▶ Frozen cooked foods should never be refrozen; likewise seafood, which spoils rapidly once defrosted.

▶ Individually freeze foods such as cookies, cookie dough, pieces of meat (like chicken), meatballs, pastries or appetizers by placing them on a baking sheet and freezing, uncovered, until hard. Wrap the food airtight in a freezer-proof plastic bag or heavy-duty foil. This technique keeps the food from sticking together, and allows you to remove as many pieces as you need at a time. Some foods must be defrosted before heating, others can be heated frozen.

▶ *Clues to whether or not frozen food has begun to deteriorate:* 1. Freezer burn—

a dry-looking surface, sometimes with pale gray spots, caused by air getting into the package; 2. Color change—indicating that the food has been frozen too long, particularly prevalent in vegetables; 3. Frost—an indicator that either the food froze too slowly, or that it has been partially thawed and refrozen; 4. Textural change—meat begins to toughen, vegetables lose their crispness, sauces separate and turn lumpy, etc.

▸ The safest method for thawing food is overnight in the refrigerator. The thawing time for some foods can be cut to a fraction of the usual by placing them in a plastic bag (if not already frozen that way), then in a large bowl of cold water. Most foods can also be defrosted in a microwave oven, following the manufacturer's directions.

▸ *See also individual listings of various foods for specific information related to freezing that food*

F

FRENCH FRIES *see* POTATOES, COOKING METHODS

FRIED EGGS *see* EGGS, COOKING METHODS

FROSTING

▸ A cake should be thoroughly cooled before being frosted.

▸ If you love extra frosting and filling, split each cake layer in half (*see* CAKES) to create four frosting surfaces instead of two (double the frosting recipe).

▸ Before frosting or otherwise decorating a cake, use a pastry brush to remove any loose crumbs.

▸ Whipped cream can be an easy, elegant frosting for many kinds of cake. You can flavor it with liqueur, sweeten it (try honey or maple syrup) or fold grated chocolate or finely chopped almond roca into it. Before adding liquid (like liqueur) to whipped cream, beat the cream to the firm-peak stage. Then gradually drizzle in the liquid while continuing to beat until it's thoroughly incorporated and the cream is very thick. Don't add more than 2 to 4 tablespoons of liquid per cup of cream or the cream may not remain stiff.

▸ Make chocolate whipped cream by combining 2 tablespoons each unsweetened cocoa powder and confectioners' sugar in a mixing bowl. Gradually stir in 1 cup whipping cream, then refrigerate for at least 30 minutes before beating.

▸ Always use a heavy pan for cooked frosting; it should hold at least double the amount of the original ingredients to allow for expansion during cooking.

▸ Stirring a boiled frosting made with sugar and water will cause it to turn grainy.

▸ If a cooked frosting starts to sugar (turn granular) on you, stir in ¼ to ½ teaspoon white vinegar or lemon juice.

- Sifting confectioners' sugar before using will prevent a lumpy frosting. If you don't have a sifter, put the sugar in a fine sieve, and push it through by stirring with a spoon.

- Don't think only milk should be used to moisten confectioners' sugar frostings. There are dozens of alternatives including strong coffee, peanut butter (with a little milk), fruit juice, jam or jelly (melted slightly), honey or maple syrup.

- Using warm liquids (milk, fruit juice, liqueur, etc.) in frostings made with confectioners' sugar will help eliminate lumps in unsifted sugar.

- If you don't like the "raw" taste of confectioners' sugar frosting, let it stand in the top of a double boiler over simmering water for about 10 minutes. Stir occasionally during that time. Remove from heat and let cool at least partially before frosting the cake.

- Beating 1 to 2 tablespoons softened butter into a confectioners' sugar frosting will keep the surface supple rather than dry and crackly (if the frosting's been heated, let it cool completely).

- If you don't want the extra fat butter adds, stir ¼ teaspoon baking powder into the confectioners' sugar before adding the liquid. The frosting will stay creamy and moist.

- If a confectioners' sugar frosting has become too thick, simply stir a little liquid into it, ½ teaspoon at a time, until the desired consistency is reached.

- Don't add chopped nuts, chocolate or fruit until after the frosting's finished, or you're liable to thin it.

- Don't worry if your cake layers are uneven—a thick frosting hides mistakes beautifully.

- It's easier to frost a cake on a serving plate so you don't risk damaging it while transferring it to the plate after it's frosted. To keep the plate clean, place several strips of waxed paper around the edges of the plate, then place the cake on top of the paper. Once the cake's frosted, carefully pull out the waxed paper strips and discard.

- If you *do* frost a cake on the rack on which it cooled, place a sheet of waxed paper under the rack. The paper will catch any drips, which can be returned to the frosting bowl (unless, of course, it has crumbs in it).

- If the cake filling is different than the frosting, don't spread it all the way to the edges or it might run into, discolor or otherwise interfere with the frosting. Spread the filling to within ½ inch of the edges (it will probably spread some when the other layer is placed on top of it); the frosting will fill any spaces.

- If a cake is extremely soft, apply a *crumb coating* by spreading a paper-thin layer of frosting over the entire cake to seal the surface, set the crumbs and fill in any imperfections. Allow this coating to dry before applying remaining frosting.

- If a cake is so delicate or crumbly that it falls to pieces when you try to frost it, freeze it until solid, then frost it. Defrost several hours before serving.
- A frosting that's too thick will tear the cake. Thin such a frosting by beating in a few drops of milk or other liquid.
- Once the frosting's on the cake, use a flexible metal pastry spatula to create decorative swirls and other finishing touches. For creamy or butter-based frostings, dip the spatula in cold water every so often so the frosting will stay on the cake and not stick to the spatula. Confectioners' sugar or cooked frostings do better if the knife is dipped into hot water first.
- Before creating a design or writing on cake frosting, use a toothpick to draw the pattern, then pipe over the lines. If you make a mistake, simply smooth the frosting with the back of a spoon and start over.

- For cupcakes, it's quicker to dip the tops in the frosting, rather than spreading frosting over each one. Just be sure all crumbs have been brushed away from the cupcake's surface. Also, the icing must be very soft or light in order to dip the cakes properly.
- To prevent plastic wrap from sticking to frosting, spray it with nonstick vegetable spray.
- Store leftover creamy or confectioners' sugar frostings in the freezer for up to 6 months. Defrost in the refrigerator overnight and beat before using.
- *See also* CAKES; PASTRY BAGS

FRUIT, DRIED

- Dried fruit will keep longer if wrapped airtight and stored in the refrigerator.
- Dried fruit will be easier to chop if you put them in the freezer for an hour.
- Dried fruit can be easily chopped in the food processor with the metal blade. If the fruit begins to stick together, add 1 to 2 tablespoons granulated sugar and continue chopping.
- Kitchen shears are great for snipping dried fruit like apples, apricots and dates. To keep the fruit from sticking, dip the shears in hot water or granulated sugar every so often.
- No matter what you use to cut dried fruit—food processor, kitchen shears or knife—you can help keep the fruit from sticking by spraying the utensil with nonstick vegetable spray.
- Hardened dried fruit can be softened by covering it with boiling water and letting it sit for 15 minutes. Drain, then blot the fruit well on paper towels before using.
- Speed-soak a cup of dried fruit by combining it with ½ cup water in a medium bowl. Cover and microwave on HIGH (100 percent power) for

90 seconds; let stand for 5 minutes before using.
- Before adding chopped dried fruit to a cake, bread or cookie batter, toss it with some of the flour called for in the recipe, separating the pieces with your fingers as you do so. This will help keep the fruit from sinking to the bottom of the batter.
- *See also* FRUIT, GENERAL; RAISINS

FRUIT, GENERAL

- Speed the ripening of soft fruits such as nectarines, peaches, pears, avocados and tomatoes by putting them in a paper bag with a ripe apple for 2 to 3 days. Pierce the bag in a few places with the tip of a knife, then fold the top to seal. The apple produces a natural ethylene gas that speeds the ripening process.
- The ripening process stops when you refrigerate fruit.
- Some fruits are coated with wax before being marketed. Waxing is done to extend shelf life, seal in moisture and improve appearance. Though such waxes are safe to eat, they may contain pesticide residues. The FDA (Food and Drug Administration) requires waxed produce to be identified with signs, but this is rarely done. Some waxed fruits are obvious by their shine and feel. If you're not sure, ask the produce manager.
- There are great fiber and nutritional advantages and almost no risk of chemical residues in eating unpeeled fruit. The FDA reports that, during annual random produce testing, 99 percent of the produce is either residue-free or well below EPA (Environmental Protection Agency) limits.
- Wash fruit just before using under cool, running water—use a vegetable brush, if necessary. Very dirty fruit can be dipped in soapy water, then rinsed thoroughly.
- Soaking fruit in water for more than a few minutes can leach out water-soluble vitamins.
- Keep cut fruit from staining your hands during preparation by spraying your hands with nonstick vegetable spray.
- Keep fruits like apples and pears from turning dark after peeling by dipping them into a bowl of cold water mixed with 3 tablespoons lemon juice.
- Removing stones (pits) from fruits like peaches and nectarines is easier if you cut the fruit from stem to stem all the way to the stone. Twist the halves in opposite directions and lift out the stone.
- Pieces of fruit are less likly to sink in a cake or bread batter if you first toss them with all-purpose flour or cake until well coated.
- Don't throw out soft, overripe fruit! Peel if necessary, cut off any bruised spots, then puree or chop finely and use as a topping for ice cream, pancakes or waffles, or for shortcake.
- Create a delicious "fruit smoothie" by combining ½ cup of your favorite

yogurt (either plain or flavored) and ¾ to 1 cup chopped fruit in a blender and processing until smooth. Pour into a glass and top off with something bubbly like sparkling water, ginger ale or champagne; stir gently.

▶ In seconds overripe fruit can also be turned into a fruit sauce to serve over puddings, cakes, etc. Just toss the fruit into a blender and puree. If necessary, add a little liquid (like fruit juice, liqueur or cream) for the sauce to reach the right consistency.

▶ For delicious fruitsicles, puree fruit (if desired, add a little water, fruit juice, milk or yogurt) and pour it into ice cube trays, or 4- to 6-ounce paper cups. When partially frozen, insert popsicle sticks in the center of each "sicle"; freeze until solid. Or freeze the puree in paper cups until solid and either push up from the bottom to eat, or peel the cup downward as you eat the frozen fruit.

▶ *See also individual fruits (such as* APPLES, APRICOTS, PEACHES, PEARS, PLUMS, *etc.);* CITRUS FRUITS; FRUIT, DRIED; RAISINS

FRUITCAKE

▶ Turn almost any fruitcake recipe into a *light* fruitcake by omitting dark spices (like cinnamon, nutmeg and cloves), substituting light corn syrup for dark corn syrup or molasses, and using only light fruits such as golden raisins, pineapple and dried apricots.

▶ Lining the bottom and sides of a fruitcake pan with foil prevents overbrowning. It's easier to grease the foil before you line the pan with it. Leave enough overlap hanging out of the pan so you can grab the edges and pull the cake out.

▶ Never fill a pan more than two-thirds full of fruitcake batter or it might rise over the edges.

▶ Make mini-fruitcakes for giving by baking the batter in paper- or foil-lined muffin tins. Reduce the baking time by one half to two thirds, checking for doneness.

▶ Fruitcakes are baked in a slow oven for a long time. To keep the outer edges from burning before the interior is baked, set the pan containing the fruitcake batter in a 13- by 9-inch baking pan filled half full with hot water.

▶ Test a fruitcake for doneness by inserting a toothpick near the center. If it comes out clean, the cake's done.

▶ Let fruitcake stand in the pan for 10 minutes after baking, then turn out, right side up, onto a rack to cool completely.

▶ Drizzle cooled fruitcake with liquor, liqueur or wine, then wrap in spirit-soaked cheesecloth. Seal airtight in foil or a heavyweight plastic bag and refrigerate for at least 3 weeks.

▶ Fruitcake will slice more easily if it's cold. Use a thin, nonserrated knife.

▶ *See also* BAKING, GENERAL; CAKE; GREASING PANS

FRYING *see* DEEP-FRYING; SAUTEÍNG; STIR-FRYING

FUDGE *see* CANDY

FUNNELS

▶ Every kitchen should have at least two funnels—narrow-mouthed and wide-mouthed. The former is for pouring liquids into a bottle, the latter for transferring chunky foods to a jar or other container.

▶ Clip off the corner of a plastic bag and it becomes an instant, disposable funnel.

▶ Make a funnel by forming a cone out of heavy-duty foil, or a double thickness of regular foil.

G

GARLIC

- There are four main types of garlic available in the United States: **American garlic**, which is white-skinned and strongly flavored; **Mexican** and **Italian garlic**, both of which have mauve-colored skins and a somewhat milder flavor; and the large, orange-sized **elephant garlic** (not a true garlic, but related to the leek) with its huge, 1-ounce cloves and extremely mild flavor.
- Whatever type of garlic you buy, look for firm, plump bulbs with dry skins. Avoid heads with soft or shriveled cloves, and those stored in the refrigerated section of the produce department.
- Store fresh garlic in an open container (away from other foods) in a cool, dark place. Properly stored, unbroken bulbs can be kept up to 8 weeks, though they'll begin to dry out toward the end of that time. Once broken from the bulb, individual cloves will keep from 3 to 10 days.
- *Garlic yields:* 1 fresh medium garlic clove = ½ teaspoon minced, ⅛ teaspoon garlic powder or dried minced garlic.
- Old garlic has a very harsh flavor. To tame its stridency, use the tip of a sharp paring knife to cut halfway through a clove, then lift out and discard the center, green-colored shoot. Boiling the garlic for 3 to 5 minutes will further reduce its harshness.
- A recipe calling for *green garlic* refers to the youngster of the species, which resembles a baby leek with its long green top and tiny white bulb. Its flavor is much softer than that of mature garlic. Green garlic is occasionally available in specialty produce markets in the spring.
- It's easy to grow your own garlic "chives." Place individual garlic cloves (point end up and ½ inch apart) in a pot of soil so that only the tips are above the soil's surface. Water only enough to keep the soil moist (not wet) and in a few weeks you'll have garlic chives. Snip and use them as you would regular chives to garnish salads, soups, vegetables and a multitude of other dishes.
- Crushing, chopping, pressing or pureeing garlic releases more of its essential oils and produces a sharper, more assertive flavor than if the cloves are sliced or left whole.
- To quickly peel garlic cloves, place the flat side of a French knife on top of the clove and give it a smack with your fist (not too hard, unless you want to crush the clove). The jolt separates the skin from the clove for easy removal. This method is good for peeling a few cloves at a time.
- If you have a lot of garlic to peel, separate the bulb into cloves, drop into

boiling water and cook for 30 seconds. Turn into a colander and rinse with cold water. Peel when cool enough to handle.

▶ Garlic skins can also be loosened in a microwave oven. Place a whole head of garlic on a paper plate, then microwave on HIGH (100 percent power) for about 1 minute, rotating the plate at 30 seconds. (The time will vary according to the size of the head and the power of the oven.) Let garlic stand in oven for 1 minute. Peel when cool enough to handle.

▶ If you've peeled a lot of garlic, don't put those papery skins in the garbage disposal or you could clog the works.

▶ For garlic cloves ready in an instant whenever you need them, peel a whole head of garlic cloves, place them in a jar and cover with olive or vegetable oil. Seal airtight and refrigerate for up to 2 weeks. When the cloves are gone, you have a delicious bonus—garlic-flavored oil that's great for salad dressings, brushing on bread, sautéing, and myriad other uses.

▶ There's no need to peel garlic cloves when you're putting them through a garlic press. Simply pop the clove, skin and all, into the press and squeeze. The garlic flesh will be forced through the mesh, while the skin stays in the press, keeping it relatively unclogged and making cleanup a breeze.

G

▶ If you don't have a garlic press, simply place a garlic clove on a piece of plastic wrap or waxed paper, fold the paper over to cover the clove, then smash it with a meat pounder, rubber mallet, heavy, flat-bottomed glass, or the flat side of a French knife (using your fist to give it a firm smack).

▶ For garlic-flavored vinegar, combine 6 to 8 sliced, peeled garlic cloves with 1 quart red- or white-wine vinegar. Let stand 2 to 4 weeks, or until the vinegar is flavored as desired. Remove and discard the garlic.

▶ Make your own garlic puree to have on hand whenever a recipe calls for minced or pressed garlic. Put the peeled cloves of 1 large head of garlic into a food processor fitted with the metal blade; drizzle with about 1 tablespoon olive oil. Process until garlic is pureed, scraping down sides of workbowl and adding oil if necessary. Refrigerate in an airtight glass container for up to 2 weeks. For an absolutely airtight seal, smooth the surface of the pureed garlic and cover with about ⅛ inch oil. If any mold appears on the garlic puree, discard immediately.

▶ If you chop garlic with a little salt, the minced garlic won't stick to the knife as much. The salt also absorbs much of the garlic juice. Be sure to reduce the amount of salt used in the dish accordingly.

▶ Want just a whisper of garlic in your salads? Cut a clove in half and rub the cut edges over the inside of the bowl.

▶ Be careful not to overbrown garlic when sautéing or it will turn pungent and bitter. Minced garlic will usually cook in less than 1 minute over medium-high heat.

- If you want just a little garlic flavor in sautéed foods, cook halved garlic cloves in oil over medium heat for 1 to 2 minutes, then remove them with a slotted spoon.
- When sautéing both garlic and onions, put the onions in the pan first. When they're almost done, add the garlic. Otherwise, the garlic will become overbrowned and bitter.
- The longer and more gently garlic is cooked, the milder it becomes. In dishes like slow-cooked stews whole garlic cloves become so soft and pastelike that they can be crushed against the side of the pot and stirred into the liquid.
- When garlic is roasted, it turns golden and buttery-soft, its flavor slightly sweet and nutty. Roasted garlic is wonderful spread like butter on bread or grilled meats, on baked and in mashed potatoes, and as an ingredient in soups, sauces and salad dressings. Either a whole head or individual cloves of garlic can be roasted. If you separate the cloves each one becomes a little caramelized. To roast 1 head garlic, gently rub off the outer layers of papery skin. Separate into cloves and place on a square of aluminum foil large enough to loosely enclose the garlic. Drizzle cloves with 1 teaspoon olive oil; loosely wrap and seal. Bake at 400°F for 25 to 30 minutes, or until soft when pierced with a metal skewer or the tip of a pointed knife. Serve warm or at room temperature. Leftovers can be refrigerated in an airtight jar for up to 10 days.
- Love eating garlic but hate the aftertaste and odor? The following remedies should help alleviate the problem: chewing on fennel seeds, a coffee bean, fresh parsley or chlorophyll tablets; or drinking lemon juice (mix it with a little sugar to soften the shock); or eating lime sherbet.
- Remove garlic odor from your hands by rubbing them with lemon, then salt. After rinsing, wash with soap and warm water.
- Deodorize a garlic-scented cutting board by rubbing it with a paste of baking soda and water.
- Though dried and oil-packed minced garlic, garlic extract, garlic juice, garlic powder and garlic salt may be convenient to use, they're a poor flavor substitute for the less expensive, readily available fresh garlic.

GARLIC PRESSES

- No need to peel garlic that will be run through a press. Simply insert the whole clove—skin and all—and squeeze. Remove and discard the skin before pressing the next clove.
- Most garlic presses are difficult to clean—even those self-cleaning units with built-in prongs. Without thorough (and time-consuming) scrubbing, residual oil from the garlic can cling to the utensil. The oil, which quickly turns rancid, can easily pass its unpleasant flavor to the next batch of garlic to be pressed. An easy solution is to buy a dishwasher-safe

garlic press, such as stainless steel, and let your major appliance do the work. Place the press in an open position on the bottom rack (laying it atop the silverware works great).

▶ It's easier to clean a garlic press right after using it, before any residual garlic dries and clogs the holes. The press can also be set in a cup of warm water until you're ready to clean it.

▶ Some garlic presses have pointed "teeth" that push garlic fragments back out through the holes, making cleaning much easier.

GARNISHING; GARNISHES

▶ Few adages about food are truer than "You eat with your eyes first." A simple but deft finishing touch can turn a dull-looking dish into one that's smashing. Garnishes add eye appeal to almost any dish and they needn't be time-consuming. A basic rule of thumb is that any garnish should be edible and, when possible, an ingredient that's intrinsic to the dish. For example, if a dish has fresh basil in it, mince some extra to use as a garnish, or arrange sprigs of basil around the side of the dish. It doesn't take much effort to create a garnish while you're preparing the dish.

▶ Always garnish food at the last minute. If you garnish a dish, then let it sit in the refrigerator several hours, the garnish won't look as fresh as it should.

▶ Before serving dishes that have been standing or refrigerated, give them a stir. This will bring the dressing, juices or whatever has settled to the bottom of the dish up to the surface, giving it a sheen and making it look tantalizingly fresh. Likewise, turn meats over to coat the top with juice to give it that succulent look. Do this just before garnishing the dish.

▶ Easy, eye-catching garnishes include julienned vegetables, toasted nuts or breadcrumbs, grated cheese, thin rings of onion or bell pepper, slices of citrus fruit, chopped pimiento, sliced or chopped olives, snipped chives or scallion greens, capers, hard-cooked egg slices, thinly sliced fresh vegetables such as zucchini or radishes, whole or halved cherry tomatoes, thinly sliced gherkins or cornichons, chopped or sieved hard-cooked egg whites or yolks, tiny boiled onions, crisp celery leaves . . . the list is endless. About the only limit is your imagination!

▶ Give sprigs of parsley a colorful border by dipping them into cold water, shaking off the excess, then dipping the leaf edges into paprika. Let dry on a plate in the refrigerator until ready to use.

▶ Make a chiffonade to garnish rice, vegetables, meats or other dishes by stacking the leaves of greens—such as chard, romaine, sorrel or spinach, rolling them up into a cigar shape, then thinly slicing crosswise. The resulting green "ribbons" make a garnish that's both flavorful and colorful.

- Use a citrus stripper to flute mushrooms by carving out strips at even intervals.
- Cutouts: Use a canape cutter or tiny cookie cutter to cut designs out of ⅛- to ¼-inch-thick slices of fruits or vegetables such as apples, carrots, citrus rind or cucumbers.
- Spirals, citrus: Using a citrus stripper or sharp knife, cut a citrus rind horizontally around and down the fruit, forming one continuous spiral. Wind the strip around a rounded handle (such as on a wooden spoon), secure with tape, and let dry for 2 hours. Slip the spiral off and use as a garnish.
- Scalloped edges: Use a paring knife or a citrus stripper to cut evenly spaced, lengthwise channels (at about ½-inch intervals) in a citrus fruit. When the fruit is sliced, the channels give the edges a scalloped effect.
- Twists: Make a fruit or vegetable twist by taking a thin slice (orange, lemon, cucumber, etc.), making one cut from the center to the edge, then twisting the slice into a spiral or S shape.
- Scallion brushes: Trim off the root end and most of the green portion of a scallion. Use a sharp, pointed knife to thinly slash both ends at ⅛-inch intervals, leaving a 1-inch uncut space in the center of the scallion. Place in a bowl of ice water in the refrigerator for 1 hour, or until the slashed tips curl.
- Chile pepper flowers: Choose small, brightly colored chiles. Wear gloves to protect your hands from the chile's volatile oils (*see* CHILES). Use a sharp, pointed knife to cut each pepper from the tip to the stem end at about ⅜-inch intervals. Remove the seeds and, if desired, trim the "petal" ends to form points. Place in a bowl of ice water for 1 hour, or until the chili peppers open into flower shapes.
- Fruit or vegetable fans: Use a sharp, pointed knife to cut the fruit or vegetable (such as pickles, radishes or strawberries) lengthwise into thin slices. Cut to within ¼ inch of the stem end. Use your fingers to fan out the fruit or vegetable.
- Radish flowers: Use a sharp knife to vertically cut thin petals of the red peel around the radish from the tip down almost to the stem end. Put radishes in a bowl of ice water, cover and refrigerate for an hour or so, or until petals pull away from the center portion.
- Soup deserves garnishing, too. Try grated cheese, toasted almond slices, a dollop of sour cream dusted with paprika or red pepper, finely snipped chives or scallion greens, minced herbs like parsley or basil, or sprigs of herbs.

GELATIN

- There are two basic types of gelatin—**powdered gelatin** and **leaf gelatin**. The latter is generally only available in bakery-supply stores and some specialty shops.

- All gelatin will last indefinitely if wrapped airtight and stored in a cool, dry place.
- *Gelatin yields:* 1 envelope powdered gelatin = 1 tablespoon powdered gelatin, 4 sheets leaf gelatin.
- A general rule of thumb is that 1 ¼-ounce envelope powdered gelatin will gel 2 cups of liquid.
- It's important to soak gelatin in cold liquid (whatever the recipe directs) for 3 to 5 minutes before dissolving it. This softens and swells the gelatin granules so they'll dissolve smoothly when heated.
- Add flavor to a dish by substituting other liquids for all or part of any water that's called for in gelatin-based dishes. Options include fruit juices, clarified vegetable or meat broths, wine, tomato juice, etc.
- Softened gelatin can be dissolved in one of several ways. You can add it to a hot mixture, or set a bowl of it inside another bowl or pan containing very hot water, or heat it in a microwave oven at HIGH (100 percent power) for about 45 seconds. Always stir the gelatin until it's completely dissolved.
- Never let a gelatin mixture boil or you'll destroy its setting capabilities.
- Certain raw foods contain an enzyme that keep gelatin from setting properly. These are figs, guava, ginger root, kiwi fruit, papaya and pineapple. Heat destroys the enzyme, however, so these foods can be used if they're cooked or canned.
- A gelatin-based dish will be easier to remove from the mold after it sets if you rinse out the mold with cold water before pouring in the mixture.
- Spraying a mold with nonstick vegetable spray will also facilitate removal of a gelled dish. This technique, however, sometimes leaves a film of oil on the dish which, though not detectable in the flavor, could slightly cloud the surface of a clear gelatin dish.
- If you're in a hurry for a dish to set, only mix enough hot liquid into the gelatin to dissolve it (¼ cup should be enough), then use ice water or other liquid for the balance.
- To speed the setting of gelatin mixtures, place the bowl containing the mixture in a larger bowl of ice water. Stir constantly until the mixture has reached the desired consistency.
- You can also speed setting by starting the mold in the freezer. Keep it there for 20 to 30 minutes, then transfer to the refrigerator. Set a timer or you're liable to wind up with a frozen dish.
- Pieces of fruit or other food won't sink in a gelatin mixture if you wait until the gelatin is partially set (the consistency of egg whites) before stirring them in.
- A gelatin mixture that has set too fast can be resoftened by placing the bowl containing the mixture in a larger bowl of warm water and stirring until the desired consistency is reached.

- When making layered gelatin molds, wait until the bottom layer is sticky to the touch—it should appear to be almost set. Then carefully spoon the second gelatin layer over the first.
- To remove a gelatin-based dish from its mold, insert a knife between the mold and the food in several places to release the vacuum. Then dip the mold in hot water up to the edge. Don't let it sit in the water for more than 5 seconds or you run the risk of melting the gelatin and losing detail. Place a plate over the top of the mold and, holding both plate and mold tightly, invert them, giving the mold a firm shake. The molded food should drop onto the dish. Sometimes it takes a minute or so for gravity to do its work. If the mold won't release, dip it into hot water again for a few seconds, or drape it with towel that was soaked in hot water and wrung out. Lift the mold away from the dish. If possible, return the dish to the refrigerator to refirm for about 20 minutes.
- It's easier to perfectly center a gelatin-based mold if you first rinse off the plate it's to be turned out on with cold water.
- Foods made with too much gelatin have a hard, rubbery texture.
- You can "recast" a leftover gelatin-based mold by putting it in a pan and heating over low heat just until melted. Add new ingredients, if desired, then pour into a smaller mold and chill until firm.

G

GIFTS, FOOD

- Always accompany a food gift with the recipe, and attach an accessory that can be used to make the food, or something that complements it. Many items can be attached to the bow as part of the wrapping. Others can be containers in which to make the food gift. For instance, gifts of candy might have a candy thermometer or wooden spoon attached to the bow. A gift of cake, pie or cheesecake could be given in a special pan (such as springform or Bundt) and accompanied by an assortment of special coffees or teas, a tea infuser, or a set of demitasse cups or cordial glasses. Bread gifts could be given on a nice cutting board, in a linen-lined bread basket, or in a muffin tin. Accessories could include a bread knife, butter dish, butter mold or stamp, honey server, cheese slicer, or selection of jams, jellies and honeys. Possible accessories for cookie gifts include cookie cutters, stamps or molds.
- For gift containers, line plastic-mesh berry or cherry-tomato baskets with colorful tissue paper, then plastic wrap; fill with homemade goodies, and finish with a ribbon and bow. Dress up the basket by weaving ribbon through the plastic mesh.
- Present your food gifts in wonderful, interesting containers that become part of the gift such as decorative tins and canisters, roll cozies, unique

baskets, crystal boxes, cookie jars, muffin tins of all sizes, bread pans, cutting boards, springform pans, special cake pans, covered cake or pie carriers, serving plates, decorative bottles and jars, or cast-iron molds (animal or corn shapes). Line the containers with silver or gold doilies to add a festive touch.

▸ Protect bows on gifts to be mailed by covering them with inverted berry baskets.

GINGER

▸ **Fresh ginger** is commonly available in two forms—young and mature. *Young ginger,* sometimes called "spring ginger," can be found in the springtime in most oriental markets. It's very tender, has a pale skin that's so thin it doesn't require peeling, and a milder flavor than its mature form. *Mature ginger,* available year-round in most supermarkets, has a tough, tan-colored skin that must be removed. Look for mature ginger with a smooth skin—if wrinkled or cracked, the root is dry and past its prime. It should have a fresh, spicy fragrance.

G

▸ Store unpeeled ginger root in the refrigerator, tightly sealed in a plastic bag in the vegetable drawer for up to 3 weeks. It can be frozen for up to a year if you wrap it in plastic wrap, then in a freezer-proof plastic bag. Slice off as much as you need and return the rest of the root to the freezer.

▸ When you peel ginger root, be careful to remove only the skin—the delicate flesh just under the surface is usually the most flavorful.

▸ Store peeled fresh ginger root by cutting it into ½-inch pieces and placing it in a small, screw-top jar. Cover with dry sherry or Madeira and refrigerate for up to 3 months. The wine will impart some of its flavor to the ginger, but that's a minor disadvantage when weighed against having peeled ginger ready and waiting to be used.

▸ The bonus to storing peeled fresh ginger root in wine is the delicious, ginger-flavored liquid that can be used in stir-fry dishes, salad dressings, sauces, etc.

▸ For almost-instant minced ginger root, put a small, peeled chunk of it into a garlic press and squeeze.

▸ Ginger contains an enzyme that prevents gelatin from setting properly. Heat destroys the enzyme, so ginger can be used if cooked before being added to a gelatin mixture.

▸ **Dried, ground ginger** has a very different flavor than its fresh counterpart and should not be substituted for fresh ginger. It is, however, delicious in many savory dishes such as soups, curries and meats, wonderful with many fruit dishes, and indispensable in baked goods like gingerbread and gingersnaps.

▶ **Crystallized** or **candied ginger**, readily found in most supermarkets, has been cooked in a sugar syrup and coated with coarse sugar. It's great in sweet baked goods or sprinkled over ice cream, but can also be used in some savory foods, since the amount of sweetness it adds is negligible in many dishes.

▶ Chop an entire jar of crystallized ginger slices at a time so the minced ginger will be ready when you want it. Place the slices in a food processor fitted with the metal blade; use quick on/off pulses until the ginger is chopped to the desired consistency. If the ginger begins to stick together, add 1 or 2 tablespoons granulated sugar and continue to process. Store chopped ginger in an airtight jar at room temperature for up to 1 year.

▶ Other forms of ginger include **preserved stem ginger**, small knobs of ginger in heavy sugar syrup; **red, sweet ginger**, preserved in a bright red syrup; and **pickled ginger**, which has been preserved in rice vinegar. The two sweet preserved gingers are usually used for desserts like cakes and ice creams, or for salad dressings. Pickled ginger is most often used in Japanese cooking, usually as a condiment. These types of ginger can be found in Asian markets and in the gourmet or ethnic section of many supermarkets.

▶ *See also* SPICES

GRAPEFRUIT

▶ Choose grapefruit that have thin, fine-textured, brightly colored skin. They should be firm yet springy to palm pressure. The heavier they are for their size, the juicier they'll be. In general, the thinner the skin, the more juicy the fruit.

▶ Don't store grapefruit at room temperature for more than a couple of days. Their quality will keep best (for up to 2 weeks) if wrapped in a plastic bag and stored in the refrigerator.

▶ *Grapefruit yields:* 1 medium grapefruit = about 1 cup juice; 1½ cups segments.

▶ A grapefruit knife and grapefruit spoons are wonderful and inexpensive tools. The knife's curved, flexible blade, serrated on both sides, is great for freeing the fruit's flesh from both rind and membrane. The serrated-tipped spoon allows you to cut away the flesh from the rind as you eat it.

▶ Grapefruit will be juicier if you roll it between your palm and the countertop for a few seconds just before eating.

▶ Or make it juicier by pricking the skin in several places with the tines of a fork, then microwaving on HIGH (100 percent power), uncovered, for about 20 seconds. Let stand 2 minutes before cutting.

► Grapefruit halves will sit more steadily on a plate if you cut a thin slice (making a flat place) off the bottoms.

► The flavor of overly acidic grapefruit can be tempered by sprinkling it lightly with salt.

► Grapefruit juice makes a great base for salad dressings.

► When you're peeling grapefruit to use the sections in a salad it's sometimes a hassle to get all the white pith off the fruit. It's much easier if you plunk the whole fruit in a pot of boiling water, remove from heat and let stand 4 minutes. Remove from the water and cool until it's easy to handle. When you peel away the skin, the pith should come right off with it. Any remnants can be pulled off with a grapefruit knife.

► Hollowed-out grapefruit halves make great individual serving dishes for fruit compotes or salads. Thick-skinned grapefruit make sturdier bowls than those with thin skins. After the flesh and membranes are removed, put the grapefruit shells in a large bowl of ice water in the fridge to make them as firm as possible. Drain and blot dry just before filling.

► *See also* CITRUS FRUITS; FRUIT, GENERAL

G

GRAPES

► Choose grapes that are plump, full-colored and firmly attached to their stems. Green (white) grapes, like Thompson seedless, are ripe when they have a slight pale yellow hue. Dark grapes should be deeply colored with no sign of green.

► Store unwashed grapes in a plastic bag in the refrigerator for up to a week.

► *Grape yields:* 1 pound seedless = about 3 cups.

► Before eating, thoroughly wash grapes and blot dry with paper towels.

► Ideally, grapes should be served at about 60°F, so it's best to remove them from the refrigerator about 30 minutes before serving.

► Frozen grapes are wonderful snacks—particularly in the summertime. Wash thoroughly and blot dry, then separate and put on a tray in the freezer. When solid, transfer the grapes to a freezer-proof plastic bag; seal and freeze for up to 3 months.

► Frosted grapes make a beautiful garnish. Beat 1 egg white until it's frothy, then dip small grape clusters (3 to 5 grapes) first into the egg white, then into granulated sugar. Using coarse decorating sugar makes the grapes really sparkle. You can coat the entire grape, or just half. Set the sugar-dipped grapes on a rack to air-dry completely before using.

► Another way to frost grapes is to use a pastry brush to paint grape clusters with honey, maple syrup or corn syrup. Dip the coated grapes into sugar, then dry on a rack. If necessary, recoat grapes with sugar a second time.

► *See also* FRUIT, GENERAL

GRATERS

▶ Spray a grater with nonstick vegetable spray (or rub with a little vegetable oil) before grating foods like cheese and citrus rind and the cleanup will be a snap.

▶ If you have several foods to grate, always start with those that won't leave much residue on the grater (like carrots); save messy foods like cheese for last.

▶ A toothbrush is the perfect tool for cleaning a grater. If it's a used toothbrush, be sure and run it through a dishwasher cycle before using.

GRAVIES *see* SAUCES

GREASING PANS

▶ Use vegetable shortening, unsalted butter or margarine, or nonstick vegetable spray to grease baking pans. Salted butter causes some baked goods to stick to pans.

▶ Too much fat on a pan can cause overbrowning. So will salted butter at temperatures over 400°F.

▶ If you don't like getting your fingers greasy, or getting shortening under your nails, use a crumpled piece of paper towel to dip into the greasing agent and spread over the pan. Or, cover your hand with a small plastic bag when greasing pans. Leave the bag in the shortening can for the next use.

▶ The recipe term "grease and flour" refers to sprinkling a greased pan with a small amount of flour, then tapping and rotating the pan or dish until the entire surface is coated with flour. Invert the container over the sink or waste basket and shake it gently to remove excess flour.

▶ Instead of "greasing and flouring" pans, use this homemade baker's magic: Beat until smooth ½ cup *each* vegetable oil, room-temperature vegetable shortening and all-purpose flour. Refrigerate in an airtight container for up to 6 months and use as necessary to coat muffin tins, cake and bread pans, etc.

▶ If you have trouble getting baked goods out of the pan, do this: Grease the pan, then line the bottom with waxed paper; then grease the waxed paper's surface. After the bread or cake is baked, and the baked good turned out of the pan, the waxed paper will peel right off.

GREEN BEANS *see* BEANS, FRESH GREEN

GREEN ONIONS *see* SCALLIONS

GREEN PEPPERS *see* BELL PEPPERS

G

GRILLING

- Never use a charcoal grill indoors, or near dry areas that might catch fire.
- Storing charcoal in airtight bags keeps it from absorbing excess moisture, which means it will ignite faster. If you don't use charcoal often, put the charcoal bag inside a large plastic trash bag and seal tightly.
- Never add charcoal lighting fluid to a fire that's already lit. And never use alcohol, gasoline or kerosene to start a charcoal fire.
- Don't wear clothes with long, flowing shirttails, sleeves, fringe, etc., that might catch fire.
- Charcoal briquettes are ready to cook with when they have a dull red glow and the surface is covered by a gray ash.
- To test the heat level of a charcoal fire, place your palm at the cooking level. If you can keep it there for 2 seconds, the coals are hot, 3 seconds they're medium-hot, 4 seconds they're medium, 5 seconds they're medium-low, and after 5 seconds the heat is low.
- If you're ready to begin cooking and the coals are too hot, use tongs to spread them apart, or remove a few of them. Closing the vents partway will also slow down a fire. Or, if you have an adjustable grill, raise the rack so it's farther away from the heat.
- Cleanup will be easier if you coat the grill with nonstick vegetable spray before beginning to cook. Don't spray the grill over the fire or you could have a flareup.
- Forestall flareups in one of several ways. Before beginning to grill, trim excess fat from meats or use lean ground meats; or place a drip pan immediately beneath meats, stacking the coals on either side. During cooking, move the coals so they're farther apart; or cover the grill, closing the air vents partway; or lightly mist the coals with water in a spray bottle, or squirt with water in a turkey baster. Don't be too vigorous with your misting or loose ashes could float up onto the food.
- If you don't have a drip pan, make one out of foil. Tear off a piece of heavy-duty (18-inch-wide) foil that's twice the length of your grill, then fold it in half crosswise. Bend all the edges up 1½ inches. Fold the corners to the inside to reinforce them.
- If you have a gas or electric grill, line any drip pan with a double layer of foil to deter a hot fire from burning through.
- For moister indirect grilling, add ½ to 1 cup liquid (wine, stock, beer, etc.) to the drip pan.
- Wood chips add a wonderful smokiness to grilled foods. Mesquite lends a delicate, sweeter nuance than the more intense (but still sweet) hickory. Other grill-compatible woods include apple, cherry, maple, peach, pecan and walnut. (Never use woods like pine or spruce, which exude noxious

G

pitch fumes that will ruin the flavor of food.) Look for wood chips and chunks wherever grilling equipment is sold.

▸ Always soak wood chips in water for an hour before using, wood chunks for 2 hours. Drain thoroughly before sprinkling over hot coals. Besides adding flavor, the damp wood chips keep a fire from burning too rapidly.

▸ Dried herbs such as oregano, tarragon or rosemary sprinkled over hot coals just before grilling add fragrance and flavor to the food.

▸ If you're short on time, give meats and dense vegetables (like potatoes) a jump-start by cooking them halfway done in the microwave oven and finishing on the grill.

▸ Grilled food will cook more evenly if there's about ¾ inch between pieces.

▸ When grilling food on a skewer, position the pieces of food about ¼ inch apart to insure even cooking.

▸ Most meats should be cooked over a medium fire since high heat tends to dry them out.

▸ If you're watching your weight or cholesterol, you'll want to remove the skin from chicken. But don't do it until after it's grilled—the skin holds in the meat's natural moisture. Chicken grilled sans skin can quickly become dry and tough.

▸ Poultry will cook more evenly if brought to room temperature before grilling.

▸ Fish dries out quickly so grill it at a lower temperature than you would meat or poultry.

▸ Thick foods like roasts require a slower fire to keep the outside from burning.

▸ Always heat any sauce with which you're going to baste meat. Cold sauces will slow down the cooking.

▸ Brush long-cooking meats with basting sauces during the last 30 minutes of grilling, basting every 10 minutes for a multilayered glaze. If the sauce is very high in sugar, don't start basting until the last 15 to 20 minutes as sugar has a tendency to burn.

▸ Don't baste food during the last 15 minutes of cooking time with a marinade that hasn't been boiled. Otherwise, the cooking time may be too short to kill any bacteria that was transferred from the raw meat to the marinade.

▸ Remove food from the grill a minute or two before it's done—the residual heat will continue to cook it.

▸ Your charcoal grill will practically self-clean if you cover the steel grid with heavy-duty foil (shiny side down) as soon as you remove the food. Close all the vents and put the cover on the grill. (For a gas grill, leave the heat on for 20 minutes.) When the grill is cool, scrub with a wire brush or crumpled foil, then wipe with damp paper towels. Grills with

porcelain or chrome grids should be cleaned according to the manufacturer's instructions.
▶ An old vinyl tablecloth makes a good substitute grill cover. Attach Velcro
at the edges to hold the cover in place.
▶ *See also* BARBECUE SAUCE; MARINATING

GROUND BEEF; GROUND MEATS IN GENERAL

▶ In the supermarket, you're likely to find a choice of ground beef—ground
sirloin, ground round, ground chuck and plain ground beef (sometimes
simply labeled "hamburger"). The name indicates the cut from which
the meat was ground; ground beef (or hamburger) is customarily a combination of several cuts. The leanest of these is **ground sirloin** (sometimes
labeled "extra lean"), which contains about 15 percent fat. **Ground
round** (labeled "lean") is next, with between 20 and 23 percent fat;
ground chuck, depending on the market (some of which label regular
ground beef as "chuck"), can range between 23 to 30 percent. **Regular
ground beef** touts a hefty 30 percent fat (as much as most sausage!). The
label will usually indicate the percentage of fat or, conversely, that of lean.
If the label doesn't list the percentage of fat, visually check the meat—
the more fat (which is white) there is, the lighter the mixture will be.
▶ Avoid ground meat that smells bad, is dry and brown-looking around the
edges, or that has discolored patches of brown or gray.
▶ When choosing ground beef or other meat, remember that fat greatly
contributes to flavor. And the lower the fat content, the drier the cooked
meat will be. Even if you're watching fat and cholesterol, high-fat ground
meat might still be an option when making dishes that require the meat
to be browned, such as meatballs. That way, much of the fat will cook
out of the meat and can be drained off.
▶ Store ground beef and other ground meats in the coldest part of the refrigerator for up to 2 days; freeze, wrapped airtight, for up to 3 months.
▶ The process of freezing and thawing meat causes it to lose some of its
natural juices, so always try to buy ground meat that hasn't been frozen.
▶ When freezing ground meat pat it out to a 1-inch-thick layer, then double
wrap and freeze. Not only will it freeze more quickly, but defrosting will
take a fraction of the time.
▶ Remember, the higher the percentage of fat in ground meat, the more
shrinkage there is after it's cooked. Take that into consideration when
making hamburger patties, meatballs or other formed, ground-meat
dishes.
▶ To insure food safety and guard against bacterial infection, cook ground
meat until well done.
▶ *See also* BEEF; HAMBURGERS; MEATBALLS; MEATLOAF; MEATS, GENERAL

HAM

- Choose firm, plump hams that are rosy pink and finely grained; country hams range in color from pale pink to deep red. Don't worry about slight iridescence on the surface—that's a reaction some curing agents have to air and light.
- Country hams undergo a special curing during which they're often smoked and aged, which makes them firmer and saltier. Many country hams require special preparation before being baked, including scrubbing, soaking, simmering and skinning. If a country ham isn't accompanied with instructions, ask your butcher about it.
- The words "natural juices added" or "added water" on a ham label are a signal that you're paying for these added weight increasers, and getting less meat.
- If you don't want to bother with the rind on a ham, have the butcher remove it for you.
- The smaller the canned ham, the more likely that it's formed from bits and pieces of ham combined with gelatin and pressed together.
- Refrigerate a whole cured ham in its original wrapping for up to 1 week; ham slices, wrapped airtight, for 3 days. Some country hams can be stored in a cool place for 1 to 2 months (follow label instructions).
- Canned hams should be stored according to label directions. Some require refrigeration; others have been sterilized and don't need to be refrigerated until after opening.
- Check the label before using a ham. Most are fully cooked and may be eaten immediately, or heated until hot (an internal temperature of 140°F—8 to 10 minutes per pound in a 350°F oven). However, some hams are labeled "cook before eating," requiring them to be heated to an internal temperature of 160°F.
- Even if a ham is "fully cooked," its flavor is greatly improved by heating.
- Always remove any paper casing from a ham that requires cooking before heating.
- Canned ham will slip out of its can more easily if you immerse it in hot water for 1 to 2 minutes before opening.
- Remove all but ¼- to ½-inch of the fat before glazing a ham.
- Sprinkling a ham's fatty layer with sieved brown sugar will give the baked ham a delicious caramelized coating.
- Slices of ham won't curl while cooking if you cut slashes through the fat along the edges at 1-inch intervals.

- Ham slices will stay juicy and tender if you cook them slowly.
- The rind can be pulled right off a cooked ham if you cut it lengthwise down the center before baking. Cook it slit side down, and remove the rind right after cooking.
- Never throw out a ham bone. Freeze it for later use to flavor soups, stews, beans or broth.
- Ham is easier to slice thinly if it's chilled.
- Freeze leftover ham for up to 6 months, slicing off what you need to flavor soups, omelets, etc., returning the rest to the freezer.
- When using ham as a flavoring in stir-frys, soups, beans, etc., you'll get more evenly distributed flavor if you finely chop the meat. A few large chunks won't broadcast the flavor as well as many small pieces.
- *See also* BACON; MEATS, GENERAL; PORK; PROSCIUTTO

HAMBURGERS

- See GROUND BEEF for purchase and storage information.
- Ground sirloin makes the leanest burgers, then ground round, ground chuck and lastly regular ground beef (or just plain "hamburger"). The leaner the ground beef, the drier the cooked burger will be.

H

- Adding 1 or 2 tablespoons vegetable oil per pound of ground sirloin will replenish the moisture and some of the fat (though the fat will be unsaturated).
- When making hamburger patties, remember that the higher the percentage of fat in ground meat, the more shrinkage there is after it's cooked. So if you're making hamburgers out of regular ground beef, form the patties so they're about ½ inch larger in diameter than the hamburger bun.
- For moister burgers, use ground meat that's coarsely rather than finely ground.
- If you don't like getting your hands messy when making a hamburger mixture, put the ingredients in a large, zip-closure plastic bag, seal, then squish the contents together *just* until well mixed.
- Don't overmix a hamburger mixture or the finished patties will be dense and heavy.
- For juicier, more flavorful burgers, add 2 to 3 tablespoons tomato or vegetable juice, beef broth or other liquid to each pound of ground meat.
- Add a smoky flavor to burgers by mixing ⅓ cup diced, crisply cooked smoked bacon or ham with the ground beef before forming into patties. Since bacon and ham are salty, don't add as much salt as you normally would.
- Add nutrition and cut on meat consumption by substituting 1 cup of lightly sautéed, finely grated potato or carrot (or half of each) for a quarter pound of the meat.

- Or add minced leftover vegetables to a burger mixture.
- After you've seasoned your meat mixture, fold in 1 stiffly beaten egg white for each pound of meat. The cooked burgers will be light and juicy.
- If you dampen your hands with water while forming hamburger patties, the meat won't stick to your fingers.
- A large ice cream scoop is a good tool for scooping up uniform amounts for hamburger patties.
- Use a light touch when shaping burgers so the mixture doesn't become too compacted and therefore produce a dense burger.
- If you want uniformly shaped hamburgers, place the meat mixture in the center of a long sheet of plastic wrap. Use your hands to form the meat into a log the diameter you want your hamburgers. Then wrap the log in plastic wrap, smoothing out its shape in the process. Freeze for 1 hour, or until the meat feels firm but not solid. Then cut the log into uniform slices.
- If you like well-done burgers with lots of crusty (seared) surface, make the patties thin and large, and cook them quickly. For succulent patties, shape the meat into thick rounds and cook more slowly.
- Put about 1 tablespoon grated cheese or cottage cheese, or a chunk of blue cheese or cold herb butter in the center of a hamburger patty, making sure the filling is completely sealed with meat. By the time the burger is done, the filling will be melted and come oozing out deliciously when the patty is cut into.
- When freezing hamburger patties (raw or cooked), separate them with squares of plastic wrap. That way you can pry the patties apart and defrost as needed.
- For a nice, crispy surface for pan-fried burgers, lightly dust the patties with flour or cornstarch just before cooking.
- For "chicken-fried" hamburgers, dip the patties in beatten egg, then in finely ground bread or cracker crumbs.
- Always preheat your pan or broiler so the meat's surface gets nicely seared.
- Unless your patties have a coating like flour or breadcrumbs, it's usually not necessary to cook them in oil or melted fat. There's enough fat in the meat to lubricate the pan, particularly if it has a nonstick surface.
- Never use a metal spatula to press down on a hamburger patty while it's cooking—you'll squeeze out much of the flavorful juices!
- When cooking hamburgers for a crowd, place the patties side by side on several baking pans (with shallow sides so the grease won't drip off onto the bottom of the oven), bake at 350°F until partway done, then finish the burgers outdoors on the grill.
- To insure food safety and guard against bacterial infection, cook hamburgers until well done.

▶ Ketchup and mustard aren't the only garnishes for hamburgers. Next time try topping them with something different like sautéed onions and bell peppers, guacamole, chutney, barbecue sauce, salsa, crisp bacon strips or chili.

▶ *See also* BEEF; GROUND BEEF; MEATS, GENERAL

HARD-COOKED EGGS *see* EGGS, COOKING METHODS

HAZELNUTS

▶ Depending on the region of the country, hazelnuts are also called **filberts** and **cobnuts.**

▶ *Hazelnut yields:* 1 pound shelled, whole = about 3½ cups.

▶ Hazelnuts have a bitter brown skin that should be removed. To do so, soak them in cold water for 1 minute. Drain (but don't dry), then bake at 400°F for 5 to 7 minutes, or until the skins begin to flake. Place a handful of the warm nuts on a dish towel, then fold the towel over the nuts and rub vigorously to remove most of the skins. Repeat with the remaining nuts.

▶ Save yourself the trouble of peeling hazelnuts and look for the packaged, chopped hazelnuts that are available in some supermarkets and specialty stores.

▶ *See also* NUTS, GENERAL *for general purchase, storage and usage information*

HERBS
Fresh herbs:

▶ Fresh herbs give a dish a pizzazz that dried herbs just can't match. When buying fresh herbs, choose those that have a clean, fresh fragrance and bright color; avoid herbs that show signs of wilting or browning around the edges.

▶ Store fresh herbs in the refrigerator, wrapped loosely in barely damp paper towel and sealed airtight in a plastic bag for up to 5 days.

▶ Bouquets of herbs—such as basil, cilantro and parsley—can be placed, stem end down, in a tall glass filled with enough cold water to cover 1 inch of the stem ends. Cover the top of the bouquet with a plastic bag, securing it to the glass with a rubber band. Alternatively, the herb bouquet may be placed in a screw-top jar in the same manner and sealed tightly. Either way, the water should be changed every 2 days.

▶ Just before using herbs, wash them, then blot dry with a paper towel.

▶ Kitchen shears are great for snipping fresh herbs into small pieces.

▶ It's always best to use restraint when adding any herb to a dish. The flavor of an herb—oregano, for example—can vary widely depending on the variety and season. You can always add more, but it's hard to salvage an overseasoned dish.

▶ If adding chopped herbs to a cold dish such as potato salad, cover and refrigerate for at least 2 hours so the flavors will have time to mingle.

▶ Many fresh herbs lose much of their flavor when heated so, if possible, add them to a long-cooking sauce or soup during the final 20 to 30 minutes of cooking time. Or add the herbs when the dish begins cooking, then stir in 2 tablespoons fresh chopped herbs just before serving to give the dish a fresh flavor.

▶ Don't automatically throw out the stems of herbs after you cut off the leaves. Mince them finely and use to flavor sauces, soups and stews. If you can't use them right away, freeze the stem pieces as directed in the next tip.

▶ Freeze fresh (washed and dried) herbs when in season by stripping the leaves from the stems, then filling muffin cups halfway with the herb leaves. (You can also finely chop the stems and process the same way.) Fill muffin tins with cold water, making sure herbs stay submerged. Freeze until solid, then pop out the frozen herb cubes, seal tightly in a plastic bag and return to the freezer for up to 6 months. When you're ready to use the herbs, place the herb cubes in a strainer and run cold water over them until defrosted. Use immediately.

▶ Fresh, cleaned herbs can also be frozen by first pureeing, then freezing. Spoon teaspoons (or tablespoons) of the pureed herb onto a plastic-wrap-lined baking sheet and freeze until solid. Then transfer the solid spoonsful of herbs to a plastic bag, seal airtight and return to freezer. Use to flavor soups, stews, sauces, salad dressings and other mixtures. Defrost before adding to cold mixtures like salad dressings; no defrosting is necessary when adding to hot mixtures.

▶ Sprigs of fried herbs (such as parsley, tarragon and marjoram) make a crunchy, flavorful garnish. The secret is to keep the oil at about 285°F so the delicate leaves won't burn. Heat at least 2 inches vegetable or peanut oil in a heavy 3-quart saucepan and drop in flour-dusted herb sprigs. Fry until golden, remove with a slotted spoon and drain on paper towel.

▶ Make your own bouquet garni by putting fresh herbs in a cheesecloth bag tied with string. Or put the herbs in a tea infuser. Add the bouquet garni to soups or other mixtures; remove just before the final seasoning.

▶ Make your own herb vinegar by immersing clean, fresh herbs in cider or wine vinegar. Seal and refrigerate for 2 weeks. Strain vinegar into another bottle; refrigerate and use as needed.

▶ Herb butter is wonderful on meats, vegetables, fish, bread—you name it. Simply add about ¼ cup finely chopped fresh herbs (or about 1½ tablespoons dried herbs) to ½ cup softened butter and beat. Cover and refrigerate for at least 3 hours before using. If the herb butter will accompany hot foods like meat, it can be served cold. For breads, however, remove it from the refrigerator 30 minutes before serving.

▶ Make a big batch of herb butter and freeze part of it for up to 6 months to use at a later date.

Dried herbs:

▶ To dry fresh herbs in a microwave oven, sprinkle about ¼ cup leaves (such as mint, oregano or tarragon) on a paper plate or napkin. Microwave on HIGH (100 percent power) for 1 to 3 minutes (depending on the herb and size of leaf), rotating every 30 seconds or so. Cool before storing in an airtight jar at room temperature.

▶ The dried herbs available at the supermarket have a stronger, more concentrated flavor than fresh herbs, but quickly lose their pungency.

▶ Crushed or ground dried herbs become lackluster more quickly than whole herbs.

▶ The biggest enemies of dried herbs are air, light and heat.

▶ Store dried herbs in a cool, dark place for up to 6 months. After 3 months, it's best to refrigerate them.

▶ The more airtight the storage container (glass, screw-top containers are the best), the longer dried herbs will last.

H

▶ To be sure how old an herb in your cabinet is, use a felt-tip marking pen to note the purchase date on the bottom of the can or jar. Or mark the date on a strip of masking tape and stick it to the bottom.

▶ If using dried herbs instead of fresh, substitute 1 teaspoon for each tablespoon fresh. Reverse the formula if substituting fresh for dried herbs, using 3 times the amount.

▶ When substituting ground herbs for dried leaf herbs, use about half the amount called for.

▶ Simplify finding your dried herbs by alphabetizing them.

▶ Buy a turntable in the kitchen-supply section of a hardware or department store, and keep your herbs on it for flick-of-the-wrist convenience.

▶ Before adding dried herbs to a mixture, intensify their flavor by crushing them between your fingers.

▶ When adding dried herbs to a cold mixture like salad dressing, give them a boost by mixing them with just enough hot water to moisten. Set aside 15 minutes before using.

▶ For a fresher flavor and color, combine dried herbs with an equal amount of minced parsley.

▶ If your dried herbs are over the hill and you don't have time to go to the store for more, just use a little more than you normally would to make up for their weak flavor.

▶ *See also* SPICES, *as well as individual herb listings*

HIGH-ALTITUDE ADJUSTMENTS

▶ Altitudes above 3,500 feet have lower atmospheric pressure, which causes cooked or baked foods to react differently.

▶ Did you know that water boils at 212°F at sea level, but at an altitude of 7,500 feet it boils at 198°F? That's because there's not as much air pressure to inhibit the boiling action.

▶ Boiled foods take longer to cook at high altitudes. Also, the liquid used for cooking may need to be increased.

▶ Foods like dried beans and peas take longer to cook at high altitudes and may require more liquid than at sea level.

▶ Meat, poultry and fish usually require a longer cooking time than at sea level.

▶ Foods stored at high altitudes dry out more quickly than those at low altitudes. That means that an ingredient such as flour is drier and will absorb more liquid. Therefore, slightly more liquid or less flour may be required for cake batters or bread and cookie doughs to reach the proper consistency.

▶ At high altitudes, leavening must also be adjusted so baked goods don't overrise. Likewise, sugar adjustments are necessary in order to prevent a porous crumb with a heavy crust.

▶ For baked goods leavened by baking powder or baking soda: *At an altitude of 3,000 feet*—reduce leavening by ⅛ teaspoon for each teaspoon, reduce sugar by ½ to 1 tablespoon for each cup, and increase liquid by 1 to 2 tablespoons for each cup; *at an altitude of 5,000 feet*—reduce leavening by ⅛ to ¼ teaspoon for each teaspoon, reduce sugar by ½ to 2 tablespoons for each cup, and increase liquid by 2 to 4 tablespoons for each cup; *at an altitude of 7,000 feet*—reduce leavening by ¼ teaspoon for each teaspoon, reduce sugar by 1 to 3 tablespoons for each cup, and increase liquid by 3 to 4 tablespoons for each cup;

▶ No recipe adjustment is suggested for yeast breads baked at high altitudes. However, letting the dough rise twice before the final pan rising allows it to develop a fuller flavor. Increasing the baking temperature by 25°F will help set the crust faster so bread will not overrise during the oven-spring that takes place the first 10 to 15 minutes of baking.

▶ Increase the baking temperature by 25°F for cakes and cookies; slightly decrease baking time.

▶ For baked goods like cakes, beat egg whites only to the soft-peak stage, rather than until stiff.

▶ For deep-fat frying, decrease the fat temperature by 3 degrees for each 1,000 feet above sea level; fry foods for a longer time.

▶ *See also* BREADS; CAKES

HONEY

▶ There are hundreds of honeys throughout the world, most of them named for the flower from which they originated. A variety of honey is available in supermarkets but for the broadest selection, check a natural food store. There you'll find a panoply of honeys that could include heather, raspberry, spearmint and thyme—each flower lending its subtle nuance to the delicately scented honey.

▶ Honey varies greatly in flavor. When using honey in cooking, it's important to know its source. For instance, buckwheat honey has far too strong a flavor to be used in a recipe that calls for orange flower honey, which has a light, delicate fragrance and flavor.

▶ Honey comes in three basic forms—*liquid honey* (extracted from the comb), *chunk-style honey* (liquid honey with pieces of the honeycomb), and *comb honey* (a square or round piece of the honeycomb, with the honey inside).

▶ Store liquid honey in an airtight container in a dry place at room temperature for up to a year; comb and chunk honey for 6 months.

▶ *Honey yields:* 1 pound = 1⅓ cups.

▶ When refrigerated, honey crystallizes forming a gooey, grainy mass.

▶ Crystallized honey can be reliquified right in the jar or bottle. Simply set the container in a pan or bowl of very hot water; stir after 5 minutes, then every minute or so until the honey is once again smooth. Or remove the metal lid from the honey jar and microwave at HIGH (100 percent power) for 15 to 60 seconds, depending on how full the container is.

▶ Lightly oil the pitcher in which you serve honey and, after you're through, every speck of what's left will slip out easily and back into the honey jar.

▶ Use the same technique when measuring honey—oil the measuring cup or spoon before you pour in the honey.

▶ If a recipe calls for a cup of honey as a sweetener and you don't have any, substitute 1¼ cups sugar plus ¼ cup more of whatever liquid is called for in the recipe. Or you can substitute another syrupy sweetener (such as light or dark corn syrup, maple syrup or molasses), depending on the flavor you want.

▶ Substituting honey for sugar in baked goods is risky business, but can be done with a little experimentation. As a general rule, don't substitute honey for more than half the sugar called for in a recipe. For each ½ cup of granular sugar, substitute ⅓ cup of honey and reduce the liquid by 2 tablespoons; add ¼ teaspoon baking soda to the dry ingredients.

▶ Honey can cause overbrowning in baked goods. If you're using a recipe that wasn't specifically formulated for honey, reduce the oven temperature by 25°F.

H

▸ The lid on a honey jar won't stick if you wipe off the rim of both the lid and the jar with a damp paper towel before resealing.

▸ Food for thought: though honey is sweeter than refined sugar (so you might use less of it), it has more calories per tablespoon (65 compared to sugar's 45) and, like sugar, contains almost no vitamins or minerals.

▸ *See also* SYRUPS

HORSERADISH

▸ Fresh horseradish is available in many supermarkets. Look for firm roots with no sign of withering.

▸ Store fresh horseradish, tightly wrapped in a plastic bag, in the refrigerator for up to 3 weeks. Freeze for up to 6 months.

▸ Peel fresh horseradish and cut out its fibrous core just before using.

▸ Avoid breathing the fumes when grating fresh horseradish or you're liable to burn your eyes and nose.

▸ Bottled commercial horseradish is available white (preserved in vinegar) and red (preserved in beet juice). It can be found in supermarket refrigerator cases.

▸ Within 4 weeks after opening, prepared horseradish begins to turn bitter and loose its hotness. If you're going to keep it longer than a month, spoon tablespoons of it onto a plastic-wrap-lined baking sheet and freeze until solid. When hard, transfer horseradish lumps to an airtight plastic bag and freeze for up to 6 months.

▸ Mix 2 to 3 tablespoons horseradish with 1 cup sour cream or whipped cream for a wonderful accompaniment for roast beef or prime rib.

▸ A small amount of horseradish mixed with applesauce makes a delicious condiment for pork.

HOT PEPPER SAUCES

▸ Unless the labeling directs otherwise, store hot-pepper sauces like Tabasco at room temperature for up to 1 year.

▸ Even though hot sauces change color from red-orange to a dark rust-red over a period of time, they still pack a spicy-hot punch.

ICE CREAM
Commercial ice cream:

▶ All commercial ice creams have "overrun," an industry term referring to the amount of air they contain. High-quality ice creams contain from 10 to 25 percent air, which gives them a dense yet creamy texture. In general, low-quality ice creams have a greater proportion of air pumped into them. Since overrun isn't listed on the carton, the only way to be sure is to weigh the carton. The weight of a pint of ice cream containing 25 percent air will be about 18 ounces (subtract about 1½ ounces for the container's weight), the weight is proportionately higher with a lower percentage of overrun. The bottom line is that a pint container of premium ice cream will weigh more than the same size of a store brand. This fact should be considered when you're calculating the so-called savings of low-priced ice cream because the truth is, you're paying for a lot of cold air.

▶ Sticky packaging is a signal that the ice cream, sherbet, or frozen yogurt has probably thawed and leaked, then refrozen. Choose another package.

▶ Ice cream begins to melt as soon as you take it from your supermarket's freezer section. It should be the last thing you put in your cart, and be sure the clerk puts it in an insulated bag. As soon as you get home, put the ice cream in the freezer.

▶ Ice cream tends to absorb other food odors and form ice crystals so it's best when consumed within 2 to 3 days. Double wrap the carton in a heavy-duty plastic bag to extend the ice cream's storage life by a couple of days.

▶ Ice crystals won't form as fast if, after using part of a carton of ice cream, you lay a sheet of plastic wrap directly on the surface of the remaining ice cream. Press the plastic wrap down so that it forms a fairly airtight seal, then replace the carton's lid and return the ice cream to the freezer.

▶ Low-fat ice creams and frozen yogurts melt faster than their caloric cousins, and quickly turn to puddles of liquid when served over desserts like hot pies and cobblers.

▶ Soften a quart of rock-hard ice cream by microwaving it at MEDIUM-LOW (30 percent power) for about 30 seconds. Test the softness by inserting a skewer or narrow knife. Hardened high-fat ice cream will soften more quickly than its less caloric cousins because microwaves are attracted to fat.

▶ If ice cream is too hard to scoop and you don't have a microwave oven, peel away the carton and cut the ice cream into slices.

▶ An electric knife makes easy work out of cutting blocks of commercial ice cream into slices.

▶ Use nonstick vegetable spray to thinly coat ice cream scoops, spoons— whatever you use to remove ice cream from the carton—and the ice cream will slip right off the utensil.

▶ Make your own premium stir-in style of ice cream by adding ½ to ¾ cup of any of the following to a softened pint of your favorite ice cream: crushed cream-filled chocolate cookies; raisins or chopped, rehydrated dried fruit; chopped nuts; chopped fresh fruit; chocolate chunks; miniature marshmallows; chopped chocolate-covered mints; the list is endless. Return the ice cream to the freezer for at least 2 hours to refirm.

▶ Melted, refrozen ice cream never tastes the same as the original. But don't throw it out—use it as a creamy topping for puddings, cakes, pies . . . even hot breakfast cereal!

▶ Next time you entertain, create an ice cream sundae dessert buffet. Provide bowls of various-flavored ice cream and sherbet balls, chopped fruit (strawberries, bananas, peaches, etc.), sauces (hot fudge and caramel), chopped nuts and whipped cream. You'll get raves!

▶ Top vanilla ice cream with warmed maple syrup and toasted pecans.

Homemade ice cream:

▶ Before preparing any homemade ice cream, check the manufacturer's directions for your particular ice cream machine.

▶ For a higher yield and creamier texture, make and chill the ice cream mixture the day before you plan to freeze it. A chilled ice-cream mixture will also freeze faster.

▶ Homemade ice cream won't form crystals if you add 1 envelope unflavored gelatin for each 6 cups liquid. Let the gelatin soften in ¼ cup of the liquid, then heat until the gelatin dissolves and stir it into the rest of the liquid.

▶ Homemade ice cream will have a lighter texture if you give it room to expand during the churning and freezing process so only fill the canister two-thirds full.

▶ When using an ice cream maker that requires rock salt and ice, use a ratio of 1 cup salt for each 6 cups of ice.

▶ As the ice melts during churning, add more salt and ice to keep the temperature cold enough.

▶ The faster the freezing process of ice cream, the smoother its texture.

▶ Before opening a canister of ice cream, remove the ice and water to well below the level of the lid. Wipe off the lid well to make sure that no salt or water gets into the ice cream as you remove it.

▶ Homemade ice cream should be "ripened" in the freezer for at least 4 hours after making to fully develop its flavor and texture.

► *See also* DESSERTS, GENERAL

ICE CUBES

► For crystal-clear ice cubes, start with water that's been boiled, then cooled to room temperature before being poured into ice-cube trays. Bottled spring water will also give you clear cubes.

► Make festive ice cubes by freezing small edibles inside. For instance, use small lemon-wedge chunks or mint sprigs for iced tea, a whole raspberry or blackberry for fruit punches, a pineapple chunk for piña coladas, a green olive in martinis, etc. You can do the same with edible flowers (*see listing*).

► Make large or decoratively shaped ice cubes (for punch bowls, etc.) by freezing water in muffin tins, madeleine pans, mini Bundt pans, tart tins, etc.

► Flavored ice cubes are great for icing drinks without diluting them. For instance, use lemonade cubes for lemonade, Bloody Mary mix for Bloody Marys, coffee for iced coffee—you get the idea.

► Get ready for a party by starting several days in advance to make ice cubes, bagging them in tightly sealed plastic bags as each batch is finished. If the cubes stick together, give the bag a whack on the countertop to separate them. Ice cubes are less likely to stick together if stored in paper bags, but you can't store them as long because air will adversely affect the flavor.

► When buying commercial ice cubes, figure on getting about 10 cubes per pound; a 25-pound bag will contain about 250 ice cubes.

► Discard old ice cubes—they'll give your drinks that unpleasant "freezer" taste. Sprinkle them around houseplants for slow watering.

► You can "speed-chill" bottled drinks (including wine) by completely submerging them in a bucket or large pot filled with half ice and half water for about 20 minutes. This chilling method is much faster than using ice alone.

► Throw a handful of ice cubes into the garbage disposal to help sharpen the blades.

ICED TEA *see* TEA

ICING *see* FROSTING

IMMERSION BLENDERS

► The immersion blender is a long, narrow, handheld appliance with rotary blades at one end. It does a good job of blending and pureeing both small and large amounts of food. Some models have accessories such as a strainer, blending bowl, spatula, whisk attachment and a beaker for mixing drinks. The whisk attachment makes it possible to use the immersion blender to whip cream and beat egg whites.

▸ One of the pluses of the immersion blender is that you can put it right into a glass, pitcher, pot of soup or bowl of cooked potatoes or other food—all of which means minimal cleanup.

▸ When processing hot foods, protect your hand from spatters by wearing an oven mitt.

▸ Always remove a pan from the heat before using an immersion blender.

▸ If your immersion blender has variable speeds, always begin at low speed, gradually increasing to high.

▸ To clean, unplug the blender, hold the blade part under hot, running water, using a little soap if the surface is oily. Never submerge an immersion blender.

▸ *See also* BLENDERS

J

JARS AND BOTTLES

▶ If a jar just won't open, turn it upside down and smack the flat top of the lid against a hard surface. Or facilitate opening by holding a jar's metal lid under hot, running water—the heat will cause the metal to expand. If you're trying to open a glass jar that's been refrigerated, begin with warm water, and gradually increase the temperature to hot in order not to crack the glass.

▶ Twist off an obstinate lid by getting a better grip on it with a damp cloth or a rubber glove. Or place a wide rubber band around the lid.

▶ If the jar or bottle neck is small enough, use pliers to open the lid. Cover plastic lids with a dish towel before applying pressure with pliers.

▶ Jar grippers—thin, pliable disks of rubber—can be purchased in many supermarkets and hardware stores.

▶ Keep the lids of jars and bottles filled with sticky ingredients (like maple syrup) from sticking by wiping the rim of both the lid and the container with a paper towel dampened with hot water before resealing.

▶ Keep your shelves clean by using a damp cloth to wipe off the sides and bottom of bottles containing ingredients like syrup or oil.

▶ Save screw-top, quart-size (or smaller) soft-drink or other narrow-necked bottles and use as "canisters" for cornmeal, granulated sugar and other dry, free-flowing ingredients. First of all, make sure the clean bottle is *completely* dry—a process that can be sped up by using a hair dryer to blow hot air into it. Then position a funnel in the bottle's neck and pour in the sugar, etc.; seal tightly. Now you can pour the ingredient right into a measuring cup or other container. If lumps form (which means either the bottle wasn't thoroughly dry or the lid's not airtight), simply shake the bottle to break them up.

▶ Clean and save screw-top jars—they make great moisture- and odor-proof storage containers for all manner of foods.

▶ Glass and plastic peanut butter jars are perfect for storing food because they're slightly wider at the top than at the bottom, which facilitates removing food from them.

▶ Never fill a glass jar or bottle with a hot mixture without warming it first with hot water. Otherwise, you're liable to crack the glass.

▶ Food freezes well in glass screw-top jars. Just be sure to leave ½ to 1 inch of headroom to allow for the natural expansion that occurs when foods or liquids are frozen.

▶ If you want to quickly defrost food that's been frozen in glass jars, immerse it in cold water, changing the water every 10 minutes or so. Never put a frozen jar of food in hot water, which will crack the glass and ruin the food.

▸ To rid jars and bottles of a lingering odor, fill them with hot water and 1 tablespoon baking soda. Let stand overnight, then rinse and dry.

▸ If you can't reach the bottom of a bottle with a bottle brush to clean it, fill it with warm, soapy water and let stand for 20 minutes. Then add a ½-inch layer of dried beans or pie weights and shake until the debris loosens.

JERUSALEM ARTICHOKES

▸ Jerusalem artichokes aren't really artichokes, but rather a member of the sunflower family—the reason many growers today are calling this vegetable "sunchoke."

▸ Buy Jerusalem artichokes that are firm and fresh-looking. Avoid those that are wrinkled, tinged with green or have soft spots.

▸ Store them in a plastic bag in the refrigerator for up to 1 week.

▸ *Jerusalem artichoke yields:* 1 pound = about 2 cups chopped.

▸ Jerusalem artichokes may be peeled but, because the skin is very thin and quite nutritious, usually only need washing before using.

▸ If you're going to peel them, use a vegetable peeler. Always peel before cooking—otherwise, too much flesh comes off with the peel.

▸ This vegetable's nutty, sweet flavor and crunchy texture makes it the perfect addition to salads. It can also be cooked by steaming, boiling or sautéing, and is wonderful in soups and stews.

▸ *See also* VEGETABLES, GENERAL

JICAMA [HEE-kah-mah]

▸ This large, bulbous root vegetable has a thin brown skin and white crunchy flesh. Choose a jicama that's heavy for its size and free of blemishes.

▸ Store jicama in the refrigerator in a plastic bag for up to 2 weeks. Peel just before using.

▸ *Jicama yields:* 1 pound = about 3 cups chopped.

▸ To peel jicama, use a sharp knife to pull off the skin (and attached white fibrous layer) in sheets.

▸ Jicama's sweet, nutty flavor is good both raw and cooked. Raw, it's good in both fruit and vegetable salads, or sliced thinly on sandwiches. It can be used cooked in stir-frys, boiled and mashed like a potato, sautéed on its own, or in soups or stews. Add it to soups near the end of the cooking time so it retains its crisp texture.

▸ If you can't find jicama in your market, the closest thing to it in texture is water chestnuts.

▸ *See also* VEGETABLES, GENERAL

JULIENNE [joo-lee-EHN]

▸ This is a technique whereby food is cut into thin, matchstick strips.

▸ First cut the food (such as a potato) into ⅛-inch-thick slices. Then stack the slices and cut them into ⅛-inch-thick strips. Those strips may then be cut into the desired length.

▸ When trying to julienne something round like a beet, first cut a thin slice from the bottom so it will sit firmly and not roll on the work surface.

▸ Julienned food is most often used as a garnish.

▸ If you don't want to bother with julienning food by hand, look in kitchenware shops for a julienne slicer—a special tool that cuts food into thin strips in one motion.

J

K

KETCHUP; CATSUP [KEHCH-uhp; KACH-uhp]

▸ Unopened ketchup can be stored indefinitely in a cool, dark place. Once opened, ketchup should be stored in the refrigerator where it will keep indefinitely.

▸ *Ketchup yields:* 1 16-ounce bottle = 1⅔ cups.

▸ Can't get the ketchup to pour out of the bottle? Insert a straw or knife with a long thin blade and rotate it once or twice. Remove, then invert the bottle.

▸ To get the last bit of ketchup from the bottle, add about 1 tablespoon water or vinegar, then shake well until the bottle is clean. Depending on whether you used water or vinegar, the mixture can be added to salad dressing, spaghetti sauce, soup, chili.

KIDNEYS

▸ Beef and veal kidneys are multilobed, while lamb and pork are single-lobed. Beef kidneys have the strongest flavor; they're also the least tender.

▸ Choose kidneys that are firm, with a rich, even color. Avoid those with dry spots or a dull surface. In general, the younger the animal, the more tender the texture and the more delicate the flavor. Kidneys from younger animals have a paler color than those from older animals.

▸ Store kidneys, loosely wrapped, in the refrigerator for up to 1 day. They're best used the day they're purchased.

▸ Before cooking, remove skin and any excess fat from kidneys.

▸ Soaking kidneys from more mature animals in cold salted water for 30 to 60 minutes helps reduce their strong odor. Drain and blot dry with paper towel before cooking.

▸ Blanching kidneys in lightly salted water also helps diminish any strong flavor. Dry thoroughly before cooking according to the recipe.

KNEADING *see* BREADS, YEAST

KNIVES

▸ A good knife should be sturdy and well balanced. In the best knives, the end of the blade (called the tang) extends all the way to the end of the handle, where it's anchored by several rivets.

▸ The best knives are made of high-carbon stainless steel or forged carbon.

▸ When shopping for a knife rack, choose one made of wood, either a free-standing or a wall model. Wood is much kinder to knives than the magnetic holders because it doesn't abrade the blade. If using a free-standing knife rack, preserve the blades by placing the knives in the slots upside down.

▶ Never keep knives in a drawer—their edges and tips get scratched and become dull.

▶ If you must store knives in a drawer, make a cardboard sheath for each one (flatten a cardboard tube from foil or waxed paper). Or you can buy knife sheaths at a cutlery or cookware store

▶ Using a sharpening steel to hone the blade *before each use* will give you a knife that cuts cleanly and safely every time. Before using, wash the blade to remove the microscopic bits of steel dust.

▶ Every so often, renew your knife's edge by using a whetstone, drawing the knife across it at a 20-degree angle, making about 6 strokes a side.

▶ A wooden cutting board is easier on a knife edge than a hard plastic board.

▶ Exposing a knife to high heat can permanently damage it.

▶ Some foods—like onions, potatoes and artichokes—will discolor carbon knives; conversely, the knives will also discolor the food.

▶ To keep your knives in the best condition, wash and dry them right after using. Never soak knives or wash them in a dishwasher.

▶ Stainless-steel knives will stay shiny if you rub them with a slice of lemon peel or a rubbing alcohol–dampened rag; wash before using.

K

L

LABEL TERMS

▶ Understanding food labels can be confusing but the following term definitions ought to dispel much of the mystery. Before beginning, however, remember the basics: Most labels list ingredients in descending order by *weight,* not by the amount of each ingredient. Therefore, a cereal that lists sugar as the second or third ingredient might actually contain a small percentage of sugar.

▶ The words *low-fat* on a label mean that the amount of fat per serving (or per 100 grams of food) is 3 grams or less. The term *percent fat free* may only be used on low-fat products.

▶ *Reduced fat* on a label indicates the product contains 50 percent (or less) of the fat found in the product's regular version. *Reduced saturated fat* means the same thing, but pertains only to saturated fat.

▶ The words *low in saturated fat* mean each serving contains 1 gram (or less) of saturated fat, and the number of calories from that source are not more than 15 percent.

▶ The term *fat-free* indicates the product has less than ½ gram fat per serving, providing there are no added fat or oil ingredients.

▶ *Reduced cholesterol* on a label means the product contains 50 percent (or less) of the cholesterol of the product's regular version.

▶ The term *low in cholesterol* means that the amount of cholesterol per serving (or per 100 grams of food) is 20 milligrams or less, and that the saturated fat is 2 grams or less.

▶ *Cholesterol-free* appears on labels of products that contain less than 2 milligrams of cholesterol and 2 grams (or less) of saturated fat per serving.

▶ *Reduced sodium* on a label indicates at least 75 percent less sodium; *low sodium* means 140 milligrams or less per serving; *very low sodium,* less than 35 milligrams sodium per serving; *sodium-free,* less than 5 milligrams per serving.

▶ The words *reduced calorie* means there are at least ⅓ fewer calories than the regular form of the product.

▶ *Low-calorie* indicates 40 calories or fewer per serving, and fewer than 0.4 calories per gram of food.

▶ *No sugar added* on a label simply means that there's no table sugar. Check the label carefully, however, for words like corn syrup, dextrose, fructose, glucose, maltose or sucrose—all of which are sugar.

▶ The virtually meaningless term *light* (or *lite*) is used in a variety of ways by individual manufacturers. According to the Food and Drug Administration, the only parameter for this term is that it must contain "less of something." *Light* or *lite* can refer to reduced calories (in which case, nutritional information must be on the label), but it can also mean a light color or flavor (as with some oils), a reduced amount of fat, sugar, alcohol, etc., or a fluffy texture.

▶ According to the FDA, the words *natural flavorings* on a label are "derived from a spice, fruit or fruit juice, edible yeast, herb, bark, bud, root, leaf or similar plant material, meat, seafood, poultry, egg, dairy product . . . whose significant function in food is flavoring rather than nutritional." Be aware, however, that those broad parameters include ingredients like hydrolyzed protein and HVP, both of which contain MSG.

▶ As of this writing, the FDA has no set definition for the word *natural* on a label. Though there's no real consistency in the labeling world, the term generally means that there are no artificial ingredients or *intentional* additives in the product. However, many foods labeled "natural" are full of sugar, fat and preservatives, so *check the ingredients*. When the term "natural" is used with meat or poultry, it simply indicates the product is minimally processed and free of artificial ingredients.

▶ *Organic* is another nebulous term that, in some states, means that crops are grown without pesticides and that there are no chemicals in animal feed or water. In some areas, however, the word organic is used without qualification.

▶ *Enriched* products are those that have lost nutrients during processing, then had them replaced (approximately) by enrichment. White flour, for example, loses 50 to 80 percent of many nutrients during processing, but then has some of them replaced.

▶ The word *fortified* on foods like breakfast cereals means that nutrients have been added that weren't originally in the ingredients.

▶ *RDA* on a label stands for "Recommended Dietary Allowance," the government-recommended daily amounts of protein, vitamins and minerals for healthy adults. Such amounts are ballpark figures and may vary slightly according to gender, pregnancy, etc.

▶ *See also* ADDITIVES

LAMB

▶ Lamb is meat from a sheep less than 1 year old. Baby lamb is slaughtered at between 6 to 8 weeks of age; spring lamb is usually 3 to 5 months old. The younger the animal, the more tender it is. Animals slaughtered at between 12 to 24 months are called yearlings; over 2 years old, mutton.

▶ Domestic lamb, which is fed on grain, has a milder flavor than the grass-fed imported lamb. Domestic lamb cuts are also larger and meatier than their imported counterparts.

▶ When purchasing lamb, let color be your guide. In general, the darker the color, the older the animal. Baby lamb will be pale pink, while regular lamb is pinkish-red. Lamb should have a fine-grained flesh and creamy white fat.

► Choose a plump leg of lamb—the ratio of meat to bone and fat will be higher.

► Thick lamb chops (1 to 1½ inches) will be more succulent than thin ones.

► Bone-in cuts are always more flavorful than boneless cuts.

► Store ground lamb and small cuts like chops, loosely wrapped in waxed paper, in the coldest part of the refrigerator for up to 3 days; larger cuts like roasts for up to 5 days. Ground lamb can be frozen 3 months; solid cuts for 6 months.

► The thin, parchmentlike coating (called *fell*) on a leg of lamb retains the meat's juices so don't remove it before cooking.

► If the flavor of older lamb is too strong for your palate, mix equal parts lemon juice and olive oil and rub all over the meat's surface. Cover and refrigerate for 2 hours, then wipe dry and cook.

► Lemon juice rubbed over the meat's surface also serves to tenderize it.

► Removing most of the excess fat from lamb cuts will not only be good on the waistline, but will also reduce any "lamby" flavor some diners don't appreciate.

► Slash the fat at ½-inch intervals along the edges of lamb chops and they won't curl while cooking.

► Lamb cooked just until medium-rare will be much more tender and succulent.

► Overcooking lamb makes it dry and tough.

► Cooked lamb can be stored in the refrigerator for up to 3 days.

► *See also* MEATS, GENERAL

LARD

► Lard is rendered and clarified pork fat, the very best of which is *leaf lard*, which comes from the fat around the animal's kidneys. Processed lard has a mild, nutty flavor and is about the consistency of vegetable shortening.

► It may be stored at room temperature for up to 8 months, in the refrigerator even longer. Check the label for storage directions. Either way, it should be tightly wrapped to prevent absorption of odors.

► Lard is richer than many other fats and therefore makes extremely tender, flaky biscuits, pie crusts and pastries.

► When substituting lard for butter or margarine in baking, reduce the amount by 20 to 25 percent.

► *See also* FATS AND OILS

LARDING; LARDING NEEDLE

▶ Many lean cuts of meat can be made succulent and juicy by larding—inserting long, thin strips of fat every inch or so throughout the flesh. The fat melts during cooking, moistening the meat.

▶ The fat used for larding is usually pork fat (known as lardons), which many butchers sell precut.

▶ Add a flavor bonus by soaking the lardons in wine or brandy, then rolling in salt, pepper or herbs before inserting.

▶ A larding needle—a special tool with a pointed tip and hollow cavity—makes this process easy.

▶ Larding can also be done by piercing the meat with a long, thin knife, then forcing the fat strips through the holes. When you do it this way, any seasoning on the lardon's surface will come off at the opening, as you're forcing it through.

▶ Always insert the lardons across the meat's grain.

▶ Slice larded cuts on the diagonal so the fat strips look like a scattering of small white dots.

▶ *See also* BARDING

LEEKS

▶ Buy leeks with crisp, brightly colored leaves and an unblemished white portion. Avoid any with withered or yellow-spotted leaves. The smaller the leek, the more tender it will be.

▶ Store leeks in a plastic bag in the refrigerator for up to 5 days.

▶ *Leek yields:* 1 pound = about 2 cups chopped.

▶ Before using, trim a leek's rootlets; trim leaf ends so about 5 inches remain. Slit the leek from top to bottom and wash thoroughly under cold, running water to remove all the dirt trapped between the leaf layers.

▶ Leeks may be cooked whole, or cut into slices. Whole leeks are best braised or steamed; sliced leeks can be sautéed.

▶ Chopped leeks are wonderful in a variety of foods including salads, stir-fries and soups.

▶ Save the tough green leek ends you trim off, put them in a cheesecloth bag and use to flavor soups.

▶ Bury a leek bulb in dirt, set it on a window ledge, keep it moist, and before long, you'll have green leek shoots that can be snipped and used like chives.

L

LEMONS

▶ Choose lemons with smooth, brightly colored skin with no tinge of green. They should be firm, plump and heavy for their size.

▶ Store lemons in a plastic bag in the refrigerator for 2 to 3 weeks.

▸ *Lemon yields:* 1 pound = about 5 medium; 1 cup juice. One medium lemon = 3 tablespoons juice; 2 to 3 teaspoons zest.

▸ Buy lemons in peak season when they're most economical and enjoy their juice throughout the year. Simply squeeze the juice and freeze it in ice cube trays. Once the lemon-juice cubes are solid, turn them into heavy-weight plastic bags, seal tightly and freeze for up to 6 months.

▸ Room-temperature lemons will yield more juice than those that are refrigerated.

▸ Need just a few drops of lemon juice? Pierce the skin with a toothpick and squeeze out what you need. To store the lemon, reinsert the toothpick, put the lemon in a plastic bag and refrigerate.

▸ To squeeze a lemon wedge over food at your plate, spear the wedge through the flesh with a fork first, then squeeze. That way, the juice won't squirt where you don't want it.

▸ For a restaurant-style presentation, set a lemon half, cut side down, on a square of cheesecloth. Bring up the cheesecloth ends and tie at the top with a small ribbon or string. Place a wrapped lemon half on each guest's plate. This presentation allows diners to squeeze out the juice without worrying about seeds or chunks of flesh spurting onto their food.

▸ Always thoroughly wash lemons to remove insecticide before using their peel (zest) for anything.

▸ Homemade dried lemon peel is easy to store and great for flavoring everything from cakes to sauces. To make your own, simply remove the zest (the colored portion), chop finely, and dry in a single layer at room temperature overnight, or until completely dry. If you're in a hurry, place grated zest on an ungreased baking sheet and bake at 200°F for about 20 minutes, stirring occasionally. Cool completely before storing in an airtight container at room temperature.

▸ Make granulated lemon zest by combining the outer peel (yellow portion only) of 1 lemon with 1 to 2 tablespoons granulated sugar in a food processor fitted with the metal blade. Process until powdery and use the sugared zest in everything from tea to desserts.

▸ Remove berry or beet stains from fingers by rubbing them with half a lemon.

▸ *See also* CITRUS FRUITS *for tips on juicing, etc.*

LENTILS

▸ Lentils are tiny, lens-shaped, dried pulses (legume seeds). The most widely available variety are grayish brown, though there are also yellow and red varieties.

▸ Store lentils in an airtight container for up to 1 year in a cool, dry place. They can be frozen indefinitely.

- Before using, put lentils in a colander and rinse. Pick through them, discarding any shriveled lentils or bits of gravel.
- Unlike dried beans and whole peas, lentils don't need soaking before cooking.
- Increase the cooking time when lentils are prepared with acidic ingredients, such as tomatoes or wine. Or add tomatoes, etc., when the lentils are almost done.
- Drain off the cooking liquid as soon as the lentils are done or they'll continue to cook.
- Lentils are great served alone, or added to soups and stews, or dressed with vinaigrette and served as a salad.
- Cover and refrigerate leftover cooked lentils and use within 5 days.
- *See also* BEANS, DRIED; PEAS, DRIED

LETTUCE *see* SALAD GREENS

LIMA BEANS

- Lima beans are sold both fresh and dried. Fresh limas are in season from June to September. They're usually sold in their pods, which should be plump, firm and dark green.
- Store fresh limas in a plastic bag in the refrigerator for up to 1 week. Shell just before using.
- *Fresh lima bean yields:* 1 pound unshelled = 1½ cups shelled.
- Shell limas by pulling on the string to open the pod. Speed the process by using scissors to cut off a thin strip of the pod's inner edge.
- Cooked fresh limas are wonderful when cooled, dressed with vinaigrette and served as a salad.
- *See also* BEANS, CANNED; BEANS, DRIED
- *See also* BEANS, DRIED

L

LIMES

- Choose limes that are brightly colored, smooth skinned and heavy for their size. Small brown areas (called "scald") on the skin won't affect flavor or succulence. However, a hard or shriveled skin will.
- The most common lime in the United States is the Persian lime; Florida's Key lime is not as widely available. The latter is smaller, rounder and has a color more yellow than green.
- Store uncut limes in a plastic bag in the refrigerator for up to 10 days. Cut limes can be stored in the same way for up to 5 days.
- *Persian lime yields:* 1 pound = 6 to 8 medium; about ½ to ⅔ cup juice. One medium lime = about 1½ tablespoons juice; 1½ teaspoons zest.

- As with all citrus fruit, limes should be thoroughly washed if you plan to use the skin.
- Lime juice can be substituted for lemon juice in most recipes.
- *See also* CITRUS FRUITS *for tips on juicing, etc.*

LIQUORS, LIQUEURS, AND MIXED DRINKS

- Ever wonder what the word "proof" on a liquor or liqueur bottle means? It's a term used to indicate the amount of alcohol; in the United States, the *proof* is exactly twice the percentage of alcohol. Therefore, a bottle labeled "86 Proof" contains 43 percent alcohol.
- Rubbing the rim of a bottle with waxed paper keeps it from dripping.
- Keeping liquors such as Scotch and gin refrigerated means your mixed drinks won't dilute as fast when poured over ice cubes because the liquor will already be cold.
- Chilling the glasses before adding the drink adds an extra dimension of cold.
- The more you stir a mixed, iced drink, the faster the ice melts and dilutes the blend.
- When making a mixed drink, always start with the least expensive ingredients first so if you make a mistake, it won't be too costly.
- Once a carbonated beverage is added to a drink, stir it very gently. Vigorous stirring produces a flat drink.
- To "frost" the rim of a glass, moisten the rim slightly with water, then dip into salt or granulated sugar. For margaritas, dip the glass rim into lime or lemon juice, then salt.
- Cucumber sticks make great swizzle sticks for Bloody Marys.
- Brandy or liqueur must be heated for flambéing. To do so, microwave 1 ounce at HIGH (100 percent power) for 15 seconds. Or heat in a small saucepan just until bubbles appear around edges of pan.

- Like your brandy warm on a cold winter night? Microwave it in the glass (make sure it isn't lead crystal) at HIGH (100 percent power) for about 10 seconds.
- *See also* ALCOHOL; BEER; CHAMPAGNE; FLAMBÉING; ICE CUBES; WINE

LIVER

- Beef and calf's liver are two of the most popular. The color of beef liver is reddish brown, compared to the paler pinkish brown of calf's liver. Liver from a mature animal is also less tender and has a stronger odor and flavor than that from a younger one. Other animal livers used for cooking are lamb, pork, poultry and goose.
- Choose liver that has a bright color and moist (but not slick) surface. It should have a fresh, clean smell.

▸ Store liver, loosely wrapped, in the refrigerator for no more than 2 days.

▸ Tenderize liver by soaking it in milk to cover for 2 hours in the refrigerator. Discard the milk and cook the liver as desired.

▸ Tomato juice also acts as a liver tenderizer. Cover the liver with the juice and refrigerate for 3 hours. If you want to use the juice as a soup or sauce base, bring it to a boil and cook for 5 minutes before doing so.

▸ Raw liver is easier to grind if you first cook it for 5 minutes. Or, cut into strips and partially freeze before grinding.

▸ Liver becomes very tough when overcooked, so it's best to slightly undercook it and let the residual heat finish the job.

▸ When making a sauce that has liver blood in it, add a teaspoon or two of lemon juice to keep it from curdling.

▸ Food for thought: Because liver acts as a clearinghouse for substances that enter the body, it tends to store and absorb unwanted chemicals, medicines and hormones that an animal is fed. The older the animal, the greater the accumulation of these unwanted and potentially dangerous substances. Whether such potential contaminants are offset by liver's nutritional value is still in question. The choice is yours.

LOBSTERS

▸ When buying live lobsters, choose those that are active; when picked up, their tail should curl under the body. If lobsters have been stored on ice, they may be sluggish, so the tail test is particularly important. Whole, cooked lobsters should have their tails curled, a sign that they were alive when cooked. Cooked lobster meat should be sweet-smelling and snow-white. Frozen tails should be in an untorn package with no sign of frost; the visible meat should be free of dry-looking spots.

▸ Ask your fishmonger when the lobsters in his tank were caught. Some markets keep lobsters for a week or more, and these won't be as succulent as those that are fresh-caught.

▸ Live lobsters should be cooked the day they're purchased. They can be stored in the refrigerator on a bed of ice covered by a damp cloth for 1 day.

▸ *Lobster yields:* 1 pound cooked lobster meat = about 2 cups pieces. Needed per serving—1 8-ounce lobster tail, or 1 1- to 1½-pound whole lobster, or 4 ounces cooked lobster meat.

▸ Before cooking, always check to make sure a lobster's still alive; bacteria forms extremely quickly in a dead lobster.

▸ Be humane and kill the lobster before cooking it. Plunge the tip of a large, sharp knife between the eyes to kill it instantly.

▸ To keep lobster tails from curling when they're cooked, insert a metal or bamboo skewer completely through the middle, removing the skewer after the lobster is cooked.

L

▶ A lobster's roe (called *coral*) and *tomalley* (its liver) are prized by many lobster lovers.

▶ To keep the surface of lobster moist while broiling, brush several times with butter.

▶ Lobster that's to be served cold will be more flavorful if slightly under-cooked, and then cooled in the cooking liquid.

▶ Overcooking lobster makes the meat stringy and tough. It's done as soon as the meat turns opaque.

▶ Before dismembering a cooked whole lobster, cover it with a dish towel so the juices won't spurt all over.

▶ Intimidated when a whole lobster is set before you at the table? Approach it this way: First eat the tail meat, then twist off the claws and pick the meat out of them. Next come the legs—break off each one and suck out the meat. Lastly, eat any meat in the body cavity, along with the tomalley and (if it's a female lobster) coral.

▶ If you're adding cooked lobster to a hot dish, do so at the last minute. Otherwise, the lobster will become overcooked and flavorless.

▶ When making a sauce for lobster, put cracked pieces of lobster shell in the liquid to be used, bring to a boil, then reduce heat and cook 30 minutes. After straining, this flavorful broth will add depth and richness to your sauce.

▶ *See also* SHELLFISH

LOW-CALORIE AND LOW-FAT COOKING *see* COOKING LIGHT

L

MANGOES [MANG-gohs)

- Choose mangoes with an unblemished, yellow skin blushed with red. The larger the mango, the higher the fruit-to-seed ratio. Ripe mangoes will yield to gentle palm pressure and have perfumy fragrance. Avoid those with a shriveled or black-speckled skin.
- Refrigerate ripe mangoes in a plastic bag for up to 5 days.
- Place underripe fruit in a paper bag (pierced with a few holes) with an apple at room temperature for 1 to 3 days. Green, rock-hard mangoes will probably never ripen.
- Mangoes have a huge, flat seed that clings tenaciously to the fruit. To remove the flesh from the seed, use a sharp knife to cut the fruit vertically, sliding the knife along the seed on one side. Repeat on the other side, which will give you 2 large pieces. Then cut away the remaining meat, and remove the peel from all the pieces. Chop or dice as desired.
- Be careful when eating mango—the juice will stain your clothing.
- *See also* FRUIT, GENERAL

MAPLE SYRUP

- There are several kinds of "maple" syrup on the market today. *Pure maple syrup* is sap that's been boiled until much of the water has evaporated. It has a more subtle flavor and isn't as sweet or viscous as artificial maple syrups. *Maple-flavored syrup* is a mixture of a low-cost syrup (such as corn syrup) and a small amount of pure maple syrup. *Pancake syrup* is nothing more than corn syrup flavored with artificial maple extract.
- Pure maple syrup is graded according to color and flavor, the highest grade being AA or Fancy. In general, the higher the grade the lighter the color and more delicate the flavor.
- Although pure maple syrup is more expensive than its imitators, its flavor is far superior.
- Pure maple syrup should be refrigerated after opening to keep mold from forming. It can be refrigerated for up to 1 year.
- Always heat refrigerated syrup (or at least bring it to room temperature) before pouring over pancakes or waffles.
- Heat a bottle (glass) of syrup by placing it in a pan of hot water over low heat. Or pour syrup into a pan and heat directly, then pour into a pitcher. Heat ½ cup of syrup in the microwave at HIGH (100 percent power) for 30 to 60 seconds, depending on how cold it is; slightly longer for a larger amount.

- Although crystallized syrup can be used, if mold develops discard it.
- The crystals in syrup will melt when the syrup's heated.
- Make a delicious maple butter by beating 1 stick (½ cup) softened, unsalted butter with a pinch of salt until creamy. Beating constantly, slowly drizzle in ¼ cup pure maple syrup.
- Maple syrup is great drizzled over ice cream, puddings, cakes, hot cereals, baked apples—you name it!
- Substitute maple syrup for honey in baked goods like cakes, pies, breads. It's also great in frostings.
- Maple syrup makes a delicious glaze for carrots, ham or ribs.
- *See also* SYRUPS

MARGARINE

- There are many different styles of margarine on the market today. *Regular margarines* are 80 percent fat; *diet margarines* contain 40 percent fat and a relatively high proportion of water. *Soft margarines* are made entirely with vegetable oil and specially processed so they're spreadable. The light, fluffy *whipped margarines* have had air (sometimes equal to half the volume) beaten into them. *Liquid margarines* have been processed to be soft enough to be squeezable when cold; they come in pliable bottles. There are also *butter-margarine blends,* which are usually proportioned 40 to 60 percent respectively.
- Margarines lowest in cholesterol are made from a high percentage of polyunsaturated *liquid* safflower or corn oil.
- If you're watching your cholesterol, check the margarine label for the word "hydrogenated," which refers to the process of hardening unsaturated oil into a semisolid. This transforms it into a saturated fat, which destroys any benefits the oil had as a polyunsaturate.
- Regular margarine can be substituted for butter satisfactorily in most recipes with the exception of certain preparations like pastries (Danish pastry, croissants and puff pastry) and toffee candy.
- Never substitute diet, soft or whipped margarine in recipes calling for regular butter or margarine. These products contain too much air and the results could be disastrous.
- Some cookies may be affected if you substitute margarine for butter. The dough will be slightly softer, which can affect cookies that should have a specific shape
- *See also* BUTTER; FATS AND OILS; LARD

MARINADES; MARINATING [MAIR-ih-nayd; MAIR-ih-nay-ting]

- Marinades flavor and tenderize foods. Most marinades contain an acid ingredient (like lemon juice, tomato juice, vinegar or wine), which tenderizes tough cuts of meat.

▶ Always marinate food in a glass or ceramic container. Most marinades contain acidic ingredients such as vinegar or lemon juice, which react with metal and cause off-flavors in the food, as well as damage to the container.

▶ The marinade should completely cover the food. If it doesn't, turn the food every couple of hours so it's evenly exposed to the marinade.

▶ To save on cleanup, marinate food in a large plastic bag with a zip-closure seal. Set the bag on a large plate and refrigerate, turning the bag occasionally to distribute the marinade. There are now 1- and 2-gallon size plastic bags, the larger being ideal for foods such as roasts and whole fish.

▶ Foods should be covered and refrigerated while they are marinating. Letting them stand at room temperature encourages bacteria growth.

▶ Larger cuts of meat, such as a beef roast, benefit from longer marinating— up to 2 days.

▶ Pricking large cuts with the tines of a fork helps the marinade penetrate the flesh.

▶ Skirt steaks will be more tender and flavorful if you cut diagonal slashes about ⅛-inch-deep in the flesh before marinating.

▶ A marinade often makes a delicious sauce for the finished fish, meat, or poultry that's been marinating in it. Just be sure to boil the marinade for 5 minutes before serving to destroy any harmful bacteria that may have been transferred from the raw food.

▶ Don't baste food during the last 15 minutes of cooking time with a marinade that hasn't been boiled. Otherwise, the cooking time may be too short to kill any bacteria that was transferred from the raw meat to the marinade. An option is to reserve some of the marinade *before* food is marinated in it and use it for late basting.

▶ Salad dressing is an easy, instant marinade for vegetables like bell peppers, mushrooms or tomatoes.

MARSHMALLOWS

▶ Store marshmallows in a tightly sealed plastic bag in the freezer and you won't have to worry about them drying out.

▶ *Marshmallow yields:* 1 pound regular marshmallows = about 60; 1 cup = 6 to 7 whole or snipped. One 10½-ounce package miniature marshmallows = 400 pieces; 1 cup = about 83.

▶ Marshmallows are easier to cut if they're frozen.

▶ Scissors are perfect for snipping marshmallows into the right size.

▶ When snipping room-temperature marshmallows, dip scissors in cold water whenever necessary.

▶ If marshmallows have gotten hard, tightly seal them in a plastic bag with 2 to 3 slices fresh white bread (not French or Italian) and let stand for 3 days.

M

▸ For kids' birthday parties, top home-baked cupcakes with a whole marsh-mallow about 3 minutes before removing them from the oven. The marshmallow will melt and form a frosting.

MARZIPAN [MAHR-zih-pan] *see* ALMOND PASTE

MAYONNAISE [MAY-uh-nayz; may-uh-NAYZ]

▸ A wide selection of mayonnaise can be found in markets today—from real to imitation, and in styles ranging from nonfat to low-fat to regular. The calorie count for 1 tablespoon ranges from 100 for the real stuff, to about 8 for the nonfat, imitation style.

▸ Commercial mayonnaise can be stored, unopened, in a cool, dark place for up to 4 months. Once opened, refrigerate for up to 6 months. Home-made mayonnaise should be covered and refrigerated for no more than 1 week. Mayonnaise will separate if frozen.

▸ Once you taste homemade mayonnaise, it'll be hard to go back to com-mercial-style mayo—they're like completely different foods. Here are a few simple tips for successful homemade mayonnaise. First of all, the eggs and oil should be the same temperature, so remove the eggs from the refrigerator at least 30 minutes before using. Beat the egg yolks (or whole egg) with the salt and *half* the vinegar or lemon juice called for in the recipe, then begin beating in the oil—a few drops at a time—until 2 to 3 tablespoons oil have been added. At that point, you can begin adding the oil in a fine stream. When all the oil has been added, lightly beat in the remaining vinegar or lemon juice.

▸ The food processor makes homemade mayonnaise foolproof. Most newer machines have a feed-tube food pusher with a tiny hole in the bottom, which was specifically designed with mayonnaise in mind. Use the metal blade to process the egg yolks, salt and vinegar, then fill the food pusher with oil and let the machine do the work. The oil will drip a steady drizzle into the running machine at the perfect speed for emulsification to take place.

▸ Extra-virgin olive oil can overpower the flavor of homemade mayon-naise. Better to use either a mild olive oil, or half extra-virgin and half vegetable oil.

▸ Homemade mayonnaise made with whole eggs won't be quite as rich as one made only with egg yolks.

▸ If you live in an area where salmonella-infected eggs are a problem (mainly in the Northeastern and Mid-Atlantic states), eating homemade mayonnaise could be harmful to your health. If your eggs are suspect and you don't want to risk food poisoning, either make homemade mayo from pasteurized liquid whole eggs or use commercial mayonnaise.

▸ To substitute pasteurized liquid whole eggs for egg yolks in a homemade mayonnaise recipe, use ⅛ cup for each egg yolk. Otherwise, if a mayo recipe calls for 2 egg yolks, use ¼ cup pasteurized liquid whole eggs. One large shell egg = ¼ cup pasteurized liquid whole eggs.

▸ If homemade mayonnaise curdles, start over with 1 beaten egg yolk and beat in separated mayo a drop at a time, beating continually.

▸ Another method for correcting curdled mayonnaise is to slowly drizzle in boiling-hot water, beating constantly. Start with about 1 tablespoon, adding only enough to reemulsify the mayo.

▸ Give a fresh taste to commercial mayonnaise by stirring in 1 to 2 teaspoons of good wine vinegar, lemon juice or lime juice.

▸ If mayonnaise is too thick (homemade or commercial), gradually stir in whipping cream or evaporated milk until it reaches the desired consistency.

▸ The next time a recipe calls for mayonnaise, try a mixture of half mayo, half sour cream. The result will be a lighter, less salty flavor. If you want to lighten the calorie count, use the low-fat versions of one or both.

▸ Lighten the calorie content of regular mayo by combining it with plain, nonfat yogurt. The proportion is up to you, depending on how piquant you like it.

▸ Many manufacturers are now producing a commercial mustard mayonnaise. Make your own by simply adding mustard to taste to homemade or store-bought mayo (start with about 1 teaspoon mustard per ½ cup mayo). Use this tangy mixture in salads (like egg or tuna) and salad dressings, as a sandwich spread, or to brush over meat such as baked ham or pork loin.

▸ Personalize mayonnaise by stirring in herbs or other flavorings. Add minced fresh herbs like basil, dill, mint or watercress; or minced fresh or sautéed garlic (cooked garlic has a milder flavor); or finely grated lemon zest; or horseradish; or minced sun-dried tomatoes; or curry or chili powder; or drained pickle relish; or mustard; or crumbled blue cheese; or chopped onions or shallots; or whatever else you like!

▸ Warm mayonnaise makes a wonderful sauce for chicken, fish or vegetables. Season it first with minced herbs, then let stand for several hours in the refrigerator to enhance the flavors. Heat gently, just until warm, then spoon over the food to be sauced.

▸ *See also* EGGS

MEASURING

▸ Accurate measurements are important in all cooking, but probably most crucial in baking recipes.

▸ Never measure ingredients directly over the mixing bowl. A slip of the wrist and flour, sugar, salt, etc., could spill over the measuring cup or spoon and into the rest of the ingredients, ruining the lot.

- There are two different types of measuring cups. *Dry measuring cups* and *liquid measuring cups*. Dry measuring cups come in nested sets which can include 2-cup, 1-cup, ½-cup, ⅓-cup, ¼-cup and ⅛-cup sizes. Liquid measuring cups range in size from 1 to 8 cups (the latter really more of a measuring "bowl").

- To use liquid measuring cups, pour in liquid, then read the measurement at eye level.

- Confused by the recipe term "dash"? For all intents, a dash is about ¹⁄₁₆ of a teaspoon. Many measuring spoon sets have ⅛-teaspoon measures, so use one and fill it about half full.

- The coffee measure that often comes with ground coffee equals 2 tablespoons (⅛ cup).

- Measure flour and confectioners' sugar by first stirring, then spooning into a dry measuring cup and leveling off with the straight edge of a knife. Don't tap or press the ingredient into the cup before measuring.

- Measure brown sugar by packing it down firmly into a dry measuring cup; level with a knife.

- For ingredients like nuts, coconut and chopped dried fruits, fill a dry measuring cup and level with your fingers.

- Measure shortening or softened butter and margarine by packing it into a dry measuring cup or measuring spoon, leveling with a knife. Butter or margarine in stick form can be measured by simply cutting off the amount needed (the wrapping will be marked)—1 stick = ½ cup or 8 tablespoons.

- To measure ground coffee, use 2 level tablespoons (1 coffee measure, ⅛ cup) for each 6 ounces (¾ cup) water.

- To determine the size of baking pans, muffin tins, etc., use a ruler to measure the diameter of the container's top from inside edge to inside edge. Measure the depth from the inside, bottom to the top.

- Measure the volume of a casserole or soufflé dish by filling it with water, then measuring the liquid. Such dishes are most commonly found in the following sizes: 1, 1½, 2 and 3 quarts.

- Before measuring syrupy sweeteners such as honey and corn syrup, lightly coat a measuring spoon or liquid measuring cup with vegetable oil. Every drop of the syrup will easily slip out. The same result can be accomplished if you measure the oil or fat called for in a recipe and then use the same (unwashed) utensil as the measure.

- If you keep a scoop (available at supermarkets or specialty shops) in each canister (flour, sugar, etc.), it makes scooping the ingredients into a measuring cup a lot easier.

- Put a sheet of waxed paper under the cup into which you're scooping sugar, flour, cocoa, etc. That way, you can easily return any spills to the canister.

M

▶ A kitchen scale comes in handy for measuring smaller amounts from a larger bag. For instance, if a recipe calls for 8 ounces of nuts, and you have a 12-ounce bag, you can measure the exact amount out in the scale.

▶ Some common measurements and equivalents:

1 teaspoon	=	⅓ tablespoon; 60 drops
3 teaspoons	=	1 tablespoon
½ tablespoon	=	1½ teaspoons
1 tablespoon	=	3 teaspoons; ½ fluid ounce
2 tablespoons	=	⅛ cup; 1 fluid ounce
3 tablespoons	=	1½ fluid ounces; 1 jigger
4 tablespoons	=	¼ cup; 2 fluid ounces
8 tablespoons	=	½ cup; 4 fluid ounces
16 tablespoons	=	1 cup; 8 fluid ounces; ½ pint
⅛ cup	=	2 tablespoons; 1 fluid ounce
¼ cup	=	4 tablespoons; 2 fluid ounces
⅓ cup	=	5 tablespoons plus 1 teaspoon
⅜ cup	=	¼ cup plus 2 tablespoons
½ cup	=	8 tablespoons; 4 fluid ounces
⅔ cup	=	10 tablespoons plus 2 teaspoons
⅝ cup	=	½ cup plus 2 tablespoons
¾ cup	=	12 tablespoons; 6 fluid ounces
⅞ cup	=	¾ cup plus 2 tablespoons
1 cup	=	16 tablespoons; ½ pint; 8 fluid ounces
2 cups	=	1 pint; 16 fluid ounces
1 pint	=	2 cups; 16 fluid ounces
1 quart	=	2 pints; 4 cups; 32 fluid ounces
1 gallon	=	4 quarts; 8 pints; 16 cups; 128 fluid ounces

▶ Use the following table to figure out metric conversions. The same number is used either way—the difference is whether you divide or multiply with it. Otherwise, when you're converting to metric (as from cups to liters), you would *multiply* the number of cups by .236 to get the equivalent in liters. If converting from metric (as from liters to cups), you *divide* the measurement being converted (liters) by .236 to get the cup equivalency. Whether converting to or from metric, it's important to adjust *all* measurements. Otherwise, the proportions of the ingredients could be critically imbalanced.

Divide:

milliliters by 4.93 to get teaspoons

milliliters by 14.79 to get tablespoons

milliliters by 29.57 to get fluid ounces

milliliters by 236.59 to get cups

liters by .236 to get cups

milliliters by 473.18 to get pints

liters by .473 to get pints

milliliters by 946.36 to get quarts

liters by .946 to get quarts

liters by 3.785 to get gallons

grams by 28.35 to get ounces

kilograms by .454 to get pounds

centimeters by 2.54 to get inches

Multiply:

teaspoons by 4.93 to get milliliters

tablespoons by 14.79 to get milliliters

fluid ounces by 29.57 to get milliliters

cups by 236.59 to get milliliters

cups by .236 to get liters

pints by 473.18 to get milliliters

pints by .473 to get liters

quarts by 946.36 to get milliliters

quarts by .946 to get liters

gallons by 3.785 to get liters

ounces by 28.35 to get grams

pounds by .454 to get kilograms

inches by 2.54 to get centimeters

M

MEATBALLS

- ▶ See the following MEATLOAF tips for general information on making a meatball or meatloaf mixture.
- ▶ To quickly and evenly shape meatballs, spoon the mixture onto a sheet of plastic wrap or waxed paper. Pat into the thickness commensurate with what you want the meatball's diameter to be. Otherwise, if you want 2-inch meatballs, form the mixture into a square that's 2 inches thick. Cut that square into 2-inch squares, then roll the cubes into balls. Using this method, you can form meatballs into smaller or larger sizes.
- ▶ Or you can form the meatball mixture into a log 2 inches in diameter (for

2-inch meatballs), then cut the log into 2-inch lengths and roll the pieces into balls.

► Or use a small ice cream scoop to shape uniform meatballs.

► Dampen your hands with cold water before rolling a meat mixture into balls.

► Use a gentle touch when forming meatballs or the mixture may fall apart on you. Conversely, it can become too compacted and the resulting meatball will not be as tender.

► Put a ½-inch chunk of cheese or cold herb butter in the center of a meatball, forming the meat around it. By the time the meatballs are done, the filling will be melted and ooze out deliciously with every bite. The center surprise can also be a small sautéed mushroom, small roasted garlic clove, a half teaspoon of chutney . . . you name it!

► *See also* GROUND BEEF

MEATLOAF

► Choose ground round for making meatloaf—it has less fat (which would be absorbed by breadcrumbs) than regular ground beef and more fat than ground sirloin, which would produce a dry meatloaf.

► For a moister, more tender meatloaf, use coarsely ground meat instead of finely ground.

► If you don't like getting your hands messy when mixing a meatloaf mixture, put the ingredients in a large, zip-closure plastic bag, seal, then squish the contents together until well mixed.

► A cup of grated cheese makes meatloaf magic when added to the mixture before baking. For a crowning touch, sprinkle the top with another ½ cup grated cheese 15 minutes before the meatloaf is done.

► For a juicy, more flavorful meatloaf, add ⅓ cup of liquid (tomato or vegetable juice, wine, beef broth, etc.) per pound of meat.

► Substituting red wine or dark beer for any liquid called for in the recipe will enrich a meatloaf's flavor.

► Using soft breadcrumbs instead of dry breadcrumbs will produce a moister, more tender meatloaf.

► Add fiber and nutrition by substituting ⅓ cup oat bran for ⅓ cup breadcrumbs. If your meatloaf recipe doesn't include breadcrumbs, add ¼ cup oat bran plus 2 tablespoons liquid such as milk, water, beef broth, etc.

► For a moist, delicious meatloaf that helps cut back on meat intake, substitute a cup of finely grated potato or carrot (or half of each) for a quarter pound of the meat. Or add ½ cup mashed potatoes to the mix.

► Double a meatloaf recipe and freeze one for future use.

► If you make meatloaf often, but don't like the idea of the meat sitting in rendered fat while it bakes, make a special "meatloaf pan." Buy an inexpensive metal loaf pan (or use an aluminum foil pan) and use an awl

M

or ice pick to punch holes in the bottom at 1½-inch intervals (punch from the inside out). Put the meatloaf mixture in the pierced pan and place it on a rack set inside a baking pan. That way, the grease will drain out as the meatloaf bakes, which gets rid of some of those pesky calories.

▶ Prevent meatloaf from sticking by spraying the pan with nonstick vegetable spray, or coat it lightly with vegetable oil. This also speeds cleanup.

▶ Make individual servings by baking meatloaf in large, greased muffin tins. Small meatloaves bake faster so watch the timing.

▶ Form a meatloaf mixture into 2 or 3 long, thin shapes about the diameter of a baguette or loaf of cocktail rye. Bake, cool, then refrigerate meatloaf until firm. Cut meatloaf thinly and serve on mustard-buttered bread slices, topped with a thin sliver of cornichon. Serve as an hors d'oeuvre.

▶ If you're planning to freeze a whole meatloaf, line the pan with foil, allowing enough overlap to cover and seal the finished loaf. Bake as usual, drain off grease and cool to room temperature before sealing the foil. Double wrap in a plastic bag and freeze for up to 6 months.

▶ Once the meatloaf mixture has been placed in the pan, press down on it firmly with the back of a large spoon to level the surface and compress the mixture.

▶ Rubbing the top of a meatloaf mixture smooth with cold water will minimize cracking.

▶ About 20 minutes before the meatloaf is done, cover the top with a 1-inch-thick layer of mashed potatoes. Brush lightly with olive oil or melted butter, or sprinkle with about ¼ cup grated cheese, and return to oven. You can also mix the cheese with the mashed potatoes before spreading them on top of the loaf. If the potato crust isn't as brown as you'd like, run it under the broiler for a minute or so.

▶ Make sure your meatloaf is done by checking it with a meat thermometer—it should register 170°F.

▶ Use a bulb baster to remove excess grease from around a cooked meatloaf.

▶ After removing the baked meatloaf from the oven, run a knife around the edges, then let it stand in the pan for 10 to 15 minutes. This allows it to "set" and makes it easier to remove and cut.

▶ If you're tired of the proverbial meatloaf sandwich, crumble leftover meatloaf and use it in chili. Or combine it with a sauce and serve over rice or noodles.

▶ *See also* GROUND BEEF

MEATS, GENERAL

▶ The average amount of meat to allow per person is: boneless meat—4 to 5 ounces; bone-in cuts like chops and steaks—8 ounces; mostly bone cuts like shanks—10 ounces.

▶ A meat cut with a high proportion of fat and bone will yield fewer servings than a boneless cut. For instance, bony meats, like spareribs, yield 1 to 2 servings per pound. Chops and bone-in steaks have a moderate amount of bone and will therefore yield 2 to 3 servings per pound, whereas you can figure about 4 servings per pound for boneless roasts, ground meats, liver, etc.

▶ Save time by having your butcher bone meat and chicken, cut meat for stew, or cut pockets in roasts and thick chops. It's a free service that will reduce your time in the kitchen.

▶ The process of freezing and thawing meat causes it to lose some of its natural juices, so always try to buy meat that hasn't been frozen.

▶ As a general rule, fresh meat should be stored in the coldest part of the refrigerator for up to 2 days for ground meat, 3 days for other cuts. Ground meats can be frozen, wrapped airtight, for up to 3 months, solid cuts for up to 6 months.

▶ When freezing ground-meat patties, steaks or chops, separate them with squares of plastic wrap. That way you can pry the pieces apart and defrost as needed.

▶ If meat has been frozen, defrost it overnight in the refrigerator. Or place the meat (still in its freezer-proof wrapping) in a large bowl of cool water. Change the water every half hour until meat is defrosted.

▶ Whether slicing meat or cutting it into chunks, you'll get the most tender result if you cut against the grain.

▶ It's easier to slice meat thinly for quick-cooking dishes like stir-frys if you first freeze the meat for 30 to 60 minutes (depending on the meat's thickness).

▶ Freezing chunks of meat for 30 minutes will also make grinding it easier.

▶ Avoid commercial meat tenderizers that contain MSG (monosodium glutamate) or salt, both of which will extract some of the meat's natural juices.

▶ Papaya contains papain, an enzyme used chiefly in meat tenderizers. Make your own tenderizer by pureeing papaya and rubbing it all over the meat's surface. Or soak the meat in papaya juice, available at many supermarkets and most natural food stores. Cover and refrigerate the meat for 3 hours. Scrape off and discard the papaya puree, pat the meat dry and cook as desired.

M

▶ Tea can also be used as a meat tenderizer, particularly for stew meat. In a Dutch oven, sear chunks of stew meat in fat or oil until very well browned. Add 2 cups strong black tea, bring to a boil, then cover and simmer for 30 minutes. Add stock or whatever liquid you wish, vegetables, herbs, etc., and continue to cook the stew as usual.

▶ Time-honored ways of tenderizing tough pieces of meat include pounding with a mallet, marinating, and long, slow, moist-heat cooking such as braising or stewing.

▶ Never tenderize a piece of meat by piercing it with a fork. During cooking, the natural juices will drain out of the holes you've created.

▶ If possible, remove meat from the refrigerator an hour before cooking.

▶ For well-browned meat (steaks, chops, etc.), make sure the meat's surface is thoroughly dry. This is particularly important with meat that's been marinated. Paper towels make an excellent blotter.

▶ Unless the cut is very lean, it's often unnecessary to add fat or oil for browning meat—simply brush the bottom of the pan lightly with oil. If more fat is necessary, make sure the temperature of the oil is very hot, but not smoking, before adding the meat. Whether or not you use added fat, the pan should be very hot when the meat is added.

▶ Dusting meat lightly with flour will facilitate browning when searing, sautéing or otherwise cooking it in a little oil.

▶ Salt leaches some of the juices from the meat, so it's best to salt toward the end of the cooking time or after the meat is cooked.

▶ When browning meat, add 1 teaspoon sugar to the fat; heat, stirring often until the fat is hot, then brown the meat in it. The sugar caramelizes and gives the meat a beautiful color and flavor with negligible sweetness.

▶ Remove excess fat from a skillet with a baster.

▶ Cutting into a steak or chop to determine its doneness releases some of its juices. Though it takes practice, you can tell whether a steak's done to your liking by using the touch technique. Press the meat lightly with your finger: if it's soft, the meat's rare; if it resists slightly but springs back, it's medium-rare; if the meat is quite firm, it's well done.

▶ Instead of braising or stewing meat cuts in water, try more flavorful liquids like wine, beer, stock or vegetable juice.

▶ Because the juices in meat shift to the center while it cooks, the exterior becomes dry. Letting the meat "rest" for 10 minutes after it's finished cooking allows the juices to redistribute throughout the flesh and set. This produces an evenly moist result and makes the meat easier to carve. Keep the meat warm during this rest period by covering it lightly with foil.

▶ Don't worry if four people show up for dinner and you only have two servings of meat. Simply cut the meat in small pieces, combine it with vegetables and a sauce, and serve over rice.

▶ Chop leftover cooked meat and use it in salads, soups, stir-fries, dumplings, omelet fillings, stuffed peppers or acorn squash, meatloaf, pasta sauce, tacos or burritos. Or simply slice and use it for sandwiches, or combine with a sauce and serve over rice.

▶ When freezing leftover meat, think about how it will be used and cut it accordingly. You may want to slice, dice or chop it. Measure the quantity (1 cup, etc.) and label the meat accordingly, including how it should be used (stew, sauté, sandwiches, etc.)

▶ The USDA's Meat and Poultry Hotline is just a phone call away for detailed information on topics including food handling, food safety and understanding meat and poultry labels. Call 1-800-535-4555 Monday through Friday from 10 A.M. to 4 P.M., eastern time. In the Washington, D.C., area, call 447-3333.

▶ *See also* BACON; BEEF; CHICKEN; GROUND BEEF; HAM; HAMBURGERS; KIDNEYS; LAMB; LIVER; MEATLOAF; PORK; POULTRY; ROASTS; ROCK CORNISH GAME HENS; STEAKS; SAUSAGE; SWEETBREADS; TURKEY; VEAL

MEAT TENDERIZERS *see* MEATS, GENERAL

MEAT THERMOMETER *see* THERMOMETERS

MELONS

▶ There are two broad classes of melons—watermelon and muskmelon, the latter of which includes cantaloupe, casaba, Crenshaw, honeydew, Persian and Santa Claus (or Christmas) melon.

▶ When ripe, muskmelons will give slightly when pressed with your finger at the blossom end; their odor will be sweet and perfumy. Choose melons that are heavy for their size; avoid those that are soft, shriveled or moldy.

▶ These characteristics indicate ripeness in the following specific melons: **cantaloupe**—a thick, well-raised, cream-colored netting over a golden-green rind; **casaba**—an even-colored yellow rind with a slightly wrinkled appearance; **Crenshaw**—a golden green, smooth, slightly ribbed rind; **honeydew**—an almost indistinguishable wrinkling on the creamy yellow rind's surface, often detectable only by touch; **Persian**—pale green rind with a delicate netting; **Santa Claus**—oval-shaped with a splotchy green and yellow skin with stripes.

▶ If you can't find a ripe melon, choose another fruit. Melons picked before they're mature will never reach their full flavor potential.

▶ To verify if a melon was picked before its time, check the perimeter of the crater at the stem end for jagged edges. That's a signal that the melon was yanked from the vine before it was perfectly ripe.

▶ Slightly underripe melons should be stored at room temperature (preferably in a paper bag pierced in several places). Adding an apple to the bag will speed ripening.

▶ Store whole, ripe melons in the refrigerator for up to 5 days.

▶ Store cut melons in the refrigerator, sealed in plastic wrap, for up to 3 days. Cut melons absorb other food odors easily, and their own odor can ruin other foods, so make sure the wrapping is airtight.

▶ Use a large spoon or an ice cream scoop to remove the seeds from a melon.

▶ Leaving the seeds in a halved melon during storage will help keep it fresh.

▶ Melon will be fuller in flavor if you serve it at room temperature, or only slightly chilled. If melon has been refrigerated, let it stand at room tem-

M

perature for 30 to 60 minutes (depending on the size) before serving.

▸ Give underripe melon more flavor by cutting it into chunks or melon balls and marinating it for 3 to 4 hours in a mixture of 2 cups orange juice, ½ cup chopped fresh mint leaves, ½ teaspoon ground cinnamon and ¼ teaspoon ground ginger. For extra sweetness, add a little sugar or honey to the mix.

▸ Hollow out a small cantaloupe half, line it with lettuce leaves and use it as a serving bowl for fruit salad.

▸ *See also* FRUIT, GENERAL; WATERMELON

MERINGUE; MERINGUES [mer-RANG]

▸ There are two fundamental kinds of meringue. **Soft meringue**, used as a topping for pies, puddings and other desserts such as Baked Alaska, is baked only until the peaks are nicely browned and the valleys golden. **Hard meringue** has a higher proportion of sugar, is formed into tiny confections or into containers for fruit, ice cream, etc., and then baked at a very low temperature (200°F). **Italian meringue**, made by beating hot sugar syrup into stiffly beaten egg whites, can be used to create either soft or hard meringue.

▸ See EGGS for general information on egg whites

▸ When adding sugar to egg whites to create meringue, first beat the whites at high speed until they form soft peaks. Beating constantly, gradually add sugar, 1 to 2 tablespoons at a time. Continue beating until sugar is dissolved and whites are glossy and stiff.

▸ Whenever adding things like grated chocolate or ground nuts to a meringue, fold them in gently so as not to deflate the mixture.

▸ Making meringue on a humid day isn't a good idea because the sugar absorbs moisture, which can create a meringue that's soft and gooey, or one that beads.

▸ To keep meringue from "weeping" (exuding moisture), blend 1 teaspoon cornstarch with the sugar before beating it into the egg whites.

▸ For high-rise meringue, blend about ½ teaspoon baking powder into the sugar before beating it into the egg whites.

M

▸ To make sure all the sugar is dissolved in a meringue, rub a little of it between your thumb and index finger. It should feel silky smooth, not gritty.

▸ Bake a soft meringue according to recipe directions unless you live in an area where bacterial contamination of eggs is a problem. In that case, here's a method that will make meringue-topped pies safe to eat: Spread an *even* layer of meringue (don't mound it in the center) over the surface of a *hot* pie filling. Bake at 350° for 15 minutes.

▸ Beads on the surface of a baked meringue can be caused by several factors: humid weather, the sugar didn't dissolve completely during the beating process (usually because it was added too fast); the meringue wasn't immediately baked or was underbaked or baked at too high a temperature; or the pie wasn't cooled slowly enough.

► Create a delicate, crispy "crust" on your soft meringue topping by sprinkling it with sifted confectioners' sugar just before baking.

► A meringue pie topping won't crack if you cool it at room temperature (away from drafts!) before refrigerating.

► A baking sheet lined with parchment paper is the best surface on which to bake hard meringues. Or grease the baking sheet with solid vegetable shortening.

► For meringue pie shells, grease the pan with vegetable shortening.

► Hard meringues are generally baked at a very low temperature (200°F) for a long period of time to dry them out and make them crisp.

► Be sure to let hard meringues dry completely in the oven. Removing them prematurely can result in a gummy, rather than crisp, texture.

► Hard meringues that are done will easily peel away from parchment paper or release from the baking sheet. If yours stick, return them to the oven for a few minutes. Wait until the meringues have cooled slightly before removing them from the paper or baking sheet.

► Check a meringue pie shell for doneness by flicking it with your finger. It'll sound hollow when it's done.

► Store hard meringues wrapped airtight first in a plastic bag, then in a sealed container, for up to 2 weeks. In humid climates meringues should be frozen, and will keep for up to 3 months.

► *See also* EGGS (*Egg whites*)

MICROWAVE COOKING

► *Note:* Timing in the following tips will depend on the wattage and size of your oven.

► Did you know that microwave ovens work by converting electric energy into microwave energy—short, high-frequency electromagnetic waves similar to those emitted by ordinary daylight and radio waves? This energy makes food molecules vibrate at an incredibly fast rate, creating the friction that heats and cooks the food. The reason microwaves travel so extraordinarily fast—and therefore cook food so quickly—is because they're so short. These waves are attracted to the fat, moisture and sugar in food, and cook from the outside in, only penetrating to a depth of about 1 ½ to 2 inches. Microwaves cook food from all directions (top, bottom and sides) at once. The center of the food is generally cooked by heat conduction.

► The most important tip for microwave cooking is to *read the instructions for your particular model.* It's vital that you know the wattage of your microwave oven. If a recipe has been tested using a 700-watt oven, and yours

M

is a 500-watt oven, the timing will need to be adjusted.

▶ Most microwave cookbooks are written for 700 watt ovens. To convert the cooking time to a lower-wattage oven: *For a 650-watt oven,* add 10 seconds (or less) for each minute stated in the recipe; *for a 600-watt oven,* add 20 seconds for each minute stated in the recipe; *for a 500-watt oven,* add 40 seconds for each minute stated in the recipe.

▶ Many characteristics affect how a microwave oven cooks food: Shape—thin pieces cook faster than thick; fat and/or bone distribution; density; starting temperature; and the amount of moisture, sugar and fat the food contains. Foods that are low in moisture and/or high in fat or sugar cook faster.

▶ Microwave timing also depends on the volume of food being cooked. You can't double a microwave recipe and expect it to cook in the same time. Two potatoes can take almost twice as long to cook as one.

▶ Most microwave ovens have spots where the waves don't cover as evenly as the rest of the space. Ovens equipped with a turntable eliminate this problem by rotating the food. If you don't have a turntable, however, it helps to know ahead of time where the hot spots are so you can turn the dish for even cooking. Check your oven by lining the bottom, corner-to-corner, with waxed paper. Spread the paper almost to the corners with a ⅛-inch layer of pancake batter. Cook at HIGH (100 percent power), checking every 30 seconds, until the batter begins to cook. In most ovens, some of the batter will be cooked through, while other spots are still wet, which tells you exactly where food cooks fastest and enables you to adjust or stir as necessary.

▶ Lining the bottom of your microwave oven with waxed paper will keep cleanup at a minimum.

▶ Inexpensive turntables are available in the kitchenware section of most department stores and many specialty shops. Be sure to measure your oven before buying one to be sure it will fit.

▶ Nonmetal containers are used in microwave ovens because microwaves pass through them (unlike metal, which deflects the waves), thus the containers remain relatively cool even though the food becomes quite hot. During long cooking periods, however, the food can heat the dish, so be careful when removing it from the microwave oven.

▶ Metal can cause arcing (sparking) in a microwave oven so don't use plates or cups that have a metallic design or trim, or containers (such as some insulated cups) that might have metal supports in the handles. Lead crystal should also be avoided because the lead deflects the microwaves, which not only slows the cooking process, but could damage the oven.

▶ If you're unsure if a dish or other container contains metal, use this test: Place 8 ounces of cool water in a 1-cup glass measure. Set it in the microwave oven next to or in the center of the dish in question. Microwave for 1 minute. If the dish remains cool, it's suitable for microwave cooking.

▶ Oddly enough, a small amount of aluminum foil can be used in microwave ovens as long as it doesn't touch the sides of the oven. If parts of a food are cooking too fast (such as the tips of chicken wings), place a tiny aluminum foil shield over them.

▶ Some foods can be cooked on paper plates or paper towels—just make sure any you use are labeled "safe for microwave cooking."

▶ Plastic containers that aren't specifically made for microwave use may warp or melt during prolonged cooking.

▶ If possible, cook food in a round dish (like a glass cake pan). Food in the corners of square or rectangular dishes overcooks because microwaves concentrate there.

▶ Using a different size or shape container than a microwave recipe directs can make a noticeable difference in how long it takes a dish to cook.

▶ As a rule of thumb, cover any food that would be covered during conventional methods.

▶ A paper plate makes a sturdy, disposable cover for microwaved food.

▶ Plastic wrap makes a great dish cover but there's some concern that at high temperatures the plasticizers in some brands could migrate to food in contact with the wrap. Though so far there's no conclusive proof of toxicity, why take a chance? Avoid the problem by not allowing the wrap to touch the food during prolonged cooking where heat gets very high.

▶ When an airtight plastic-wrapped container is removed from the microwave oven, the wrap often collapses onto the food. This problem can be avoided simply by poking a tiny hole in the center of the plastic wrap after it's stretched tight over the container. Or the dish can be vented by turning back a corner of the plastic to allow some of the steam to escape while the food is cooking.

▶ When removing plastic wrap from a dish that's been in a microwave oven, always fold back the side away from you first to avoid the escaping scalding-hot steam. Only use plastic wrap that's labeled "microwavable."

▶ Waxed paper is a good food cover when you want much of the steam to escape.

M

▶ Microwave-safe paper towels are great for covering foods that spatter, such as bacon.

▶ Seal microwave cooking bags with unflavored dental floss in lieu of twist ties.

▶ Use your microwave probe to heat liquids, such as those in which to dissolve yeast (105° to 110°F), or for scalding milk (180°F).

▶ Room-temperature food cooks faster than refrigerated or frozen foods.

▶ Most vegetables cook beautifully in a microwave oven—they keep their color and nutrients better than with most other cooking methods.

▶ Cut food into uniform pieces so that it will cook evenly. Small or thin pieces will cook more quickly than large pieces.

▶ Because microwaves cook food at the outer edge of a plate first, always arrange the thickest or densest part at the outside of the dish. For instance, arrange the meaty part of chicken legs at the edge of a plate, with the drumsticks pointed toward the center.

▶ Likewise, it's important to stir foods like casseroles and puddings to distribute the food for even cooking.

▶ Dishes of foods that can't be stirred should be rotated a half turn (unless the oven has a turntable) halfway through the cooking time. This allows for any hot spots in a microwave oven.

▶ Never microwave foods like egg yolks, chicken livers or whole potatoes or tomatoes without first piercing them with a fork. Foods with an unpierced skin (or membrane in the case of the egg yolk) form pressure within their casing and can easily explode, making a mess of your microwave oven.

▶ Get a head start on grilling large cuts of meat or whole chickens by cooking them in the microwave partway while the coals preheat.

▶ To allow for variances in oven wattage, always check food for doneness at the minimum cooking time given in a recipe.

▶ Don't omit the standing time called for in some microwave recipes. It's important because it allows heat conduction to finish the job of cooking.

▶ The microwave oven is great for melting chocolate. Four ounces of chocolate will take about 3 minutes at MEDIUM (50 percent) power in a 650- to 700-watt oven. The timing will vary depending on the oven and the type and amount of chocolate. White chocolate has a tendency to scorch easily, so should be handled with care.

▶ Thaw frozen juice concentrate in a flash by turning it into a glass measuring cup and cooking it at HIGH (100 percent power) for 30 to 60 seconds, stirring halfway through.

▶ Quickly bring a chunk of cheese to room temperature by heating at MEDIUM (50 percent power) for about a minute.

▶ To melt butter in a 600- to 700-watt oven at HIGH (100 percent power): 2 tablespoons cold butter will melt in about 45 seconds, ¼ cup in about 50 seconds, and ½ cup in about 1½ minutes. Residual heat will continue to melt the butter even after it's removed from the oven. Cover the container in which the butter is melting with a piece of waxed paper to protect against spatters.

▶ Soften a stick of butter to the spreadable stage at MEDIUM-LOW (30 percent power) for about 20 seconds.

▶ Caramelizing sugar is easy and fast in the microwave oven. Put the sugar in a glass measuring cup. No fuss, no muss!

▶ Crystallized honey or other syrups can be reliquified right in the jar or bottle. Simply remove the metal lid and cook at HIGH (100 percent power) for 15 to 60 seconds, depending on how full the container is.

▶ One of the microwave oven's best functions is reheating leftovers. Watch the food carefully—you don't want it to "cook," simply reheat.

▶ *See also* COOKING, GENERAL

MILK

▶ When you buy milk, check the pull date on the carton—you want the latest date. For instance, if it's June 1, choose a carton that's dated June 8 over one that's dated June 5.

▶ Pull dates are purposefully conservative—properly stored, most milk will be fine to use a week after the carton's date.

▶ To give fluid milk the longest life, make it the last thing you pick up before checking out of the market; refrigerate it as soon as you get home.

▶ The flavor of milk can be altered by ordinary daylight—even indirect light. Keep that in mind if you buy milk in clear glass or plastic bottles, keep them in the dark as much as possible.

▶ Extend storage life by up to a week by transferring milk in a cardboard carton to a screwtop glass container.

▶ Milk absorbs odors easily so always close opened containers.

▶ For the best flavor, serve milk icy cold from the refrigerator.

▶ Milk's storage life is reduced when allowed to sit out at room temperature for more than 30 minutes, as it would when put in a pitcher for serving. Instead of returning that milk to the carton, cover the pitcher with plastic wrap, refrigerate, and use within a couple of days.

▶ Though freezing changes milk's consistency, you can freeze a whole quart-carton of milk, double wrapped in a plastic bag, for up to 6 months. Or pour 1-cup amounts in small, zip-closure, freezer-proof bags and freeze. Defrost in the refrigerator.

▶ *Milk substitutions:* For 1 cup nonfat (skim) milk—⅓ cup dry nonfat milk plus ¾ cup water; for 1 cup sour milk—1 tablespoon lemon juice or white vinegar plus milk to equal 1 cup (let stand 5 minutes); for 1 cup whole milk—1 cup nonfat (skim) milk plus 2 tablespoons melted unsalted butter or margarine, or ½ cup evaporated whole milk plus ½ cup water, or ¼ cup dry whole milk plus ⅞ cup water.

▶ Milk that's begun to sour doesn't taste good to drink, but is perfectly fine to use in recipes for baked goods.

▶ Slightly soured milk can be substituted for buttermilk in baking recipes.

▶ Scalding milk was originally done to kill bacteria in milk—a process that's been rendered obsolete with pasteurization. Today, scalding most often serves to speed preparation and cooking time—for instance, warm milk melts fat and dissolves sugar more quickly.

- Before heating milk, rinse the pan with cold water to keep it from scorching and sticking.
- Milk scorches easily because the whey proteins sink and stick to the pan's bottom. Cooking over medium heat or in a double boiler will diminish the problem.
- Keep a skin from forming on heated milk either by covering the pan or by beating the milk so that a froth forms on the surface.
- There's no cure for the flavor of scorched milk. If that happens, throw it out and start anew.
- Milk products tend to curdle easily, especially when combined with certain foods. Fruits and vegetables, for instance, contain acid, which contributes to curdling.
- Warm milk before combining it with flour or other starch and it won't clump as easily.
- *See also* BUTTERMILK; CREAM; DRY MILK; EVAPORATED MILK; SWEETENED CONDENSED MILK; YOGURT

MINT

- The two most widely available varieties of mint today are peppermint and spearmint. There are several ways to distinguish them from each other. **Peppermint** has bright green leaves and purple-tinged stems. It has a slightly peppery flavor and is the more pungent of the two. **Spearmint** leaves can be either gray-green or true green; they have a milder flavor and fragrance.
- Choose mint with evenly colored leaves that show no sign of wilting.
- Store a bunch of mint in the refrigerator, stems down in a glass of water with a plastic bag over the leaves, for up to a week. Change the water every 2 days.
- Don't think of mint only for sweet dishes. It's wonderful in all manner of savory dishes and has long been used in many Asian cuisines.
- Mint has a particular affinity for tomatoes. The next time you make a tomato salad, add a little minced mint to the dressing. Or toss chopped mint with tomatoes, then dress the salad. Fresh tomatoes, mint and lemon zest make a wonderful pasta sauce.
- Mint makes an attractive garnish for fruit compotes or salads, some meats (like lamb) and drinks (the classics being iced tea and mint juleps).

MIXED DRINKS *see* LIQUORS, LIQUEURS AND MIXED DRINKS

MOLASSES

- Molasses comes in three basic forms: **dark molasses** is darker, thicker and less sweet than the milder flavored **light molasses; blackstrap molasses** is very thick, dark and somewhat bitter.

- ▸ The robust flavor of dark molasses makes it perfect for classics like gingerbread, shoofly pie, Indian pudding and Boston baked beans. The milder-flavored light molasses is often used as a pancake and waffle syrup. Blackstrap, most often found in natural food stores, is rarely used in cooking; in the United States, it's more commonly used as cattle food.
- ▸ Whether or not molasses is labeled "sulfured" or "unsulfured" depends on whether sulfur was used in the processing. In general, unsulfured molasses is lighter and has a cleaner sugarcane flavor.
- ▸ Store molasses, tightly sealed, in a cool, dark place at room temperature for up to 2 years.
- ▸ *Molasses yields:* 1 pound = 1⅓ cups.
- ▸ Light and dark molasses are interchangeable in recipes, the latter having a slightly more robust flavor.
- ▸ Before measuring molasses, lightly coat the measuring cup or spoon with vegetable oil. That way, the molasses will slide right out instead of clinging to the measuring implement. Or, measure the fat (shortening, butter, etc.) called for in a recipe and then use the same (unwashed) utensil to measure molasses.
- ▸ To counterbalance the natural acidity of molasses, add 1 teaspoon baking soda to the dry ingredients for each cup of molasses in recipes for baked goods.
- ▸ Baked goods with a high percentage of molasses tend to overbrown. Be on the safe side and reduce oven heat by 25°F.
- ▸ Molasses butter is wonderful on muffins, pancakes, waffles, etc. Beat 1 stick softened butter, 1 tablespoon brown sugar, ½ teaspoon pure vanilla extract and a pinch of salt together until creamy. Slowly drizzle in 1 tablespoon light or dark molasses, beating constantly until thoroughly incorporated. Cover and refrigerate for up to 5 days. Remove from refrigerator 30 minutes before serving.
- ▸ *See also* SYRUPS

MORTAR AND PESTLE [MOR-tuhr and PEHS-tuhl; PEHS-tl]

- ▸ Ceramic or marble mortars and pestles are superior to those made of wood because they don't absorb food odors and are easier to clean.
- ▸ If you use a mortar and pestle often, it's handy to have several sizes. Some are sold in nested sets of 3 mortars and 1 pestle. The smallest mortar is ideal for spices and seeds, the largest for mixtures such as pesto or brandade.

MSG (Monosodium Glutamate) [mon-uh-SOH-dee-uhm GLOO-tuh-mayt]

- ▸ MSG is derived from glutamic acid, one of the twenty-two natural amino acids.

M

▸ Though it has no pronounced flavor of its own, MSG has the ability to intensify the flavor of savory foods.

▸ Some people have negative MSG reactions, including headache, dizziness, flushing and burning sensations.

▸ If you're MSG-sensitive, you should know that MSG is hidden in many foods under other names. The Food and Drug Administration (FDA) doesn't require a separate MSG listing when any of the following (MSG-laden) ingredients are present: hydrolyzed vegetable protein, hydrolyzed plant protein, Kombu extract, and natural flavoring or seasoning.

MUFFINS

▸ Make greasing muffin cups a breeze by using nonstick vegetable spray.

▸ If you don't want to get your fingers messy, use a crumpled piece of paper towel dipped into shortening for greasing muffin cups.

▸ Never grease muffin cups that won't be used—the grease will burn and make a mess of your pan.

▸ Put 2 or 3 tablespoons water in unused muffin cups to keep the pan from warping.

▸ For perfectly rounded muffin tops, only grease the bottoms and *halfway* up the sides of the muffin cup.

▸ Save on cleanup by using paper or foil baking cups.

▸ Always preheat the oven 10 to 15 minutes before beginning to bake muffins. Turn the oven on before you begin to mix the batter.

▸ Substituting buttermilk or yogurt for milk in a muffin batter will yield light, tender muffins. Be sure to add ½ teaspoon baking soda for each cup of buttermilk or yogurt you use.

▸ Any muffin can be made lighter by separating the eggs. Mix the yolks with the other moist ingredients; beat the whites until stiff and fold them in after the rest of the ingredients are combined.

▸ Stirring muffin batter too vigorously creates tough muffins with pointed, peaked tops. Only stir the batter until all the dry ingredients are moistened. There will still be lumps—don't worry, they'll disappear during baking.

▸ Turn any muffin into a "cinnamon surprise" by mixing together ½ cup brown sugar, ⅓ cup finely chopped walnuts or pecans and ½ to 1 teaspoon ground cinnamon. Fill a muffin cup halfway with batter, put a teaspoon of the sugar-nut mixture in the center, then top with the remaining batter. Sprinkle any leftover sugar-nut mixture over the top of the batter before baking.

▸ If you fill muffin cups more than three-quarters full, you're liable to get "flying saucer" tops.

▸ If your oven runs hot, place a small pan with a cup of hot water on the bottom shelf while you're baking the muffins. The added steam will help prevent the muffin edges from overbrowning.

► Check muffins for doneness by inserting a toothpick in the center. If it comes out clean, the muffins are done.

► To remove muffins from their cups, run a dinner knife around the edges, then under the muffin to tilt it out of the pan.

► If your muffins are stuck on the bottom and absolutely won't come out of the pan, set the hot muffin tin on a wet towel for 2 minutes. The muffins should be easier to remove.

► To keep the bottoms of baked muffins from getting soggy by steaming in their muffin cup, tilt them slightly in the pan until cool enough to handle.

► To cool muffins completely, transfer them to a rack.

► Keep just-baked muffins warm for a few minutes by slightly tilting each one in the pan and returning to the turned-off oven with the door ajar.

► Store leftover muffins in a tightly sealed plastic bag at room temperature for up to 3 days.

► Freeze muffins in a single layer in heavy-duty foil or freezer-weight plastic bags for up to 3 months.

► Reheat leftover muffins—loosely wrapped in foil—in a 325°F oven for about 10 minutes. Or microwave at HIGH (100 percent power) for 15 to 30 seconds, or until warmed through. Be careful not to over-microwave, or you'll turn the muffins into stones.

► For delicious muffin crisps, thinly slice leftover muffins, place the slices on a baking sheet, and toast both sides under the oven broiler. Or place the slices in a toaster oven and toast until golden brown.

► Split leftover savory muffins, toast under the broiler, and top with a creamed mixture for lunch or dinner.

► *See also* BAKING, GENERAL; BAKING POWDER; BAKING SODA; BISCUITS; BREADS, GENERAL; BREADS, QUICK; GREASING PANS; HIGH-ALTITUDE ADJUSTMENTS; POP-OVERS

MUSHROOMS

M

► The common cultivated mushroom (ranging from white to brown) is what's most often found in most U.S. supermarkets. However, more and more wild mushrooms are showing up in markets, some of the most popular being chanterelle, enoki, morel, oyster and shiitake.

► When choosing common cultivated mushrooms, look for those that are firm and evenly colored with tightly closed caps. If all the gills underneath are showing, the mushrooms are past their prime, but certainly still usable. Avoid mushrooms that are broken, damaged or have soft spots. If the mushrooms are to be cooked whole, select those of equal size so they'll cook evenly. You'll have more control of the product if you hand-select mushrooms, rather than buying them prepackaged.

▶ Tips for buying some of the more popular wild mushrooms: **chanterelle** (shan-tuh-REHL), trumpet-shaped with a bright yellow to orange color—choose whole, plump, spongy specimens; **enoki** [en-NAHK-ee], clumps of long, spaghettilike stems topped with tiny, snowy white caps—choose those that are firm and white; **morel** [muh-REHL], a cone-shape, beige to dark brown cap that's spongy, honeycombed and golden brown—choose firm, slightly spongy mushrooms; **oyster**, a fan-shape cap that varies in color from pale gray to dark brownish gray—choose firm specimens, the young, small (1½ inches in diameter) ones are considered best; **shiitake** [shee-TAH-kay], a dark brown, floppy cap that can be as large as 8 to 10 inches in diameter—choose plump mushrooms with edges that curl under.

▶ Store fresh mushrooms, unwashed, in the refrigerator for up to 3 days. Place them in a single layer on a tray; cover with a damp paper towel. Mushrooms will stay firmer if there's air circulating around them so they can "breathe." Storing them in a plastic bag speeds deterioration. Fresh mushrooms stored over 3 days will still certainly be usable, but they begin to dry out.

▶ Dried mushrooms can be stored in a cool, dark place for up to 3 months.

▶ Clean mushrooms just before using. If using water, never immerse mushrooms, as they're very absorbent and become mushy. Simply rinse under cold running water and blot dry with paper towels. Or you can simply wipe off mushrooms with a damp paper towel. Trim about ¼ inch off the stem ends, except for enokis, which should be separated at the stem end from the base. Shiitakes have very tough stems that should be removed completely (save them to flavor stocks or soups).

▶ If you don't need the mushroom stems right away, cover and refrigerate them for up to 3 days for use in soups, sautés or sauces. The stems can also be frozen for up to 6 months.

▶ *Fresh mushroom yields:* 1 pound = about 6 cups sliced; 2 cups sliced and cooked. One pound of mushrooms will serve about 3 people.

M

▶ Don't peel mushrooms or you'll lose much of their flavor.

▶ White mushrooms will stay that way if you wipe them with a paper towel dipped in lemon water.

▶ Air quickly begins to darken a mushroom's flesh. So, if you're cutting mushrooms to be used raw in a salad or as crudités, do so at the last minute. Or you can take a more labor-intensive approach and cut them ahead of time, wiping the cut surface with a paper towel dipped in lemon juice.

▶ Make slicing a one-step process by using an egg slicer (stem the mushroom first). For mushroom wedges, use an egg wedger.

▶ Sautéing mushrooms brings out and concentrates their flavor. Make sure the pan and oil are hot and don't overcrowd—mushrooms exude a lot of moisture during cooking and you want to be able to stir them around in the pan. Otherwise they'll steam, rather than sauté.

▶ Marinate small, cleaned button mushrooms in your favorite vinaigrette for 2 days in an airtight container in the refrigerator. They're great in salads, as a garnish, or with before-dinner drinks.

▶ Puree leftover raw or cooked mushrooms (add a little vegetable or chicken broth, if necessary) and freeze in ice cube trays. Turn mushroom cubes into a plastic bag and freeze until ready to use. Great for flavoring sauces, soups, casseroles, etc.

▶ For a simple garnish, vertically cut large, cleaned mushrooms with stems into quarters.

▶ Dried mushrooms can be rehydrated by covering them with warm water and soaking for about 30 minutes. Before using, rinse and blot thoroughly with paper towel; cut off tough stems.

▶ Don't throw out the liquid in which you've soaked wild dried mushrooms. It's great for flavoring soups, stews and sauces. Label and freeze it until you're ready to use it.

▶ *See also* VEGETABLES, GENERAL

MUSKMELONS *see* MELONS

MUSSELS

▶ Buy live mussels with tightly closed shells or those that snap shut when tapped—otherwise they're not alive. Avoid those with broken shells, that feel heavy (meaning they're full of sand) or that feel light and loose (signaling the mussel is dead). In general, smaller mussels will be more tender than larger ones.

▶ Choose shucked mussels that are plump, their liquor (liquid) clear.

▶ Store live mussels in a single layer on a tray in the refrigerator covered only with a damp cloth for up to 2 days. Discard any dead mussels before cooking.

▶ Store shucked mussels in the refrigerator up to 3 days. They should be covered completely with their liquor. If you need more liquid, combine 1 cup water with ½ teaspoon salt and pour this brine over the mussels to cover. Shucked mussels can be frozen in their liquor for up to 3 months.

▶ Get rid of sand by soaking mussels in cold, salted water (use ⅓ cup salt per gallon of water) for 1 hour.

▶ Before cooking, use a stiff brush to scrub mussels under cold, running water. Pull out the dark threads (beard) that protrude from the shell. Mussels die when debearded so don't do so until just before cooking.

▶ Like all shellfish, mussels should be cooked gently to prevent toughening.

M

▶ Mussels cooked in their shells are done when their shells open. Discard any with unopened shells.

▶ *See also* SHELLFISH

MUSTARD, PREPARED

▶ In general, prepared mustard is made from powdered mustard, a liquid such as water, vinegar, wine or beer, and various seasonings. Mustards come in a wide variety of flavors and textures (from smooth to grainy) and run the gamut from very mild to mouth-scorching hot. Grainy mustards get their texture from the addition of crushed or whole mustard seeds.

▶ **American-style mustard**—the ballpark (hot dog) mustard—is made from mild white (also called yellow) mustard seeds, sugar, vinegar and turmeric (which produces its characteristic bright yellow color). American-style mustard has a smooth texture and mild flavor.

▶ **Dijon mustard**—a smooth-textured, pale grayish yellow mixture hailing from Dijon, France, and known for its clean, sharp flavor, which can range from mild to hot. It's made from brown mustard seeds, white wine, unfermented grape juice and a blend of seasonings. Dijon mustards are usually spicier and more pungent than their American counterparts. Mustards labeled "Dijon-style" are made in the same way, but are not from Dijon.

▶ **English mustard** is made from both white and brown or black mustard seeds, flour and turmeric. It's bright yellow and extremely hot.

▶ **German mustard** can range in color from pale yellow to brown and in texture from smooth to coarse. Its spicy, slightly sweet flavor can range from mild to hot.

▶ **Chinese mustard**—primarily used as a dipping sauce for Chinese dishes—can be created at home by making a paste from powdered mustard and water, wine or vinegar. The paste must be made at least 15 minutes before using in order for the flavor and "heat" to develop. This type of mustard generally loses its potency after about an hour, so a fresh batch should be made before each use.

▶ Prepared mustard can be stored for at least 2 years; refrigerate after opening.

▶ It's important to use the type of mustard a recipe calls for. Otherwise, you could end up with a completely different flavor than was intended.

▶ Make your own flavored mustard by adding finely chopped herbs (like basil, dill or tarragon), garlic, shallots, onions, olives, fennel seeds, capers, green peppercorns, grated lemon zest, etc., to a good Dijon mustard.

▶ For a great spread for meat sandwiches, create a horseradish mustard by mixing 1 part horseradish to 3 parts mustard. Use a teaspoon of this fragrant mustard in your next Bloody Mary for a great change of pace.

M

▸ Make your own mustard mayonnaise by adding mustard to taste to home-made or commercial mayo (start with 2 to 3 teaspoons mustard per ½ cup mayo).

▸ Use mustard mayonnaise as a sandwich spread, in salads (like egg or tuna), salad dressings, or to brush over meat such as baked ham or pork loin.

▸ Make mustard butter by blending 2 to 3 teaspoons of your favorite pre-pared mustard with ½ cup softened butter. Add about ¼ cup minced fresh herbs for herbed mustard butter.

▸ Mustard butter is great for basting for meats, poultry and fish, for cooking scrambled eggs, on sandwiches, melted over cooked vegetables, etc.

▸ Make a delicious glaze for ham by combining your favorite mustard with maple syrup, honey or melted orange mamalade or other preserves.

▸ Mustard adds a mysterious piquancy to all manner of dishes including seafood salads, soups and stews, potato or bean salads, savory soufflés, quiches, bread doughs, quick bread batters, baked beans, etc. It's best to err on the side of caution when adding mustard—powdered or prepared—to a dish. You can always add more, but there's no way to correct an over-mustarded dish.

▸ *See also* MUSTARD SEEDS

MUSTARD SEEDS; POWDERED MUSTARD; MUSTARD OIL

▸ Mustard seed comes in three main types—white (also called yellow), brown and black. White or yellow mustard seeds are larger than the darker varieties, but also less pungent. Brown seeds have a strong flavor; the slightly milder black seeds are most often used by Indian cooks.

▸ Powdered mustard is made from mustard seeds that have been finely ground.

▸ Mustard oil is pressed directly from mustard seeds. This pale golden, ar-omatic oil is extremely hot and pungent.

▸ Whole white mustard seeds and powdered mustard are commonly avail-able in supermarkets. Black seeds can be found in Indian markets; the brown seeds are occasionally available in specialty gourmet markets. Mus-tard oil is available in ethnic markets, specialty gourmet shops and many supermarkets.

▸ Store mustard seeds in a cool, dark place for up to 1 year; powdered mus-tard for up to 6 months. Mustard oil should be stored in the refrigerator to preventy rancidity.

▸ You can make your own mustard by combining about 2 parts powdered mustard with 1 part liquid (such as water, wine or vinegar); stir until the mixture is the consistency of a smooth paste. If desired, add fresh herbs, garlic or other seasonings. Let stand about 15 minutes before using for the flavor to develop. Taste the mustard—if it's too hot, stir in 1 teaspoon

M

each cream and granulated or brown sugar. This type of mustard quickly loses its potency and should be made fresh before each use.
▸ Add a touch of intrigue to your next stir-fry by using mustard oil, fresh ginger and garlic. Just add a touch of mustard oil—it's very hot and pungent.
▸ A soupçon of mustard oil in salad dressing adds both flavor and piquancy.
▸ *See also* MUSTARD, PREPARED

M

N

NECTARINES

▶ Choose fragrant, brightly colored nectarines that give slightly to palm pressure. Avoid those with bruises or other blemishes as well as any that are hard or overly green.

▶ Store ripe nectarines in the refrigerator for up to 5 days.

▶ Ripen underripe nectarines at room temperature. To speed ripening, place nectarines in a paper bag with an apple; pierce bag in several places with the tip of a knife. Let stand at room temperature until ripe.

▶ *Nectarine yields:* 1 pound = 4 small, 3 medium; 2½ cups chopped.

▶ Wash nectarines just before using; they don't require peeling.

▶ A nectarine's flesh will discolor after being cut. If you're not combining the nectarine with an ingredient containing acid (such as a salad dressing), dip the nectarine pieces quickly in and out of acidulated water (3 tablespoons lemon juice per quart of cold water).

▶ In the height of their season, make nectarine (rather than strawberry) shortcake. Flavor the whipped cream with a little nutmeg and amaretto and you'll get raves.

▶ *See also* FRUIT, GENERAL

NUTMEG; NUTMEG GRATERS

▶ Nutmeg is sold ground or whole in a market's spice section.

▶ Freshly grated nutmeg is much more pungent than its canned, ground counterpart. Use in vegetables, soups, stews, breads and desserts.

▶ There are several styles of nutmeg graters and grinders, which are commonly found in specialty kitchenware shops. Most graters have a fine-rasp, slightly curved surface over which a whole nutmeg is rubbed. Many graters store the whole nutmegs in containers attached to the bottom or back of the unit. Nutmeg grinders use a spring-mounted post to hold a whole nutmeg against a sharp blade that, when a crank is rotated, grates the nutmeg.

▶ A toothbrush is the perfect tool for cleaning nutmeg graters and grinders.

▶ Did you know that the spice mace is the dried, ground outer membrane that covers the nutmeg seed? That's why mace tastes and smells like a pungent version of nutmeg.

▶ *See also* SPICES *for general purchase and storage information*

NUTS, GENERAL

▶ When buying unshelled nuts in bulk, choose those that are heavy for their size, with solid shells sans cracks or holes.

▸ Shelled nuts should be plump, crisp and uniform in color and size. Avoid those that are shriveled or discolored. Packaged shelled nuts are harder to test for freshness. If they're in a cellophane bag, snap a couple through the wrapping. If they bend, rather than break crisply, the nuts are past their prime. Once you get the cellophane-packaged nuts home, double bag them in a plastic bag to keep them as fresh as possible.

▸ *Nut yields:* As a general rule, 4 ounces of most nuts = 1 cup chopped nuts.

▸ Nuts have a high fat content and, therefore, the attendant problem of rancidity. For that reason, store nuts airtight in a cool place. Shelled nuts can be refrigerated in this manner for up to 4 months, frozen up to 8 months. As a general rule (and depending on their freshness at the time of storage), unshelled nuts will keep twice as long as shelled.

▸ Rancid nuts will ruin whatever food they flavor so be sure to buy in small amounts from a supplier with rapid turnover. Always taste nuts before using them.

▸ Place hard-to-crack nuts in a large saucepan and cover with water. Bring to a boil, then remove from heat, cover and set aside for at least 15 minutes, or until cool. Blot the nuts dry, then crack, positioning the cracker on opposite ends.

▸ If you want to shell nuts so that the nutmeats are relatively unscathed, gently press on the middle of the shell with a nutcracker, rotating the nut 3 or 4 times as you do.

▸ To eliminate bits of shell in freshly hulled nuts, turn the nuts into a large bowl of cool water. The shells will float and can be poured or skimmed off. Drain and dry the nuts thoroughly before using.

▸ Nuts are easier to chop when they're warm. Either heat in microwave oven at HIGH (100 percent power) for 2 to 3 minutes or in a conventional oven at 325°F for 5 minutes.

▸ Toasting nuts before using in recipes intensifies their flavor and adds crunch. Another bonus—toasted nuts aren't as likely to sink in cakes, breads and other batter-based foods.

▸ Another way to keep chopped nuts from sinking in batters is to toss them with 1 or 2 tablespoons of the flour called for in the recipe.

▸ Toast nuts or seeds in an ungreased skillet over medium heat, stirring frequently, until golden brown. Or, oven-toast at 350°F, stirring occasionally, for 10 to 15 minutes.

▸ Microwave-toasted nuts and seeds barely change color, but they *taste* toasted (but wait until they're cool to taste). Place 1 cup chopped nuts on a paper plate. Microwave, uncovered, at HIGH (100 percent power) for 3 to 4 minutes, or until nuts *smell* toasted. Rotate plate a half turn after 2 minutes.

▸ Use the food processor to make quick work of chopping nuts. Place about 1 cup whole nuts or large nut pieces in a food processor bowl fitted with the metal blade. Process, using quick on/off pulses, until nuts are desired texture. Don't overprocess or you'll wind up with nut butter.

▶ Because of the shape of the jarlike container, it's hard to chop nuts in a standard blender container without turning at least part of them into paste. First rule—never chop more than 1 cup of nuts at a time, and process with short on/off bursts of power. Adding 1 tablespoon flour, cornstarch or sugar will also help keep the nuts separate.

▶ Some blenders come with 1-cup containers in addition to the standard large size. These small containers work well for chopping nuts. Only fill them two-thirds full and use quick on/off pulses until the nuts reach the desired texture.

▶ Add flavor to baked goods like breads, cakes and cookies by substituting ⅓ cup finely ground nuts for ⅓ cup of the flour.

▶ Ground nuts are great in meatballs, meatloaf and burgers.

▶ For super-crunchy seasoned nuts to serve with aperitifs or as snacks, beat 1 egg white until stiff. Fold in 2 cups nuts and 2½ to 3 teaspoons mixed seasonings (such as chili powder, ground ginger or cinnamon, cayenne, curry powder or cumin), using a rubber spatula to mix until nuts are well coated. Spread in a single layer on a baking sheet and bake at 275°F for 30 to 40 minutes, stirring every 10 minutes. Cool completely before serving. Store airtight.

▶ You can also make cocktail nuts in a skillet. Sauté 2 cups nuts in 2 tablespoons oil or melted butter over medium-high heat, stirring often, until they begin to brown. Sprinkle with your choice of seasonings (salt, pepper, cayenne, curry powder, etc.), tossing the nuts with a wooden spoon, then turn out onto paper towels to cool. Store airtight.

▶ To add a delicious flavor to pastry pie crusts, once the pie dough is in the pan and fluted, sprinkle the bottom and sides with about ¼ cup ground or finely chopped, toasted nuts. Use your fingers or the back of a spoon to gently press the nuts into the pie crust; bake or fill as usual.

▶ Make your own nut butter by grinding nuts in a food processor or blender. When the nuts are pastelike, add enough vegetable oil to create the texture you desire. Honey and maple syrup add sweetness to nut butters and salt will enliven the flavor.

▶ When using chopped nuts for a garnish, put them in a strainer first and toss them a few times to remove bits of nuts and skin that would mar the look of whatever you're decorating.

N

▶ *See also* ALMONDS; BRAZIL NUTS; CHESTNUTS; HAZELNUTS; PEANUTS; PECANS; PISTACHIOS; WALNUTS

OATS

- Store oats in an airtight container in a cool, dry place for up to 6 months. Oat bran should be stored no longer than 3 months. Oat products may be double wrapped and frozen for up to 1 year.
- *Rolled oat yields:* 1 pound = 5 cups; 1 cup = 1¾ cups cooked.
- **Old-fashioned (rolled) oats** have been steamed, then flattened into flakes.
- **Quick-cooking oats** have been cut into several pieces before being steamed and flattened.
- Old-fashioned oats take about 15 minutes to cook; quick-cooking oats take 5 minutes. The texture of the former is slightly firmer than the short-cut oatmeal.
- Old-fashioned oats and quick-cooking oats can usually be interchanged in recipes.
- **Instant oats** have been cut into very small pieces, precooked and dried so they need no real cooking. This processing makes them unsuitable as a substitution in recipes for old-fashioned (rolled) or quick-cooking oats. Using them can turn baked goods like muffins or cookies into gooey lumps.
- **Steel-cut oats** (also called Irish oatmeal or Scotch oats) are oats that have been cut, but not rolled. They take a longer time to cook (about 20 to 30 minutes) and have a decidedly chewy texture.
- **Oat flour** is the finely ground grain. It doesn't contain gluten, and must be combined with a flour that does when used for baked goods that need to rise (like yeast breads).
- **Oat bran** is the ground outer casing of the grain and is particularly high in soluble fiber.
- Give oats a toasty flavor by roasting them in a dry skillet over medium-high heat until golden brown. Cool before adding to recipes.
- Toasted oats make a delicious addition to cookies, muffins and other baked goods.
- Give cookies, muffins, etc. a nutritional boost by adding ¼ cup oat bran to the ingredients.

OKRA

- When buying fresh okra, look for firm, brightly colored pods under 4 inches long. Larger pods may be tough and fibrous. Avoid dull, limp or blemished pods.

▸ Store unwashed okra in a plastic bag in the refrigerator for up to 3 days.

▸ Before cooking, wash okra pods and trim stem ends. Okra can be cooked whole or cut crosswise into slices.

▸ *Okra yields:* 1 pound = 2¼ cups chopped.

▸ Cut okra gives off a viscous substance that thickens any liquid in which it's cooked.

▸ Okra is usually boiled (either alone or in soups, stews, etc.), sautéed or cooked in a microwave oven.

▸ Okra makes a perfect partner with tomatoes, onions or corn.

▸ Marinate cooked okra slices in your favorite vinaigrette overnight and toss it in a salad the next day.

▸ For a delicious change of pace, grill okra the next time you're grilling meat. Simply brush whole pods with olive oil, then place the okra crosswise over the grill grids. Cover grill and cook over medium-high heat for 3 minutes, then turn and cook the other side 2 to 3 minutes.

▸ *See also* VEGETABLES, GENERAL

OILS *see* FATS AND OILS

OLIVE OIL *see* FATS AND OILS

OLIVES

▸ Unopened olives can be stored in a cool, dark place for 1 year. Once opened, refrigerate olives for up to 1 month.

▸ If olives are in a can, transfer them and their brine to an airtight glass jar before refrigerating.

▸ Extend olive storage life by floating a thin layer of vegetable oil on the surface of the brine.

▸ Bulk olives can be put in a jar and covered with oil. Sealed airtight, they'll keep in the refrigerator for up to 2 months.

▸ If a white film develops on an olive brine's surface, simply skim it off; rinse off any film on the olives.

▸ Discard olives once they begin to turn soft.

▸ Pitting olives: Lay an olive on a work surface, hold the flat side of a French knife on top of it, and give the knife a gentle but firm whack with your other palm or fist. The pit should slip right out, leaving the flesh reasonably intact. You can also roll over the olive with a rolling pin.

OMELETS *see* EGGS, COOKING METHODS

O

ONIONS

▸ There are two main classifications—dry onions and scallions (*see separate listing*), also called green onions.

▶ When buying dry onions, choose those that are heavy for their size with dry, papery skins. Avoid onions with soft areas, moist or spotted skins, or that have begun to sprout.

▶ Among the more mild-flavored onions are the yellow- or white-skinned Bermuda and Spanish, and the red or Italian. Three particularly sweet and juicy onions (often available only by mail order outside their area) are the Maui (Hawaii), Vidalia (Georgia) and Walla Walla (Washington).

▶ Store whole onions in a cool, dry place with good air circulation for up to 2 months, depending on their condition when purchased. Spring and summer onions have a milder flavor and shorter storage life than fall and winter onions. Humidity breeds spoilage in dry onions.

▶ Cut off the top of an old (clean) pair of pantyhose, drop onions into a leg and hang in a cool, dry place. The hose lets air circulate, which helps keep the onions longer.

▶ *Onion yields:* 1 pound = 4 medium; 2 to 3 cups chopped.

▶ An easy way to peel pearl onions is to drop them into boiling water and cook 1 to 2 minutes, depending on their size. Drain and turn onions into a bowl of ice water. Pinch onion at root end and it will pop out of its skin.

▶ Or put pearl onions and about ¼ cup water in a 1-quart covered casserole and microwave at HIGH (100 percent power) for about 3½ minutes, stirring halfway through cooking time. Drain onions and turn into a bowl of ice water until cool enough to handle.

▶ To peel a large, dry onion, cut a small slice off the top and root ends. Then hold the onion under warm running water, pulling the skins off as you do. Or you can use the same boiling water–ice water technique in the previous pearl-onion tip.

▶ Don't put papery onion skins in the garbage disposal or you could clog the works.

▶ Tricks for keeping tears at bay while cutting onions: freeze onions for 20 minutes before chopping; hold a wooden kitchen spoon between your teeth; bite down on 2 kitchen matches, sulphur tips pointing out, so they're positioned under your nose; turn on the stovetop exhaust fan and chop on top of the stove; buy a pair of safety goggles from the hardware store.

▶ If you only use part of an onion, leave the skin on the unused portion to help keep the onion fresh in the refrigerator.

▶ The sharper your knife and the quicker you chop, the fewer tears you'll experience.

O

▶ Make chopping an onion a breeze by first cutting it in half from the top to the root. Place halves cut side down, then cut into parallel vertical slices. Holding slices together, slice crosswise to your original cuts.

▶ Leaving the stem end intact while you slice an onion will hold it together until you get to the end.

▸ Decrease the harshness of onions by slicing, then soaking them in ice water for 30 to 60 minutes, changing the water 2 or 3 times during that period. Thoroughly blot dry before using. This process is particularly effective for onions that are to be served raw.

▸ To keep onions from becoming bitter in dishes like salads, dips or spreads, place the chopped onions in a bowl with 4 cups cold water mixed with 1½ tablespoons white or cider vinegar. Let stand 5 minutes, stirring every minute or so. Drain well before using.

▸ Once cut, an onion should be tightly wrapped, refrigerated, and used within 5 days.

▸ The best storage container for a raw onion after it's cut is an airtight screw-top *glass* jar (plastic lets out the odor). Refrigerate a cut onion this way for up to 1 week.

▸ Chopped, raw or sautéed onions can be frozen in an airtight container and frozen for up to 3 months. Add them directly to dishes like soups and stews without thawing; thaw and blot dry before sautéing those frozen raw.

▸ For almost-instant onion juice, cut a peeled onion into chunks, puree it in a food processor, then strain off the juice.

▸ Make your own dried onions by cutting an onion into paper-thin slices (a food processor works great), then separate the slices into rings. Arrange the rings in a single layer on a baking sheet and place in a 275°F oven until dry and golden brown (30 to 60 minutes, depending on the onion's natural moisture content). Refrigerate these flavor-intensive onions in an airtight container for up to 1 month, adding to dishes as needed.

▸ Whole onions will stay intact during boiling if you first cut an X about ¼-inch deep in the stem end.

▸ Boiled onions will keep their shape better if they're simmered, rather than cooked at a rapid boil.

▸ If you're boiling onions that are particularly sharp and pungent, cook them for 2 minutes and drain off the water. Repeat this process twice, letting the onions complete their cooking time in the third change of water. The result will be deliciously mild, sweet cooked onions.

▸ If you've overcooked boiled onions until they're soft, immediately drain and plunge them into ice water. They'll firm up a little in about 60 seconds.

▸ Before adding onions to dishes like casseroles, soups and stews, briefly sauté them in olive oil or butter. This 5-minute process will greatly improve their flavor in the finished dish. Stir 1 teaspoon sugar into the oil or butter before adding the onions for a delicious caramelized flavor.

▸ One of the most important secrets for super-crisp onion rings is to keep the oil right around 375°F. After breading the onion rings, let them air-dry for 30 minutes in the refrigerator before frying. Don't crowd the on-

O

ion rings in the pot of oil, or you'll bring the oil temperature down and wind up with greasy rings. Transfer fried onion rings to a paper-towel-lined baking sheet and keep warm in a 300°F oven until all the rings are fried (*see* DEEP-FRYING).

▶ Alleviate a lingering onion smell from your kitchen by putting a pot of water on to boil to which you've added 1 cup vinegar and 1 teaspoon ground cloves.

▶ To help remove onion odor from your hands, rub them with lemon wedges, parsley, salt and vinegar, or a stalk of celery that has been cut in half lengthwise. Wash with soap and hot water after any of these processes.

▶ To get rid of the proverbial "onion breath," eat several sprigs of vinegar- or salt-dipped parsley. Or you might find chewing on fennel seeds, coffee beans or chlorophyll tablets more enjoyable.

▶ *See also* CHIVES; LEEKS; SCALLIONS; SHALLOTS; VEGETABLES, GENERAL

OPENING JARS AND BOTTLES *see* JARS AND BOTTLES

ORANGES

▶ The two most popular types of oranges in the United States are sweet oranges and loose-skinned oranges. **Sweet oranges**, prized both for eating and for their juice, are generally large; their skins are usually more difficult to remove than their loose-skinned relatives. Among the more popular sweet oranges are the seedless navel, the juicy, coarse-grained Valencia, and the red-fleshed blood orange. **Loose-skinned oranges** have skin that readily slips off the fruit; their segments are also loose and divide easily. Members of the mandarin orange family are all loose-skinned and include the thick-skinned tangerine, the multiseeded Dancy, the almost seedless satsuma and the tiny clementine.

▶ No matter the variety, choose oranges that are firm and heavy for their size. Avoid any with mold or spongy spots. A rough, brownish area (called russeting) on the skin doesn't affect flavor or quality; neither does slight greening, which sometimes occurs in fully ripe oranges. Because oranges are sometimes dyed with food coloring, a bright color isn't necessarily an indicator of quality.

▶ Before you buy that economical bag of oranges, remember that you can't see all of the areas on each orange. If there's a moldy orange or two in the bag they can speed detrioration of the entire lot.

▶ Oranges can be stored at a cool room temperature for a couple of days, but they'll last up to 2 weeks when refrigerated.

▶ *Orange yields:* 1 pound = 3 medium; about 1 cup juice. One medium orange = about ⅓ cup juice; 1 to 2 tablespoons zest.

▶ Before squeezing the juice from oranges, use a citrus zester to remove the outer colored portion of the peel. Freeze this zest for up to 6 months to use later to flavor both sweet and savory dishes.

▸ Did you know that all forms of orange juice—frozen concentrate, fresh-squeezed or pasteurized—contain the same proportion of vitamin C? And orange juice retains up to 90 percent of its vitamin C for up to 1 week if you store it in the refrigerator.

▸ Frozen orange juice concentrate will retain its vitamin C for up to a year if stored at 0°F or lower.

▸ *See also* CITRUS FRUITS *for tips on juicing, etc.*

OVENS, CONVENTIONAL

▸ Oven Temperature Terminology:

Very slow	250°–300°F	121°–149°C
Slow	300°–325°F	149°–163°C
Moderate	350°–375°F	177°–190°C
Very hot	450°–475°F	233°–246°C
Extremely hot	500°–525°F	260°–274°C

▸ Oven temperatures can be off as much as 50° to 100°F, a discomfiting thought, since baked goods can be seriously affected by oven variances. That's why a good oven thermometer is an excellent investment (*see* THERMOMETERS).

▸ To check oven accuracy, place the thermometer on the center rack and preheat the oven for 15 minutes. If the thermometer reading doesn't agree with the oven setting (for example, if it reads 400°F when the oven is set at 350°F), you know that your oven runs 50°F hot. Therefore, when a recipe requires a 350°F temperature, set your oven to 300°F.

▸ If you don't want to buy an oven thermometer, here's an old-time method for testing oven temperatures: Sprinkle 1 tablespoon flour over the bottom of a metal pan and place it in a preheated oven for 5 minutes. If the flour turns tan, the temperature is 250 to 325°F; golden brown, 325 to 400°F; dark brown, 400 to 450°F; darkest brown, 450 to 525°F.

▸ If you're in a hurry, turn on the oven the second you walk through the door. That way it can be preheating while you begin meal preparations.

▸ Preheat an oven for 15 minutes before baking foods such as breads, pastries, soufflés and cakes. Foods requiring 1 hour or more of baking can usually be started in a cold oven. If you start baking in a cold oven, be sure to factor that fact into the recipe's baking time.

O

▸ Most ovens have hot spots. To insure even baking, rotate baking dishes and pans from top to bottom, and from front to back.

▸ Line the oven floor with heavy-duty aluminum foil. When the foil gets dirty, throw it out. Make sure you don't cover any vents with the foil or you could throw the temperature off.

▶ Oven spills will come up more easily if you immediately pour salt on them. Wait until the oven cools before wiping up the spill.

▶ Ovens without automatic- or self-cleaning units are less of a chore to clean if you heat to 200°F, then turn off the oven and set a shallow glass bowl containing ½ cup ammonia on the middle shelf. Close the oven and let stand overnight. The next day, open the oven and let it air out before you wipe it clean with damp paper towels.

▶ Clean the inside of your oven window by dampening a cloth, then dipping it into a small bowl of baking soda and scrubbing in a circular motion.

▶ To get rid of unpleasant cooking (or even oven cleaner) odors in your oven, peel an orange and lay the strips of peel on the oven racks. Heat the oven to 350°F, and leave peels in the oven for 30 minutes. Turn off the oven and leave peels until cool.

▶ *See also* BAKING; BROILING; CONVECTION OVENS; MICROWAVE COOKING

OVEN THERMOMETERS *see* THERMOMETERS

OYSTERS

▶ Live oysters should be as fresh as possible and therefore should be purchased from a store with good turnover. Reject any with broken shells or that don't have tightly closed shells, or with shells that don't snap shut when tapped with your fingernail. The smaller an oyster is for its species, the younger and more tender it will be.

▶ Shucked oysters should be plump, uniform in size, have a good color and smell of the sea; their liquor (liquid) should be clear.

▶ Store live oysters in the refrigerator (larger shell down), covered with a damp towel, for up to 3 days. The sooner they're eaten, the better they'll taste. If any shells open during storage, tap them—if they don't close, throw them out.

▶ Store shucked oysters, covered by their liquor, for up to 2 days; in the freezer for up to 3 months.

▶ If there's not enough liquor to cover the shucked oysters, make your own by dissolving ½ teaspoon salt in 1 cup water.

▶ *Oyster yields:* 1 dozen shucked oysters = about 1 cup; 1 quart shucked oysters = about 50.

▶ Scrub live oysters under cold, running water before opening.

▶ Oyster and clam shells will open more easily if frozen for 10 to 20 minutes.

▶ Or ready oysters for opening by placing them, hinge facing out, around the rim of a 10-inch plate and microwaving at HIGH (100 percent power)

O

for about 30 seconds—just until the shells open slightly.
- ▶ The pointed end of a can or bottle opener works well for prying oysters open.
- ▶ Poached oysters should be cooked only until their edges curl; their bodies should be plump and opaque.
- ▶ Oysters become tough when they're overcooked, so watch carefully.
- ▶ *See also* SHELLFISH

O

PANCAKES

- Instead of using milk in your batter, try substituting an equal amount of fruit juice. Orange juice makes wonderful pancakes, particularly with the addition of 1 tablespoon orange zest. Or try peach nectar, with ½ cup minced fresh peaches.

- When making a fruit-juice substitution, baking soda should be used to counteract the fruit's natural acidity. If there isn't already baking soda in the recipe, reduce the baking powder by ½ teaspoon and add ½ teaspoon baking soda.

- Create maple-flavored pancakes by substituting ¼ cup pure maple syrup for ¼ cup of the milk or other liquid in the recipe.

- Add ½ teaspoon each cinnamon, nutmeg and vanilla to your favorite pancake batter for a spicy start to the day. Two tablespoons brown sugar in the batter will sweeten it slightly. Add the spices to the dry ingredients, the vanilla and brown sugar to the wet ingredients.

- For gingerbread pancakes, substitute 2 tablespoons molasses for an equal amount of milk, and add ½ teaspoon ground ginger and ¼ teaspoon each ground cinnamon and allspice to the dry ingredients.

- For ultralight pancakes, substitute room-temperature club soda for the milk. Mix a club-soda batter just before you use it because it won't keep its punch long.

- Pancakes will also be fluffier if you separate the eggs and mix the yolks in with the rest of the liquid. Combine the wet and dry ingredients as usual. Then beat the egg whites until stiff and fold into the batter at the last minute.

- Beating the batter until smooth will produce tough pancakes. Pancake batter should be blended only until the dry ingredients are moistened, which means the batter will still be lumpy.

- Most pancake batters can be covered and refrigerated overnight. If the batter thickens too much, gently stir in 1 to 2 tablespoons milk.

- A batter stored for more than a day will need a leavener boost—mix in ¼ teaspoon baking powder that has been blended with 1 teaspoon cold milk.

- For maximum pancake panache, make them right at the table on an electric griddle or skillet.

- Making pancakes is a breeze if you use a nonstick griddle or skillet. Simply use a paper towel to lightly rub the griddle surface with about ½ tablespoon oil. Excess oil causes pancakes to brown unevenly and makes the edges crisp. Oiling a nonstick griddle between pancake batches is usually unnecessary.

▶ A pancake griddle should be very hot. To test it, flick a few drops of cold water on the griddle—if the water dances on the surface, the griddle is ready.

▶ Use a ¼-cup dry measure to pour the batter onto the griddle. Depending on the batter's thickness, ¼ cup of batter will make pancakes 3 to 4 inches in diameter.

▶ Use a wide-mouthed pitcher to mix and pour pancake batter.

▶ Make kids of all ages happy by forming fun shapes with pancake batter. Spoon or pour the batter onto the griddle in the form of a teddy bear, a child's initial, a heart—your imagination is your guide.

▶ Cook pancakes until bubbles break all over the surface. Flip the cakes, cooking the second side only until golden brown.

▶ *Never* press a pancake down with a metal spatula. Doing so will compress the cake and make it heavy.

▶ Turning a pancake more than once toughens it.

▶ If you're not cooking pancakes on an electric griddle at the table to be served as you make them, place the cooked cakes in a single layer on a large baking sheet lined with a dish towel. Keep them warm in a 200°F oven until ready to serve.

▶ Help keep pancakes warm by heating the syrup. One-half cup syrup will heat in a few minutes on stovetop, 30 to 60 seconds in the microwave at HIGH (100 percent power).

▶ There are dozens of pancake toppings other than maple syrup. Try finely chopped fresh strawberries or other fruit, your favorite jam or jelly thinned with a little fruit juice or melted until liquefied, sour cream or crème fraîche sweetened with a little brown sugar, a simple dusting of powdered sugar, or honey, just to name a few.

▶ Cool leftover pancakes, then place them in a freezer-proof container separated by waxed-paper squares. Seal and freeze for up to 3 months.

▶ Reheat frozen pancakes in a single layer on a baking sheet at 325°F for about 8 minutes, or until warmed through. A toaster oven works well, too, and a toaster can be used for sturdy pancakes.

▶ Or cover frozen pancakes lightly with waxed paper and microwave on HIGH (100 percent power) for 10 to 30 seconds. Don't over-microwave or you'll turn the pancakes into Frisbees.

▶ Leftover (unsweetened) pancake batter can be used to thicken a sauce or soup. Simply whisk it into a hot mixture and stir until thickened.

▶ *See also* MAPLE SYRUP

P

PANCAKE SYRUP *see* MAPLE SYRUP; SYRUPS

PAN SIZES

▶ There are times when most cooks don't have the size pan called for in a recipe. Substitutions can be made, but it's important to remember that baking times will need to be adjusted when pan sizes are changed.

▶ To measure the volume of a pan or dish, fill it with water, then measure the liquid. The dimensions of a pan are measured from inside edge to inside edge. Measure the depth by standing the ruler in the pan and checking the distance to the rim (don't slant the ruler, as with a pie pan).

▶ Once you know the volume or dimensions, mark the measurements right on the outside bottom of the pan. Scratch the information into metal pans; use a waterproof marking pen on glass or ceramic pans.

▶ The following table will help determine substitutions of pans of similar sizes. Otherwise, if a recipe calls for a 8-inch square baking pan (which has a 6-cup volume), you can see by this table that a 9-inch round cake pan holds approximately the same volume.

COMMON PAN SIZE	APPROXIMATE VOLUME
1¾" by ¾" mini muffin cup	⅛ cup
2¾" by 1⅛" muffin cup	¼ cup
2¾" by 1⅜" muffin cup	scant ½ cup
3" by 1¼" giant muffin cup	⅝ cup
8" by 1½" pie	4 cups
8" by 1½" round cake	4 cups
9" by 1½" pie	5 cups
8" by 2" round cake	6 cups
9" by 1½" round cake	6 cups
8" by 8" by 1½" square	6 cups
11" by 7" by 2" rectangular	6 cups
7½" by 3" Bundt	6 cups
8½" by 4½" by 2½" loaf	6 cups
9" by 5" by 3" loaf	8 cups
9" by 2" pie (deep dish)	8 cups
9" by 2" round cake	8 cups
8" by 8" by 2" square	8 cups
9" by 9" by 1½" square	8 cups
9" by 3" Bundt	9 cups
8" by 3" tube	9 cups
9" by 9" by 2" square	10 cups
9½" by 2½" springform	10 cups
10" by 2" round cake	11 cups
10" by 3½" Bundt	12 cups

P

9" by 3" tube	12 cups
10" by 2½" springform	12 cups
13" by 9" by 2" rectangular	15 cups
10" by 4" tube	16 cups

PAPAYAS [puh-PY-yuhs]

▶ Choose richly colored papayas that give slightly to palm pressure. If all you can find are slightly green fruit, don't worry—they'll ripen quickly at home.

▶ Speed the ripening of papayas by placing them in a paper bag with an apple at room temperature. Pierce the bag in a couple of places with the tip of a knife, then seal.

▶ Store ripe papayas in a plastic bag in the refrigerator for up to 1 week.

▶ Ripe papaya is best eaten raw; slightly underripe fruit can be cooked as a vegetable.

▶ Before using, use a sharp knife to peel the papaya, then cut it in half and use a spoon to scoop out the seeds.

▶ Though the papaya's shiny, grayish black seeds are usually discarded, they have a peppery taste and make a delicious salad dressing. Combine some of the seeds with your favorite vinaigrette in a blender and process until pureed.

▶ Papaya contains an enzyme that prevents gelatin from setting properly. Heat destroys the enzyme, so cooked papaya can be added to a gelatin mixture.

▶ Papaya contains papain, an enzyme used chiefly in meat tenderizers. Make your own tenderizer by pureeing papaya and rubbing it all over the meat's surface. Or soak the meat in papaya juice, available at many supermarkets and most natural food stores. Cover and refrigerate the meat for 3 hours. Scrape off the papaya puree, pat the meat dry and cook as desired.

▶ Scoop out most of the flesh from a papaya and use the shell as a serving container for salads or fruit compotes.

▶ *See also* FRUIT, GENERAL

PAPRIKA (pa-PREE-kuh; PAP-ree-kuh)

▶ Paprika is a powder made by grinding dried, aromatic sweet red peppers. Its flavor can range from mild to hot, the color from bright orange-red to blood-red. Most commercial paprika comes from Spain, South America, California and Hungary.

▶ The full-flavored Hungarian variety is considered superior, and comes in both mild and hot forms. Hot Hungarian paprika packs a punch similar to cayenne.

P

▶ Increase paprika's flavor by roasting it in a dry skillet for a few minutes. Cool before using.

▶ *See also* SPICES *for purchase and storage information*

PARBOILING

▶ Parboiling food is done by partially cooking it in boiling water, then plunging it into cold water to stop the cooking process. This method is particularly useful for dense foods like carrots which, if parboiled, can be combined with quick-cooking ingredients like celery in sautés and stir-frys. This technique insures that all the ingredients will complete cooking at the same time.

▶ Make sure the water is boiling rapidly before beginning to parboil. Test the food for degree of doneness by piercing it with a fork.

▶ Have a bowl of ice water ready so you can fast-cool the parboiled food in order to stop the cooking.

▶ After cooling, parboiled food can be covered and refrigerated for 24 hours before being used when necessary. Make sure it's the same temperature as the other foods with which it's being cooked.

▶ *See also* BLANCHING

PARSLEY

▶ The two most popular varieties of this herb are **curly-leaf parsley** and the more strongly flavored **Italian** or **flat-leaf parsley.**

▶ Choose parsley with bright green leaves with no sign of wilting.

▶ Thoroughly wash fresh parsley and shake off excess moisture; wrap in paper towels, then in a plastic bag. Parsley can be stored in this manner for up to 1 week.

▶ A parsley bouquet can also be stored by placing it, stem ends down, in a tall glass filled with enough cold water to cover 1 inch of the stem ends. Cover the top with a plastic bag, securing it to the glass with a rubber band. Change the water every 2 days.

▶ Wilted parsley can be revived by cutting off ½ inch of the stems, then standing the parsley in a glass of ice water. Refrigerate for at least 1 hour.

▶ There's no need to meticulously tear parsley leaves from their stems before chopping. Simply cut off the stems of an entire bunch as close to the leaves as possible. Parsley stems are relatively tender so a few won't be noticeable in a batch of minced parsley.

▶ Make sure parsley leaves are thoroughly dry and chopping will be much easier.

▶ Finely chopped parsley will stay fluffy and light if you squeeze it in a double thickness of paper towel to remove all excess moisture. Rewrap in more paper towel, then in a plastic bag; refrigerate for up to 2 days.

P

▶ *See also* HERBS

PARSNIPS

► Choose firm, small to medium, well-shaped parsnips. Avoid those that are limp, shriveled or spotted.

► Store parsnips in a plastic bag in the refrigerator for up to 2 weeks.

► Peel and trim ends just before using.

► *Parsnip yields:* 1 pound = 4 medium; 2 cups peeled and chopped.

► Parsnips, which have a naturally sweet flavor, can be used as you would carrots.

► Though one of the most popular ways to prepare parsnips is to cook and mash them, they're wonderful chopped and quickly sautéed with chopped, tart apples.

► Add chopped parsnips to soups and stews, or blanch, cool and use in salads.

► Parsnips quickly turn mushy when overcooked, so be sure to add them to soups, stews and sautés toward the end of the cooking time.

► *See also* VEGETABLES, GENERAL

PASTA [PAH-stuh]

► Whether buying fresh or dried pasta, read the label and only buy brands made with durum wheat (also called semolina). This is the pasta of preference because it absorbs less water, has a mellow flavor and retains a pleasant "bite" when cooked. When buying dried pasta, always check the package to make sure the pieces are unbroken. If it looks crumbly or dusty, air has gotten to it—it's stale.

► Dried pasta will last almost indefinitely if stored in an airtight glass or plastic container in a cool, dark place. Dried whole-wheat pasta is the exception, and may turn rancid if stored for more than 1 month.

► Fresh pasta can be wrapped airtight in a plastic bag and refrigerated for up to 5 days, or double wrapped and frozen for up to 4 months. Frozen fresh pasta should go directly from freezer to boiling water.

► *Pasta yields:* 1 pound dry, 1-inch macaroni-style (shells, elbows, etc.) = about 9 cups cooked. One pound dry spaghetti-style noodles = about 7 cups cooked.

► How much pasta to buy per serving depends on whether it's fresh or dried (fresh pasta is heavier because it contains moisture). Generally, the formula is: Dried pasta—2 ounces per side-dish serving, 4 ounces per main-dish serving. Slightly larger amounts of fresh pasta are required—about 3 ounces per side-dish serving, 5 ounces per main-dish serving.

► If you don't have a pasta pot with a removable, perforated inner basket, use a colander, large strainer or French-fry basket inside a pot of boiling water in which to cook pasta. That way, you can simply lift the basket out and shake it to drain off excess water.

P

- Use about 4 quarts water per pound of pasta. Have the water boiling rapidly before adding the pasta, and stir the noodles a few times to keep them moving so they cook evenly. Once the water returns to a rolling boil, stirring isn't necessary because the water moves the pasta.
- Unsalted water will reach a boil faster than salted water, so add salt to rapidly boiling water just before adding the pasta.
- Adding 1 tablespoon vegetable oil to the cooking water keeps pasta from sticking together while cooking. It also keeps the water from boiling over.
- Rubbing vegetable oil around the top of the pot will also prevent boil-overs.
- No need to break long pasta like spaghetti and fettuccine into shorter pieces to fit in the pot. Simply set it in the boiling water and, as it softens (in just a few seconds) ease it around and down into the pan.
- After you add pasta to boiling water, covering the pot will speed the water returning to a boil. Take the cover off as soon as the boil has returned.
- The key to successful pasta is not to overcook it. Most commercial dried pasta needs less time to cook than the package recommends, while some fresh pastas may take less than a minute. The best way to test pasta for doneness is to bite into a piece. Perfectly cooked pasta should be al dente—tender, but still firm to the bite. If there's a noticeable "line" running through the thickest part of the pasta, it's not done. When you're testing for doneness, remember that residual heat continues to cook the pasta for a few seconds after it's removed from the water.
- When preparing pasta to be used in a dish requiring further cooking—such as a casserole or soup—reduce the cooking time by a third. The pasta will continue to cook and absorb liquid in the final dish.
- Cooking twice as much pasta at one time gives you a head start on the next night's meal. Thoroughly drain the portion you're not using, then put it in a bowl of ice water to stop the cooking. Drain thoroughly, then toss with 1 to 2 teaspoons oil. Cover and refrigerate for up to 3 days. You can use it in a salad, add it to soup (at the last minute), or toss it with your favorite sauce.
- Be sure to thoroughly drain cooked pasta. Excess cooking water clinging to the pasta will dilute the sauce.
- If cooked pasta sticks together, spritz it gently with hot running water for just a few seconds. Drain thoroughly before saucing.
- If the pasta will be used for salad, rinse it under cold running water to remove excess starch and keep the pieces from sticking together.
- Count on about 2 cups sauce per pound of pasta.
- If you're using a long-cooking sauce, prepare it before putting the pasta on to boil. Pasta that waits around for the sauce to finish can become overcooked.

P

- When saucing pasta, a general rule is: Thin or smooth noodles require a light, smooth sauce that won't overpower or weigh down the pasta; sturdy shapes like rotini can handle chunkier sauces.
- Next time you make pasta sauce, try doing so in a 12- or 14-inch skillet. That way you can turn the drained pasta right into the skillet and have plenty of room to toss it.
- Try serving the pasta and sauce separately, letting diners serve themselves according to taste.
- Pasta cools quickly, so always heat the serving bowl or plates before you dish it up. Dishes can be heated in a 250°F oven until warm, about 10 minutes. Or fill a serving bowl with very hot water, then pour it out and dry the bowl just before serving.
- There are several ways to reheat unsauced pasta. You can microwave it right in the storage container (if it's a plastic bag, open one corner, if it's a lidded casserole, leave the cover on) at HIGH (100 percent power) for 2 to 4 minutes, stirring halfway through. The timing depends on the amount and temperature of the pasta. Room-temperature pasta can also be reheated simply by tossing it with hot sauce. Or put it in a colander and run hot water over it, draining well before saucing. Sauced pasta can be reheated in a covered saucepan over low heat or in the microwave, as previously suggested.
- Make a gratin out of leftover pasta by placing it in a shallow baking dish and layering with sautéed mushrooms or green peppers or other vegetables. Moisten with sauce of your choice and top with breadcrumbs and grated cheese. Bake at 350°F until warmed through and the top is golden brown, about 25 minutes.
- The trick to eating long ribbon pasta is to start with just a few strands near the edge of the plate, positioning your fork vertical to the plate's surface. Then begin twisting your fork, winding the long strands into a tight, bite-sized bundle. All that's left is to eat it!

PASTA SHAPES

The hundreds of different shapes and sizes of pasta can be confusing, and the fact that manufacturers often use different names for the same shape (fusilli and rotini, for example) simply complicates matters. The following pasta-shape glossary should help you with those pastas most commonly available in supermarkets and Italian markets.

Acini di Peppe—"Peppercorns." Tiny peppercorn-shaped pasta.

Agnolotti—"Priests' caps." Small, crescent-shaped stuffed pastas.

P

Anellini—Tiny pasta rings.

Bavettine—Narrow *linguine.*

Bucatini—Hollow, spaghettilike strands.

Cannaroni—Wide tubes; also call *zitoni.*

Cannelloni—"Large reeds." Large, round tubes generally used for stuffing.

Capelli d'Angelo; Capellini—"Angel hair." Long, extremely fine strands.

Capelveneri—Very thin noodles.

Cappelletti—"Little hats." Hat-shaped stuffed pasta.

Cavatappi—Short, thin, spiral macaroni.

Cavatelli—Short, narrow, ripple-edged shells.

Conchiglie—"Conch shells." Shell-shaped pasta, sometimes called *maruzze.*

Coralli—Tiny tubes, generally used in soup.

Ditali—"Thimbles." Small macaroni about ½ inch long.

Ditalini—Smaller *ditali.*

Elbow Macaroni—From small to medium tubes.

Farfalle—"Butterflies." Bow- or butterfly-shaped pasta.

Farfallini—Small *farfalle.*

Farfallone—Large *farfalle.*

Fedelini—"Little faithful ones." Very fine spaghetti.

Fettucce—Flat egg noodles about ½ inch wide; the widest of the *fettuccines.*

Fettuccelle—Narrow (about ⅛ inch wide), flat egg noodles; the thinnest of the *fettuccine* family.

Fettuccine—"Little ribbons." Thin, flat egg noodles about ¼ inch wide.

Fideo—Thin, coiled strands of pasta that, when cooked, resemble vermicelli.

Fusilli—"Little springs." Traditional *fusilli* comes in spaghetti-length spiral-shaped noodles. Cut *fusilli* is about 1½ inches long.

Gemelli—"Twins." Short, 1½-inch twists that resemble 2 strands of spaghetti twisted together.

Gnocchi—Small, ripple-edged shells.

P

Lasagne—Long, very broad noodles (2 to 3 inches wide); straight or ripple-edged.

Linguine—"Little tongues." Very narrow (⅛ inch wide or less) ribbons.

Lumache—"Snails." Large shells intended for stuffing.

Macaroni—Tube-shaped pasta of various lengths.

Maccheroni—The Italian word for all types of macaroni, from hollow tubes, to shells, to twists.

Mafalde—Broad, flat, ripple-edged noodles.

Magliette—"Links." Short, curved tubes of pasta.

Manicotti—"Little muffs." Very large tubes, used for stuffing.

Margherite—"Daisies." Narrow flat noodles, with one rippled side.

Maruzze—"Seashells." Shell-shaped pasta that comes in several sizes, from tiny to jumbo.

Mezzani—Very short, curved tubes.

Mostaccioli—"Little mustaches." Pasta tubes about 2 inches long.

Orecchiette—"Little ears." Tiny disk shapes.

Orzo—Pasta grains, the size and shape of rice.

Pappardelle—Wide noodles (about ⅝ inch) with rippled sides.

Pastina—"Tiny dough." Any of various tiny pasta shapes (such as *acini de pepe*), generally used in soups.

Penne—"Pens" or "quills." Diagonally cut tubes with either smooth or ridged sides.

Perciatelli—Thin, hollow pasta about twice as thick as spaghetti; similar to *bucatini*.

Pezzoccheri—Thick buckwheat noodles.

Quadrettini—Small flat squares of pasta.

Radiatore—"Little radiators." Short, chunky shapes (about 1 inch long and ½ inch in diameter) that resemble tiny radiators with rippled edges.

Ravioli—Square-shaped stuffed pasta.

Rigatoni—Large grooved macaroni about 1½ inches wide.

Riso—Rice-shaped pasta, similiar to *orzo*.

Rotelle—"Little wheels." Small, spoked-wheel shapes.

Rotini—Short (1 to 2 inches long) spirals.

P

Ruote; Ruote de Carro—"Cartwheels." Small, spoked-wheel shapes.

Semi de Melone—"Melon seeds." Tiny, flat melon-seed shapes.

Spaghetti—Long, thin, round strands.

Spaghettini—Very thin spaghetti.

Tagliarini—Long, paper-thin ribbons, usually less than ⅛ inch wide.

Tagliatelle—Long, thin, flat egg noodles about ¼ inch wide.

Tagliolini—Another name for *tagliarini*.

Tortellini—"Little twists." Small stuffed pasta, similiar to *cappelletti*.

Tortelloni—Large *tortellini*.

Trenette—A narrower, thicker version of *tagliatelle*.

Tripolini—Small bow ties with rounded edges.

Tubetti—"Little tubes." Tiny, hollow pasta tubes.

Vermicelli—"Little worms." Very thin strands of spaghetti.

Ziti—"Bridegrooms." Slightly curved tubes, ranging in length from 2 to 12 inches.

PASTRY BAGS

▶ Pastry bags come in a variety of sizes and can be found in gourmet shops, some supermarkets and the kitchenware section of most department stores. The most popular materials for pastry bags are clear plastic (which are disposable), nylon and plastic-lined cotton or canvas.

▶ Use a small, zip-closure plastic bag for a quick, disposable pastry bag in one of several ways. Spoon the frosting into the bag and seal, then snip off one of the corners and pipe your design onto the dessert being decorated. Or snip ¼ to ½ inch from a corner and insert a piping tip into the opening. Fill the bag with frosting and seal.

▶ Make an instant, disposable pastry bag by folding a square of waxed paper in half diagonally to form a triangle. Shape the triangle into a cone, securing the top edge with Scotch tape or a paper clip. Fill two-thirds full with frosting, melted chocolate, etc., fold down the top of the bag, then snip off the pointed end so the hole is the desired diameter.

▶ Filling a pastry bag is much easier if you can use two hands. Twist about 2 inches of the tip end so the filling won't come out. Set the bag, twisted end down, in a wide-mouthed jar or 4-cup measuring cup; fold the cuff of the bag over the jar's rim. Fill the bag about two-thirds full, then twist the top closed and lift the bag out of its holder.

P

▶ After you fill a pastry bag, put your finger over the opening and give it a shake to compact the filling and eliminate air pockets.

▶ If you want to make a melted-chocolate design on a dessert, put finely chopped chocolate or chocolate chips in a small, heavy-duty plastic bag (a regular-weight bag could melt). Set the unsealed bag upright in a small bowl and microwave at MEDIUM (50 percent power) until the chocolate is almost melted; let stand 5 minutes until completely melted. Or *seal* the bag and set in a bowl of very hot water until chocolate is melted (make sure that no water gets into the chocolate). Thoroughly dry the bag with paper towels, then snip a tiny hole in a corner of the bag and pipe directly onto the dessert.

▶ Pipe a mixture from a pastry bag by applying pressure from the top, continually twisting it tight to the filling as the bag empties.

PASTRY BRUSHES

▶ An untreated natural-bristle paintbrush can be substituted for a pastry brush.

▶ Always smell a pastry brush before using it to make sure no rancid odor remains from its last use. An off odor can transfer easily to foods.

▶ Make quick work out of greasing pans, baking sheets and muffin tins by using a pastry brush dipped in oil or melted shortening.

▶ Wash pastry brushes in hot, soapy water to rid them of any oil or other ingredient that might turn rancid. Be sure to rinse brushes throughly after washing.

PEA *see* PEAS

PEACHES

▶ Peaches fall into two classifications—**freestone**, in which the stone or pit easily comes away from the flesh, and **clingstone** or **cling**, where the fruit adheres stubbornly to the pit. Freestone peaches are the more commonly available in markets, while clings are widely used for commercial purposes.

▶ Choose intensely fragrant fruit that gives slightly to palm pressure. Avoid those that are hard, or have soft spots (bruises), or show signs of greening.

▶ Store ripe peaches in a plastic bag in the refrigerator for up to 5 days.

▶ Ripen underripe peaches at room temperature by placing in a paper bag with an apple; pierce bag in several places with the tip of a knife.

▶ *Peach yields:* 1 pound = 4 medium; 2¾ cups sliced; 2¼ cups chopped.

▶ The flavor of a peach is intensified at room temperature so take it out of the fridge at least 30 minutes before eating.

P

- If you're eating a peach out of hand, it's up to you whether or not to peel it. Always wash it well; in doing so, much of the fuzz will rub off.
- Always peel peaches that will be cooked or the skin will become tough and ruin the texture of the pie, preserves, or whatever.
- To peel a peach, dip it in boiling water for 20 to 30 seconds; remove with a slotted spoon and immediately plunge into a bowl of ice water. Use a paring knife to pull off the skin. If the skin doesn't come off readily, repeat the process, or simply use the knife to peel the skin that resists.
- The flesh of a peach will discolor rapidly after being cut or peeled. If not combining peaches with an ingredient containing acid (such as a salad dressing), dip them quickly in and out of acidulated water (3 tablespoons lemon juice per quart of cold water); drain well.
- Few fruit desserts are better than the classic peach Melba—poached peach halves and vanilla ice cream topped with raspberry sauce.
- For great peach shortcake, beat 1 or 2 tablespoons seedless raspberry jam into whipped cream just before it's stiff and spoon over layers of shortbread and sliced peaches that have been tossed with a little Chambord (raspberry-flavored liqueur).
- *See also* FRUIT, GENERAL

PEANUT BUTTER

- Did you know that peanut butter was promoted as a health food at the 1904 St. Louis World's Fair?
- Unopened, peanut butter can be stored in a cool, dry place for at least 1 year. Once opened, regular peanut butter will stay fresh for about 3 months. After that, it should be refrigerated to keep the oil from turning rancid. Natural peanut butter—made without salt, sugar, stabilizers or additional fats—must be refrigerated, and will keep for about 6 months.
- Because it doesn't contain stabilizers, the oil in natural peanut butter separates and often rises to the top of the jar. To save calories, some people pour off the oil, but this leaves you with a rather dry spread. If you want the peanut butter the way it was intended, simply stir the oil back into the mixture.
- Make your own peanut butter by chopping peanuts (plain or dry roasted) in a food processor or blender. When the nuts are very finely ground, add a little vegetable or peanut oil, processing until the mixture reaches the desired consistency.
- Peanut butter in soup is an old southern favorite. Stir a tablespoon or two into the next chicken soup you make and see how you like it.
- Add an exotic touch to poultry and meat sauces and marinades by stirring in 1 or 2 tablespoons peanut butter.
- Morning toast spread with peanut butter and drizzled with a little honey

P

or maple syrup is delicious and much more nutritious than using butter or margarine.

▸ Make a special bread pudding by spreading the bread slices with peanut butter before layering them with the custard mixture.

▸ Tired of peanut butter and jelly sandwiches? Next time, mix a little chutney or mashed banana with the peanut butter, or put a layer of potato chips, dill pickle slices or rashers of crispy bacon on top of the peanut butter.

▸ Don't throw out used peanut butter jars—their wide-mouth openings make them great for food storage.

PEANUTS

▸ Did you know that peanuts aren't really nuts . . . they're legumes!

▸ Though there are several varieties of peanut, the two most popular are the small, round **Spanish peanut,** and the larger and more oval **Virginia peanut.**

▸ Choose unshelled peanuts that have clean, unbroken, unblemished shells; they shouldn't rattle when shaken. Shelled peanuts, often available in vacuum-sealed jars or cans, are usually roasted and sometimes salted.

▸ Store unshelled peanuts, tightly wrapped, in the refrigerator for up to 6 months.

▸ Store unopened, vacuum-packed shelled peanuts at room temperature for up to 1 year. Once opened, shelled peanuts should be refrigerated airtight and used within 3 months.

▸ *Peanut yields:* 1½ pounds of unshelled peanuts = about 1 pound shelled nuts; 3½ to 4 cups.

▸ Raw peanuts in the shell can be roasted by spreading them in a single layer in a shallow pan and baking at 350°F for about 30 minutes. Stir once or twice during that time.

▸ Don't just think of peanuts for sweets like candy. They're great in main dishes (everything from meatloaf to soups), tossed in salads, in a stuffed acorn squash filling, in muffins or as a garnish for vegetables like carrots.

▸ *See also* NUTS, GENERAL

PEARS

▸ Choose pears that are fragrant and free of blemishes and soft spots. Buy pears that are firm, but not hard. Pears for out of hand eating should be just slightly soft at the stem end. Those to be used for cooking should be somewhat firmer.

▸ Store ripe fruit in a plastic bag in the refrigerator for up to 5 days.

▸ Ripen pears at room temperature by placing them in a paper bag with an

P

apple. Pierce the bag in several places with the tip of a knife. Unlike most fruit, pears are ripe when they're still fairly firm.

▶ *Pear yields:* 1 pound = 3 medium; 3 cups sliced.

▶ If you're eating a pear out of hand, there's no need to peel it. Just wash it thoroughly and enjoy.

▶ The skin of a pear darkens and toughens when heated, so it should always be removed for cooked dishes. Use a vegetable peeler or sharp paring knife to remove the thin skin.

▶ When you core a pear, make sure to get all the gritty flesh around the core.

▶ A pear's flesh discolors rapidly when exposed to air. If not combining pears with an ingredient containing acid (such as a salad dressing), dip them in acidulated water (3 tablespoons lemon juice per quart of cold water).

▶ *See also* FRUIT, GENERAL

PEAS, DRIED; FIELD PEAS

▶ Field peas are a variety of yellow or green pea grown specifically for drying. These peas are dried and usually split along a natural seam, in which case they're called *split peas*.

▶ Dried peas can be stored in an airtight container for up to 1 year in a cool, dry place. They can be frozen indefinitely.

▶ Before using, pick through dried peas; discard any that are discolored or shriveled. Tiny holes signal bugs.

▶ Dried *whole* peas need to be soaked before cooking to rehydrate them. For the overnight method, put the whole peas in a large bowl or pot and cover with at least 3 inches of cold water; soak overnight. (If flatulence is a problem, change the water at least twice during the soaking process.)

▶ If you don't have time to soak the peas overnight, use the quick-soak method: Put them in a large pan, cover with water and bring to a boil. Remove from heat, cover and let stand for 1 to 2 hours. Then cook according to the recipe directions.

▶ Always drain off the soaking water and add fresh water in which to cook the peas.

▶ Unlike whole peas, split peas don't need soaking before being cooked.

▶ Salt dried peas after they're cooked. Adding salt to the cooking liquid slows down the cooking and toughens the peas.

▶ Smoked sausage, ham or bacon are perfect flavor partners for split peas and split-pea soup.

▶ As soon as the peas are done, drain off the hot cooking liquid or they'll continue to cook. Unless, of course, you're cooking split peas for soup, in which case it doesn't matter if they're soft.

P

▶ Cover and refrigerate leftover cooked whole or split peas and use within 5 days.

▶ *See also* BEANS, DRIED; LENTILS; PEAS, FRESH GREEN

PEAS, FRESH GREEN

▶ Fresh green peas are also known as **English peas, shell peas** and **garden peas.** Purchase fresh green peas that have firm, plump, unblemished, bright green pods; avoid pale or shriveled pods. The peas inside should be glossy, crunchy and sweet (not starchy). The tiny, young *petits pois* are generally only available in specialty produce markets. Peas begin the sugar-to-starch conversion process the moment they're picked so it's important to buy them as fresh as possible.

▶ Store fresh green peas, unwashed, in a plastic bag in the refrigerator for no more than 2 days.

▶ *Fresh peas yield:* 1 pound peas in the pod = about 1 cup shelled peas.

▶ Shell peas just before using. To remove the peas, snap off the stem end and use it to "unzip" the pod by pulling on the string. Press on the seam, which will pop open to reveal the peas, then run your thumb or finger under the peas to free them.

▶ Don't throw out the pods after shelling the peas. Toss them in a pot of chicken or vegetable stock and simmer for 1 hour before removing the pods. They'll add a nice flavor to the broth, which can be the base for your next pot of soup. The broth can be frozen until you're ready to use it. Or you can freeze the pea pods for up to 3 months for use at a future date.

▶ Don't add baking soda to the cooking water for peas. It may keep them green, but will leach out valuable nutrients in the process, not to mention affect their flavor.

▶ Peas will lose their gorgeous bright green color if cooked with acidic ingredients (like lemon juice, wine or tomatoes) in a covered pot.

▶ Be careful not to overcook peas—they should be crisp-tender when done. Overdone peas will lose their bright green color and much of their fresh flavor.

▶ Young green peas are perfectly wonderful raw in salads.

▶ Frozen green peas—especially the tiny, sweet petit pois—don't need defrosting before being added to a cooked dish. Simply stir them into the dish 2 to 3 minutes before the cooking time is finished. The heat of the dish will cook them just enough—so they're still crisp-tender instead of mushy. For pea salads, simply pour cold water over the frozen peas and let stand about 5 minutes, or until peas are defrosted. Drain well before adding to the salad.

▶ *See also* PEAS, DRIED; PEAS, POD

P

PEAS, POD

▶ This type of pea is entirely edible—pod and all. The two main varieties of pod peas are snow peas and sugar snap peas.

▶ The **snow pea** (also known as **Chinese pea pod**) is thin, crisp and has an almost translucent, bright green pod. It's flatter than the **sugar snap pea**, which is a cross between the snow pea and the English pea (common green pea). The sugar snap has a plump, crisp, bright green pod in which the peas are more prominent.

▶ Choose snow and sugar snap peas that fit the descriptions in the preceding tip. Avoid pods that are limp or broken.

▶ Store unwashed snow and sugar snap peas in a plastic bag in the refrigerator for up to 3 days.

▶ Before using, wash pod peas, then snap off the stem ends, using them to pull on and remove the string, if necessary.

▶ Pod peas should either be served raw or cooked only briefly. When using in dishes like stir-frys, add during the last minute or so of cooking time.

▶ *See also* PEAS, FRESH GREEN

PECANS

▶ Pecans have a fat content of over 70 percent—higher than any other nut.

▶ Pecans will be easier to crack if you cover them with water, then bring to a boil. Remove from heat, cover and set aside for at least 15 minutes, or until cool. Blot the nuts dry, then crack end to end.

▶ *See also* NUTS, GENERAL *for general purchase, storage and usage information*

PEPPER; PEPPERCORNS

▶ There are three basic types of peppercorn (the *Piper nigrum* family)—black, white and green. The strongest flavored of the three is the **black peppercorn**, which is picked when the berry's not quite ripe, then dried until it shrivels and darkens; it's slightly hot with a hint of sweetness. Among the world's best black peppers are the Tellicherry and the Lampong. **White peppercorns** are the fully ripe berries from which the skin has been removed; they have a milder, less pungent flavor. Black and white peppercorns are available whole, cracked and coarsely or finely ground. **Green peppercorns,** the soft, underripe berry, are usually preserved in brine and have a fresh, "green" flavor. They're also sold dried.

▶ Unrelated to black, white and green peppercorns are cayenne pepper, Szechuan pepper and the pink peppercorn. **Cayenne pepper** (also called **red pepper**) is ground from a variety of chile peppers, therefore its hot, spicy flavor. **Szechuan pepper** berries come from the prickly ash tree and resemble black peppercorns but with a tiny seed; they're mildly hot and have a distinctive flavor and fragrance. **Pink peppercorns** are actually

P

the dried berries from the *Baies* rose plant; they're pungent and slightly sweet.

► Whole dried peppercorns can be stored in a cool, dark place for at least 1 year. Green peppercorns packed in brine should be refrigerated once opened and can be kept for 1 month; green water-packed peppercorns for 1 week. Freeze-dried green peppercorns can be stored in a cool, dark place for about 6 months.

► Preground pepper loses its flavor fairly quickly and should be stored in a cool, dark place for no more than 3 months.

► Nothing compares to the flavor of freshly ground pepper. If you don't have a pepper grinder, use a mortar and pestle to crush the peppercorns. Alternatively, you can use a rolling pin, mallet, or even the side of an unopened can to crush the peppercorns on any work surface.

► Use white pepper if you don't want to mar the appearance of light-colored sauces and other preparations.

► Adding ½ teaspoon peppercorns to a shaker full of ground pepper will freshen the flavor and keep it shaking freely.

► *See also* SPICES

PERSIMMONS

► The two most widely available persimmon varieties in the United States are the Hachiya (also called Japanese persimmon) and the Fuyu. The **Hachiya** is large and round, with a slightly elongated, pointed base; the **Fuyu** is smaller and more tomato-shaped.

► Choose plump persimmons with a glossy, brilliant red-orange skin; their caps should be green. The Hachiya should be quite soft (but not mushy) when ripe, whereas a fully ripe Fuyu will be firm, yet give to gentle palm pressure.

► Store ripe persimmons in a plastic bag in the refrigerator for up to 3 days.

► Ripen persimmons by putting them in a pierced paper bag with an apple at room temperature. Overripe persimmons turn mushy, so watch them carefully.

► Cold temperatures have an amazing effect on persimmons—it makes them sweeter. If you want to puree persimmons for use in a recipe but the fruit's a little underripe, speed up the process by putting the persimmon in a freezer-weight plastic bag and freezing until solid. Thaw at room temperature and the persimmons will be sweet and ready to go.

► If eating a persimmon out of hand, wash it thoroughly. If you plan to cook with it, peel the fruit first.

► If the Hachiya is eaten even slightly underripe, it will pucker your mouth with an incredible astringency. The Fuyu, on the other hand, is not at all astringent.

P

- Some Hachiyas contain a few black seeds, which should be removed before using the flesh in baked goods, etc.
- For persimmon "sherbet," cut the fruit in half, wrap each half in plastic wrap, and freeze for about 4 hours, then eat right out of the skin. Or peel (and seed, if necessary), cut into chunks and freeze. When the persimmon chunks are solid, puree in a food processor.
- Persimmons are usually pureed before being used in cooking or for baked goods. Add 1 to 2 teaspoons lemon juice to the puree to keep the fruit from darkening.
- *See also* FRUIT, GENERAL

PHYLLO [FEE-loh]

- Phyllo (also spelled filo) is tissue-thin pastry dough. It's usually sold in 1-pound boxes and can be found fresh in many Middle Eastern markets and frozen in most supermarkets.
- Tightly wrapped phyllo can be stored in the refrigerator for up to a month. Once opened, use phyllo within a few days.
- Phyllo can be frozen for up to 1 year. Thaw frozen phyllo overnight in the refrigerator. Phyllo becomes brittle if refrozen.
- Phyllo sheets become dry and brittle quickly so don't remove them from their wrapping until all the other ingredients are ready.
- Always keep those phyllo sheets you're not working with covered with waxed paper topped by a slightly damp cloth (don't let cloth touch phyllo—it will make it soggy and unmanageable). This keeps the phyllo from drying out.

PICNICS

- Carry a large plastic bag in case there are no trash barrels.
- If you think the ground might be damp, take along a plastic tarp or several large plastic bags to spread out underneath the tablecloth or blanket.
- Wrap a napkin around each place setting (fork, spoon and knife) and tie with a 6-inch piece of colorful yarn.
- Dampen inexpensive cloth napkins, fold and wrap in a plastic bag, and use as an after-picnic cleanup for hands.
- If you don't have a cooler, line a picnic basket or cardboard box with a thermal blanket and then a large plastic bag. Fill with blue-ice packs and the food or drink that requires chilling.
- If you don't have blue ice to chill picnic foods, soak sponges in water, then put them in plastic bags, seal, and freeze until solid. In an insulated cooler, they should last for up to 3 hours, depending on the size of the sponge.
- In lieu of blue ice, fill clean milk cartons with water and freeze. Or line large, shallow plastic storage containers with foil or plastic wrap, fill with

P

water, and freeze until solid. Then place the chunk of ice in a zip-closure plastic bag.

▶ Large chunks of ice melt more slowly than ice cubes.

▶ Make sure any food to be packed in a cooler is well chilled.

▶ Always double wrap raw poultry, meat or fish to make sure juices don't leak and contaminate other foods.

▶ If the trip is long, freeze raw chicken and meat (to be grilled) and put it frozen into the cooler. It will thaw during the journey.

▶ Keep beverages in one cooler and food in another for easy access.

▶ A full cooler will stay cold longer than one that's only partially filled.

▶ If possible, put the cooler and picnic basket inside the car during the trip to the picnic site. The trunk gets too hot.

▶ At the picnic site, put the cooler in the shade and cover it with a blanket.

▶ The more you open the cooler lid, the faster the temperature will rise.

▶ Keep hot foods hot by insulating the containers with a layer of heavy-duty foil, then several layers of newspaper.

▶ Make portable, disposable salt and pepper shakers by filling separate paper straws with the seasoning, then tightly twisting the ends to close.

▶ Use a muffin tin as a condiment server, each section holding something different—ketchup, mustard, chopped onions, sliced pickles, relish, etc.

▶ An egg carton makes a handy container for small, bruisable items that need protection such as apricots, plums, tomatoes and deviled eggs (individually wrap the latter in plastic wrap).

▶ If bugs are getting into your drinks, cover the glass with foil, then poke a straw through the foil.

▶ Bacteria grows rapidly at warm temperatures, so at the picnic's end, throw out perishables such as lunch meats, potato or pasta salad, and meat or poultry.

PIE CRUSTS

▶ A cool kitchen will add to your success in making successful pastry crusts.

▶ Pie crust ingredients (even flour) should be cold to produce the very best results.

▶ The best flour for pie pastry is all-purpose or pastry flour. Bread flour has too much gluten to make a tender crust; cake flour is too soft and won't give the proper body.

▶ Lard and shortening will produce a shorter (more tender) crust than butter or margarine. If you want the best of both worlds, use half lard or shortening and half butter.

▶ A vegetable-oil crust won't be as flaky as one made with solid fat such as butter, shortening or lard.

▶ Sugar in a pastry dough not only contributes to its sweetness, but tenderizes it as well.

- ▶ Personalize your pastry dough by adding flavor enhancers such as ground cinnamon, nutmeg or ginger, or—for savory pies—chili or curry powder, or crushed dried basil or tarragon leaves, etc. Stir these flavorings into the flour before cutting in the fat.
- ▶ It's the tiny pockets of fat encased in flour that make a pie crust crisp and flaky. Use a pastry blender or 2 knives to cut the butter (or other shortening) into the flour mixture *only* until the mixture resembles coarse crumbs. For the flakiest crust, cut in half the fat to the coarse-crumb stage, then add the remaining fat and cut to pea-sized pieces. Body heat will melt the fat and toughen the crust so touch the dough with your hands as little as possible.
- ▶ Making pastry dough in the food processor is a cinch, providing you don't overprocess. Using the metal blade, combine the dry ingredients with a couple of quick on/off pulses. Add chunks of *cold* fat, processing with quick on/off pulses until the pieces are the size of large peas. Add the cold liquid and process with quick on/off pulses *just* until the dough begins to gather on the blades. (Processing the dough until it forms a ball will produce a tough crust.) Turn the crumbly mixture out onto a piece of plastic wrap, folding edges over and lightly form dough into a disk. Refrigerate until ready to roll out.
- ▶ Anytime you add water to a pie dough, it must be iced. *Any* liquid should be ice cold.
- ▶ Once the liquid has been added to a pie crust mixture, blend *only* until the dough begins to hold together. Overworking pie dough will make it tough.
- ▶ Substitute icy-cold sour cream or whipping cream for water for an extra-flaky crust.
- ▶ If your dough is too wet because you've added too much liquid, place it between two sheets of plastic wrap, flatten to about ½ inch, and freeze until firm, but not rock hard. Once firm, the dough can be rolled out with ease. Note that too much water causes pastry to shrink, so make allowances.
- ▶ Pie dough can be made ahead, wrapped and refrigerated for up to 4 days.
- ▶ Chilled pastry dough rolls out more easily than room-temperature dough. Form it into a ½-inch-thick disk, wrap in plastic wrap and refrigerate for 30 minutes.
- ▶ A large pastry board and heavy rolling pin make rolling out doughs a breeze. Marble and textured acrylic boards are the easiest to work with. Both the pin and board should be lightly floured.
- ▶ Or roll the dough out on a lightly flour pastry cloth; or use a stockinette cover (available at kitchenware shops) on your rolling pin.
- ▶ Cornstarch is a good substitute for flour to keep dough from sticking to both the work surface and rolling pin. It works great, doesn't give a

P

starchy aftertaste, and is easier to clean up than flour.

► Rolling out dough on a waxed-paper-covered countertop makes cleanup a breeze. To keep the waxed paper from slipping, sprinkle a few drops of water on the countertop before arranging the paper.

► Most doughs can be rolled out on a smooth countertop without sticking if you spray the surface beforehand with nonstick vegetable spray. A soapy sponge or cloth makes cleanup a breeze.

► Roll out dough by placing the rolling pin in the center of the disk of dough, then roll firmly and evenly out to the edge. Continue rolling from the center outward until the dough circle is 3 inches larger than the pie pan's inside diameter.

► Chilled dough is easier to roll if you first give it a few whacks with your rolling pin, making ridges in the disc of dough. Press down with the pin and start rolling from one of the ridges, rotating the dough a quarter turn after each roll.

► A pizza cutter is great for cutting strips of pie dough for lattice-top pies.

► Use a pastry scraper or a large metal spatula to loosen stuck dough from a pastry board.

► To transfer dough from pastry board to pan, fold dough circle in half, gently lift dough and position it so the fold is across the pan's center. Unfold the dough, easing it into the pan. Or, you can drape the dough over a flour-dusted rolling pin, position it over the pie pan, and remove the pin.

► Don't stretch the dough as you place it in the pan—stretched dough shrinks.

► If you find holes or particularly thin spots in the dough once it's in the pan, patch with bits of leftover dough, pressing down gently with your fingertips.

► To crimp the edges, start by using a knife to trim the edge of the top crust, creating a ¾- to 1-inch overhang. Fold the overhang under, then form a raised edge by pressing the dough gently between your thumb and index finger. Decoratively crimp or flute the edge as desired.

► If you have trouble getting the edges of the top crust to stick to the bottom crust, lightly brush the edge of the bottom crust with water before pressing the two together.

► For prebaked pie shells, use a fork to prick the bottom and sides of the unbaked shell at ½-inch intervals. Refrigerate the unbaked crust for 30 minutes (or freeze for 15 minutes) before baking. For filled baked pies, don't prick the dough.

► If you don't have time to refrigerate the crust before baking, place a sheet of foil on top of the unbaked crust, molding it to fit the crust. Pour about 1½ cups of pie weights (available at gourmet kitchen shops), dried beans or rice onto the foil. Bake the shell about 8 minutes, remove the foil and

P

weights, then continue baking 4 to 5 minutes, or until the pie shell is golden brown.

▶ To prevent a soggy crust, refrigerate the unbaked crust for 15 minutes. Or brush it with slightly beaten egg white, which serves as a sealant, then refrigerate for 15 minutes.

▶ If the crust won't be prebaked, pour the filling into the pie shell *just* before baking to keep it from becoming soggy. Setting the pie pan on a metal baking sheet during baking also helps prevent soggy crusts.

▶ You can line a pie pan with pastry, then put it in a plastic bag or other airtight wrapping and refrigerate for up to 4 days, freeze for up to 6 months.

▶ Always defrost a pie shell before filling and baking. If using a glass pie pan, make sure it's close to room temperature so it won't crack when put in a hot oven.

▶ Custard pies are notorious for creating soggy crusts. One remedy is to prebake the unpricked crust for 5 minutes, then letting it cool for 15 minutes before filling. Using a heavyweight, freezer-to-oven glass pie pan also helps, because glass absorbs heat better than metal and produces a well-baked crust.

▶ Add a nutty nuance to your bottom crust by sprinkling toasted ground nuts over the bottom. Use the back of a dinner tablespoon to press the nuts lightly into the dough before adding the filling. The nuts also help keep the crust from becoming soggy.

▶ You can also press fine cookie crumbs into a pastry dough before baking. The cookie crumbs work best for single-crust pie shells that are baked blind.

▶ The upper crust: Give the top crust of your pastry a sheen by brushing it with lightly beaten egg white or cold milk. Brushing it with whipping cream or an egg yolk beaten with 1 teaspoon water will produce a glossy, dark golden brown crust. A mixture of 2 tablespoons water and 1 table-spoon granulated sugar will produce a crisp, sweet top crust. Brushing it with plain water will make it crisp. Make sure no puddles of sugar or egg glaze remain on the crust—they tend to overbrown. Don't brush glaze on the crimped edges of a crust until the last 10 to 15 minutes of baking time or they might get too dark.

▶ For a sweet, spicy top crust, sprinkle it with 1 tablespoon sugar and ground cinnamon or nutmeg to taste. Savory pies can be sprinkled with caraway, poppy or sesame seeds.

▶ If the fluted edges of your crust begin to brown too fast, make a shield by cutting a 12-inch-wide piece of foil 3 inches longer than the pan's diameter (for example, an 11-inch length of foil for an 8-inch pie pan). Cut out a center circle that's 2 inches smaller than the pan's diameter. When

P

the crust begins to brown, place the foil over the pie, gently curving the excess to cover the fluted edge.

► Create a delicious snack by rolling out leftover pie crust to a ⅛- to ¼-inch thickness and sprinkling generously with ground cinnamon and granulated sugar. Cut into strips or irregular shapes and bake in a 350°F oven until golden brown. You can also brush the dough with maple syrup, honey or melted, cooled jelly. Whatever the topping, it's great comfort food!

► Leftover pie dough can also be frozen airtight for up to 6 months. It can be used in small amounts to top cobblers, mini potpies, etc. Or it can be combined with other batches of leftover dough and used for a pie crust. If you just have a few scraps of leftover dough, use canapé cutters or small cookie cutters to cut out decorative garnishes for soups and stews. Remember, however, that rerolling the dough will reduce its tenderness.

► Many cookie doughs make fine pie crust—and you don't have to roll them out. Simply press the cookie dough into the pan, making a raised and flutted edge, if desired. Work quickly and use a light touch so as not to overwork the dough and create a tough crust. Refrigerate the dough for at least 30 minutes before baking.

► Though most pastry-dough crusts don't require the pan to be greased, graham- and cookie-crumb crusts need a well-greased pan.

► If you like graham cracker or cookie crusts but think they're too sweet, substitute ½ cup of them with Ritz or saltine cracker crumbs; omit any salt from the crust recipe.

► You can use Oreo cookies—including the filling—to make a wonderful pie crust that doesn't require extra sugar. Just combine 1½ cups Oreo cookie crumbs (about 22 cookies) with 3 tablespoons melted butter and press into the pan as usual.

► Another easy way to firmly pack the crumbs into a pie pan is to use the back of a dinner tablespoon or a rubber spatula. Or spread the crumbs in place, then press them down with another pie plate (of course, then you have to wash the second pie plate).

► Prebaking a crumb crust for 10 minutes at 350°F will help keep it crisp. Completely cool a prebaked crumb crust before filling.

► Seal a prebaked crumb or pastry crust by using the back of a dinner teaspoon to spread 2 to 3 ounces melted semisweet chocolate over the bottom of the crust and halfway up the sides. Pop the coated crust in the refrigerator for about 10 minutes to set the chocolate before filling.

► A pie crust made with cookie or graham cracker crumbs will sometimes stick to the pan when the pie is chilled. A quick remedy is to soak a dishtowel in very hot water, wring it out, and wrap it around the base of

P

the pie plate for 5 minutes. The heat will soften the butter in the crust, thereby loosening it for easy removal.

▶ *See also* CRUMBS, GENERAL; PIE PANS; PIES, GENERAL

PIE PANS

▶ Not sure about the size of your pie pan? Measure the diameter from the inside edge of the rim. Pie-pan measurements may vary up to ½ inch—a 9-inch pan is often only 8½ inches in diameter.

▶ Glass, dark-metal and dull-metal pans absorb heat and produce a crisp, golden-brown crust; shiny aluminum pans produce a paler crust.

▶ When using glass pie pans, reduce the oven heat by 25°F.

▶ Lightweight foil pans are usually smaller than regular pie pans. Extra filling may be poured into individual muffin tins.

▶ Unless otherwise indicated in a recipe, pie pans do not need to be greased.

▶ *See also* PAN SIZES; PIE CRUSTS; PIES, GENERAL

PIES, GENERAL

▶ Before beginning to bake a pie, position the oven rack in the middle of the oven; preheat oven for 15 minutes. Use an oven thermometer for accurate oven temperature

▶ Always taste the fruit before making a fruit-pie filling. If the fruit isn't sweet enough, slice it very thinly so there'll be more surfaces to absorb the sugar.

▶ Add a new dimension to pumpkin pie by adding ¼ cup pure maple syrup, and decreasing the sugar and liquid by 2 tablespoons each.

▶ When a pie recipe calls for dotting the surface with butter, you'll get more even coverage by rubbing a cold stick of butter over the coarse side of a grater and sprinkling the grated butter over the top.

▶ When making a pie with super-juicy fruit, stir 1 tablespoon quick-cooking tapioca into the filling. During baking, the tapioca will absorb and thicken some of the excess juice and keep the filling from bubbling over.

▶ To prevent a fruit pie's juices from spreading when you dish it up, fold 1 egg white, beaten until stiff with 2 tablespoons of the sugar in the recipe, into the filling before baking.

▶ Fruit pie juices often bubble up and cause the crust to stick to the pan. To prevent this, grease and flour the pie pan before the bottom crust goes in.

▶ Freeze a pie filling during the summer months when fruit is plentiful and enjoy fruit pie during the winter. Simply line a pie pan with heavy-duty foil, leaving plenty of overlap to cover the top. Fill the foil-lined pan with the fruit filling of your choice, seal and freeze. When solid, remove the foil-wrapped filling from the pie pan, label the contents, and return to the freezer for up to 6 months. When ready to bake, unwrap and place

P

frozen filling in pie crust, then position and flute top crust. Cover the edge with foil. Bake at 425°F for 30 minutes; remove foil and bake 25 to 30 minutes longer, or until crust is golden brown.

▶ When making any kind of custard pie (including pumpkin), stir the mixture only until it is well combined. Beating it until frothy will cause unsightly bubbles to form on the surface of the baked pie.

▶ Have your fruit-and-cheese course in a pie! Sprinkle ½ to 1 cup grated cheddar over the top of an apple or pear pie before positioning the top crust. The cheese will melt down over the fruit during baking and add a delicious flavor.

▶ Never pour a filling into the pie shell until just before baking. Combining the two ahead of time and letting the unbaked pie stand contributes to a soggy bottom crust. The crust and filling can be covered and refrigerated separately until ready to bake.

▶ To prevent boilovers in super-juicy fruit pies, stick 3 or 4 pieces of raw tubular macaroni through the top crust in a circle about 1 inch from the center. The macaroni tubes allow the steam to vent, thereby releasing the pressure that would force out the juices. Short pieces of paper drinking straws will also do the trick. Needless to say, remove the macaroni or straws from the pie after baking.

▶ To save on messy oven cleanup, bake pies that tend to boil over—such as fruit pies and those with liquid sweeteners like molasses—on a baking sheet that's been coated lightly with nonstick vegetable spray.

▶ To prevent a custard filling from spilling as you put the pie in the oven, pull out the oven rack a few inches, place the unfilled pie shell on the oven rack, then pour in the filling. Very gently return the rack to its original position.

▶ It's important that oven heat circulate freely and evenly. If baking two pies on one shelf, position the pans so there's at least 2 inches between each other and the sides of the oven. If baking on two shelves, position the pans so that one doesn't sit directly beneath another.

▶ There are two ways to test a custard pie for doneness. The first is to insert a dinner knife into the pie about an inch from the center. If the knife comes out clean, the pie's done. The second "jiggle" method is done by holding the edge of the pie pan with a potholder and gently shaking the pie. If you can't get a grip on the pan, shake the oven shelf. If the center inch of the pie shows a gentle (rather than sharp) wave, remove it from the oven. Residual heat will continue to cook the filling as the pie stands.

▶ Cool pies on a rack so air can circulate underneath and speed the cooling.

▶ Quick-cool pies by filling a 9- by 13-inch pan with ice cubes, then setting the pie plate atop the cubes. Watch to make sure that, as the ice melts, the water doesn't reach the top of the pie plate.

P

► Glaze single-crust fruit pies or tarts by lightly brushing the surface with warm, light corn syrup 10 minutes after removing the pie from the oven. Or, depending on the fruit's flavor and color, you can brush the surface with melted currant or apple jelly. Apple or pear pies are wonderful when glazed with warm maple syrup.

► After cooling to room temperature, refrigerate custard pies to avoid spoilage.

► Always store pumpkin pie in the refrigerator; leftovers should be stored for no more than 3 days.

► For cream pies where the pie shell and filling are cooked separately, be sure to cool both completely before pouring the filling into the shell to prevent the crust from becoming soggy.

► When decorating the top of a pie, always place the garnishes (strawberries, chocolate leaves, etc.) between where the cuts will be so you won't have to cut through or remove a garnish in order to serve the pie.

► Cream pies will cut more cleanly if you wipe the blade often with a piece of damp paper towel.

► Meringue won't "weep" if you blend a teaspoon of cornstarch with the sugar before beating it into the egg whites.

► Spreading the meringue all the way to the edge of the crust will help prevent shrinkage and watery edges.

► Create a delicate, crispy "crust" on your meringue pie topping by sprinkling it with sifted confectioners' sugar just before baking.

► A meringue pie topping won't crack if you cool it at room temperature (away from drafts!) before refrigerating.

► A meringue topping won't stick to the knife if you dip the knife in very hot water between cuts. Rubbing the knife with vegetable oil or butter also works.

► Refrigerate leftover meringue pie by covering it with plastic wrap that has been rubbed with vegetable oil so it won't stick to the surface.

► Cover fruit pies with foil or plastic wrap and store at room temperature for up to 3 days.

► Add that just-baked touch by reheating fruit pies in a 300°F oven for 10 to 15 minutes before serving.

► Ice cream pies are fast and delicious. Bake and cool a homemade or commercial pie crust (or use a graham-cracker crust) and fill with slightly softened ice cream or sherbet, mounding high in the center. Drizzle or sprinkle with your favorite topping such caramel or fudge sauce, chopped nuts, crumbled cookies or M&M candies; freeze until solid. Fresh fruit toppings should be spooned over the pie just before serving. Once the pie is frozen solid, wrap and store for up to 1 week. Let stand at room temperature for 5 to 10 minutes to facilitate cutting.

► *See also* MERINGUE; PIE CRUSTS; PIE PANS

P

PIMIENTOS [Pih-MYEHN-toh; pih-MEN-toh]

▶ Store an unopened jar of pimientos in a cool, dark place for up to 1 year. Once opened, refrigerate for up to 2 weeks.

▶ Leftover pimientos will keep longer if you rinse them off with water and drain thoroughly. Then put them in a small screw-top jar and cover with vegetable oil.

▶ Leftover pimientos can also be covered with oil and frozen for up to 6 months.

PINEAPPLE

▶ Choose pineapples that are slightly soft to the touch with a full, strong color and no signs of greening. The stem end should smell sweet and aromatic; the leaves should be crisp and green with no yellow or brown tips. Avoid pineapples with soft or dark areas on the skin.

▶ Pineapple should be picked ripe because once it's off the plant, the starch won't convert to sugar—it won't really ripen. If you keep slightly under-ripe pineapples at room temperature for several days, it will decrease the fruit's acidity (tartness), though it won't increase its sweetness.

▶ Store whole, ripe pineapples, tightly wrapped, in the refrigerator for up to 3 days.

▶ Once cut, store pineapple, tightly sealed, in the refrigerator for up to 3 more days.

▶ *Pineapple yields:* 1 medium pineapple, peeled and cored = about 3 cups chunks.

▶ To peel and cut a pineapple, be sure the knife you use is very sharp. Cut off both the base and the leaves, then stand the pineapple on one end and cut off strips of the skin from top to bottom. The easiest way to remove the eyes is to cut a wedge-shaped groove on either side of the eyes, following their pattern, which spirals diagonally. Cut away as little of the pineapple's flesh as possible.

▶ Or you can slice the pineapple, then cut away the peel.

▶ Or you can buy a relatively inexpensive gadget available in kitchenware shops that cores and peels the pineapple at the same time.

▶ To core a pineapple, cut the peeled fruit in quarters, then stand the quarters on one end and cut downward to remove the core.

▶ Don't throw out a fresh pineapple core. It's tough, but it can make great swizzle sticks for fruit drinks. Cut it lengthwise into quarters unless it's a very thin core.

▶ If you find that a pineapple is simply too acidic to eat, make a sugar syrup of 2 parts water to 1 part sugar; bring mixture to a boil. Be sure and make enough syrup to cover the pineapple. Cut the pineapple into chunks or slices; put in a flat-bottomed bowl. Pour the hot sugar syrup over the

P

pineapple, cool to room temperature, then cover and refrigerate overnight. Drain the pineapple before using in salads, compotes, etc.

▶ Pineapple contains an enzyme—bromelain—that prevents gelatin from setting properly. Heat destroys the enzyme, so cooked pineapple can be used in a gelatin mixture.

▶ That same enzyme is a natural meat tenderizer. Add pineapple juice to marinades, or simply marinate meat in the juice alone. The pineapple flavor is particularly compatible with pork.

▶ Give the edges of pineapple chunks a beautiful blush by cutting a pineapple into spears, then laying them in a shallow ceramic or glass dish. Pour strawberry, raspberry or cranberry juice over the spears; cover and refrigerate for 24 hours. Drain the spears, then cut into chunks and use in salads, compotes or as a garnish.

▶ *See also* FRUIT, GENERAL

PISTACHIOS

▶ When buying unshelled pistachios make sure the shells are partially open for two reasons: 1. It's a help in retrieving the nutmeat; 2. Closed shells signal an immature nut.

▶ The shells of pistachios are either an off-white or dyed red. According to the California Pistachio Commission, pistachios are dyed for two reasons: 1. Many people find that form most familiar; or 2. so they're easier to spot in a bowl of mixed nuts (their words).

▶ *See also* NUTS, GENERAL *for general purchase, storage and usage information*

PITA BREAD [PEE-tah]

▶ For an almost-instant Greek pizza, separate a pita bread in half horizontally, sprinkle with cheese—half grated mozzarella and half crumbled feta, capers, sliced olives and crumbled oregano. Broil for about 3 minutes, or just until cheese melts. Cut into wedges.

▶ Make pita chips by separating the rounds horizontally, lightly brushing the insides with olive or canola oil, and seasoning to taste with salt and pepper. Stack the rounds, then cut the stack into 12 wedges. Arrange wedges in a single layer on a lightly oiled baking sheet and bake at 350°F for 8 to 10 minutes, or until golden brown. Cool on paper towels and store airtight for up to 5 days.

PIZZA [PEET-suh]

▶ Does your favorite commercial pizza arrive with a limp crust? Next time, try sautéing the slices in a large, lightly oiled skillet until it recrisps. Or place pizza on a rack set on a baking sheet and bake at 400°F for 5 minutes. The skillet method produces a crisper crust without overcooking the topping. Use two skillets for a large pizza, and put a second round of slices on to crisp over low heat while you're eating the first round.

▸ To prevent a homemade pizza crust from getting soggy, lightly sauté vegetables like mushrooms, bell peppers, onions and spinach (all of which have a high water content) before using them as toppings.

▸ For the crispest crust, try putting a thin layer of cheese *under* the sauce and toppings; top with more cheese, if desired. The bottom cheese layer provides a buffer between the crust and moist toppings.

▸ If you don't have a pizza cutter, make quick work of cutting pizza by using kitchen scissors.

PLASTIC WRAP

▸ Storing plastic wrap in the freezer will keep it from sticking to itself.

▸ If plastic wrap won't adhere to ceramic, glass or metal containers, dip your finger in water and moisten the dish's rim, then cover with the wrap.

▸ Plastic wrap doesn't stick well to plastic or acrylic surfaces. Cover such containers with a plastic bag, twisting and sealing the top with a wire fastener.

▸ Protect yourself and your kitchen from spatters when whipping cream by laying a sheet of plastic wrap (with a hole cut for the beater stems) on top of the bowl.

▸ Place a sheet of plastic wrap between layers of stored candy.

▸ Separate layers of decorated, moist or sticky cookies with plastic wrap to prevent their sticking together.

▸ Use sheets of plastic wrap to separate layers of cookies before freezing.

▸ Shape a ground-meat mixture into burgers or meatballs by spooning a portion between 2 sheets of plastic wrap, then forming the desired shape. Your fingers won't get messy and neither will the countertop.

▸ *See also* ALUMINUM FOIL; WAXED PAPER

PLUMS

▸ Choose firm plums that give slightly to palm pressure; the color should be good for its variety. Avoid plums with skin blemishes such as cracks, soft spots or brown discolorations. Don't worry about any pale gray filmy-looking coating on the skin—that's natural and doesn't affect quality.

▸ Store ripe plums in a plastic bag in the refrigerator for up to 5 days.

▸ Ripen underripe plums by placing in a paper bag with an apple at room temperature. Pierce the bag in several places with the tip of a knife.

▸ *Plum yields:* 1 pound = 6 to 8 2-inch whole plums; 3 cups sliced or chopped.

▸ Plums don't need peeling, but wash them thoroughly before using.

▸ Plums are great quartered, sautéed in a little butter (and sprinkled with

P

¼ to ⅓ cup sugar) just until they begin to soften, then spooned over vanilla-bean ice cream.
- ▶ *See also* FRUIT, GENERAL

POACHED EGGS *see* EGGS, COOKING METHODS

POACHING

- ▶ A method of cooking whereby food is cooked in a liquid that's at the simmering point. Among those foods most commonly poached are eggs, fruit, fish and chicken.
- ▶ Poaching produces a particularly delicate flavor in foods.
- ▶ During poaching, the food is flavored by the liquid, and the liquid takes on the food's flavor. For that reason, chicken is usually poached in chicken stock (sometimes with the addition of wine), fruit in a sugar syrup, fish in fish stock, etc.
- ▶ Only use enough poaching liquid to cover the food.
- ▶ The pan used for poaching should be just large enough to accommodate the food and liquid to cover. Too large a pan would require more poaching liquid, which would mean the resulting broth, stock, etc., would be diluted.
- ▶ A whole fish will keep its shape better if you wrap it in cheesecloth before poaching. Drape the ends of the cheesecloth over the top of the fish as it cooks and use the extra cheesecloth to lift the cooked fish out of the pan. There are also special cheesecloth fish-poaching bags available in specialty kitchenware shops.
- ▶ If you put a whole fish directly into hot water, the skin will split apart.
- ▶ Begin poaching fish and poultry in a cold liquid. That way, the outside doesn't get overdone before the inside is cooked. It also helps prevent fish from falling apart during cooking.
- ▶ High-fat fish like butterfish or sablefish aren't suitable for moist-heat cooking like poaching because they're inclined to fall apart. Lean fish like cod, flounder, perch, red snapper or sole is a better choice.
- ▶ Poached fish is extremely delicate so handle it gently when removing from the pan. If it's a large piece, use 2 slotted metal spatulas; a slotted spoon for small pieces.
- ▶ Bones add a lot of flavor to flesh and to the poaching liquid, so you may want to cook some meats with the bone in.
- ▶ Never throw out a poaching liquid. It can be used either to make a sauce for the poached food or as a soup base.
- ▶ If you're poaching bone-in chicken to use in salads, save the chicken bones, put them back in the poaching liquid and cook for 30 minutes to

extract as much flavor as possible. Strain, cool and use the liquid for soups, sauces, etc.

▶ If you're not going to use a poaching liquid within a couple of days, freeze it for up to 6 months. Be sure and label it so you don't wind up with "mystery" packages in the freezer.

▶ *See also* EGGS, COOKING METHODS (POACHED)

POLENTA *see* CORNMEAL

POMEGRANATE [POM-uh-gran-uht]

▶ Pomegranates—nature's most labor-intensive fruit—can be eaten as fruit, pureed for the juice, or used as a garnish for salads, meats, fruit compotes, drinks or desserts.

▶ Choose pomegranates that are heavy for their size and have a bright, fresh color and blemish-free skin.

▶ Store whole pomegranates in a cool, dark place for up to 1 month; refrigerate for up to 2 months.

▶ Pomegranate seeds can be frozen for up to 1 year.

▶ Whenever working with a pomegranate protect yourself with an apron. The vivid-red juice makes nasty stains.

▶ If you don't want red-tinged fingers and nails, use gloves while working with a pomegranate.

▶ To open a pomegranate, cut it in half, then into quarters. Use your fingers to pry out the pulp-encased seeds, removing any of the light-colored membrane that adheres.

▶ You can juice a pomegranate in a couple of ways. One is to cut it in half and juice it like an orange. Or remove the seeds, pop them into a blender and process until pulverized. Strain the juice before using.

▶ Refrigerate freshly squeezed juice and use within 2 to 3 days.

▶ Store pomegranate juice in glass containers—plastic ones may stain.

▶ Pomegranate juice adds a sweet-tart nuance to salad dressings, savory sauces, marinades and dessert sauces.

▶ *See also* FRUIT, GENERAL

POPCORN

▶ Popcorn is a special variety of dried corn that pops when heated because of the natural moisture trapped inside the hull. In simple terms, when the corn's heated, the moisture vaporizes, which causes immense pressure. When the pressure becomes too great, the hull bursts open and the kernel's starchy contents explode outward, expanding in volume while turning the kernel inside-out.

▶ Unpopped popcorn can be stored at room temperature for about a year,

P

but it retains its natural moisture better if kept in an *airtight* container in the refrigerator or freezer. Popcorn that keeps its moisture produces larger popped kernels.

▶ Popcorn commercially packaged with oil in its own "pan" should be stored no longer than about 3 months at room temperature. Longer than that and you risk having the oil turn rancid.

▶ *Popcorn yields:* One tablespoon oil plus ½ cup corn kernels = about 4 cups popped corn (using a 4-quart pan).

▶ If you're getting lots of unpopped kernels (old maids) it's usually because the corn has lost its natural moisture. Dried-out kernels won't pop. Help restore dry popcorn by combining 3 cups popcorn with 1 tablespoon cool water in a screw-top jar. Shake the contents every 15 minutes until the water is absorbed. Set the jar in a cool, dark place for a couple of days before using the popcorn. An abbreviated version of this technique is to cover popcorn with cold water for 5 minutes, blot well with paper towels, then cook as usual.

▶ Popcorn produces steam as it pops so for the crispest popcorn, leave the pan lid ajar about ¼ inch so the steam can escape without letting the corn pop out. To prevent soggy popcorn, remove the pan lid the second the popping stops.

▶ Personalize your popcorn by adding herbs and spices to the oil in which the corn will be popped. Stir in the corn kernels, coating them well with the oil and condiments, then pop as usual. Anything from grated Parmesan cheese to dried oregano leaves to chili or curry powder can add pizzazz to popcorn.

▶ Add a quartered garlic clove to the butter as it melts for garlic-buttered popcorn. Be sure to remove the garlic with a slotted spoon before you pour the butter over the popcorn. A half teaspoon chili powder stirred into the butter gives you Southwest-style popcorn.

▶ Having trouble getting salt and other dry flavorings to stick to air-popped popcorn? Next time spritz it lightly with nonstick vegetable spray before seasoning.

▶ Store leftover unbuttered popcorn in an airtight plastic bag at room temperature for up to 2 weeks; refrigerate buttered popcorn.

▶ To recrisp popcorn, place in a single layer in a baking pan with shallow sides (a jelly-roll pan is perfect) and heat at 325° for 5 to 10 minutes.

▶ Food for thought: 1 cup plain popcorn = about 30 calories; 1 cup buttered popcorn = 90 to 120 calories (depending on the amount of butter).

POPOVERS

▶ Unlike most other breads, popovers are leavened by eggs and steam. They're extremely easy to mix and bake.

- Bring the milk and eggs to room temperature before mixing a popover batter. If you've forgotten to do so, heat the milk just until lukewarm, and put the eggs in a bowl of very warm water for 10 minutes.

- Be sure measurements are precise for popover batter. And don't use extra-large or small eggs if the recipe calls for large. (Most recipes that don't specify an egg size use large eggs.)

- Popover batter can be made ahead, covered tightly and refrigerated for a day. Before using, let the batter stand at room temperature for 30 to 60 minutes and stir well before pouring into baking cups.

- Generously grease (use about ½ teaspoon grease per popover) the containers in which you bake the popovers, otherwise, they'll stick badly.

- There are special popover cups (or pans), or you can use custard cups or a muffin tin. If using separate popover or custard cups, place them on a heavy baking sheet before filling.

- Because popovers puff so high, don't fill the baking cups more than half full with batter.

- Popovers should be baked on the center rack of the oven at 400° to 450°F. If using glass baking cups, reduce heat by 25°F.

- It's important to leave the oven door shut during the first 20 minutes of baking. Drafts can easily collapse popovers.

- Bake popovers until they're nicely browned and firm to the touch. Underbaking can cause popovers to collapse after they're removed from the oven.

- As soon as popovers are done, remove them from the oven and prick in several places with a fork to let the steam escape. This keeps the insides from steaming and becoming too soggy.

- Popover interiors are naturally moist. If you want drier, crisper popovers, after they've been pricked return them to the turned-off (but still warm) oven for about 10 minutes. Leave the oven door ajar 1 to 3 inches so the popovers don't overbrown.

- Loosen popovers from their baking cups by running a knife around the edge.

- Whether or not you're going to use them all, remove popovers from the pan so the bottoms won't get soggy.

- Leftover popovers can be frozen in an airtight plastic bag for up to 3 months. Reheat by placing frozen popovers on a baking sheet and heating in a preheated 400°F oven for 10 to 15 minutes.

- Split popovers (leftover or fresh-baked) and fill the cavities with poached or scrambled eggs, creamed chicken or tuna, or fruit salad.

- *See also* BAKING, GENERAL; BREADS, GENERAL; GREASING PANS; HIGH-ALTITUDE ADJUSTMENTS

P

POPPY SEED

▶ Did you know that there are about 900,000 tiny poppy seeds in each pound?

▶ To keep poppy seed from becoming rancid, store in an airtight container in the refrigerator for up to 6 months.

▶ Augment the flavor of poppy seed by toasting it, either in a dry skillet over medium heat, or in a 350°F oven. Stir occasionally, toasting only until seed begins to brown. Poppy seed used as a topping for baked goods doesn't need pretoasting because the oven does the job.

PORK

▶ When buying pork, look for meat that's pale pink with a small amount of marbling and white (not yellow) fat. The darker pink the flesh, the older the animal.

▶ Store fresh pork that will be used within 6 hours of purchase in the refrigerator in its store packaging. Otherwise, remove the packaging and loosely wrap with waxed paper; store in the coldest part of the refrigerator for up to 2 days. Ground pork and pork sausage shouldn't be stored for more than 1 or 2 days.

▶ Pork can be frozen for 3 to 6 months; larger cuts have longer storage capabilities than chops or ground meat.

▶ Thanks to modern technology, trichinosis in pork is now rarely an issue. Take normal precautions, however, such as thoroughly washing in hot, soapy water anything (hands, knives, cutting boards, etc.) that comes in contact with raw pork. Never taste uncooked pork.

▶ Cooking pork to an internal temperature of 137°F will kill any trinchinae. However, to allow for a safety margin for thermometer inaccuracy, most experts recommend an internal temperature of from 150° to 165°F. This range produces pork that's juicy and tender, whereas the 170° to 185°F range recommended in many cookbooks produces dry, overcooked meat.

▶ The best way to test pork's doneness is with a meat thermometer. Cutting it to see if it's still pink lets too many good juices run out.

▶ If you want succulent chops, choose those that are about 1 inch thick. Thin chops have a tendency to dry out no matter how careful you are.

▶ To cut a pocket in pork chops for stuffing, choose loin or rib chops that are about 1½ inches thick (have your butcher cut some if those displayed aren't thick enough). Cutting from the fat side, use a sharp, pointed knife to make a horizontal slit about 3 inches wide almost to the bone. Make the inside pocket larger than the actual slit. Fill the pocket with stuffing and secure the opening with toothpicks.

P

▸ Leftover pork dishes should be refrigerated within 2 hours of cooking and used within 2 days.

▸ *See also* BACON; HAM; MEATS, GENERAL; ROASTS

POTATOES

▸ When buying potatoes, choose those that are firm, well-shaped for their type, and blemish-free. Avoid potatoes that are wrinkled, sprouted or cracked. A slight green tinge is indicative of prolonged light exposure and of the presence of solanine, an alkaloid that can be toxic if eaten in quantity. This bitter green portion can be cut or scraped off and the potato used in the normal fashion.

▸ Choose potatoes by how you're going to use them. The low moisture, high-starch **russet** or **Idaho** potato (long, slightly rounded ends, rough, brown skin with numerous eyes) is excellent for baking and frying. The similarly shaped **long white potato** (thin, pale brown skin with almost imperceptible eyes) can be boiled, baked or fried. The medium-size, thin-skinned **round red and round white** potatoes (also commonly referred to as **boiling potatoes**) have a waxy flesh with less starch and more moisture than the russet or long white, making them better suited for boiling; they can also be roasted or fried. **New potatoes**—the youngsters of any variety—have a crisp, waxy texture and thin, undeveloped wispy skins; they're excellent boiled or roasted. Because they retain their shape after being cooked and cut, new potatoes are the best choice for potato salads.

▸ Store potatoes in a cool, dark, well-ventilated place for up to 2 weeks. If the storage area is around 50°F, the potatoes will keep for up to 3 months. New potatoes should be used within 3 or 4 days of purchase.

▸ Refrigerating potatoes causes them to become overly sweet and to turn dark when cooked. Warm temperatures encourage sprouting and shriveling.

▸ Cut off a leg of an old (clean) pair of pantyhose, drop potatoes into it and hang in a cool, dark, dry place. The hose lets air circulate, which helps keep the potatoes longer.

▸ Because of the interaction of their natural gases, storing potatoes and onions together can cause the potatoes to rot more quickly.

▸ *Potato yields:* 1 pound russet-sized potatoes = 3 medium; about 3½ cups chopped; 2 to 3 cups mashed (depending on type of potato and amount of liquid added). One pound new potatoes = 8 to 10.

▸ Whether baking, boiling, steaming or microwaving, whole potatoes will cook more evenly and get done at the same time if they're relatively the same size.

▸ A potato's peel has lots of flavor and nutrients so don't remove it if you don't have to.

P

- If you're using potatoes with the skin on, use a vegetable brush to scrub them well.
- Get a jump on the next night's meal by cooking twice as many potatoes as you need for one meal. The leftover potatoes can be used in a salad or soup, mashed, tossed with other vegetables, etc.
- The flesh of a potato darkens when exposed to air. If you want to cut potatoes ahead of time, first dip them in a mixture of 1 quart cool water and 3 tablespoons lemon juice. Drain, cover and refrigerate until ready to use.
- If you've cut potatoes ahead of time and their flesh has darkened, cooking them in milk will whiten them again (don't let the milk boil). After cooling, the milk can be refrigerated for up to 3 days for use in sauces, soups, etc.
- A teaspoon or two of lemon juice in the cooking water will keep potatoes white after cooking.
- Potato skins are easier to remove while the potatoes are still hot.
- Never throw away the water in which you boil potatoes—it makes a delicious, nutritious soup base and wonderful, moist breads.
- When cooking potatoes that are to be mashed, cook them with the skins on. Remove the skins and return them to the water. When cool, puree the potato skins and water, then freeze for future use. The skins add both flavor and nutrition.
- Food for thought: One 6-ounce potato contains only about 120 calories but packs a nutritional punch. It's low in sodium, high in potassium and a storehouse of minerals, vitamins C and B-6, and complex carbohydrates.
- *See also* POTATOES, COOKING METHODS; POTATO SALAD; SWEET POTATOES; VEGETABLES, GENERAL

POTATOES, COOKING METHODS
Baked potatoes:

- Russet potatoes are best for baking.
- Scrub well, blot dry with paper towels, and use the tines of a fork to prick potatoes about 1 inch deep in several places to let the steam out during baking.
- If you rub a little butter, bacon fat, or vegetable or olive oil on the skin of potatoes to be baked, the skin will be crisper and browner. Oiled potatoes also bake slightly faster.
- Wrapping potatoes in foil to bake them doesn't allow the steam (produced by a potato's natural moisture) to escape, therefore the skin will be soft, not crisp.

P

▶ Place potatoes to be baked right on the oven rack.

▶ If you have a lot of potatoes to bake at one time, stand them on end in a 12-cup muffin tin.

▶ For crispier skins, bake potatoes at 425°F for 45 to 60 minutes, depending on the size.

▶ Cut a potato's baking time by almost a third by skewering it with an aluminum potato nail (but not in a microwave oven).

▶ If you're in a hurry, put pierced potatoes in a microwave oven; cook at HIGH (100 percent power) for 3 minutes for 1 potato, 4 minutes for 2, 5 minutes for 3, etc. Remove from microwave and immediately place in a preheated 425°F oven for 20 to 25 minutes.

▶ If you're in a *real* hurry, you can completely cook potatoes in a microwave oven, although they won't have exactly the same texture of *baked* potatoes. Pierce 6- to 8-ounce potatoes with a fork and cook at HIGH (100 percent power) for: 1 potato, 4 to 6 minutes; 2 potatoes, 6 to 8 minutes; 3 potatoes, 8 to 10 minutes; 4 potatoes, 10 to 12 minutes, etc. (These are approximate cooking times and will depend on the size of the potatoes and the wattage of the oven.) Let potatoes stand for 5 minutes in the microwave oven before serving.

▶ To test potatoes for doneness, insert the tines of a fork deep into the center of the potato; there should be no resistance.

▶ Bake more potatoes than you need and dice the leftovers (with skins on) for hash browns the next day.

▶ Use a sharp knife to slit a baked potato down the center as soon as it's done. Just before serving, squeeze both ends together to open the potato and expose the flesh.

▶ Watching calories? Use low-fat instead of regular sour cream.

▶ Two tablespoons salsa mixed with 1 cup sour cream makes a zesty baked-potato topping.

▶ For a low-calorie sour cream substitute, try Quark—a soft, unripened cheese with the texture and flavor of sour cream. It comes in two versions—low-fat and nonfat. Quark isn't as tart as yogurt and its texture is richer than either low-fat sour cream or yogurt.

▶ Or put some cottage cheese and a little milk in the blender and process until smooth. Season to taste with salt and pepper.

▶ Personalize your potato topping by combining sour cream, Quark, etc. with any of a dozen additions including: chopped basil, chives, dill, scallions or watercress; crumbled bacon; grated cheddar, Jack, Parmesan or Swiss cheese; crumbled feta or blue cheese; toasted caraway, celery, fennel, poppy or sesame seed; curry; cayenne or chili powder; freshly ground pepper; or diced, seeded tomatoes.

▶ For real comfort food, top a baked potato with chili.

P

▸ For leftover whole baked potatoes, cool to room temperature, then wrap well and refrigerate for up to 3 days. To reheat, soak potato in hot water for 1 minute, then bake at 350°F for about 20 minutes.

▸ Whole baked potatoes can be frozen (after cooling) for up to 3 months by wrapping in heavy-duty foil, then in a plastic bag. Thaw overnight in the fridge, then bake foil-wrapped potatoes at 350°F for 30 minutes. Or bake frozen, foil-wrapped potatoes at 350°F for about 45 minutes. Remove foil for final 10 minutes of baking time.

▸ For quick potato snacks, scrape flesh out of leftover baked potato skins and brush them with olive oil. Use scissors to cut the skins into ½-inch-wide strips, then sprinkle with salt, pepper and a little chili powder; bake at 400°F until crispy (about 10 minutes). These crispy strips are great for snacks and appetizers. When crumbled, they make a nice garnish for soups and salads.

▸ Cut leftover baked potatoes into ½-inch pieces and toss with a little olive oil. Bake uncovered at 425°F, turning occasionally, until crisp and golden brown, about 45 minutes. Season to taste with salt and freshly ground pepper; or use other seasonings such as chili powder, cayenne or minced fresh herbs.

French fries:

▸ See DEEP-FRYING tips before preparing French fries.

▸ Russets are the best potatoes for frying.

▸ Allow 1 medium potato per person when making French fries.

▸ After cutting potatoes into ¼- to ½-inch-thick lengthwise strips, soak them in a bowl of cold water for 30 minutes to remove excess starch.

▸ Use paper towels to *thoroughly* dry the potatoes. Any trace of water will cause the fat to spatter and boil up violently.

▸ Before beginning to fry potatoes, line a couple of baking sheets with a double layer of paper towels.

▸ Drop about one third of the potatoes at a time into 375°F oil. Too many potatoes at once will lower the temperature of the oil, which means the potatoes will get greasy. Fry until potatoes are golden brown, transfer to paper-towel-lined sheets.

▸ Keep potatoes warm in a 275°F oven while you fry the rest.

▸ Always reheat oil between batches.

▸ Season French fries with salt (and pepper, if desired) as soon as you put them on the baking sheet to drain.

▸ For the crispiest results, fry the potatoes twice: first in 340°F oil for about 3 minutes, or until golden. Drain on paper towels. Once cool, cover and let stand at room temperature for up to 4 hours. Just before serving, heat

P

oil to 375°F. Fry potatoes in batches until golden brown. Transfer to paper-towel-lined baking sheets; keep warm in oven while frying remaining potatoes.

▶ For oven French fries, follow directions in previous tips up to the point of frying. Toss potato sticks with just enough oil (or half oil, half melted butter) to coat. Arrange in a single layer on baking sheets. Bake at 400°F for 20 minutes; turn and bake another 20 minutes.

▶ Food for thought: Ounce for ounce, French fries contain 12 times the fat and almost 3 times the calories of a baked potato.

Mashed potatoes:

▶ Russets make the best mashed potatoes.

▶ Leaving the skin on adds flavor and nutrition to mashed potatoes. Be sure to cut the potatoes into small cubes before you cook them so large pieces of skin won't clog the beaters or potato ricer.

▶ For extra-rich mashed potatoes, cook the potatoes in milk.

▶ Add a ham hock, piece of raw bacon or smoky sausage link to the cooking water for potatoes, bring water to a boil and cook for 5 minutes before adding potatoes. Remove ham, bacon or sausage; your potatoes will have a delicious smoky nuance.

▶ Cook the potatoes only until they're fork-tender; drain immediately so they don't absorb excess moisture.

▶ After draining the potatoes, return them to the pan and cook over low heat for about 1 minute, shaking the pan often, to evaporate excess moisture and steam.

▶ You don't have to use boiled potatoes to make mashed potatoes—baked potatoes also work great.

▶ Many pundits declare that if cold milk is added to potatoes the potatoes will get gluey. Not so if you slowly add the milk, beating constantly as you do. You won't usually be adding enough milk to noticeably affect the temperature of the potatoes; if so, a few minutes in the oven will heat them right up.

▶ Though most recipes call for adding milk to potatoes for mashing, you can be virtuous and add evaporated skim milk or naughty and use heavy or sour cream.

▶ Only beat potatoes until they're light; overbeating will cause them to turn sticky and starchy.

▶ For a thoroughly decadent treat, fold ½ cup whipping cream, whipped until stiff, into mashed potatoes just before serving.

▶ For lighter, fluffier mashed potatoes, beat in more milk and leave out the butter.

P

- If you plan on using mashed potatoes for piping a border or as a garnish, they'll hold their shape better if you add 1 lightly beaten egg to the potatoes while you're beating them.
- To update your mashed potatoes with color and flavor, just before serving, fold in ¼ to ½ cup minced herbs or vegetables like basil, watercress, red or green bell peppers, or fennel. The heat of the hot mashed potatoes will "cook" the additions, and the flavor will be wonderfully fresh.
- Stirring in 1 cup shredded cheddar at the last minute adds flavor as well as beautiful streaks of color.
- Mashed potatoes are best served immediately, but you can make them 15 to 20 minutes ahead and reheat in a microwave oven. Cover the potatoes and cook at HIGH (100 percent power) for 1 to 2 minutes, depending on the amount of potatoes. Stir potatoes before serving.
- Or put mashed potatoes in an ovenproof dish, brush with melted butter, cover and place in a 250°F oven for 30 minutes.
- If you're going to hold mashed potatoes, as in the previous tip, don't stir in any extras (minced herbs, grated cheese, etc.) until just before serving.
- Form leftover mashed potatoes into patties, dip in beaten egg, then breadcrumbs and let dry in the refrigerator for 1 hour. Then fry until golden brown and crispy on both sides and enjoy the raves.
- Leftover mashed potatoes make a great soup or sauce thickener.

Roasted potatoes:

- Russets, long whites and new potatoes are all suitable for roasting.
- Halve small potatoes; cut larger ones into quarters, sixths or eighths. Pour ¼ to ⅓ cup olive oil, melted butter and oil combination, pan drippings or other fat into a shallow baking dish or pan. Add potatoes and toss to liberally coat with oil. Roast in a preheated 375°F oven for 1 to 1½ hours, or until crisp and brown on the outside and fork-tender.
- One secret for perfectly roasted potatoes is to turn them often—about every 15 minutes—so they get evenly crisp and brown.
- Pan drippings or lard add great flavor to roasted potatoes.

POTATO SALAD *see* SALADS

POULTRY, GENERAL

- "Poultry" is a generic term for any domesticated bird used for food, the most common being chicken, Rock Cornish game hen, duck and turkey.
- Choose meaty, full-breasted poultry—a scrawny bird means you're paying proportionally for too much bone. The skin should be smooth and soft, not bruised or torn. Generally, the younger the bird, the more tender the meat and the milder the flavor; the pinker the bone ends,

P

the fresher the bird. Avoid poultry with an off odor. If buying pre-packaged poultry, make sure the cellophane isn't torn and that the package isn't leaking. Check the pull date on the label to be sure the bird isn't past its prime.

▸ Also check for the USDA (U.S. Department of Agriculture) inspection stamp on the package label, an indication that the bird is wholesome and accurately labeled. The USDA also has three grades for poultry—A, B and C. Grade A, which is what is most often found in markets, is the highest quality—an indicator that the bird is essentially defect-free.

▸ Always add an extra ounce per serving of boneless poultry to allow for shrinkage. Add another 2 ounces per serving to allow for bone. There-fore, if you plan on 4-ounce, bone-in portions, buy enough for 7-ounce servings.

▸ Store poultry in the coldest part of the refrigerator (40°F or below) as soon as you get it home from the market. If it's packaged tightly in cellophane and you're not going to use it within a few hours, either loosen the pack-aging or remove it and loosely rewrap the poultry in waxed paper. Raw poultry can be refrigerated for up to 2 days, cooked poultry up to 3 days.

▸ Freezing causes a loss of natural juices in poultry and can reduce tender-ness. If you have to freeze chicken, seal it airtight in a freezer-proof plastic bag or foil. If using foil, press it closely to the meat. If using a plastic bag, use one with a zip-closure and close all but ½ inch. Insert a straw and suck out as much air as possible, so that the bird becomes "vacuum-packed." Having the wrapping as close to the bird as possible prevents the formation of ice crystals. Freeze uncooked chicken for up to 6 months; cooked chicken for up to 3 months.

▸ When thawing frozen poultry, do so in the refrigerator and allow about 5 hours per pound. Thawing poultry at room temperature means you run the risk of bacteria formation.

▸ You can also submerge frozen poultry (still in its freezer wrapping) in a large container of cold water. Allow 30 minutes per pound and change the water every 30 minutes.

▸ Poultry sometimes gets an unpleasant "refrigerator" smell. Refresh it by squeezing lemon juice inside the cavity.

▸ Let refrigerated poultry sit at room temperature for 15 to 30 minutes to take some of the chill off before cooking.

▸ Bacteria flourish in poultry at temperatures between 40° and 140°F, so don't let it sit out at room temperature too long before cooking.

▸ Poultry shears are often much easier to use than a knife when cutting up poultry such as chicken or duck.

▸ Toss all the poultry parts you're not planning to use (giblets, tail, back-bone, skin, etc.) into a saucepan along with a handful of parsley and a

P

chopped carrot, cover with water and bring to a boil. Cover, reduce to simmer and cook for 30 to 60 minutes, or until the liquid has reduced by half. Strain the stock and refrigerate to solidify the fat. After removing the fat, freeze, if desired, and use the stock when you want to enrich soups or sauces.

▶ Freeze chicken or duck livers as you get them until you get enough to make a pâté or other dish. Simply put the livers in a freezer-proof, airtight container, cover with milk and freeze. Add more livers as you get them (covering with more milk) until you're ready to use them. Defrost overnight in the refrigerator.

▶ Out of string and want to truss a bird? Try using unflavored dental floss.

▶ Or don't truss at all—simply tuck the wing tips under the bird's back.

▶ Commercial salad dressing makes an easy, instant marinade for all kinds of poultry.

▶ To prevent bacteria growth, don't stuff poultry until just before cooking. You can make the dressing and prepare the bird separately, combining them at the last minute.

▶ Only stuff a bird three-quarters full to allow for the stuffing to expand during cooking.

▶ Bacteria on raw poultry can contaminate other food it comes in contact with so it's vital that you *always* use hot, soapy water to thoroughly wash your hands, cutting board and any utensils used in the preparation of poultry. Never let any raw juices come in contact with cooked poultry.

▶ Don't salt poultry until after cooking. Salt draws out the juices from the meat and will make it drier if added before cooking.

▶ Let the bird baste itself by covering it with a double layer of cheesecloth that's been soaked with canola or olive oil (melted butter if you're not watching cholesterol); baste as necessary. At the end of the roasting time when the cheesecloth is removed, the bird will be moist and golden brown. Removing the cheesecloth 30 minutes before the bird is done will produce a crisp, brown skin.

▶ White meat cooks slightly more quickly than dark meat, so if you're cooking poultry pieces add the white-meat portions about 5 minutes after the rest.

▶ Boneless poultry will cook in a third to half the time of that needed for bone-in birds. For instance, boneless chicken breasts will cook in 20 to 30 minutes in a 350°F oven, while bone-in breasts need from 30 to 40 minutes.

▶ When grilling or boiling, leave the skin on during cooking. It keeps the juices in and creates a more tender result. Remove the skin after the dish is cooked.

▶ A general rule for poultry doneness is when the juices run clear and the meat near the bone at the thickest part is no longer pink. Drumsticks should twist easily in their sockets. Large birds can be tested with a meat thermometer, which should register 180°F when inserted in the thigh's thickest part. Be sure not to touch the bone when inserting the thermometer or it will throw the reading off.

▶ Letting poultry "rest" for a few minutes after it's finished cooking allows the juices to redistribute throughout the flesh and set. This produces an evenly moist result and makes the bird easier to carve. Allow about 10 minutes for small birds, 20 minutes for larger ones. Keep the poultry warm during this rest period by covering it lightly with foil.

▶ In cooked poultry, bones that have dark splotches are an indicator that the bird's been frozen. When poultry is frozen, the blood cells in the bone marrow rupture. Upon thawing, the ruptured cells leak, which causes the discoloration. Cooking turns the red spotches dark brown.

▶ Don't leave cooked poultry sitting out at room temperature for more than 2 hours. To prevent bacterial growth, it should either be kept hot (145° to 165°F) or put in the refrigerator.

▶ Removing cooked poultry from the bones before refrigerating will keep the flavor fresher longer.

▶ Put all the bones in a large pot, cover with water and bring to a boil. Reduce heat, cover and simmer for 1 hour. Cool to room temperature, strain, then refrigerate or freeze for use in soups, stews, sauces, etc.

▶ Thoroughly heat leftover poultry (to about 180°F) and gravy (bring it to a boil and cook 5 minutes).

▶ Dice leftover cooked poultry and sauté with diced potatoes, onions and green peppers for a great hash that can be served for breakfast or dinner.

▶ The USDA's Meat and Poultry Hotline is just a phone call away for detailed information on topics including food handling, food safety and understanding meat and poultry labels. Call 1-800-535-4555 Monday through Friday from 10 A.M. to 4 P.M., eastern time. In the Washington, D.C., area, call 447-3333.

▶ *See also* CHICKEN; DUCK; ROCK CORNISH GAME HENS; TURKEY

POWDERED SUGAR *see* SUGAR

PRESSURE COOKERS; PRESSURE COOKING

▶ Pressure cookers have a locking, airtight lid and a valve system to regulate internal pressure. They operate on a principle whereby the steam that builds up inside the pressurized pot cooks food at a very high temperature. The more pounds of pressure, the higher the internal temperature and the quicker the food cooks. This cooking method reduces preparation time by as much as two thirds while retaining the food's nutritional value.

P

▸ Traditionally designed cookers are equipped with detachable pressure regulators, whereas the more modern designs feature built-in valves and indicator rods that indicate the pressure. Before starting to cook with a pressure cooker, it's vital that you thoroughly read the manufacturer's instruction booklet.

▸ When buying a pressure cooker, look for one with a 6-quart or larger capacity. Anything smaller will limit the cooked yield of foods like beans, which can only fill a cooker halfway. A cooker with two handles is convenient for moving the pot from stove to sink.

▸ Pressure cookers are great for quickly tenderizing inexpensive, tough cuts of meat and older poultry like stewing hens. They make quick work of soups, stews and rice dishes like risottos and pilafs. Beans and whole grains cook (without presoaking) in about 30 minutes.

▸ A general rule is to only fill the cooker two-thirds full, especially with high-liquid foods like soups. Of course, general rules always have exceptions—foods like beans and grains shouldn't fill more than half the cooker, whereas other foods can fill it three quarters.

▸ The more food there is in a cooker, the longer it will generally take to reach full pressure. However, once high pressure is reached, a large quantity of food cooks just as quickly as a small quantity.

▸ When cooking soups and stews, start the liquid heating while you're chopping the other ingredients. This will reduce the time it takes for the pressure to reach the proper level once the lid is locked on.

▸ The pressure won't rise unless the lid is securely locked into place.

▸ After cooking is completed, the pressure in traditional cookers can be reduced either by letting the pot sit off the heat (which can take up to 20 minutes for a full pot of soup or stew) or by running cold water over the cooker. The second method usually releases the pressure in under a minute. Some of the newer pressure cooker models have a "quick-release" lever or button.

▸ Thoroughly wash your cooker after each use, taking particular care to make sure the vent isn't clogged.

▸ When storing your pressure cooker, don't lock the lid to the pan. Instead, turn it upside down and set it on top of the pan.

▸ *See also* COOKING, GENERAL

PRETZELS [PREHT-zuhls]

▸ Why spend money on an expensive specialty item like chocolate-coated pretzels when it's so easy to make your own? For every 6 ounces of pretzels (the small, twisted ones look prettiest), melt 12 ounces white or dark chocolate with 1 tablespoon vegetable oil. Dip half the pretzel into the melted chocolate and place on a waxed-paper-lined baking sheet. If desired, sprinkle chocolate-dipped portion with jimmies, colored sprinkles, or other decorative topping. Refrigerate just until chocolate sets, then store, tightly covered, in a cool, dry place.

PROSCIUTTO [proh-SHOO-toh]

▶ Prosciutto is the Italian word for "ham."
▶ This special Italian-style ham has been seasoned, salt-cured (but not smoked) and air-dried. It's available in gourmet and Italian markets and some supermarkets.
▶ Italian prosciuttos are designated *prosciutto cotto,* which is cooked, and *prosciutto crudo,* which is raw but ready to eat because of its curing.
▶ Prosciutto should be golden-pink and moist-looking; its fat should be pure white.
▶ Store a whole prosciutto in a cool, dry place for up to 1 year. Once cut, wrap and store prosciutto in the refrigerator; use within a few weeks.
▶ Only buy sliced prosciutto as needed—the thin slices dry out quickly.
▶ If planning to use prosciutto in cooked dishes, have it sliced slightly thicker than usual, then cut it into strips or chunks.
▶ In general, prosciutto shouldn't be cooked. It's classically served with figs or melon as a first course.
▶ If using prosciutto in cooked dishes, stir it in at the very last minute; prolonged cooking toughens it.

PRUNES

▶ Choose prunes that are slightly soft and somewhat flexible. They should have a bluish-black skin and be blemish-free.
▶ Store prunes airtight in a cool, dry place for up to 6 months. Refrigerate for up to 9 months, freeze up to 1 year.
▶ *Prune yields:* 1 pound dried prunes = 2½ cups; 4 to 4½ cups cooked.
▶ Adding a couple of lemon wedges to the cooking water gives the prunes a brighter flavor.
▶ Prunes will become mushy if overcooked.
▶ Before stuffing prunes, soften them by covering them with boiling water, orange juice or other liquid. Cover and let stand until cool. Blot prunes dry with paper towels before stuffing.
▶ Chopped prunes make a delicious addition to all kinds of foods including savory stuffings, breads, cakes, cookies, stews, etc.
▶ Prune butter (also called "lekvar") is simply pureed prunes. It can be found in the jam, baking or ethnic section of your supermarket. Store unopened prune butter at room temperature for up to 1 year. Once opened, refrigerate and use within 2 weeks.

P

▶ Prune butter can be substituted—measure for measure—for butter or other fat in baked goods, thereby cutting fat by 75 to 90 percent. However, since fat contributes tenderness, baked goods without it tend to have a rubbery texture. A good compromise is substituting three-quarters of the fat with prune butter.

▶ To make your own prune butter, combine 8 ounces (about 1⅓ cups) pitted prunes and ⅓ cup water in a blender or food processor fitted with the metal blade. Process until the prunes are pureed, scraping down the sides of the container as necessary.

▶ Put pitted prunes in a saucepan, cover with port or red wine like Cabernet or Zinfandel. Heat just until bubbles form around the edges; cover and let cool to room temperature. Refrigerate covered prunes and wine for at least 1 day (up to 1 week). Taste for sweetness, adding sugar if desired, and heat just until warm. Spoon warm prunes and their liquid over ice cream, pound cake, puddings, etc.

▶ Spirit-plumped prunes also make a wonderful garnish for meats like chicken, duck and pork.

▶ *See also* FRUIT, DRIED

PUMPKINS

▶ Choose pumpkins that are brightly colored and heavy for their size; their rinds should be free from blemishes. In general, the flesh from smaller pumpkins will be sweeter and more tender and succulent than that from the larger of the species. If you plan to use pumpkin for cooking, choose a variety specifically grown for its eating quality, such as the sugar pumpkin.

▶ Store whole pumpkins at room temperature for up to 1 month, refrigerate for up to 3 months.

▶ *Pumpkin yields:* 1 5-pound pumpkin = about 4½ cups mashed, cooked pumpkin. One 16- to 17-ounce can = about 2 cups mashed.

▶ Pumpkin can be prepared in almost any way suitable for winter squash (as a soup, vegetable, etc.). Likewise, winter squash (such as acorn or hubbard) can be substituted for pumpkin in recipes.

▶ Use an electric mixer to beat cooked pumpkin—any strings will wind around the beaters and can easily be rinsed right off.

▶ Don't throw out those seeds you remove from raw pumpkin. Rinse them clean of all pulp and strings, then spread in a single layer on a large baking sheet. Thoroughly air-dry (about 4 hours), then hull. Toss the hulled seeds with 2 tablespoons vegetable oil, spread in a single layer on a baking sheet, and bake at 350°F for about 30 minutes, or until golden brown. Stir seeds every 5 to 10 minutes during roasting time. Salt to taste and cool to room temperature before using.

P

- ▸ Halloween pumpkins will keep longer if you spray them with antiseptic inside and out.
- ▸ Always store pumpkin pie in the refrigerator; leftovers should be stored for no more than 3 days.
- ▸ *See also* SQUASH, WINTER; VEGETABLES, GENERAL

P

Q

QUARK [QWARK]

▶ Quark is a soft, unripened cheese with the texture and flavor of sour cream. It has a milder flavor and *much* richer texture than yogurt. The texture of low-fat Quark is richer than that of low-fat sour cream.

▶ Store Quark in the coldest part of the refrigerator and use within a week of the date on the carton.

▶ Quark comes in two versions—low-fat and nonfat. The numbers for 1 ounce of low-fat Quark versus regular and low-fat sour cream (the sour cream figures are in parenthesis) are: calories—35 (61/35), fat grams—2 (6/3), cholesterol milligrams—3.4 (13/8). One ounce of nonfat Quark has 18 calories and 1 gram cholesterol.

▶ Besides being a low-calorie topping for baked potatoes, Quark is a great sour cream substitute in a variety of dishes including cheesecakes, dips, sauces, salads and salad dressings.

▶ *See also* CHEESE

RADISHES

- Choose radishes that feel firm when gently squeezed. If a radish gives to pressure, the interior will likely be pithy instead of crisp. Any attached leaves should be green and crisp.
- Store radishes in a plastic bag in the refrigerator for up to 1 week. Remove and discard leaves before storing.
- Wash radishes and trim both ends just before using.
- *Radish yields:* ½ pound = about 1⅔ cups sliced.
- For added crispness, cover radishes with ice water and refrigerate for 2 hours.
- Make radish flowers for a garnish by cutting thin petals of red peel from the tip almost all the way down to the root end all the way around the radish. Put radishes in a bowl of ice water, cover and refrigerate for an hour or so, or until "petals" pull away from the center portion.
- Radish sprouts can be found in some supermarkets and specialty produce stores. They add a peppery accent to salads and other cold dishes.
- Don't only think of radishes as raw vegetables. They're wonderful thinly sliced, sautéed quickly (just until crisp-tender) in butter or olive oil, and seasoned simply with a sprinkling of sugar, freshly ground pepper and salt.
- *See also* VEGETABLES, GENERAL

RAISINS

- The most common grapes used for raisins are Thompson seedless. The tiny Zante grape is used primarily for dried currants.
- Dark raisins are sun-dried for several weeks, thereby gaining their dark color and shriveled appearance. Golden raisins have been treated with sulphur dioxide (to prevent darkening) and dried with artificial heat, which leaves them plumper and moister than dark raisins.
- Store raisins in a tightly sealed plastic bag at room temperature for several months, refrigerate or freeze for up to 1 year.
- *Raisin yields:* 1 pound = about 3 cups.
- Freeze raisins first and they'll be easier to chop.
- Rather than taking time to chop raisins, substitute currants. Their small size and similar flavor will produce the same results.
- Plump raisins or currants by covering with liquid, then bringing the liquid to a boil. Cover, remove from heat and let stand 10 minutes.
- Or combine raisins or currants with soaking liquid in a medium bowl.

R

Cover and microwave at HIGH (100 percent power) for 30 seconds; let stand for 5 minutes before using.

▸ If you use raisins or currants in baked goods often, put them in a large, screw-top jar and cover with brandy, rum or liqueur. Store at room temperature or in the refrigerator; blot well before using.

▸ If raisins clump together, put them in a strainer and spray hot, running water over them. Or pop them in the microwave and heat at HIGH (100 percent power) for 10 to 20 seconds.

▸ Before adding raisins or currants to a cake, bread or cookie batter, toss with some of the flour called for in the recipe, separating the pieces with your fingers as you do so. This will help keep the fruit from sinking to the bottom of the batter.

▸ *See also* FRUIT, DRIED

RASPBERRIES

▸ Choose brightly colored, fresh-smelling, plump berries sans hull. Attached hulls are a sign that the berries were picked too early and will undoubtedly be tart. Avoid soft, shriveled or moldy berries.

▸ Store in the refrigerator for up to 3 days. Remove any moldy raspberries before storing so the fungus doesn't spread to the other berries.

▸ *Raspberry yields:* ½ pint = 1 cup.

▸ Though the most commonly available raspberry is red, there are also black and golden varieties. The latter are usually available only in specialty produce markets. If you can find all three colors, combine them in a compote, kissed by a dollop of softly whipped cream, for a spectacular dessert.

▸ *See* BERRIES, GENERAL *for complete storage and cleaning information*

RHUBARB [ROO-barb]

▸ There are two kinds of rhubarb on the market: *Hothouse*—with pink to pale red stalks and yellow-green leaves, and *field-grown*—with cherry red stalks, bright green leaves and a more pronounced flavor.

▸ Choose rhubarb that has crisp, brightly hued stalks. The leaves should be fresh-looking and blemish-free.

▸ Store rhubarb in the refrigerator, tightly wrapped in a plastic bag, for up to 3 days.

▸ *Rhubarb yields:* 1 pound = 3 cups chopped, raw fruit; 2 cups chopped, cooked fruit.

▸ Wash and remove the leaves just before using. The leaves, which are poisonous, should never be used in food.

▸ Field-grown rhubarb has tough, fibrous strings that must be removed before using.

▶ Rhubarb lovers can enjoy it out of season by cutting it into 1-inch chunks and freezing in a freezer-proof plastic bag for up to 9 months.

RICE

▶ Rice is classified by its size: long-, medium- or short-grain. **Long-grain rice** has a length 4 to 5 times that of its width; when cooked, it produces light, dry grains that separate easily. **Short-grain rice** has fat, almost round grains with a high starch content; when cooked, it's quite moist and the grains tend to stick together. **Medium-grain rice** has a size and character between the other two—shorter and moister than long-grain, not as starchy as short-grain.

▶ **Brown rice** is the entire grain with only the inedible outer husk removed. The nutritious, high-fiber bran coating gives brown rice a light tan color, nutlike flavor and chewy texture. Brown rice takes at least twice as long to cook than regular white long-grain rice. There's a *quick brown rice* that cooks in about 15 minutes.

▶ **White rice** has had the hull and bran layers completely removed. *Converted or parboiled white rice* has undergone a steam-pressure process that makes a fluffy, separated cooked grain; it takes slightly longer to cook than regular white rice.

▶ **Instant** or **quick-cooking rice** has been fully or partially cooked, then dehydrated; it only takes a few minutes to cook but its flavor and texture don't match that of regular rice.

▶ Store white rice in an airtight container in a cool, dark place for up to 1 year. Brown rice, which is susceptible to rancidity because of the oil in the bran layer, can be stored the same way for up to 6 months. In warm climates, or for longer storage, refrigerate or freeze rice.

▶ Rice that has been stored for a long time at low humidity may lose some of its natural moisture and therefore require more liquid and a longer cooking time.

▶ *Rice yields:* 1 cup regular rice = 3 cups cooked; 1 cup converted rice = about 3½ cups cooked; 1 cup instant rice = 2 cups cooked; 1 cup brown rice = 4 cups cooked.

▶ To make a pilaf-style rice, first sauté rice in oil or butter (about 2 tablespoons per cup of rice) over medium heat for 3 to 5 minutes. (If you want a nuttier flavor, sauté the rice until golden brown.) Then add boiling liquid, cover pan and cook as usual.

▶ You can also bake rice, rather than cook it on stovetop. Simply combine rice (sautéed, if desired) and boiling liquid in an ovenproof casserole, cover tightly, and bake at 375°F until liquid is absorbed, about 25 minutes.

▶ A teaspoon or two of lemon juice in the cooking water will make cooked rice whiter.

R

- Rice cooked with highly acidic ingredients such as tomatoes often requires extra liquid and cooking time.
- Cooking rice in chicken, beef or vegetable broth adds a flavor bonus. Or substitute wine, sherry or beer for part of the cooking water.
- One or 2 teaspoons vegetable oil added to the cooking water will keep it from boiling over.
- Adding oil or butter to the water will also keep the rice grains separated.
- Add a ham hock, piece of raw bacon or smoky sausage link to the cooking water for rice, bring water to a boil and cook for 10 minutes. Remove meat, add ½ cup more water and bring to a boil again before adding rice.
- The lid for the pan in which you cook rice should be nice and tight. If yours is loose, cover the pan with 1 or 2 layers of waxed paper, punch a hole in the center, then put the pan cover on, pressing down to seat it firmly.
- Lifting the lid to peek while rice is cooking lets out valuable steam and slows the cooking process.
- Unless a recipe states otherwise, don't stir rice while it's cooking. Doing so will release the grain's starch and make it sticky.
- Test rice for doneness by biting into it. It should be firm but tender.
- If your finished rice is too firm and all the liquid has been absorbed, add about ¼ cup hot liquid, cover and cook until absorbed. Repeat if necessary.
- If the rice is done, but there's still moisture left, remove the cover and cook over low heat, fluffing rice with a fork, until the liquid evaporates.
- If rice has scorched, the best thing to do is start over. But if you don't have time, gently spoon the rice into a clean, ovenproof casserole or pan, being careful not to scrape up any of the scorched portion. Immediately cover rice with a single layer of either fresh white bread slices or onion skins. Cover bread or onions with a piece of paper towel; put a lid on the casserole or pan. Place in a 250° oven for about 10 minutes; remove and discard towel and bread or onions, and serve.
- Tossing just-cooked rice with a fork before serving lets the steam escape, which helps keep the grains separate.
- To hold cooked rice for up to 30 minutes, remove it from the heat, toss it with a fork, cover the pot first with a dish towel, then with the pan lid. The towel prevents condensation from falling into the rice and making it sticky. Or cover with a towel and lid and place in a 250°F oven to keep warm.
- Rinsing rice after it's cooked causes a loss of some of the nutrients.
- Make a double batch of rice so you can use leftovers in the next night's meal as the basis for a stir-fry, salad or simply as a side dish.
- If you're adding leftover rice to soups or stews, do so at the last minute so the rice doesn't get soft and mushy.

▶ Leftover rice can be pureed with a little liquid and used to thicken soup.

▶ Freeze leftover rice in 1-cup portions in freezer-proof plastic bags for up to 3 months.

▶ Reheat leftover rice with 1 to 2 tablespoons liquid (such as water or chicken broth) to restore its fluffy tenderness. The heating can be done in a covered saucepan, or in a covered casserole in a microwave oven.

▶ Or put leftover rice in a colander or sieve; set in a pan over simmering water, being careful not to let rice touch water. Cover and let steam for 5 to 10 minutes; fluff with a fork.

▶ When heating frozen leftover rice in a microwave oven, defrosting isn't necessary. Simply microwave at HIGH (100 percent power) for about 2 minutes per cup, tossing the rice halfway through the cooking time.

▶ Leftovers make great fried rice. Bring rice to room temperature, then sauté in a little oil with other minced ingredients like scallions, mushrooms, maybe a little smoked sausage, some minced ginger root, etc.

▶ Give leftovers a different look by creating a mold out of leftover rice salad. Firmly pack the salad into a well-oiled mold (large- or individual-size), cover with foil or plastic wrap, and weight down with full cans. Refrigerate for at least 1 hour before unmolding onto a serving plate.

▶ Short-grained rice makes great rice pudding because it has a higher proportion of starch, which results in a creamier texture.

▶ For fluffy, cold rice pudding, fold softly whipped cream into chilled rice pudding.

▶ *See also* WILD RICE

RISOTTO [rih-SAW-toh; ree-ZAH-toh]

▶ Make this creamy, classic northern Italian dish with short-grain, high-starch rice. Arborio is the variety most commonly used in the United States.

▶ Never rinse rice before making risotto or you'll wash off some of the grain's starch, so valuable in this creamy dish.

▶ Before beginning to cook risotto, sauté the rice in a couple tablespoons of oil for 2 minutes, or just until the rice is opaque.

▶ The technique for risotto is to add hot liquid to the rice, about ½ cup at a time, stirring constantly until the rice absorbs the liquid before adding the next ½ cup liquid.

▶ Have the broth sitting over low heat so it stays hot and ready to be added to the rice as necessary.

▶ If you're adding other ingredients to the rice, sauté them beforehand just until barely done. Stir them into the risotto a minute or two before serving.

▶ Risotto can be made in the microwave oven. This technique produces a slightly less creamy risotto, but then you also don't have to stand over the pan and stir it constantly. Cook rice in oil (see third tip) at HIGH (100 percent power) for 1 minute (in a 600- to 700-watt oven). Stir in two thirds of the liquid; cook at HIGH (100 percent power), uncovered, for about 12 minutes (for 1 cup uncooked rice), stirring halfway through. Add remaining liquid; cook at HIGH (100 percent power) for about another 6 minutes. Stir and let stand, uncovered, for 5 minutes.

▶ *See also* RICE

ROASTS; ROASTING

▶ The most popular beef, lamb or pork cut for roasting is the rib roast, also called a rack. Loin (pork and veal) and leg (lamb, pork and veal) roasts are also favorites.

▶ A roast should be relatively large so it remains tender and moist during this dry-heat cooking process.

▶ The next time you buy a boneless roast, remember that bones deliver a big flavor bonus to the meat. What you gain in carving convenience, you lose in flavor.

▶ A bone-in roast won't take as long to cook as one that's boneless—the bone acts as a heat conductor to the meat's center.

▶ Remove a roast from the refrigerator 2 to 3 hours before cooking.

▶ Always cook a roast fat side up so the melting fat will naturally baste the meat during roasting.

▶ If your roast doesn't already have a layer of fat on it, cover the top of it with something like fatback or lightly salted bacon. Fat not only insulates the meat from drying out but flavors it, as well.

▶ Rub all exposed meat with olive or vegetable oil to help retain the meat's natural moisture.

▶ Whenever possible, elevate a roast so the heat and air can circulate underneath. If you don't have a roasting rack to set inside the baking pan, use a small cooking rack or several canning jar rings.

▶ Salt leaches the juices from meat, so don't salt a roast before cooking.

▶ Searing a pot roast until nicely browned not only seals in the juices but contributes flavor as well.

▶ The next time you prepare a roast for cooking, cut tiny pockets in any external fat and insert slivers of fresh garlic. The garlic will flavor both meat and drippings.

▶ A light sprinkling of sugar over the meat before roasting will contribute to browning and improve the meat's flavor. Both results are due to the caramelization of the sugar as it heats.

▶ Starting a roast in a thoroughly preheated oven will help insure that the juices are sealed in.

▶ Cooking a roast at a low temperature for a relatively long time will produce a roast with a uniform temperature (medium, medium-rare, etc.).

The disadvantage is that the exterior of a slow-cooked roast is not well browned.

▶ Slow-cooked roasts shrink less than those cooked at higher temperatures.

▶ Roasting meat at high temperatures for a relatively short time creates a beautifully browned crust and a more succulent, flavorful flesh. The finished roast will also have a range of temperatures (such as from well-done to medium-rare or rare). The disadvantage is that you'll get more shrinkage with high-temperature roasting.

▶ If you want the best of all possible worlds, start a roast at high heat, then reduce it after 20 minutes.

▶ Turning a roast at least twice during cooking helps it to brown evenly. Baste it often with the pan juices.

▶ Instead of using water when making pot roast, substitute something more flavorful such as beer, wine, stock, tomato or vegetable juice, or tomato sauce (mixed with water or broth).

▶ Basting with too much liquid (stock, wine, etc.) will create excess moisture in the oven cavity and you'll end up steaming rather than roasting the meat.

▶ When you check a roast's temperature for doneness, allow for the fact that residual heat will continue to cook the meat after it's removed from the oven. Count on the internal temperature increasing by 5° to 10°F.

▶ Because meat juices shift to the center of a roast while it cooks, the exterior becomes dry. Letting the roast rest for 10 to 15 minutes after it's finished cooking allows the juices to redistribute throughout the flesh. This also makes the roast easier to carve. Keep it warm during this rest period by covering it lightly with foil.

▶ *See also* MEATS, GENERAL

ROCK CORNISH GAME HENS

▶ Rock Cornish game hens (also called **Cornish game hens**) are miniature, 4- to 6-week-old chickens that weigh from 1½ to 2½ pounds. They're a hybrid of Cornish and White Rock chickens.

▶ Typically, a game hen is just enough for one serving.

▶ The good news: Rock Cornish game hens look elegant and take less time to cook than a whole chicken. The bad news: you get less cluck for your buck—they're more expensive and have less meat per pound than a regular chicken.

▶ To flatten a game hen, use a sharp knife to cut it down the backbone, then use your palm to press down on the breastbone until the bird lies flat.

▶ When stuffing a game hen, count on about 1 cup dressing per bird.

▶ *See also* CHICKEN; POULTRY, GENERAL

S

SAFFRON

▶ Saffron—the yellow-orange stigmas from a small purple crocus—is the world's most expensive spice. That's because each flower provides only three stigmas (which must be painstakingly handpicked and dried), and it takes 14,000 of these tiny threads for each ounce of saffron!

▶ Saffron comes either powdered or in threads (the whole stigmas). Powdered saffron loses its flavor more readily and can easily be adulterated with less expensive powders like turmeric.

▶ Don't assume your market is out of saffron if you can't find it on the shelves with the other spices. Because it's so expensive, and packaged in such small containers (making it easy to shoplift), many stores keep this precious spice in the manager's office. Ask a clerk to get you some.

▶ Buying cheaper saffron won't save money in the long run, since more will be needed for the same flavor impact.

▶ Crush saffron threads just before using.

▶ Heat releases saffron's flavor essence, so increase its impact by mixing it with 1 tablespoon very hot water; let stand for about 10 minutes before using.

▶ *See also* SPICES *for information on storing*

SALAD DRESSINGS

▶ Don't think you have to make salad dressings with only the common red- or white-wine vinegar. There's a dazzling array of vinegars on the market today including those made with fruit (like blueberries, cranberries and raspberries) or herbs (such as basil, dill, rosemary or tarragon). The mild Asian rice vinegars also complement many salads. Experiment to see what you like best.

▶ The classic ratio for a vinaigrette is 3 parts oil to 1 part vinegar, lemon juice, etc.

▶ Wine is acidic and can be substituted for all or part of the vinegar or lemon juice.

▶ The next time a dressing recipe calls for lemon juice or vinegar, try using lime juice—it makes magic when combined with salad greens. Avocado and greens with a lime-juice dressing is fantastic.

▶ If you substitute yogurt for sour cream in a dressing, use a little less vinegar to compensate for the yogurt's natural acidity.

▶ Fruit juices—such as pineapple, orange or mango—make great salad dressings. Simply combine the juice with a dash of vegetable oil, a sprinkle of nutmeg and maybe a little honey. Great for fruit salads, as well as mixed greens or seafood.

▶ For an extra smooth vinaigrette, combine the ingredients and an ice cube in a screw-top jar and shake vigorously. Discard the ice cube once the dressing is mixed.

▶ Cut down on the oil content of any salad dressing by substituting up to a third of the oil with wine, vegetable or defatted chicken broth, vegetable or tomato juice, hot water, etc. Whisk the substituted ingredient into the dressing after the other ingredients are combined.

▶ Salad dressings with less oil usually have a much thinner texture. Add body by putting the dressing in a blender and adding ¼ to ½ cup over-cooked rice or 1 or 2 chunks cooked potato. Process in the blender until smooth.

▶ You don't have to bother with mixing up a dressing separately. Simply toss the greens with enough oil to lightly coat the leaves, then sprinkle lightly with vinegar, lemon juice, etc., to taste. A little salt and pepper and you're ready to go.

▶ Adding 1 or 2 teaspoons minced fresh ginger root is an easy way to give an exotic flavor to salad dressing.

▶ Make a quick avocado dressing by combining half an avocado with 1 cup vinaigrette dressing in a blender and processing until smooth.

▶ For a super-zesty dressing, mix half and half pickle juice and vegetable oil.

▶ If you're using a salad-dressing mix, combine it with 2 to 4 tablespoons boiling water, stirring until combined. Cool to room temperature before adding remaining liquid. This technique releases the flavors almost instantly.

▶ Give a commercial dressing a homemade touch by mixing in some minced fresh herbs, garlic or shallots.

▶ *See also* FATS AND OILS; VINEGARS; SALAD GREENS; SALADS

SALAD GREENS

▶ There are literally hundreds of lettuces and salad greens grown through-out the world and, because their seasons peak at different times of year, there's always a wide variety available. Besides the many lettuces (like butterhead, iceberg, romaine and red-tip), there's a plentitude of greens that can be used in salads including arugula, Belgian endive, curly endive, frisee, escarole, dandelion greens, mâche, mustard greens, radicchio, spin-ach and watercress.

▶ The general rule when buying lettuce or other greens is to look for those that are crisp and free of blemishes. They should smell fresh, never sour.

▶ Greens will last longer if they're washed as soon as you get them home.

▶ The easiest way to clean greens is to cut off the bottom to separate the leaves, then put them in a sink or large container full of cold water. Swish the greens around with your hands, then let them stand for a few minutes for any dirt to sink to the bottom.

▸ Iceberg lettuce should be cleaned differently. First remove the core by firmly smacking it against the countertop. Then grab the core with your fingers, twist and lift out. Run cold water into the resulting cavity, flushing thoroughly. Invert the head to let the water drain out.

▸ All greens must be thoroughly dried before using or storing. The easiest way to dry greens is in a salad spinner, which is one of the best fifteen-dollar investments you can make. Rather than overload the spinner (which won't get the greens as dry as you want), do the greens in batches.

▸ You can also dry greens by shaking off excess moisture, laying them out on a double layer of paper towels (or a dish towel), then blotting the surface dry.

▸ Store clean greens, wrapped loosely in dry paper towels, in a tightly sealed plastic bag. Remove as much air as possible from the bag before sealing it, then refrigerate for up to 1 week.

▸ *Greens yields:* 1 pound = about 6 cups pieces.

▸ To renew greens that have begun to wilt, place them in ice water to which you've added 2 tablespoons lemon juice; cover and refrigerate for 1 hour. If you have time, wrap the dried greens in dry paper towels and refrigerate for about 4 hours.

▸ Many kitchen pundits have long insisted that lettuce leaves must be torn by hand or their leaf edges will turn brown. Not true, if you do it right. Using a *sharp* stainless-steel knife to cut lettuce won't cause browning any faster than if you tear it. The main difference is in the appearance—many people feel that torn leaves have more eye appeal than those that are cut.

▸ If you're lining a plate with large lettuce leaves, add a little color by dipping the edges in water (shake off well), then into a saucer of paprika. Just a little paprika—you want the effect to be subtle not overt.

▸ Don't think of greens just for salads. They're wonderful sautéed, stir-fried or braised, and served as a side dish.

▸ *See also* SALAD DRESSINGS; SALADS

SALADS

▸ The best salad is a study in contrast and balance of textures, colors and flavors. Mix crunchy ingredients with those that are soft, tangy flavors with mild or slightly sweet, and bright colors with those more muted. The result will be eye-pleasing, palate-teasing and downright delicious.

▸ Salads don't have to consist of greens. There are dozens of fresh vegetables that you can make a delicious salad with including broccoli, cauliflower, celeraic, corn, cucumbers, fennel, green beans, jicama and turnips. Simply peel if necessary, and dice, chop or shred.

- Always dress salad greens just before serving so they won't become soggy.
- Don't overdress your salads. Too much dressing will weigh down the ingredients and mask their flavor. The dressing should highlight, not overpower, the salad ingredients.
- Save on cleanup by refrigerating cleaned salad greens in a large plastic bag then, just before serving, pour the dressing over the greens, seal the bag, and toss. Arrange the dressed salad on individual plates and serve.
- Another work-saver idea is to mix the dressing right in the salad bowl, then add the salad ingredients and toss.
- When making pasta salad, always cook the pasta very al dente. This will allow the pasta to absorb some of the dressing and still be firm, not mushy. Hot pasta can be combined with vinaigrette dressing, but let it cool to room temperature before adding other ingredients (fresh herbs, vegetables, etc.) to keep them from wilting.
- If you're using long noodles in pasta salad, it's a good idea to rinse them under cold, running water to remove excess starch. It's the starch that makes the noodles stick together into unwieldy clumps.
- New potatoes are the best choice for potato salads, next comes boiling potatoes. Both hold their shape better than russets.
- Potatoes for potato salads will absorb more dressing if you dress them while they're hot, then refrigerate.
- Personalize deli-bought potato salad by adding finely chopped red or green bell peppers, cucumbers, dill or sweet pickles, hard-cooked eggs, grated cheddar cheese or herbs such as basil, cilantro, dill or parsley.
- Substitute leftover cooked fish for recipes that call for canned salmon or tuna.
- Use hollowed-out large tomato or bell pepper halves as edible containers for bean, rice, tuna or other salads.
- The presentation of a salad is almost as important as its flavor. An easy way to add color is with edible flowers (*see* FLOWERS, EDIBLE). The flowers can be used whole, or the petals can be scattered over the top of the salad. The key when using flowers is subtlety, not cuteness.
- Chilling the salad plates or serving bowl will keep your salads crisp longer.
- Use leftover meat, fish or poultry as the base for a main course salad the next day. Add salad greens or chopped fresh vegetables, croutons and your favorite dressing and, voilà!, a meal in minutes.
- Use leftover bean, pasta, rice, meat, fish or vegetable salads to stuff pita pockets for an instant sandwich the next day.
- Do you always throw out leftover tossed salad because it gets limp and soggy? Next time, recyle the salad into soup by pureeing it, then adding broth and chopped vegetables.
- After cleaning wooden salad bowls, rub them with a crumbled piece of waxed paper to seal the surface.

▸ *See also* COOKING LIGHT; FLOWERS, EDIBLE; SALAD DRESSINGS; SALAD GREENS; VEGETABLES; GENERAL

S

SALMON [SAM-uhn]

▸ Most of the North American salmon are found off the Pacific coast and about 90 percent come from Alaskan waters. **Chinook** or **king salmon** is considered the finest and is the most expensive; its soft-textured, high-fat flesh ranges in color from off-white to bright red. The **coho** or **silver salmon** has a high-fat (but lower than chinook), firm-textured, pink to red-orange flesh. The moderate-fat **sockeye** or **red salmon** has a firm, deep red flesh that's highly prized for canning. Among those low-fat varieties are the pink-fleshed **pink** or **humpback salmon**—the most delicately flavored of the Pacific varieties, and **chum** or **dog salmon**, which has the lightest color and lowest fat content.

▸ Whenever you grill or poach salmon, cook twice the amount you need for dinner. Chill half the salmon and use the next day, cut into strips or chunks and served over greens for a cold salmon salad.

▸ Or toss leftover cooked salmon pieces with a chunky pasta like radiattore or rotini and salad dressing for a pasta salad,

▸ Toss leftover salmon chunks with hot pasta, fresh dill and a little olive oil for a delicious entree.

▸ *See also* FISH, GENERAL (*for buying, storing and cooking information*); FISH, COOKING METHODS; SMOKED FISH

SALSA [SAHL-sah]

▸ In general, salsa is a highly seasoned, cooked or uncooked sauce, used either for dipping or as a garnish. Though the original mixtures were made with a base of chopped tomatoes, today recipes and menus abound with "salsas" made with almost everything, including fruit.

▸ *Salsa cruda* on a label or menu indicates an uncooked mixture.

▸ *Salsa verde* means "green sauce," and refers to mixtures made with tomatillos, green chiles, cilantro and various seasonings.

▸ A wide variety of salsas are available in most supermarkets. They may be fresh or cooked and range in spiciness from mild to hot.

▸ Store fresh salsas, tightly covered, in the refrigerator for no more than 5 days. Cooked salsas may be stored at room temperature for up to 6 months. Once opened, refrigerate for up to 1 month.

▸ Add pizzazz to cooked vegetables such as corn, green beans and summer squash by tossing with 2 to 3 tablespoons salsa.

▸ Salsa is great spooned atop baked potatoes or tossed with hash browns; stir it into mashed potatoes to update an old-fashioned favorite.

▸ Bring salsa to room temperature and use as a garnish for sautéed, grilled or broiled meat, chicken or fish.

▶ Stir several teaspoons salsa into sour cream (low-calorie or regular) or yogurt for an almost instant dip for crudités or chips.

▶ Toss your favorite salsa with greens for a snappy, low-fat salad dressing.

▶ Salsa make a great sandwich spread—just make sure it's not too liquid or your bread will get soggy.

S

SALT

▶ Salt helps balance and brighten the flavors of a dish. There are many different kinds of this most popular seasoning. **Table salt** is a fine-grained, refined salt with additives that make it free-flowing; **iodized salt** is table salt with added iodine. **Kosher salt** is a coarse-grained salt that's usually additive-free; many chefs and gourmet cooks prefer its texture and flavor. **Sea salt** does, as its name indicates, come from the sea; many culinary experts prefer its fresh, distinct flavor. It's available fine- or coarse-grained and most of that available in the United States is imported. **Rock salt** has a grayish cast because it's not highly refined; its chunky crystals are used predominately as a bed for oysters and clams and in combination with ice to make ice cream in crank-style makers. **Pickling salt** is additive-free and fine-grained and used to make brines for pickles, sauerkraut, etc.

▶ Never salt a sauce or other preparation that will be reduced, a process which concentrates flavors, until the end of the cooking time.

▶ Cold dishes usually require more salt than hot ones because chilling mutes the flavor of foods.

▶ The best way to prevent oversalting is to season dishes at the end of the cooking or preparation time. Many foods contain a high level of natural sodium, or taste saltier when combined with other ingredients.

▶ If you've ruined a dish by oversalting it, try stirring in 1 teaspoon each sugar and vinegar; cook for a few minutes and taste.

▶ For an oversalted liquid preparation such as soup or stew, add a sliced, peeled raw potato and simmer for 10 to 15 minutes. Use a slotted spoon to remove the potato before serving the soup.

▶ Oversalted soups can also be helped by adding more liquid or vegetables. Or quickly cook some rice in water, puree it with a little liquid, then stir it into the soup.

▶ Always retaste foods you've made ahead of time—flavors have a way of shifting and changing during refrigeration or standing time.

▶ If you're on a low-salt diet, season foods by adding more herbs, garlic and/or lemon juice.

▶ A few rice grains (about 10 for an average shaker) in your salt shaker will keep salt from clumping in humid climates.

▶ One tablespoon cornstarch combined with a box of salt will also keep it pouring freely.

S

- If a salt shaker pours *too* freely, plug up several holes by cleaning the lid, then painting over the excess holes (on the inside) with clear nail polish. Let the polish air-dry at least 1 day so there won't be any residual odor.
- *See also* COOKING LIGHT

SANDWICHES

- Frozen bread is easier to cut into very thin slices for the calorie-conscious.
- Create a "two-faced" sandwich by using 1 slice white bread and 1 rye or wheat.
- Always cut off the crusts before rolling bread flat for canapés.
- Sandwiches don't always have to be on "regular" bread. Wrap your sandwich ingredients in a softened flour tortilla or egg roll wraper, or in lettuce leaves. Or spoon a sandwich filling into a split pita bread, or atop a bagel. Toasted, split croissants or brioche make elegant sandwich breads.
- Cut calories by blending together half butter or margarine and half nonfat imitation mayonnaise for a sandwich spread. Even better, use half nonfat mayo and half low- or nonfat cream cheese.
- Stir chopped chutney into cream cheese for a great ham or turkey sandwich spread.
- Snap up the flavor of grilled sandwiches by spreading the side of the bread to be grilled with mayonnaise instead of butter.
- Always "seal" bread to keep it from getting soggy with moist fillings by spreading the slices all the way to the edges with butter, margarine or cream cheese.
- Finely chop meat or fish from the night before and combine with mayo, celery and pickle relish for a meat- or fish-salad sandwich.
- To make messy sandwiches like Sloppy Joes less *sloppy,* buy unsliced buns and cut off the top quarter of each bun. Hollow out the bottom portion, then spoon the filling into it and replace the bun's top.
- Anytime you make sandwiches in advance, be sure to wrap them airtight and refrigerate. They'll keep for at least a day that way.
- Making crustless sandwiches ahead for a party? The edges will stay fresher if you wait until just before serving to cut off the crusts. Stack 2 or 3 sandwiches at a time and cut the crusts off all at once.
- When making sandwiches to be eaten later (as for a lunchbox or picnic), keep them from becoming soggy by packing additions like tomato and pickle slices in separate plastic bags. Add the extras to the sandwiches just before eating.
- The bread won't get soggy on made-ahead sandwiches if you spread mustard, pickle relish or ketchup between cheese or meat slices, instead of directly on the bread.
- You can make several meat sandwiches at a time and freeze them in sandwich bags, then in a larger, freezer-weight bag for up to 1 month. Don't

use mayonnaise or cream cheese as a spread—they separate when frozen. Mustard or ketchup is fine; so are butter and margarine. You can put cheese on sandwiches to be frozen, but many will become crumbly after defrosting. Your best bet is processed cheese, which is pretty indestructible. Take the frozen sandwich out in the morning and it'll be thawed by lunchtime. Pack additions like lettuce and pickle and tomato slices separately.

SAUCES AND GRAVIES

▶ Many sauces and gravies are based on roux—a mixture of flour and fat that's cooked over low heat. The color and flavor of a roux are determined by the length of time the mixture's cooked. *White roux* and *blond roux* are both made with butter or oil—the former cooked just until it begins to turn beige, the latter until pale golden. Light rouxs take from 5 to 15 minutes to cook. The fuller-flavored *brown roux* can be made with butter, pork or beef fat, lard or drippings. After being cooked, its color can range from deep golden-brown to mahogany-brown. The darkest roux, which takes on a nutty flavor, sometimes takes up to 1 hour to cook—it's most often used for specialties like Cajun gumbo.

▶ A shortcut to a darker, more richly flavored roux is to cook the flour, stirring often, in a dry skillet or saucepan over medium heat until well browned. Add the fat (oil, drippings, etc.) and cook for 3 to 4 more minutes.

▶ A basic white sauce is made by stirring milk into a butter-flour roux. The thickness of the sauce depends on the proportion of flour and butter to milk. For 1 cup milk, use 1 tablespoon each butter and flour for a thin sauce; 2 tablespoons each butter and flour for a medium sauce; and 3 tablespoons each for a thick sauce.

▶ When thickening a sauce or gravy with flour or cornstarch, always make a paste by first combining the flour or cornstarch with a little broth, wine, water, etc. Otherwise, you could end up with lumps of flour in the mixture.

▶ Use a whisk when adding a flour-, cornstarch- or other starch-based paste to a hot liquid. Whisk the liquid rapidly while drizzling in the starch mixture and you won't get lumps.

▶ Use the cooking liquid from vegetables or meats, or leftover pan juices as a sauce base. The liquid can be frozen until you need it.

▶ Reducing a liquid (such as wine or stock) intensifies and enriches its flavor dramatically. Professional cooks use reductions as the base for sauces or as the sauce itself. To reduce a liquid, simply boil it until the volume is at least halved. Additions such as minced shallots or herbs are often cooked in the liquid for added flavoring.

▶ Deglazing a pan creates an almost-instant sauce. Here's what you do: After

S

food has been sautéed, remove it and any excess fat from the pan. Deglaze the pan by heating a small amount of liquid (wine, stock, etc.) in the pan and stirring to loosen browned bits of food on the bottom. Cook for a few minutes to reduce and thicken the liquid and drizzle over the sautéed food.

▶ Puree leftover soups, stews, meats or vegetables and use as a sauce base.

▶ For more flavor the next time you make a sauce or gravy from giblets, finely chop the gizzard, heart, neck, etc., then sauté the mixture in a little oil before adding the liquid and remaining ingredients.

▶ Give almost any sauce a satiny texture by whisking in 1 or 2 tablespoons butter just before serving. The same amount of heavy whipping cream also works nicely.

▶ If a sauce to which you've added meat blood begins to curdle, stir in 1 or 2 teaspoons lemon juice.

▶ A sauce that begins to separate while cooking can be saved by processing the mixture at low speed in a blender just until smooth, about 30 to 60 seconds. Return the sauce to the pan and continue cooking over very low heat.

▶ Save a hollandaise that's begun to separate by adding a little boiling water and whisking until once again smooth.

▶ Add color to a pale sauce or gravy by stirring in a few drops of Kitchen Bouquet, which is readily available in supermarkets.

▶ One or 2 teaspoons instant coffee powder or unsweetened cocoa powder adds both color and a rich flavor to sauces and gravies.

▶ After stirring sour cream or yogurt into a hot sauce, heat it gently and only until the mixture is warmed through. Boiling will cause it to curdle.

▶ Sour cream, yogurt and other milk products won't separate as easily in flour-based sauces.

▶ For an "almost-instant" pasta sauce, sauté 1 pound Italian sausage or ground chuck with 1 medium chopped onion until browned, drain off fat, stir in 16 to 24 ounces commercial spaghetti sauce, and cook until heated throughout.

▶ Adding salt and pepper after a sauce is done allows for reduction (which intensifies flavor) and prevents overseasoning.

▶ An over-salted sauce can be helped in several ways: 1. Add a peeled raw potato, cut into eighths, stir and cook for 5 to 10 minutes, then remove potatoes; 2. Stir in ½ teaspoon sugar, then taste, and add more sugar—a little at a time—if necessary; 3. One teaspoon vinegar added with sugar also helps balance oversaltiness; 4. Best idea—season the sauce just before serving to allow for other ingredients that may add a salty flavor, as well as intensified flavor because of natural reduction.

▶ *See also* ARROWROOT; CORNSTARCH; FLOUR

SAUERKRAUT [SOW-uhr-krowt]

► Precooked sauerkraut is available in jars and cans on supermarket shelves. Fresh sauerkraut is sold in delicatessens and in cryovac packages in a supermarket's refrigerated section. Fresh sauerkraut generally has a milder flavor than its canned counterpart.

► Store precooked, canned sauerkraut in a cool, dark place for up to 6 months. Refrigerate fresh sauerkraut and use within 1 week.

► To reduce sauerkraut's briny flavor, put it in a sieve and rinse it well under cold, running water. Drain well before using.

► Taste fresh sauerkraut—if it's too salty for your palate, soak it for 15 to 30 minutes in cold water; drain well before using.

► To cook fresh sauerkraut, put it in a large saucepan with just enough liquid (broth, wine, beer, water, etc.) to cover. Simmer, covered, for about 30 minutes, or until tender.

► To heat precooked sauerkraut, place in a saucepan with its liquid and cook over medium heat until hot, 5 to 10 minutes. If the sauerkraut liquid is too salty, drain it off and cover sauerkraut with water, wine or beer.

► Caraway seeds make a nice complement for sauerkraut—so does crumbled, crisp bacon.

► Roast pork is a natural partner for sauerkraut.

► Apples are also delicious with sauerkraut. Simply cut them into chunks and cook with the kraut.

► Or add chopped apples and onions to cooked and cooled sauerkraut and serve cold as a salad.

SAUSAGE

► Sausage can be fresh or cured; curing extends storage life. Some sausages are also dried; the longer a sausage is dried, the firmer it becomes. Sausage comes in several forms—fully cooked (ready to eat), partially cooked (enough to kill any trichinae) and uncooked, which may or may not require cooking depending on how or whether it's been cured.

► Refrigerator storage for sausages depends on its type: *uncooked, fresh sausages* (like pork sausage) are very perishable and should be refrigerated, well wrapped, for no more than 2 days; *uncooked, smoked sausage* (like mettwurst) for up to 1 week; *cooked sausage* (such as braunschweiger) for 4 to 6 days; *cooked, smoked sausage* (like knockwurst) in unopened vacuum-sealed package for 2 weeks, 1 week after opening; *dry and semidry sausage* (like pepperoni) for up to 3 weeks.

► Sausage can be frozen for about 2 months.

► Some sausages use fillers such as cereal, soybean flour and dried-milk solids to stretch the meat. Read the label to make sure of what you're buying.

S

▶ Hard sausages like pepperoni will last longer if you only cut off what you need at one time.

▶ Cook uncooked sausage patties over medium-low heat until the juices run clear; turn once during the cooking time.

▶ For extra-crispy sausage patties, dip them first into flour.

▶ Uncooked link sausage should be placed in a covered, cold skillet with about ½ inch of water. Bring to a boil, then reduce to a simmer. Cook until juices run clear. (Prepared this way, the casing won't burst.) Drain thoroughly, then cook over medium-high heat, turning often, until well browned.

▶ Another way to keep link sausages from bursting during cooking is to use the tines of a fork to puncture the casing in several places, then sauté over medium-low heat. The punctures allow steam and rendered fat an exit.

▶ Or you can boil link sausages for 5 minutes, drain well, then fry. This helps prevent shrinkage.

▶ Broiling link sausage is easy if you put several links on a skewer. That way, you can flip several sausages with one turn.

▶ To taste homemade sausage for seasoning, fry a little of it until well done, cool, then taste. *Never* taste uncooked sausage.

▶ *See also* MEATS, GENERAL

SAUTÉING [saw-TAY; saw-TAY-ing]

▶ Sauté means to cook food quickly in a very small amount of oil or other fat.

▶ Use a skillet or sauté pan with a handle and low sides; those with high sides can steam food before it's sautéed.

▶ For the crispest results when sautéing, thoroughly heat the oil before adding the ingredients.

▶ How do you know when oil is hot enough to begin cooking? Drop a chunk of vegetable (such as onion or bell pepper) into the pan. If it sizzles, the oil's ready.

▶ Room-temperature food browns faster and more evenly, and absorbs less fat than refrigerated food. Cold food will also stick to the pan more than room-temperature ingredients.

▶ Parboil dense foods like carrots or potatoes so they can be combined with quick-cooking ingredients like celery in sautés. This insures that all the ingredients will complete cooking at the same time, to the same degree of doneness.

▶ Be sure the food you plan to sauté is as dry as possible.

▶ Salt impedes browning, so salt food after it's been sautéed.

▶ Sprinkle a little sugar over meat before sautéing and the sautéed meat will be browner; the sugar also improves the flavor. Both results are due to the caramelization of the sugar as it heats.

▶ Rather than overcrowding one pan, sauté food in two pans—it will cook more evenly, brown better and won't have a tendency to steam, as it will if crowded.

▶ While the food is sautéing, grab the handle and shake the pan often so the food moves around and gets evenly browned.

▶ Use a bulb baster to remove any excess grease (from rendered fat in meat) from the pan.

▶ Sautéed foods shouldn't be covered during cooking. Covering the pan creates steam, which means the food will be limp.

▶ After food has been sautéed, transfer it to a plate or other container and remove any excess fat from the pan. Make a quick sauce by deglazing the pan—a technique of heating a small amount of liquid (wine, stock, etc.) in the pan and stirring to loosen browned bits of food on the bottom. This flavorful liquid may either be used as a sauce base, or reduced until slightly thick and simply spooned over the food.

▶ *See also* COOKING, GENERAL; DEEP-FRYING; STIR-FRYING

SCALLIONS (GREEN ONIONS) [SKAL-yuhns]

▶ Scallions are a distinct variety of the onion family, though some markets sell immature (green) onions as scallions. True scallions have a milder flavor than young onions. They can also be identified by the fact that the sides of the base are straight, whereas the others are usually slightly curved, showing the beginnings of a bulb. The bottom line is that scallions and young onions can be used interchangeably, if you don't mind the slightly stronger flavor of the latter.

▶ Choose scallions with crisp, bright green tops and a firm white base. Those no larger than ½ inch in diameter are best.

▶ Store, unwashed, in a plastic bag in the refrigerator for up to 5 days.

▶ Before using, trim off the roots; discard the outer white layer of the scallion.

▶ *Scallion yields:* 9 small to medium scallions with tops = about 1 cup sliced.

▶ The entire scallion—white and green part—is edible. The white portion of a scallion has a slightly stronger flavor than the green stems.

▶ Use a knife to slice the white portion of a scallion.

▶ An easy and quick way to cut the green ends is to snip them with scissors. The scissor technique also keeps the scallion greens a nice round shape.

▶ Cutting a green onion in half lengthwise before chopping will give you smaller pieces with which to season foods.

- Snipped scallion greens make a colorful garnish. They're also a flavorful addition to tossed green salads.
- Add the green portion of scallions during the final few minutes of cooking time so they'll keep their bright color.
- A scallion's white portion can be chopped and frozen raw (or sautéed) in an airtight container for up to 3 months. (The green portion becomes limp and turns dark when frozen.) Add directly to dishes like soups and stews without thawing. If sautéing, thaw and blot dry before doing so.
- Whole scallions make a delicious side dish when sautéed briefly in olive oil and seasoned with salt and pepper. Before cooking them this way, trim their green portions to a length of 3 to 4 inches.
- For a showy, easy garnish, make scallion brushes. Start by trimming off the root end and most of the scallion's green top. Use a sharp, pointed knife to thinly slash both ends, leaving uncut a 1-inch space in the scallion's center. Place in a bowl of ice water in the refrigerator for 1 hour, or until the slashed tips curl.
- *See also* CHIVES; ONIONS; VEGETABLES, GENERAL

SCALLOPS

- Though there are many species, scallops are classified in two broad groups: **bay scallops**—with meat about ½ inch in diameter, are sweeter, more succulent and more expensive than the larger, more widely available (but less tender) **sea scallops**, the meat of which averages 1½ inches in diameter. The small **calico scallops**—though they're deep-sea creatures—are often sold as bay scallops on the West Coast.
- Because scallops perish quickly out of water, they're usually sold shucked. Look for those with a sweet smell and a fresh, moist sheen. Avoid any with a strong sulfur odor. Scallops can range in color from pale beige to creamy pink to orangey. Avoid those that are stark white—it's a sign that they've been soaked in water, a marketing ploy to increase the weight.
- Refrigerate shucked scallops immediately after purchase and use within 1 or 2 days.
- *Scallops yields:* bay scallops = 100 per pound; sea scallops = 30 per pound.
- If sautéing scallops, first pat them dry with paper towels.
- Scallops cook very quickly (about 1 to 3 minutes) and, like all shellfish, toughen when overcooked.
- *see also* SHELLFISH

SCRAMBLED EGGS *see* EGGS, COOKING METHODS

SERVING *see* ENTERTAINING

SESAME SEED

- African slaves brought sesame seed to America; they called it **benne seed.** Today, there are still recipes—mostly in the South—that call for benne seed.
- Though the most common color of sesame seed is grayish-ivory, it also comes in shades of brown, red and black. These more exotic sesame seeds can be found in ethnic markets.
- To keep sesame seed from becoming rancid, store in an airtight container in the refrigerator for up to 6 months.
- Bring out the flavor of sesame seed by toasting it, either in a dry skillet over medium heat, or in a 350°F oven. Stir occasionally, toasting only until seed begins to turn golden brown.
- Sesame seed used as a topping for baked goods doesn't need pretoasting because the oven does the job.

SHALLOTS [SHAL-uhts]

- Shallots taste like a combination of onion and garlic, but milder than either. They're formed more like garlic than onions, with a head composed of multiple cloves, each covered with a thin, papery skin.
- Choose shallots that are plump and firm with dry skins. Avoid those that are wrinkled or sprouting.
- Store shallots in a cool, dry, well-ventilated place for up to 1 month.
- A recipe that calls for 1 shallot usually means 1 clove, not the whole head.
- If you have a lot of shallot cloves to peel, drop them in boiling water and let stand 1 minute. Turn into a colander and rinse with cold water before peeling.
- Cook shallots over low heat just until soft; too much heat will scorch them.

SHELLFISH

- The shellfish family is broken into two basic categories—crustaceans and mollusks. **Crustaceans** have elongated bodies and jointed crustlike shells (like crabs, lobsters and shrimp). **Mollusks** are divided into three groups: *gastropods* (or univalves), such as abalone, have a single shell and single muscle; *bivalves,* like the clam and oyster, have two shells hinged together by a strong muscle; and *cephalopods,* such as the squid, which have tentacles and ink sacs.
- *See also:* ABALONE; CLAMS; CRABS; FISH; LOBSTERS; MUSSELS; OYSTERS; SCALLOPS; SHRIMP

SHORTENING *see* FATS AND OILS

SHRIMP

S

► Choose raw, shelled shrimp that are firm, moist and translucent. Un-shelled shrimp should have shiny, firm shells; avoid those with black spots. Shrimp should smell of the sea with no hint of ammonia. Choose cooked, shelled shrimp that look plump and succulent. As a rule, the larger the shrimp, the larger the price.

► Count on about ¾ pound unshelled shrimp per serving; ⅓ to ½ pound shelled shrimp.

► On the average, you can figure that 3 pounds of shrimp will weigh only half as much after peeling and cooking.

► Before storing fresh, uncooked shrimp, rinse them well under cold, run-ning water; drain thoroughly. Refrigerate, tightly covered, for up to 2 days. Cooked shrimp can be refrigerated for up to 3 days.

► Shrimp can be frozen for up to 3 months; thaw overnight in the refrig-erator. Or place a sealed package of frozen shrimp in a bowl of cold water; change water every 10 minutes until shrimp is defrosted.

► How many shrimp you get per pound depends on the size. Though it varies from market to market, the average number per pound for: colossal shrimp—10 or fewer; jumbo—11 to 15; extra large—16 to 20; large shrimp—21 to 30; medium shrimp—31 to 35; small—36 to 45; and min-iature—60 to 100.

► In the United States, colossal and jumbo shrimp are sometimes referred to as "prawns," although prawns are a separate species.

► Though there are slight differences in texture and flavor, the various sizes of shrimp (except the miniatures) can usually be substituted for each other.

► Raw shrimp are easier to peel and devein than those that are cooked.

► To shell shrimp (either before or after cooking), start at the large end and peel away the shell. The tail fin may or may not be left on the shrimp.

► Don't throw out those flavorful shrimp shells. Wash them well, put them in a skillet with butter or oil, and cook for about 10 minutes. Strain the butter or oil and discard the shells; use the shrimp-flavored fat for sau-téing or flavoring seafood dishes, pasta, etc.

► Or place washed shrimp shells in a saucepan, cover with water and bring to a boil. Reduce to simmer, cover and cook for 30 minutes. Let shells cool in the liquid, then strain and discard shells. Use shrimp-flavored broth as a base for soups or sauces. Freeze until ready to use, for up to 6 months.

► Or cook the shrimp shells in water for 10 minutes, strain and discard shells, then use the water to cook the shrimp in.

► Whether or not to devein shrimp is a matter of personal preference. In general, small and medium shrimp don't need deveining except for cosmetic purposes. However, because the intestinal vein of larger shrimp contains noticeable grit, it should be removed.

► To devein shrimp, use a sharp, pointed knife to cut a shallow slit down the middle of the outside curve. Pull out the dark vein, then rinse the slit under cold, running water.

► Shrimp cooked in its shell is more flavorful than shrimp shelled before cooking.

► Simmering unshelled shrimp in beer gives it a wonderful, slightly sweet flavor.

► As with all shellfish, shrimp should be cooked briefly or it becomes tough and rubbery. Cook only until the flesh turns opaque; whole shrimp should just begin to curl. If the shells are on, they should turn pink.

► An iodine flavor tells you that the shrimp has fed on dead plants.

► *See also* SHELLFISH

SIEVES [sihvs]

► When buying a sieve, look for one with strong handles and frame; it should have a hook or other extension for resting the sieve on top of bowls or pans. Buying one that's dishwasher-safe will save on tedious washing.

► Some foods require a little help to go through a sieve. Always use a wooden spoon—it's easier on the sieve than a metal one.

► The container into which you're straining food should be deep enough so that the bottom of the sieve won't touch the liquid being strained.

► If a recipe for a moist ingredient calls for a fine sieve or strainer and you don't have one, line a colander or coarse sieve with several layers of cheesecloth that have been moistened with water and squeezed out. You can also line it with the leg section of an old, clean pair of pantyhose.

► If you don't have a flour sifter, spoon the flour into a fine sieve, then shake or tap it over a measuring cup set on a piece of waxed paper. This also works with confectioners' sugar. If necessary, use the back of a wooden spoon to stir the flour or sugar so it goes through easier.

► Find yourself without a colander or sieve? Create one by using an ice pick or pointed knife to poke holes in an aluminum pie plate. This substitute is only appropriate for liquid mixtures.

► As soon as you're through using a sieve, wash it. Otherwise, dried food will clog the tiny holes and make cleaning difficult. A clogged sieve can be cleaned by soaking it in hot, soapy water, then scrubbing with a vegetable brush. Trouble-free cleaning is a snap in the dishwasher (bottom shelf), but only if your sieve is dishwasher-safe.

SIMPLE SYRUPS *see* SUGAR SYRUPS

S

SLOW COOKERS (CROCKPOTS)

► The slow cooker—also known as a Crockpot—is comparable to an electric casserole in that it cooks food with slow, steady, moist heat (the low setting is about 200°F). It's designed to slowly cook food over a period of about 8 to 12 hours. Slow cookers have tight covers, which keeps food moist during long hours of cooking. Most have adjustable heat levels, allowing you to turn the heat up when you get home to finish the dish, if necessary.

► Slow cookers come in a range of sizes, from 1 to 6 quarts—the average size is 3½ quarts. The 1-quart cooker is good for cooking for 1 to 2 people, or for keeping party foods like dips and meatballs warm. Large families will most probably need the 6-quart cooker.

► Always read the manufacturer's guidelines for your particular slow cooker, particularly those for converting conventional recipes to slow cooking.

► Two great advantages of the slow cooker is that it doesn't heat up the kitchen, and the dish can be cooking all day while you're at work.

► A disadvantage to the slow cooker is that some vegetables (like celery) may become mushy by the time the other ingredients in the dish are done.

► Dense vegetables like potatoes and carrots should be cut into pieces no larger than 1 inch thick. Otherwise, they may not cook through.

► Leaving the peel on slow-cooked vegetables not only retains nutrients, but also helps them keep their shape. Simply scrub the skins of potatoes, carrots, etc., before chopping and adding to the pot.

► Slow-cooked food at elevations over 3,500 feet usually takes longer to get done than at lower altitudes.

► If you're going to be away from home longer than the cooking time, plug your slow cooker into an automatic timer (available at any hardware store). Set the timer to start the cooker while you're gone. Always place *chilled* food into a cooker that has a delayed starting time. Never let the food stand for more than 2 hours before the cooking starts.

► Putting cold ingredients in a hot cooker can crack the crockery insert.

► Always let the crockery insert cool completely before removing and washing (it can be put in the dishwasher). Trying to cool a hot container quickly by filling it with cool water can crack it.

► Never immerse the outside electric unit in water. Simply wipe clean with a damp paper towel or sponge.

► *See also* COOKING, GENERAL

SMOKED FISH

- Though smoked salmon is probably the most popular smoked fish in the United States, other smoked fish that can be found include mackerel, trout and whitefish.
- Buy smoked fish that looks fresh, not dry around the edges.
- Plan on 2 slices smoked fish per serving.
- Store smoked fish, tightly wrapped, in the refrigerator for up to 3 days.
- Thin slices of smoked fish are easier to separate when cold.
- Smoked whole fish is easier to skin and bone while it's cold.
- Arrange slices of smoked fish on a serving plate, cover with plastic wrap, and let stand at room temperature for 30 minutes to bring out the natural, rich flavors of the fish.
- Some accompaniments for smoked fish are capers, caviar, lemon wedges, sour cream, melon slices, or finely chopped chives, cucumbers, dill, red onion or tomatoes.

SNAILS

- Fresh snails are cultivated in the United States and are available year-round in specialty markets. They must be soaked, trimmed and cooked before they can be substituted for canned snails in recipes.
- Canned snails with a bag of shells attached are sold in gourmet markets and some supermarkets. The best canned snails come from France.
- Buy fresh snails the day you plan to use them and store in the refrigerator until ready to prepare.
- *Snail yields:* 1 pound fresh American snails = about 48 canned (American snails are smaller than European snails).
- To prepare live snails, soak them in a shallow pan of lukewarm water to cover for about 10 minutes. Discard any snails that haven't begun to emerge from their shells after that time. Drain remaining snails, cover with cold water mixed with 1 teaspoon salt and let stand at room temperature for 1 hour. Prevent snails from crawling out by dampening the edge of bowl and coating with salt. Scrub the shell's exterior and rinse well in cold water.
- Place snails in boiling water, then reduce heat to simmer and cook 5 minutes. Drain, then use a snail fork or skewer to remove the snails from their shells. Snip off head, black tails and any bit of green gall; rinse snails. Poach snails in water to cover (or use half wine or beef broth) for 1½ to 2 hours, or until tender. Add a bay leaf, 1 chopped small carrot and 1 chopped celery stalk to the liquid, if desired. Cool snails in broth to room temperature. Now the snails are ready to be used in recipes calling for canned snails.
- Clean empty snail shells by covering them with 1 quart water mixed with

S

2 tablespoons baking soda and 1 tablespoon salt. Bring to a boil; cover and simmer 30 minutes. Drain, rinse well and dry thoroughly before using.

▸ Snail shells can be used over and over again if they're carefully washed and dried after each use.

▸ Canned snails are better if you rinse them with cold water, then put them in a bowl of salted water with a little fresh garlic. Cover tightly and refrigerate overnight; blot dry with paper towels before using.

SNOW PEAS *see* PEAS, POD

SOFT-COOKED EGGS *see* EGGS, COOKING METHODS

SOUFFLÉS [soo-FLAYS]

▸ A cold soufflé is really more of a mousse; it's based on gelatin and stiffly beaten egg whites. Such soufflés can be served frozen or simply chilled in the refrigerator. Cold soufflés are usually served as dessert.

▸ A baked soufflé is comprised of stiffly beaten egg whites, which give it the traditional light texture, and a base mixture, which provides flavor.

▸ Position the oven rack in the middle of the oven for baked soufflés. If it's a particularly high-rising soufflé, position the rack in the lower third of the oven. Preheat oven for 15 minutes, using an oven thermometer for accuracy.

▸ A classic soufflé dish is best because the straight sides force the expanding soufflé upward. It's important to use the size dish called for in the recipe.

▸ To prepare a collar for a soufflé dish, cut a piece of foil or parchment paper (foil is easier to handle) 2 inches longer than the circumference of the dish to be used. Fold the foil lengthwise in thirds; lightly butter one side. Wrap foil, buttered side in, tightly around the buttered soufflé dish. Press foil so that it conforms to the shape of the dish. The collar should rise 2 to 3 inches above the rim of the dish. Securely fasten foil with tape or string. If using string, tie it about ½ inch below the rim of the dish; use a paper clip to secure the top edge of the foil.

▸ Always butter a soufflé dish unless otherwise indicated.

▸ For dessert soufflés, sprinkle about 2 tablespoons granulated sugar into the buttered soufflé dish. Rotate and tilt the dish until sugar coats inside of dish and collar.

▸ For savory soufflés, sprinkle the dish and collar with dry breadcrumbs or finely grated cheese.

▸ The components of a soufflé may be prepared in advance for easy last-minute assembly. Butter and sugar the soufflé dish; set aside the unbeaten egg whites in a covered container. Prepare and cover the base mixture. Allow both egg whites and base mixture to stand at room temperature at least 30 minutes before using. Be sure to preheat your oven. At the last minute, simply beat the egg whites, fold them into the base mixture and bake the soufflé.

▸ Recipes calling for more egg whites than egg yolks insure lighter soufflés.

▸ When doubling a soufflé recipe, add an extra egg white to insure proper rising. For example, if the original recipe calls for 3 egg whites, use 7 egg whites in the doubled recipe.

▸ The egg whites must be beaten in a manner to incorporate as much air as possible, but not so overbeaten that they become dry or collapse (*see* EGGS).

▸ Immediately after beating egg whites, fold them into the base mixture. If the beaten whites are allowed to stand, they'll begin to deflate, and your soufflé won't be as light as it could be.

▸ Stir a small amount of the beaten egg whites into the soufflé base to lighten the mixture and make it easier to fold in the remaining egg whites.

▸ Don't overblend the mixture once the egg whites have been gently folded in or the soufflé won't rise as high.

▸ To create a soufflé with a "crown," once the mixture has been turned into the soufflé dish, run a knife vertically through the mixture (almost all the way to the bottom) about 1 to 1 ½ inches from the dish edge.

▸ Never open the oven door to check a soufflé's progress. If there's no window in the oven door, don't open it before three quarters of the baking time has passed.

▸ If the top of your soufflé is browning too quickly, butter a piece of foil slightly wider than the soufflé dish. Open the oven and quickly place foil, buttered side down, over the soufflé.

▸ Soufflés may be served in the European manner—slightly underdone, with a custardy center. Or for those who prefer light, airy soufflés, they may be cooked until the center is well done and dry.

▸ To check a soufflé for doneness, insert a long skewer or a sharp knife into the center. It will be moist if the soufflé is slightly underdone; dry if it is well done.

▸ A soufflé must be taken to the table as soon as it's removed from the oven. The collar may be removed in the kitchen, but the soufflé will begin to deflate. For this reason, you may choose to take the soufflé to the table with the collar still attached to the dish. Have a plate ready on which to place the foil and string, and remove the collar at the table with ceremony and flair.

▸ To serve a soufflé, use two forks, back to back, to gently separate it into serving portions, then scoop out each portion with a large spoon.

▸ If your soufflé collapses before you get it to the table, just pretend that's the way it's supposed to be. If it's a hot dessert soufflé, drizzle it with sauce or top with whipped cream and call it a "baked pudding." If it's a cheese soufflé, sprinkle it with grated cheese, broil the top until bubbly, and call it a "cheese torte."

S

SOUPS AND STEWS

► Soups makes an elegant first course for any special meal. Choose one that will complement the flavors of the other dishes in the meal. For example, a creamy bisque is the perfect prelude for simply grilled meat and sautéed vegetables, but would be too much with a rich entree like stroganoff.

► If you can, make soups and stews a day ahead and refrigerate overnight. The extra time allows the flavors to meld and heighten.

► Refrigerating soups before serving also allows any fat to float to the surface and solidify, making it easy to lift off before the soup's reheated.

► The biggest timesaver when making soups is the food processor. It chops and slices vegetables in a fraction of the time it would take most of us by hand. If different vegetables go into the pot at different times, chop or slice them separately, transferring each one to a dish, paper plate or sheet of waxed paper as it's cut. Always start with the least messy vegetable. Mushrooms, for example, should be cut and set aside before chopping something moist like bell peppers or onions. Wiping out the workbowl between vegetables is optional. If it's all going into the same pot anyway, why bother?

► Save and freeze leftover poultry and meat bones to make stock for soups and stews. (Refer to any general cookbook for stock recipes.)

► Add a husky richness to soups by making a smoked chicken broth using the bones and skin from a smoked chicken (which must often be specially ordered through your meat market or supermarket).

► When using canned broth as a soup base, be aware of the type you pur-chase. There are two basic styles: ready to serve (which is already diluted) and condensed (which requires added water or milk). If you use con-densed broth, undiluted, you'll wind up with an unpalatably salty soup.

► Keep canned broth in the refrigerator so the fat will congeal and be easy to lift off the surface before using. Who wants the extra calories?

► Full-flavored beers, or wines like sherry and Madeira, make flavorful ad-ditions to soups and stews.

► Add flavor to vegetable soups by substituting a vegetable juice like V-8 for a third to half of the water in the recipe.

► Roasted soup bones (baked at 400°F until brown) add a rich flavor to soups and stews.

► For maximum flavor, put soup bones in the soup or stew liquid (water, stock, etc.) before you begin heating it.

► Use the cooking liquid from vegetables or meats as a nutritious base for soups or stews. The liquid can be frozen until you need it.

► Save and freeze leftover pan juices to enrich soups or stews.

► Help clarify stocks by adding 2 to 3 eggshells and simmering for 10 minutes. Strain off the shells before adding other ingredients.

► Browning meats and vegetables give soups and stews a richer flavor. Try adding 1 teaspoon sugar to the fat, then heat, stirring often until the fat is hot, before browning the meat and vegetables. The sugar caramelizes and gives everthing a beautiful color and flavor with negligible sweetness.

► Unless you want vegetables to loose their texture, add them toward the end of the cooking time.

► Finely chopped vegetables and meat will cook much faster than large chunks.

► Save leftover vegetables for soup the next night.

► Make your own bouquet garni by putting herbs in a cheesecloth bag tied with string; remove it before final seasoning.

► Try cooking stew, covered, in a 350°F oven instead of on the stovetop. There's not as much pot-watching because the heat surrounds and cooks the stew evenly.

► Once you stir sour cream or yogurt into a hot soup, heat it gently and only until the mixture is warmed through. Allowing the mixture to boil will cause curdling. Milk products won't separate as easily in flour-thickened soups and stews.

► To help prevent curdling, always add acidic ingredients (such as tomatoes, lemon juice or wine) to a milk-based soup, rather than adding the milk product to the acidic ingredients. A little whipping cream will also help prevent curdling.

► Another way to stop curdling in milk-based soups is to make a thin, syrupy paste of flour and water and whisk it into the milk before adding acidic foods.

► If you do overheat a soup containing milk products and the liquid curdles, simply strain it into a blender jar and process until smooth. Don't fill the blender more than two-thirds full with a hot liquid, be sure to put the lid on the container, and always begin blending at low speed, gradually increasing to high.

► When adding acidic ingredients like wine, lemon juice or tomatoes to a flour- or cornstarch-thickened soup, do so after the mixture has been thickened.

► Some herbs—like basil—lose much of their flavor and aroma when cooked for more than about 15 minutes. Always taste the soup at the end of the cooking time and, if necessary, stir in 1 or 2 tablespoons chopped fresh herbs before serving.

► Pasta in soup can turn mushy when left in the broth too long. The best kind to use is pasta made with 100 percent semolina flour. Small, compact shapes like ditali (tiny macaroni), orzo (rice shape), radiatori (chunky, radiator shape) and rotini (small spirals) do better than noodle-style pasta.

S

- Add minced clams to soups and stews at the last minute so they won't toughen.
- Soup or stew too garlicky? Place a handful of parsley in a tea infuser or a cheesecloth bag tied with string and simmer in the soup or stew for 10 minutes.
- For a rich taste and texture without *too* many calories, stir 1 tablespoon butter or 2 tablespoons heavy cream into soup just before serving.
- Evaporated non- or low-fat milk (undiluted) adds a rich sensation to soups without excess calories.
- Heighten the flavor of lackluster soups or stews by adding chicken or beef extract or bouillon.
- Rescue oversalted soups by adding a peeled, thinly sliced raw potato and simmering for 10 to 15 minutes. Remove the potato before serving the soup. Of course, the best way to prevent oversalting is to season after the soup is done.
- Balance the flavor of oversalted soups and stews by stirring in 1 teaspoon each vinegar and brown sugar for each quart of liquid.
- Create instant soup by combining leftover vegetables with chicken or beef broth in a blender and processing until smooth.
- For soup in minutes, add chicken or beef broth to leftover rice, risotto or beans, and stir in some lightly sautéed vegetables. Heat just until warmed through.
- Remove excess fat from the surface of hot soups by adding 4 to 6 ice cubes. As the ice melts, the fat will congeal around them; use a slotted spoon to remove ice and solidified fat. You can also wrap several ice cubes in cheesecloth or heavyweight paper towel and run it across the soup's surface.
- Fat can also be removed from the surface by siphoning it off with a baster, or soaking it up with a fat "mop" (available in gourmet shops), or sheets of paper towel.
- Lettuce leaves also act like a sponge for fat. Add 2 or 3 of them to the finished soup and let stand for a few minutes before removing.
- Darken pale-colored soups and stews by stirring in 1 to 3 teaspoons caramelized sugar or instant coffee powder.
- Always remove as much fat as possible before thickening soups.
- Thicken vegetable and other soups with a vegetable puree. Simply cook more vegetables than you'll need, remove them from the soup with a slotted spoon, and puree them in a blender with a little liquid. Stir the puree back into the soup. It's a low-calorie, high-nutrition way to thicken soup.
- Leftover cooked potatoes or rice also make good soup thickeners. For smooth bisque-style soups, add the potatoes or rice before pureeing. Combine the cooked rice or potatoes with a little liquid; puree, then stir into

the soup. Check and correct seasoning before serving.

▸ Instant mashed potato flakes make an almost-instant, low-fat soup thickener. Stir in 1 tablespoon at a time, cook for 1 minute, then add more if necessary.

▸ Soft, crustless breadcrumbs can also be used to thicken soups. Start with ¼ cup and add more if necessary. Quick-cooking oatmeal can be used in the same way. Or you can use leftover cooked oatmeal.

▸ For a quick thickener, stir 2 to 3 tablespoons liquid (water, milk, sherry, etc.) into ¼ cup cornstarch in a small bowl. Stirring constantly, gradually add the cornstarch mixture to the hot soup a little at a time until the desired thickness is reached.

▸ Or make a thin paste with flour and water or other liquid and stir it into hot soup. Cook for at least 5 minutes before serving.

▸ Add an intriguing nuance to hearty soups and stews by stirring in ½ to 1 cup crushed gingersnap cookies (for 4 to 6 servings) 30 to 60 minutes before the dish is done. The cookies will also slightly thicken the soup.

▸ When keeping a cream- or milk-based soup warm—or if reheating it—do so in the top of a double boiler over hot water. It'll keep the soup from scorching over direct heat.

▸ When making cold soups, remember that chilling food mutes its flavor, so be sure to taste just before serving and adjust the seasoning if necessary.

▸ Keep in mind that most cold soups will be thicker than when they were hot.

▸ Always garnish soup—it not only adds eye appeal, but can also contribute flavor and textural contrast. Easy, last-minute garnishes include finely snipped chives or scallion greens, a dollop of sour cream dusted with paprika for color, minced herbs like parsley or basil, and toasted, sliced almonds.

▸ Another easy garnish is to float croutons or a crostini (toasted, thinly sliced baguette) atop soup. If desired, sprinkle the croutons or crostini with grated Parmesan.

▸ A favorite soup garnish for kids of all ages is popcorn.

▸ Grated cheese makes a simple, delicious garnish for soup. Or pass small cubes of cheese for diners to drop into their soup. In minutes the cheese cubes will melt, adding both texture and flavor to the soup.

▸ For real comfort food, make a big batch of mashed potatoes, make a mashed-potato nest in a soup bowl, and spoon a hearty stew into the indentation.

▸ Stretch a thick stew by serving it over rice.

▸ Add panache by serving soup in edible containers such as a hollowed-out large tomato (best for cold soups), or toasted French roll, or an acorn-squash half.

▸ Add a touch of freshness to leftover soup by stirring in 1 to 2 tablespoons chopped, fresh herbs just before serving. The same amount of wine, sherry or Madeira will also add magic to second-day soup. Add spirits at the beginning, as you're reheating the soup.

▶ It's easy to give leftover vegetable soup a new look and flavor. For instance, you can puree it in the blender, add grated cheese, and serve "country cheddar soup." Potato soup can be transformed into "vichyssoise" by adding some minced leeks (preferably sautéed), pureeing and thinning with milk, then refrigerating until cold. Or create a "stew" by thickening a thin soup and adding chunks of sautéed beef or pork and a splash of wine.

▶ The microwave oven makes quick work of reheating soup right in individual soup bowls. Though it's usually not necessary to cover microwave-heated soup, be sure to stir it after about a minute to distribute the heat. Thick soups like split pea often have little explosive bursts while heating so it's better to cover the bowl with waxed paper or plastic wrap. Don't seal tightly if using plastic wrap.

▶ To freeze soup, place a freezer-weight plastic bag inside a bowl, pour in soup, then freeze. When solid, lift the plastic bag out of the bowl, seal and return to freezer for up to 3 months.

▶ Freeze leftover soups and stews in individual portions to be heated in minutes in the microwave.

▶ Even if you don't have enough soup left over for a couple of servings, freeze it. You can add other leftover soups to it, then puree the lot and use as a soup base in the future.

SOUR CREAM

▶ Regular commercial sour cream contains from 18 to 20 percent fat. There are also light (30 to 50 percent less fat than regular) and nonfat versions.

▶ Store sour cream in its carton in the refrigerator for up to 1 week after the pull date on the carton.

▶ *Substitutions for 1 cup sour cream for use in cooking or baking:* 1 cup plain whole-milk yogurt; ¾ cup sour milk, buttermilk or low-fat plain yogurt plus ¼ cup butter; 1 tablespoon lemon juice plus evaporated whole milk to equal 1 cup.

▶ Bring sour cream to room temperature before adding to a hot mixture.

▶ Always stir sour cream into a hot soup or sauce just before serving. Heat it gently and only until the mixture is warmed through. Allowing the mixture to boil will cause curdling. Milk products won't separate as easily in flour-based mixtures.

▶ For a low-calorie sour cream substitute, try Quark, a soft, unripened cheese with a texture and flavor close to sour cream. It comes in two versions—low-fat and nonfat—and its texture is richer than low-fat sour cream or yogurt.

► *See also* CREAM

SOYBEAN CURD *see* TOFU

SPICES

► Ground spices quickly lose their aroma and flavor, so it's wise to buy them in small quantities.

► Some spices, such as allspice, cloves and nutmeg, can be purchased whole and ground as needed. Whole spices that are ground fresh have more punch than those that are preground.

► Store spices in airtight containers in a cool, dark place for no more than 6 months. *Never* store your spices over the stovetop or in any other hot location.

► If you know you're going to store ground spices for more than 6 months, refrigerate them as soon as you buy them. This is especially important for spice blends like chili and curry powder.

► To be sure how old a spice in your cabinet is, use a felt-tip marking pen to note the date purchased on the bottom of the can or jar. Or mark the date on a strip of masking tape and stick it to the bottom.

► Simplify finding your spices by alphabetizing them.

► Buy a turntable in the kitchen-supply section of a hardware or department store, and keep your spices on it for flick-of-the-wrist convenience.

► Intensify the flavor of whole spices like allspice berries or peppercorns by roasting them in a 350°F oven for about 10 minutes. Alternatively, you can pan-roast them over medium-high heat for about 5 minutes, stirring often. Cool completely before using.

► *See also* HERBS, *as well as individual spice listings*

SPINACH

► Spinach leaves may either be curled or smooth, depending on the variety. The smaller New Zealand spinach has flat, spade-shaped leaves that are often covered with a fine fuzz.

► Choose spinach with crisp, dark green leaves that have a nice fresh fragrance. Avoid leaves that are limp, damaged or that have yellow spots.

► Before storing, wash spinach by pulling the leaves off the stems, or cut off the stems. Put the leaves in a sink or large container full of cold water. Swish the leaves around with your hands, then let them stand for a few minutes for any dirt to sink to the bottom. Lift the leaves out of the water. If the spinach is very gritty, repeat the process.

► Thoroughly dry spinach leaves, either in a salad spinner, or by shaking off excess moisture, laying them out on a double layer of paper towels (or a dish towel), then blotting the surface dry.

► Store spinach leaves wrapped loosely in paper towels and tightly sealed in a plastic bag in the refrigerator for up to 3 days.

► *Spinach yields:* 1 pound = 10 to 12 cups torn pieces; about 1 cup cooked. One 10-ounce package frozen = about 1½ cups.

► Spinach will discolor if you chop it with a carbon blade knife (stainless steel is best), cook it in an aluminum pan or serve it in silver. Those metals will also discolor should they come in contact with spinach.

► Sauté spinach leaves briefly in bacon fat, salt and pepper to taste and garnish with crumbled, crisp bacon.

► For the fullest flavor, cook spinach only until it begins to go limp.

► Freshly grated nutmeg makes magic with spinach. Add it at the beginning of the cooking time.

► Thoroughly drain cooked spinach so excess moisture doesn't transfer to other foods on the plate.

► Garnish cooked spinach with sieved, hard-cooked eggs—a perfect partner.

► To remove excess moisture from frozen spinach, hold it over the sink and squeeze it with your hands. Then put the spinach in a double layer of paper towel, bring up the edges and twist the topknot until all the liquid is expelled. If you want the liquid from the spinach for soups, etc., squeeze over a bowl.

► Spinach leaves make great salad greens. Or make an entire salad out of spinach leaves, tossed with minced, hard-cooked eggs and crumbled, crisp-cooked bacon.

► Food for thought: spinach is a rich source of vitamins A and C, calcium, potassium and other nutrients but it also contains oxalic acid, which inhibits the body's absorption of calcium and iron (don't worry—spinach doesn't affect calcium absorption from other foods). Bottom line—enjoy your spinach, but get your calcium from other sources.

► *See also* SALAD GREENS; VEGETABLES, GENERAL

SPROUTS

► Edible sprouts are produced from a variety of seeds and beans and can be found in produce markets, natural food stores and many supermarkets. The most popular sprouts are alfalfa, lentil, mung bean, pea, radish and wheat.

► Choose crisp-looking sprouts with the buds attached. Avoid musty-smelling, dark or slimy-looking sprouts.

► Store sturdy types—like mung-bean sprouts—in a plastic bag in the refrigerator for no more than 3 days. More delicate varieties—such as alfalfa sprouts—should be refrigerated for no more than 2 days in the ventilated plastic container in which they're usually sold.

▶ Wash sprouts just before using, thoroughly blotting dry on paper towels.

▶ Cut off any roots on sprouts; the seed or bean end of a sprout need not be removed.

▶ For optimum crispness, sprouts should be eaten raw. They add both flavor and texture to salads and sandwiches.

▶ The only sprouts that are firm enough to cook without immediately wilting are mung-bean sprouts. Even so, add them last to a stir-fry or other dish and only cook them for a few seconds.

SQUASH, SUMMER

▶ Squash are divided into two categories—summer squash and winter squash. Summer squash have thin, edible skins and soft seeds. The most widely available varieties are crookneck, pattypan and zucchini.

▶ Choose firm summer squash with bright-colored skin free of spots and bruises. In general, the smaller the squash, the more tender it will be.

▶ Store summer squash in a plastic bag in the refrigerator for no more than 5 days.

▶ *Summer squash yields:* 1 pound = about 3 medium; 2½ cups chopped.

▶ Just before cooking, wash summer squash and trim both ends; peeling isn't required (except for the chayote, also called *mirliton*). Blot dry with paper towels if using in salads or sautéing. Squash that's to be cooked with a moist-heat method doesn't require drying.

▶ The tender flesh of summer squash has a high water content and doesn't require long cooking. It can be steamed, baked, sautéed or deep-fried.

▶ Zucchini is wonderful stuffed and baked. Cut in half lengthwise, scoop the flesh out of the center, leaving a ½ inch shell. Chop the zucchini flesh and combine with sautéed onions, bell peppers and breadcrumbs. Add some chopped, seeded tomatoes, season to taste and fill the zucchini cavities. Sprinkle with grated cheese bake at 400°F for about 30 minutes. You can also stuff zucchini halves with a meat and rice filling, or simply cheese and chopped zucchini.

▶ *See also* VEGETABLES, GENERAL

SQUASH, WINTER

▶ Winter squash have hard, thick skins and seeds. Their deep yellow to orange flesh is firmer than that of summer squash and therefore requires longer cooking. The most popular varieties are acorn, buttercup, butternut, hubbard, spaghetti and turban.

▶ Choose winter squash that are heavy for their size. Their rinds should be hard, deep-colored and free of blemishes or spots that are moldy or soft.

- Store winter squash in a cool, dark, well-ventilated place for up to 1 month.
- *Winter squash yields:* 1 pound = about 2 cups cooked pieces, 1 cup mashed squash.
- The skin of winter squash is extremely hard and requires a heavy knife to cut through it. First slice off the stem, then cut down through the stem to halve the squash.
- Winter squash are easier to cut if microwaved at HIGH (100 percent power) for 1 to 2 minutes; let stand for 3 minutes before cutting. Pierce the rind in a couple of places before heating.
- Use a large spoon to scoop out the seeds and membranes from the cavity; discard.
- If you wish to peel winter squash, the task is much easier after they're cooked.
- Very large squash, such as hubbard, can be cut into smaller pieces before cooking.
- Winter squash can be baked, boiled, steamed or simmered.
- Always pierce the rind of acorn squash with a fork in several places before baking it whole. This technique, which allows steam to escape, is particularly important when microwaving squash to prevent it from exploding.
- Pumpkin can be used in most recipes calling for winter squash.
- Fresh ginger root or ground ginger have a natural affinity for winter squash.
- *See also* PUMPKINS; VEGETABLES, GENERAL

SQUASH BLOSSOMS

- The flowers from both summer and winter squash are edible and delicious. They come in varying shades of yellow and orange, with flavors that hint of the squash itself.
- Squash blossoms can be found from late spring through early fall in specialty produce markets and some ethnic markets.
- Choose those that look fresh (they're naturally soft and limp) with closed buds.
- Store squash blossoms in a sealed container (not a plastic bag) in the refrigerator for no more than 1 or 2 days.
- Squash blossoms may be used as a garnish (whole or slivered) for everything from salads to soups to main dishes.
- The blossoms are most often cooked by dipping them into a light batter and frying or deep-frying. They're often stuffed with a soft cheese before being cooked.
- Cooked squash blossoms can be served as a side dish for dinner, or with honey for breakfast.
- *See also* FLOWERS, EDIBLE

STEAKS

▶ You'll get more value if you buy a porterhouse steak with the largest tenderloin attached to it.

▶ It's usually more economical to buy a round steak and have the butcher "cube" it than it is to buy cube steak.

▶ Remove steak from the refrigerator 1 hour before cooking. Room-temperature meat cooks faster and more evenly and browns better.

▶ Prevent steak from curling during cooking by slashing the fat almost all the way to the meat at 1-inch intervals.

▶ Don't trim off all the fat bordering a steak. Fat greatly contributes to the flavor of the steak.

▶ For well-browned steak, make sure the surface is thoroughly dry, particularly if it's been marinated. Use a paper towel to blot off excess moisture.

▶ Salt steak toward the end of the cooking time or the salt will leach some of the juices from the meat.

▶ When using a dry-cooking method like broiling or grilling, remember that the longer the meat cooks the tougher it gets.

▶ Position the broiler rack farther from the heating unit when broiling thick steaks so they'll cook through before burning on the outside.

▶ When panbroiling steak, it's not necessary to add fat or oil, unless the cut is very lean. Use a heavy skillet and simply brush the pan with oil. The pan should be very hot before adding the meat. A light dusting of flour on the meat will also facilitate browning.

▶ Cutting into a steak to determine its doneness releases some of its juices. Though it takes practice, you can tell whether a steak's done to your liking by using the touch technique. Press the meat lightly with your finger: if it's soft, the meat's rare; if it resists slightly but springs back, it's medium-rare; if the meat is quite firm, it's well done.

▶ Cooked flank steak requires careful slicing in order to get the most tender, attractive cut. Always slice across the grain for tenderness; position the knife at a 45-degree angle for slices that look ample rather than meager.

▶ *See also* BEEF; MEATS, GENERAL

STEAMING

▶ Steaming is probably the most nutritious method of cooking because it doesn't wash away water-soluble nutrients, like boiling does.

▶ The food to be steamed must be on a rack at least 1 inch above the boiling liquid. The water should never directly touch the food.

▶ If you don't have a vegetable steamer, improvise by using a footed colander or large, flat-bottomed sieve.

▶ The pan in which you steam food must be large enough to allow the steam to circulate freely. Otherwise, the food won't cook evenly.

- Make sure the cover to the pan in which you steam food fits tightly. Otherwise, some of the steam will escape and impede cooking. If the cover doesn't fit tightly, cover the pot with a sheet of foil, then position the lid on top of the foil, seating it firmly.
- During the steaming time, shake or stir the ingredients once or twice to make sure they cook evenly.
- Watch the liquid to make sure it doesn't boil away, leaving a dry pan. Keep a separate pot of boiling liquid to replenish that in the steamer, if necessary.
- Food can also be steamed by sealing it in a moisture-proof wrapping like foil or parchment paper, then baking. Although the food may be lightly coated with oil or butter, it can be packaged with only 1 or 2 tablespoons liquid before being sealed. The heat produces steam from the food's natural moisture, thereby producing a moist, succulent end result.
- *See also* COOKING, GENERAL

STEWS *see* SOUPS

STIR-FRYING

- The stir-fry method of cooking consists of quickly frying small pieces of food in a large pan over very high heat while constantly and briskly stirring the food.
- You don't have to have a wok for stir-frying—any large, deep skillet will do. The important thing is to have enough room to rapidly stir and toss the ingredients as they cook.
- If you do buy a wok, there are several things you should consider. If you have an electric range, a flat-bottom wok is best for even heat distribution. Gas ranges can accommodate either flat- or round-bottom woks. When you use a round-bottom wok, place the ring stand, narrow side up, over a large burner. Electric woks are free-standing.
- To season a steel wok, start by thoroughly scrubbing the wok and lid inside and out to remove the rust-resistant coating. Rinse and dry well, then pour in 2 tablespoons vegetable oil, rotating the pan to coat it thoroughly and evenly. Heat over high heat until the oil is very hot. Let cool, then use a crumpled paper towel to rub in the oil. Season the lid (removing any nonmetal handles) in the same manner, placing it directly on the burner. After each use, clean and thoroughly dry the wok (heat-dry it on the range). Then reseason by rubbing in about 1 teaspoon oil.
- Before starting to cook, heat the oil until a piece of vegetable sizzles when tossed into the pan.
- Reduce calories by spraying the room-temperature pan with nonstick vegetable spray first. After heating the pan, stir-fry the vegetables, then add a small amount of oil to cook the meat.

▶ When buying fish for stir-frying, choose varieties that have a firm flesh, such as monkfish, sea bass, shark, swordfish or tuna.

▶ For almost-instant stir-frys, chop and refrigerate the ingredients (all in separate plastic bags) the night before. Then everything will be ready and you'll have a meal in minutes.

▶ Choose stir-fry vegetables that are harmonious both in color, texture and flavor. The cooking time will depend on how the vegetables are cut. Matchstick pieces will take less time to cook than chunks of food. Always start with the vegetable that will take the longest to cook. Carrots (which are dense) will take much longer to cook than delicate bean sprouts.

▶ Parboiling (*see* listing) particularly dense vegetables before stir-frying will help get everything done at the same time.

▶ If you have a large amount of meat to cook, it's better to cook it in two batches. Otherwise, the pan can become too cool, and the meat will end up braising, rather than frying. Cook one batch until *almost* done to your liking, then transfer it to a plate and cook the second batch.

▶ Make magic with leftovers by turning stir-fries into soups (add broth), salads (toss with your favorite dressing and salad greens), or main dishes (combine with a sauce and serve over noodles or rice).

▶ *See also* COOKING, GENERAL

STRAINERS *see* SIEVES

STRAWBERRIES

▶ Choose brightly colored, plump strawberries that still have their green caps attached. They should have a potent strawberry fragrance; those without it aren't fully ripe and won't ripen after being picked. Avoid soft, shriveled or moldy berries.

▶ Wash strawberries *before* hulling.

▶ *Strawberry yields:* 1 pint = 1½ to 2 cups sliced or chopped.

▶ My talented editor, Harriet Bell, shared this unconventional way to store strawberries for up to a week. Wash and air-dry the berries, leaving the stem intact. When berries are *completely* dry, put them in a large, screw-top jar. Place a paper towel on top of the berries (to absorb excess natural moisture), seal the jar tightly and refrigerate. Unwashed berries can also be stored in this manner. If you wash them first, however, the berries will be ready and waiting for hungry snackers.

▶ When making strawberry pie, always wash, then hull the berries, letting them drain upside-down on paper towels for 30 minutes. That way, you'll remove as much excess moisture as possible and not end up with a soggy pie.

▶ *See* BERRIES, GENERAL *for complete storage and cleaning information*

STRING BEANS *see* BEANS, FRESH GREEN

S

STUFFED EGGS *see* DEVILED EGGS

SUGAR

▸ Sugar comes in myriad shapes and forms, the most common being granulated or white sugar, brown sugar and confectioners' (or powdered sugar). **Granulated (or white) sugar** is dry and free-flowing and comes in fine or superfine forms; it's also available in cubes of various sizes. **Brown sugar** is soft and moist, the result of granulated sugar being combined with molasses. **Confectioners' sugar** is granulated sugar that's been crushed into a fine powder; a small amount (about 3 percent) of cornstarch is added to prevent clumping.

▸ If stored airtight, all sugar can be kept in a cool, dry place almost indefinitely.

▸ Besides its sweetening value, sugar adds tenderness to bread, cookie and other doughs, stability to mixtures like beaten egg whites, a golden-brown surface to baked goods, and—in sufficient quantity—acts as a preservative for some foods.

▸ When caramelizing sugar, do so in a light-colored or shiny saucepan. That way you can see the color of the caramel, something that's hard to do in dark aluminum pans.

▸ If you're avoiding sugar, check food labels carefully—just because the word "sugar" isn't used doesn't mean it's not there. Look for the words dextrose, fructose, lactose, maltose and sucrose—all of which are sugars. Of course corn syrup, honey, maple syrup and molasses are also forms of sugar.

▸ *See also* SUGAR SUBSTITUTES

Brown sugar:

▸ Brown sugar comes in light and dark granulated forms. In general, the lighter the brown sugar, the more delicate the flavor. The very dark or "old-fashioned" style has a more pronounced molasses flavor. There's also a liquid form of brown sugar, which cannot be substituted for granulated brown sugar called for in recipes.

▸ Store brown sugar in a thick plastic bag in a cool, dry place. If it comes in a box, immediately transfer it to a plastic bag.

▸ *Brown sugar yields:* 1 pound = 2¼ cups firmly packed.

▸ Unless a recipe otherwise states, always measure brown sugar by packing it firmly into a measuring cup.

▸ If brown sugar begins to harden, add an apple wedge to the bag. Seal and let stand until the sugar softens, 1 to 2 days; remove apple.

▸ Soften brown sugar in a microwave oven by placing 1 cup of it in a covered dish and heating it at HIGH (100 percent power) for 30 to 60 seconds (depending on the amount of sugar); repeat if necessary. Watch carefully so that it doesn't start to melt.

▸ Or put hardened brown sugar on a pie plate and heat in a 250°F oven for about 5 minutes.

▸ Use a food processor with a metal blade to break up lumps in brown sugar. A blender also works, though you'll either have to process the sugar in small batches, or keep stopping the blender to move the top sugar down toward the blades.

▸ Substituting brown sugar for granulated sugar will produce a slightly moister baked good with a slight butterscotch flavor.

▸ *Substitutions:* 1 cup firmly packed brown sugar = 1 cup granulated sugar; 1 cup light brown sugar = ½ cup dark brown sugar plus ½ cup granulated sugar.

Confectioners' (or powdered) sugar:

▸ Confectioners' sugar is called "icing sugar" in Britain and *"sucre glace"* in France.

▸ *Confectioners' sugar yield:* 1 pound = 4 cups unsifted; 4½ cups sifted.

▸ Confectioners' sugar labeled XXXX is slightly finer than that labeled XXX; they can be used interchangeably.

▸ Some recipes call for confectioners' sugar to be sifted before using. If you don't have a sifter, spoon the sugar into a fine sieve, then shake or tap it over a measuring cup set on a piece of waxed paper. If necessary, use the back of a wooden spoon to stir the sugar so it "sifts" easier.

▸ Quick-sift confectioners' sugar by tossing it into a food processor with a metal blade and whirling until light. Gently spoon the "sifted" sugar into the measuring cup.

▸ Put confectioners' sugar in a salt shaker for those times when a recipe calls for "dusting" the top of a dish with it. Or buy a special sugar dredger—a perforated screw-top container (metal or glass) found in kitchenware stores.

▸ Or put it in a fine sieve and gently shake the sieve to dust desserts.

▸ Never sprinkle confectioner's sugar over a moist cake, pudding or other dessert until just before serving. The moisture will liquefy the sugar and turn it an unappealing pale gray color.

▸ See the following *granulated sugar* listing for a tip on making vanilla-flavored confectioners' sugar.

▸ *Substitution:* 1¾ cups confectioners' sugar = 1 cup granulated sugar.

Granulated sugar:

▸ *Granulated sugar yield:* 1 pound = 2¼ cups.

▸ Superfine sugar dissolves almost instantly, making it perfect for making meringues and sweetening cold liquids

► Create *superfine sugar* by processing granulated sugar in a food processor with the metal blade until powdery.

► Superfine sugar is known as "castor sugar" in Britain.

► Make your own vanilla sugar by burying 2 vanilla beans in a pound of granulated or confectioners' sugar. Store at room temperature in an airtight container for at least 1 week, stirring once or twice. Remove the beans and reuse in this fashion for up to 6 months. The deliciously fragrant vanilla sugar can be used as a recipe ingredient, for decorating cookies and cakes, or for sweetening coffee, fruit or desserts.

► Make citrus-flavored sugar by mixing ¼ cup finely grated orange or lemon peel with 2 cups granulated sugar. Stir well, then let stand for at least 1 week before using. Stir again before using in coffee or desserts, or sprinkled atop fruit, cakes, cookies, etc.

► *Substitutions:* 1 cup regular granulated sugar = 1 cup superfine sugar, or 1 cup firmly packed brown sugar, or 1¾ cups confectioners' sugar.

SUGAR SNAP PEAS *see* PEAS, POD

SUGAR SUBSTITUTES

► The two most common types of sugar substitutes on the market today are **aspartame** (180 times sweeter than sugar) and **saccharin** (300 times sweeter than sugar).

► Aspartame, which is synthesized from two amino acids, breaks down and loses its sweetness when heated. It is, however, excellent for sweetening cold dishes, and can be added to cooked foods (like pudding) after they're cooked and slightly cooled.

► A new granulated form of aspartame sugar substitute looks and measures like sugar. Spoonful for spoonful, it provides the same sweetness as sugar but contains only about ⅛ the calories.

► Saccharin has a slightly bitter aftertaste that becomes more pronounced when food sweetened with it is heated.

► Always check the instructions on a package of sugar substitute to determine its equivalent to sugar.

► Be careful when adding sugar substitute to food—a little goes a lot further than you might expect. A dish can be ruined by adding too much sugar substitute.

► Don't try to replace sugar with a sugar substitute in baked goods and expect the same result. Sugar is necessary for structure and volume in baked goods—substitutions can be disasterous. Always check the label to see what's recommended for that particular sugar substitute.

SUGAR SYRUPS

▸ Sugar syrups (also called **simple syrups**) can be variously flavored and have many uses including soaking cakes, glazing baked goods, poaching or preserving fruit, etc. They're also the foundation for most candies.

▸ Sugar syrups are made in various densities: thin (3 parts water to 1 part sugar), medium (2 parts water to 1 part sugar) and heavy (equal parts water and sugar).

▸ To make a sugar syrup, cook sugar and water together over low heat until clear, then boil for a minute or so.

▸ *See also* CANDY

SUNCHOKES *see* JERUSALEM ARTICHOKES

SUN-DRIED TOMATOES *see* TOMATOES

SUNFLOWER SEEDS

▸ Sunflower seeds are sold shelled and unshelled, roasted and raw, salted and unsalted.

▸ By weight, sunflower seeds are 47 percent fat; they're 24 percent protein.

▸ Because of their high fat content, all sunflower seeds should be stored in an airtight container in the refrigerator or freezer. Roasted seeds can be refrigerated for up to 4 months, frozen for up to 8 months. Raw and unshelled sunflower seeds can be refrigerated for up to 6 months, frozen for 1 year.

▸ Sunflower seeds can be eaten as a snack, used in salads or sandwich spreads, or added to a variety of cooked dishes or baked goods.

▸ When sunflower seeds are combined with baking soda in baked goods, a chemical reaction occurs that causes the baked product to take on a blue-green tinge. Though the color isn't esthetically appealing, there's no toxic threat.

SWEETBREADS

▸ Sweetbreads are the thymus glands of veal, beef, lamb and pork. Those from milk-fed veal or young calves are considered the best. Those from young lamb are quite good, but beef sweetbreads are tougher and pork sweetbreads (unless from a piglet) have a rather strong flavor.

▸ Choose sweetbreads that are white (they become redder as the animal ages), plump and firm. In general, sweetbreads from younger animals are the most tender.

▸ Sweetbreads are highly perishable and should be refrigerated, tightly sealed, for no more than 1 day before using.

▶ Sweetbreads must undergo several steps before being cooked. First soak them in cold, acidulated water (1 quart water mixed with 3 tablespoons lemon juice) for at least 1 hour to draw out any blood.

▶ Sweetbreads must then be blanched for 3 to 5 minutes, then plunged into cold water to firm them.

▶ When cooled, drain the sweetbreads; trim away and remove the outer membrane and any connective tissue.

▶ Sweetbreads will retain their shape better during cooking if you put them on a plate, cover with something flat like a small cutting board, weight down with a couple of 1-pound cans, and refrigerate for about 2 hours. If the sweetbreads are very large, cut them into slices before weighting.

▶ Sweetbreads can be braised, grilled, poached and sautéed. They're also sometimes used in pâtés and soufflés.

SWEETENED CONDENSED MILK

▶ Sweetened condensed milk is whole milk from which about 60 percent of the water has been removed; it's mixed with sugar, which the latter is about 40 percent of the volume.

▶ Store unopened cans of condensed milk at room temperature for up to 6 months.

▶ Once opened, transfer unused milk to an airtight container, such as a screw-top jar, and use within 5 days.

▶ *Sweetened condensed milk yields:* 1 15-ounce can = 1⅓ cups.

▶ Sweetened condensed milk is used in candies, custards, puddings, pies and some baked goods.

▶ Drizzle sweetened condensed milk over baked apples 15 minutes before they're done for a delicious, shiny glaze.

▶ When heated (by microwave, oven or stovetop), sweetened condensed milk becomes thick, turns a rich golden color, and takes on the flavor of caramel. *Microwave oven method:* Pour milk into a 2-quart glass or ceramic container. Cook at MEDIUM (50 percent power) for 4 minutes, stirring halfway through. Reduce power to MEDIUM-LOW (30 percent power); cook 12 to 18 minutes, stirring briskly every 2 minutes until smooth, thick and caramel-colored. The cooking time will depend on the wattage of your oven. *Oven method:* Pour sweetened condensed milk into a 9-inch pie plate and cover with foil. Place the pie plate in a larger pan; fill pan with hot water that reaches halfway up the side of the pie plate. Bake at 425°F for 1½ hours, or until thick and caramel-colored. *Stovetop method:* Pour milk into the top of a double boiler and cook over simmering water for 1½ hours. At the end of the cooking time (whichever method you use) beat the caramel until smooth.

▶ Never heat sweetened condensed milk in an unopened can, which can explode when heated.

▶ Don't substitute sweetened condensed milk for evaporated milk or vice versa. The sugar in the former would ruin the flavor of dishes calling for evaporated milk.

▶ *See also* EVAPORATED MILK; MILK

SWEET POTATOES

▶ The two most widely grown sweet potatoes in the United States are a pale variety and a darker-skinned species that many Americans erroneously call "yam." Pale sweet potatoes have a thin, light yellow skin and pale yellow flesh. Their cooked texture is dry and crumbly, much like a white baking potato, and their flavor isn't sweet. The darker variety has a thicker, dark orange skin and vivid orange, sweet flesh that, when cooked, is much moister.

▶ Choose firm sweet potatoes that are small- to medium-sized with smooth, unblemished skins that are free of soft spots.

▶ Store sweet potatoes in a cool, dry, well-ventilated place for up to a week. Under perfect temperature conditions (dry and around 55°F), they can be kept for up to 4 weeks. Do not refrigerate.

▶ The pale variety of sweet potato can be substituted for regular potatoes in most recipes.

▶ After peeling raw sweet potatoes, keep them from turning dark by letting them sit in cold acidulated water (1 quart water mixed with 3 tablespoons lemon juice) for a few minutes. Drain well before using. If the potatoes are to be fried, thoroughly blot dry with paper towels.

▶ Sweet potatoes are more nutritious if cooked in their skins.

▶ Peeling boiled sweet potatoes is easy—just drain off the hot water, then immediately plunge the potatoes into cold water. The skins will slip right off.

▶ Large sweet potatoes are often very fibrous. If you use an electric mixer to beat cooked sweet potatoes, the stringy fibers will wind around the beaters, thereby leaving the potatoes smooth.

▶ Sweet potatoes have a natural affinity for maple syrup and freshly grated nutmeg.

▶ *See also* VEGETABLES, GENERAL; YAMS

SYRUPS; SYRUPY SWEETENERS

▶ Before measuring syrupy sweeteners such as honey and corn syrup, lightly coat the measuring cup or spoon with vegetable oil. Every drop of the syrup will easily slip out instead of clinging to the sides of the cup. The same thing can be accomplished if you measure the shortening called for in a recipe and then use the same (unwashed) utensil to measure a syrup.

S

▶ Use clear measuring cups for syrups; bend down and read the measurement at eye level.

▶ Use hot water to rinse the caps of honey, maple syrup or corn syrup bottles and they'll be easier to remove the next time.

▶ Keep a syrup pitcher from dripping by dabbing some oil or butter on the inside of the pouring spout.

▶ Use a damp cloth to wipe off the sides and bottom of syrup bottles before returning them to the cupboard.

▶ *See also* CORN SYRUP; HONEY; MAPLE SYRUP; MOLASSES; SUGAR SYRUPS

TABLE SETTINGS *see* ENTERTAINING

TANGERINES *see* ORANGES

TAPIOCA [tap-ee-OH-kuh]

▶ Tapioca is a starch extracted from cassava roots. It's commonly available in three forms—pearl tapioca (which comes in both small and large sizes), quick-cooking tapioca and tapioca (also called cassava) flour or starch. Pearl and quick-cooking tapioca are available in most supermarkets, whereas the flour is more commonly found in natural food stores and Asian and Latin American markets.

▶ Stored airtight in a cool, dry place, tapioca will keep indefinitely.

▶ **Pearl tapioca** is generally used to make puddings; it must be soaked for several hours to soften it before cooking.

▶ **Quick-cooking tapioca** is in a granular form. It's most often used as a thickener and doesn't require presoaking.

▶ Both pearl and quick-cooking tapioca are done when they're absolutely clear.

▶ Tapioca flour and quick-cooking tapioca are excellent thickeners for sauces, fruit fillings, soups, glazes, etc. Tapioca-thickened sauces don't need stirring during cooking, can withstand long cooking times, and don't get cloudy. Unlike cornstarch- and flour-thickened preparations, tapioca-based mixtures don't break down when frozen, then reheated. However, quick-cooking tapioca leaves tiny pieces of tapioca suspended in whatever it thickens, whereas the flour produces a smooth mixture.

▶ If you can't find tapioca flour, and don't like the small, cooked bits that quick-cooking tapioca leaves in soups, sauces, etc., process quick-cooking tapioca in a blender until powdery.

▶ To thicken mixtures with tapioca flour, first make a thin paste by combining it with water, then stir it into a hot liquid.

▶ Once tapioca is added to a liquid, don't let the mixture boil or the tapioca may get stringy.

▶ Overstirring a tapioca mixture while cooling produces a sticky, gelatinous texture.

TEA

▶ Teas are available today in a variety of forms—tea bags, loose-leaf tea, regular or decaffeinated tea, instant tea, flavored tea and so-called "herbal

T

tea." The latter isn't biologically a tea, but rather a tisane—a tealike drink made by steeping any of various herbs, flowers, spices, etc. in boiling water.

▸ Store tea, tightly sealed, in a dark, cool place for up to 1 year.

▸ Give tea bags or loose tea your personal touch by storing them in an airtight jar with cinnamon sticks or other spices, citrus peels or vanilla beans.

▸ Begin the tea-making process by filling a kettle with fresh, cold water; bring to a boil. Count on 6 ounces of water per cup of tea.

▸ Use a china, glass or ceramic teapot—metal can affect the tea's flavor.

▸ Always warm a teapot before beginning the steeping process by pouring in some boiling water, swirling it around the pot, then discarding.

▸ For a perfect cup of tea, use 1 heaping teaspoon loose tea per cup, plus 1 teaspoon for the pot. If using tea bags, count on 1 per cup.

▸ If you don't want to strain tea before serving, put the loose leaves in a tea caddy (also called an *infuser*).

▸ Put the tea infuser or tea bags in the warmed teapot, add boiling water and give it a quick stir. Replace the teapot lid, cover with a tea cozy, and let steep 4 to 6 minutes, depending on the tea and your palate.

▸ Remove the tea infuser or tea bags, give the tea a gentle stir, then pour through a strainer (if using loose tea) into a cup.

▸ To keep a cup of tea hot, warm the cups with hot tap water before pouring in the hot tea.

▸ If you wish to use milk in tea, use whole milk—not skim milk or cream. Whole milk has the perfect textural balance for tea.

▸ For a delightful difference, try sweetening your tea with maple syrup instead of honey or sugar.

▸ Always remove tea from a teapot as soon as you're through to avoid staining.

▸ If your teapot smells stale, fill it with a mixture of boiling water and 2 teaspoons baking soda. Cover and let stand until cool. Wash as usual with soap and water.

▸ Storing a teapot with a sugar cube inside also keeps it fresh—the sugar absorbs odors.

▸ Remove teapot stains by rubbing the inside with a paste of baking soda and water; wash well with soap and hot water.

▸ Lime deposits can be removed from a tea kettle by filling it with equal amounts of white vinegar and water, bringing the mixture to a boil, then letting the kettle stand overnight. The next morning, wash and use as usual.

▸ Drill a hole in the bottom of an old teapot and turn it into a planter.

► Or put ¾ inch aquarium gravel in the bottom of a tea pot and cover with soil.
► Use approximately twice as much tea when making iced tea.
► For clear iced tea, combine tea leaves or bags with cold water; cover and refrigerate for at least 24 hours. Strain as you pour the tea into glasses.
► "Sun tea" is also a clear brew—combine tea and water in a clear pitcher or jar; cover and let stand in the sun about 4 hours.
► If you make iced tea with boiling water, and refrigerate it while hot, the tea will become cloudy. Clear it by stirring in a little boiling water. Or keep hot-brewed tea from becoming cloudy by simply letting it cool to room temperature before refrigerating.

TEMPERATURES, FAHRENHEIT AND CELSIUS (OR CENTIGRADE)

► To convert Celsius (centigrade) temperatures to Fahrenheit, multiply the Celsius number by 9, divide by 5, and add 32.
► To convert Fahrenheit temperatures to Celsius (centigrade), subtract 32 from the Fahrenheit reading, multiply by 5, and divide by 9.
► Use the following quick-reference chart for equivalent Fahrenheit and Celsius temperatures:

	FAHRENHEIT	CELSIUS
WATER FREEZES	32°	0°
	40°	4.4°
	50°	10°
	60°	15.6°
	70°	21.1°
	80°	26.7°
	90°	32.2°
	100°	37.8°
	110°	43.3°
	120°	48.9°
	130°	54.4°
	140°	60.0°
	150°	65.6°
	160°	71.1°
	170°	76.7°
	180°	82.2°
	190°	87.8°
	200°	93.3°
WATER BOILS	212°	100°
	250°	121°
	300°	149°

350°	177°
400°	205°
450°	233°
500°	260°

T

▶ *see also* OVENS; THERMOMETERS

THERMOMETERS
Candy/Deep-fat thermometers:

▶ A candy/deep-fat thermometer is indispensable for candymaking and deep-fat frying. Most of these thermometers are in the shape of a long glass tube with a small bulb at the end. Choose a clearly marked, easy-to-read thermometer with an adjustable clip to secure it to the pan.

▶ To use a candy/deep-fat thermometer, stand it upright in the candy syrup or fat so the bulb is completely immersed. Don't let the bulb touch the bottom of the pan or the temperature readout could be affected. Stoop down so you can read the thermometer at eye level. Watch the thermometer carefully—it can look like it's not moving for several minutes, then surprise you by shooting up above the necessary temperature.

▶ Check your thermometer's accuracy every so often by placing it in boiling water for 3 minutes. If it doesn't measure 212°F, calculate the difference and adjust your recipe temperature accordingly. For example, if your thermometer reads 202°F in boiling water, it's recording temperatures 10 degrees lower than they actually are. So if a recipe specifies a candy temperature of 250°F, cook the mixture until your thermometer reads 240°F. (Note: The boiling temperature of water at high altitudes will be about 2 degrees lower per 1,000 feet above sea level.)

Freezer/Refrigerator thermometers:

▶ A freezer/refrigerator thermometer reads temperatures from about −20° to 80°F. It's an important kitchen tool because, unless frozen food is maintained at a temperature of 0°F or below, it will begin to deteriorate, losing both quality and nutrients.

▶ Position the thermometer near the top and front of the freezer. Leave it there for at least 6 hours without opening the door before checking the readout.

▶ If the thermometer's temperature doesn't read 0°F or below, adjust the temperature regulator as necessary; check the reading in another 6 hours.

▶ Refrigerator temperature may be checked in the same way, and should register at 40°F.

Meat thermometers:

▸ There are two types of meat thermometers—regular and instant-read. Whatever type you buy, look for one that has an easy-to-read scale indicating at what temperature each type of meat (beef, lamb, pork, etc.) is done.

▸ A regular meat thermometer can be inserted in the meat at the beginning of the cooking time and left in throughout.

▸ Instant-read thermometers record the temperature in just a few seconds. These are inserted into the meat toward the end of the cooking time.

▸ Choose a thermometer with a thin probe—it makes smaller holes in the meat from which fewer juices can escape.

▸ For an accurate reading, insert the probe so at least half of it is inside the meat.

▸ Always insert a thermometer in the thickest section of meat. If you hit a bone, gristle or fat pocket, the reading will be distorted.

Oven thermometers:

▸ There are two kinds of oven thermometers—the spring-operated dial types and the mercury-style glass tubes. Glass tube thermometers are usually much more expensive, but then they're also consistently more accurate.

▸ Place the thermometer on the center rack and preheat the oven for 15 minutes. If the thermometer reading doesn't agree with the oven setting, you'll need to make an adjustment. For example, if it reads 400°F when the oven is set at 350°F, you know that your oven runs 50°F hot. Therefore, when a recipe requires a 350°F temperature, set your oven to 300°F.

▸ It's a good idea to leave an oven thermometer in the oven, but be sure and remove it before using any automatic cleaning cycle.

TOFU [TOH-foo]

▸ Also known as **bean curd** and **soybean curd**, tofu is made from curdled soy milk, an iron-rich liquid extracted from ground, cooked soybeans. It has a bland, slightly nutty taste that has the chameleonlike capability to take on the flavor of whatever food it's cooked with.

▸ Tofu is available in natural food stores, Asian markets and supermarkets. It's sold packaged in water, vacuum-packed and in bulk in large crocks. Unrefrigerated tofu sitting out in water invites unfriendly bacteria, so it's safest to buy it in sealed, refrigerated packages.

▸ Tofu is sold in blocks or cakes in three textures—soft, firm and extra-firm.

▸ Because it's highly perishable, tofu should be refrigerated for no more than a week. If it's packed in water, drain and cover with fresh water. All tofu should be covered with water, which should be changed daily. Tofu can be frozen (sans water) for up to 3 months, but will have a slightly chewier texture when thawed.

▶ When stir-frying, add cubes of firm or extra-firm tofu during the last few minutes to keep it from breaking up.

▶ Soft tofu is so light that it can be whipped and stirred or folded into puddings, scrambled eggs, soups, etc.

TOMATILLOS [tohm-ah-TEE-ohs]

▶ Also called *Mexican green tomatoes*, tomatillos resemble small green tomatoes in size, shape and appearance except for their thin parchmentlike husks. Their flavor hints of a lemon-apple-herb combination.

▶ Choose firm, evenly colored tomatillos with dry, tight fitting husks; avoid shriveled fruit. Tomatillos can ripen to yellow, but are more generally available (and used) green.

▶ Store tomatillos in a paper bag in the refrigerator for up to 1 month.

▶ Before using, remove husk and thoroughly wash tomatillos. They should still be quite firm.

▶ Though tomatillos are often used raw in salads and salsas, cooking enhances their flavor and softens their skin.

TOMATOES

▶ Buy tomatoes that are firm, well-shaped, richly colored (for their variety) and noticeably fragrant. They should be free from blemishes, heavy for their size and give slightly to palm pressure.

▶ Store ripe tomatoes, stem side down, at room temperature away from direct sunlight and use within a few days. Never refrigerate tomatoes! Cold temperatures make the flesh pulpy and destroy the flavor.

▶ *Tomato yields:* 1 pound = about 3 medium globe tomatoes; 8 small plum tomatoes; 25 to 30 cherry tomatoes; 2 cups chopped.

▶ Because vine-ripened tomatoes are very perishable, most supermarkets carry tomatoes that have been picked green and ripened with ethylene gas. Gassed tomatoes never have the texture, aroma and taste of vine-ripened fruit.

▶ Ripen tomatoes by putting them with an apple in a paper bag pierced with a few holes. Let stand at room temperature for 2 to 3 days.

▶ If you can't find good, ripe tomatoes for use in a cooked dish, buy quality canned tomatoes. Canned Italian plum tomatoes have a wonderful flavor that beats the heck out of underripe or out-of-season fresh tomatoes. Canned tomatoes can even be used in salads.

▶ You can cut whole canned tomatoes right in the can by snipping them with kitchen scissors.

▶ A good tomato knife with a sturdy, 4- to 5-inch serrated blade is relatively inexpensive and makes slicing tomatoes—even those with slightly tough skins—a breeze. The next best bet is to use a very sharp, pointed knife—pierce the skin with the knife tip, then cut into the pierced point.

▶ Peeling tomatoes isn't necessary if you're going to use them raw in such preparations as salads and salsas and on sandwiches. Just wash the skin thoroughly before you stem and core the tomato.

▶ In cooked dishes, tomato skins shrivel and toughen, adding an unpleasant texture to most dishes. If the tomatoes are to be chopped finely, then it's your option whether or not to peel. The tiny bits of skin won't usually be objectionable.

▶ A super-quick peeling method is to skewer a cored tomato with a large two-pronged fork and hold it over a gas flame, turning continually, just until the skin begins to split. This can take anywhere from 30 to 60 seconds, depending on the size and variety of tomato. Pull off the shreds of puckered skin.

▶ Another way to peel tomatoes is to use a sharp knife to cut a shallow X-shaped slash on the bottom. Then drop them in a pot of boiling water for about 5 seconds for very ripe tomatoes, 10 seconds for firmer tomatoes. Use a slotted spoon to transfer tomatoes to a bowl of ice water; let stand for about 1 minute. When tomatoes are cool enough to handle, use a paring knife to pull off the skin.

▶ A tomato peel can be loosened in a microwave oven by heating the tomato at HIGH (100 percent power) for 15 seconds; let stand 1 minute before peeling.

▶ To seed a tomato, cut it in half horizontally. Set a strainer over a bowl and gently squeeze the seeds into it. The strainer will trap the seeds while any juice goes into the bowl for use in sauces, salad dressings, etc.

▶ Or, if you want to seed a tomato and leave the shell intact, cut off the top ½ inch. Use a grapefruit spoon or dinner teaspoon to scoop out seeds and core.

▶ Seed cherry tomatoes by cutting them in half, then sticking your thumb or finger into the halves and flicking out the seeds.

▶ Tomato slices will hold their shape better and exude less juice if you slice vertically, from stem end to blossom end.

▶ Always add tomatoes to a tossed green salad just before serving so its natural juices don't make the greens soggy or dilute the dressing.

▶ Raw or cooked tomatoes that lack natural sweetness can be improved by adding a pinch of sugar and a dash of salt. Both bring out a tomato's natural flavors. A small amount of sugar will temper overtly acidic tomatoes.

▶ Never cook tomatoes or a tomato-based sauce in an aluminum pan—it causes the tomatoes to loose their bright color and gives the mixture a bitter undertaste.

- For stuffed tomatoes, either cut the tomato in half, or cut a slice off the top. Either way, scoop out the seeds and pulp with a spoon. Turn the hollowed-out tomatoes upside down on paper towels to drain for at least 15 minutes before stuffing.
- To give added support to stuffed tomatoes while baking, cut them vertically, stuff, then ⌐lace in lightly greased muffin tins and bake as usual.
- If you find yourself with too many tomatoes to eat before they begin to spoil, cook and freeze them. Bring them out midwinter for a refreshing taste of summer.
- To prevent tomato-based foods such as spaghetti sauce from staining plastic utensils and storage containers, liberally spray the containers with nonstick vegetable spray.
- Sun-dried tomatoes are either dried in the sun or by other methods. The result is a chewy, intensely flavored, sweet, dark red tomato. Sun-dried tomatoes are usually either packed in oil or dry-packed in cellophane.
- Rehydrate dry-packed sun-dried tomatoes by covering with hot water and letting stand for 30 minutes. Drain before using, but don't throw out the flavorful water—save it for soups or sauces.
- Or you can moisten dry-packed sun-dried tomatoes by covering them with a good olive oil and letting stand at room temperature for at least 24 hours. Save the oil for sautés or salad dressings, or simply to drizzle over French bread.
- If you're cutting just one or two sun-dried tomato halves, use kitchen shears to snip them into the desired size.
- The flavor of sun-dried tomatoes is quite intense—a little goes a long way.

TOMATO PASTE; TOMATO PUREE; TOMATO SAUCE

- **Tomato paste** is made of tomatoes that have been cooked for several hours, strained and reduced to a deep red, richly flavored concentrate. It's available in cans or tubes.
- **Tomato puree** is made of tomatoes that have been cooked briefly and strained, resulting in a thick liquid.
- **Tomato sauce** is a slightly thinner tomato puree, often with seasonings and other flavorings added so that it's ready to use without diluting in soups, sauces, etc.
- To make tomato sauce from tomato paste, combine ⅜ cup tomato paste with ½ cup water.
- The next time a recipe calls for a small amount of tomato paste, buy it in a tube instead of a can. Because so little of the tubed paste is exposed to the air, it can be tightly sealed and refrigerated for up to 1 year. A boon for those who use only 1 or 2 tablespoons of tomato paste at a time and can't stand to waste the rest.

▶ If you do have leftover tomato paste from a can, do this: Line a pie pan with plastic wrap. Place level tablespoons of paste at 1-inch intervals on the plastic wrap. Freeze, uncovered, until solid. Fold over the edges of the plastic wrap to cover the tomato paste, place the contents in a plastic bag and freeze until ready to use. The tablespoons of frozen paste can be dropped right into hot mixtures like soups and sauces.

T

TORTILLAS [tor-TEE-yuhs]

▶ Tortillas are available in the refrigerated section of most supermarkets in a variety of forms. Corn tortillas are made from corn flour (masa), flour tortillas are made with all-purpose or whole-wheat flour. There are also low-cholesterol tortillas, which are made without lard.

▶ Tortillas can be eaten plain or wrapped around various fillings.

▶ To warm tortillas, stack them on top of each other, wrap in foil, and heat at 350°F for 10 to 15 minutes.

▶ Or wrap tortillas loosely in waxed paper or a plastic bag and microwave at HIGH (100 percent power)—15 seconds for 2 tortillas, 30 seconds for 4, 1 minute for 8.

▶ Make your own tortilla chips by lightly brushing flour or corn tortillas with olive or canola oil, season to taste with salt and pepper or chili powder, then stack the tortillas and cut the stack into 12 wedges. Arrange wedges in a single layer on a lightly oiled baking sheet, salt and pepper, and bake at 350°F for 5 to 10 minutes (flour tortillas don't take as long as corn), or until crisp. Cool on paper towels and store airtight at room temperature for up to 5 days.

TUNA

▶ Fresh tuna has a tender, firm-textured, rich-flavored flesh. There are several types found in markets, generally from late spring to early fall: the high-fat, mild-flavored, white-fleshed **albacore;** the stronger-flavored, pale-pink **yellowfin;** the moderately flavored **bluefin;** and the moderate-to high-fat, strongly flavored **bonito.**

▶ Canned tuna is precooked and can be water- or oil-packed. Albacore tuna is the only one that can be labeled "white meat." Canned tuna comes in three grades, the best being *solid* or *fancy* (large pieces), followed by *chunk* (smaller pieces) and *flaked* (bits and pieces).

▶ Water-packed tuna not only contains many fewer calories than oil-packed, but it also has a fresher flavor.

▶ If you're making tuna sandwiches, don't waste money on solid- or chunk-style tuna since the mixture will be broken up anyway.

▶ *See also* FISH, GENERAL *(for buying, storing and cooking information)*

TURKEY

- See POULTRY for general information on buying, storing and cooking.
- Buying two small turkeys instead of one large one offers a double bonus: more drumsticks, thighs, wings and giblets, and a shorter cooking time.
- How much turkey to buy per serving depends on the bird's size and form. For boneless cuts, count on about ⅓ pound per serving; bone-in breast, ⅓ to ½ pound; bone-in thigh or drumstick, ½ pound; whole 6- to 12-pound turkeys, ¾ to 1 pound; whole turkeys over 12 pounds, ½ to ¾ pound.
- Allow 2 to 3 days for a frozen turkey to thaw in the refrigerator.
- Remove a whole turkey from the refrigerator about 1 hour before cooking.
- When stuffing a turkey, count on about 1 cup dressing per pound.
- Never stuff a turkey until right before roasting. Doing so invites the growth of harmful bacteria that can result in food poisoning.
- Try packing the stuffing between the skin and the meat. The bird might look puffy, but the resulting crisp, brown skin and moist breast meat is worth it.
- Turkey will almost baste itself if you cover it with a double layer of cheese-cloth that's been soaked with butter or canola or olive oil. When the cheesecloth's removed at the end of the roasting time, the bird will be moist and golden brown. For a crisp, brown skin, take off the cheesecloth 30 minutes before the bird is done.
- Plastic oven-cooking bags can reduce a turkey's cooking time by up to 1 hour. They also produce a beautifully browned bird.
- Cooking time can also be reduced by baking the stuffing in a separate pan, thereby allowing oven heat access to the turkey cavity.
- Pop-up timers found in many turkeys can often be broken or otherwise unreliable, so use a meat thermometer to test a whole turkey for doneness. The breast temperature should be 170°F, the thigh should read 180°F. If the bird is stuffed, the dressing should be at a temperature of about 160°F.
- After cooking, let turkey "rest" at room temperature for 20 minutes to allow its natural juices to redistribute throughout the flesh and set. This produces an evenly moist result and makes the bird easier to carve. Keep the poultry warm during this rest period by covering it lightly with foil.
- Always remove stuffing from the turkey before storing leftovers.
- For more information on turkey, call the Butterball Turkey Talk-Line at 1-800-323-4848. Or call the USDA's Meat and Poultry Hotline at 1-800-535-4555; in the Washington, D.C., area, call 447-3333.
- *See also* CHICKEN; POULTRY, GENERAL; THERMOMETERS

TURNIPS

- The true turnip has a white skin with a purple-tinged top. The so-called "yellow turnip," though a turnip relative, is actually a rutabaga.

▶ Small, young turnips have a delicate, slightly sweet taste. Look for those that are about 2 inches in diameter and heavy for their size. They should be firm and have unblemished skins; the greens (if attached) should be brightly colored and fresh-looking.

▶ Turnips can be stored in a plastic bag in the refrigerator for up to 2 weeks. They do best, however, if stored in a cool (55°F), dark, well-ventilated place.

▶ Before storing turnips, remove any greens. Remove the leaves from the midrib; wash greens and pat dry with paper towel. Wrap loosely in dry paper towels, then put in a tightly sealed plastic bag and refrigerate for up to 3 days.

▶ *Turnip yields:* 1 pound = about 2½ cups chopped.

▶ Before using, trim turnip stem and root ends. Baby turnips can simply be scrubbed and cooked whole; larger turnips should be peeled and quartered or chopped before cooking.

▶ Turnips may be boiled or steamed, then mashed or pureed. They're also delicious cubed and sautéed, either alone or with other vegetables. Chopped turnips add texture and flavor to soups and stews.

▶ Never cook turnip greens in an aluminum pan—it'll darken the greens and give them a metallic flavor.

▶ Add crunch to salads with cubed or julienned raw turnips.

▶ A salad of tossed greens (including turnip greens) and julienned turnips packs a double flavor whammy.

▶ *See also* VEGETABLES, GENERAL

V

VANILLA

▸ Always buy **pure vanilla extract,** which is clear, dark brown and richly fragrant. **Imitation vanilla** is made entirely of artificial flavorings and often has a harsh, bitter aftertaste. Yes, pure vanilla extract is more expensive than its imitator, but you only have to use half as much.

▸ Products labeled "natural vanilla flavoring" contain only pure vanilla extract. The words "vanilla flavoring" mean that a blend of pure and imitation vanilla was used, whereas "artificial-flavored" tells you it's entirely imitation.

▸ Vanilla extract can be stored indefinitely if sealed airtight and kept in a cool, dark place.

▸ Vanilla beans should be wrapped tightly in plastic wrap, placed in an airtight jar and refrigerated. Stored in this way, they'll keep for about 6 months.

▸ To use a vanilla bean in foods like ice cream mixtures, custards, cake batters and sauces, use a pointed knife to slit it lengthwise down the center. Scrape out the minuscule seeds and add directly to the mixture.

▸ Or you can split the vanilla bean (leaving the seeds intact) and drop it into a cooked mixture such as custard. Remove the bean before serving.

▸ Don't throw out a vanilla bean that you've used whole to flavor a sauce or custard. Simply rinse it well, dry and store for future use.

▸ The flavor of vanilla extract diminishes greatly when cooked, so always add it to a hot mixture like custard after it's cooled slightly.

▸ Make your own vanilla extract by placing a split vanilla bean in a jar containing ¾ cup vodka. Seal tightly and let stand in a cool, dark place for 4 to 6 months before using. Shake the jar occasionally during the time.

▸ Vanilla sugar is wonderfully fragrant and can be used as an ingredient in a dish, for decorating cookies and cakes, or for sweetening fruit, desserts and coffee. Make it by burying 2 vanilla beans in 1 pound granulated or confectioners' sugar. Store at room temperature in an airtight container for at least a week, stirring once or twice. Remove the beans and reuse in this fashion for up to 6 months.

▸ Love the smell of vanilla? So will your refrigerator. Put a few drops on a cotton ball, set it in a custard cup and put it at the back of a shelf. The next morning, all will smell sweet.

▸ Food for thought: Vanilla was once considered an aphrodisiac, and was so rare that it was reserved for royalty.

VEAL

▶ Though there are no precise age standards for veal, the term is generally used to describe a young calf from 1 to 3 months old. However, many markets sell meat from animals up to 9 months old when slaughtered as veal. Milk-fed veal is considered premium, and comes from calves that have been raised on milk. Their delicate flesh is firm and creamy white with a pale grayish-pink tinge. Other calves are fed grain or grass, which results in a slightly coarser texture and stronger flavor—the flesh is a pale pink color. In general, the darker the meat, the older the calf.

▶ Choose fine-textured veal that's ivory-colored with a pink to creamy pink tinge; the fat should be very white.

▶ To store veal: If it will be cooked within 8 hours of purchase, it may be left in its store wrapping. Otherwise, remove the packaging and wrap loosely with waxed paper. Store in the coldest part of the refrigerator for no more than 2 days. The object is to let the air circulate and keep the meat's surface somewhat dry, thereby inhibiting rapid bacterial growth.

▶ Veal scallops should be pounded before cooking to make them as thin as possible.

▶ Because veal is so delicate, it must be cooked very gently—more like poultry than beef. Moist-cooking methods like braising are perfect for very lean meats like veal. Low-temperature roasting and brief sautéing are also appropriate.

▶ Breading cutlets and chops helps seal in veal's precious moisture.

▶ A veal roast needs to be barded, (fat tied around the roast, your butcher can do it) to keep it moist. Or you can lay strips of salt pork over the roast's surface.

▶ Always let veal roast rest at room temperature for about 15 minutes after cooking to set the juices. While resting, the meat will continue to cook, during which time the internal temperature can rise from 5° to 10°F. Because of this, it's wise to cook veal roast only to an internal temperature of 160°F.

▶ Ground veal needs added fat or it becomes too dry during cooking.

▶ Overcooking any cut of veal will toughen and ruin its delicate texture.

▶ The flavor of veal is so delicate it will be overpowered by a strongly flavored sauce (such as barbecue sauce) or side dishes (like curried rice).

▶ *See also* BEEF; MEATS, GENERAL

VEGETABLES, GENERAL

▶ Research indicates that the family of cruciferous vegetables may provide protection against certain cancers. Those vegetables—all high in fiber, vitamins and minerals—include broccoli, Brussels sprouts, cabbage, cauliflower, chard, kale, mustard greens, rutabagas and turnips.

▶ The "baby vegetables" that are available in many markets today can be one of two things—they're either the early-harvested youngsters of the species, or specially developed miniature yet mature vegetables.

▶ In general, the smaller the vegetable, the younger it is and the more tender it will be.

▶ Some vegetables—such as bell peppers and cucumbers—are coated with wax before being marketed. Waxing is done to extend shelf life, seal in moisture and improve appearance. Though the waxes are safe to eat, they may contain pesticide residues. The FDA requires waxed produce to be identified with signs, but this is rarely done. Some waxed vegetables are obvious by their shine and feel. If you're not sure, ask the produce manager.

▶ Buying vegetables in prepackaged bags is a risk—you can't check them for signs of spoilage or other detrimental factors.

▶ If you buy root vegetables like beets and carrots with their leaves attached, remove them as soon as you get home. These greens leach moisture from the vegetable.

▶ Leaving the peel on washed vegetables and fruits gives you a bonus of fiber and nutrition. Don't worry about any chemical residues on vegetable peels. The FDA reports that, during annual random produce testing, 99 percent of the produce is either residue-free or well below EPA (Environmental Protection Agency) limits. The FDA advises that simply scrubbing the vegetables with tap water and a vegetable brush will reduce or remove any chemical residue.

▶ Limp vegetables like carrots and potatoes regain much of their crisp texture if soaked in ice water for at least 1 hour.

▶ Save time by chopping enough vegetables or herbs (like bell peppers, carrots, onions and parsley) to use for two meals. Cover and refrigerate part of the vegetables to use in a second meal the next day.

▶ Don't add baking soda to the cooking water for green vegetables such as green beans and peas. Though it may help keep them green, it will leach out valuable nutrients in the process.

▶ To keep the bright green color in vegetables like broccoli and green beans, cook them uncovered and never with acidic ingredients like lemon juice, vinegar or wine. Both the condensation that forms on the pan lid (and drips back onto the vegetables) and the acid in the water cause a chemical reaction that makes the vegetable's color drab.

▶ On the other hand, the natural acid in lemon juice preserves and improves the naturally white color of vegetables like cauliflower and potatoes.

▶ Keep blanched vegetables bright and crisp by draining off the hot water, then immediately turning them into a bowl of ice water. Let stand in water only until cool, then drain. Lengthy water contact will waterlog vegetables.

▶ Parboil dense vegetables like carrots that will be sautéed with other vegetables. The parboiling partially cooks the vegetables so they'll get done at the same time as other, less dense vegetables like mushrooms.

▶ Salting the cooking water for vegetables can draw out some of their vitamins—salt them after they're cooked.

▶ Adding ½ to 1 teaspoon sugar to cooked vegetables such as carrots, corn, and peas reduces starchy flavors and highlights natural sweetness.

▶ Don't throw out the fibrous ends of vegetables like asparagus. Cook them until tender, then puree, strain, and use for preparations like soups or sauces.

▶ Frozen vegetables such as corn and peas don't require thawing before being added to dishes like soups and casseroles. Such frozen vegetables can also be added to stir-frys and sautés, providing they'll be cooked long enough to thaw—usually only 1 to 2 minutes.

▶ Save any liquid in which you've cooked vegetables and use for soups, stews or sauces. If you don't want to use it right away, freeze the liquid for up to 6 months.

▶ Make your own pickled vegetables by marinating cauliflower florets, carrot or cucumber sticks, strips of green pepper, etc., in leftover pickle juice for 3 days.

▶ *See individual vegetable listings for specific buying and storage information*

VINEGARS

▶ There are a multitude of vinegars on the market today. Among the more commonly available are the fruity **apple cider vinegar** made from fermented apple cider, the harsh-tasting **distilled white vinegar** made from a grain-alcohol mixture, and the pleasantly pungent **wine vinegar** which can be made from either red or white wine. Then there's **malt vinegar** obtained from malted barley, the mild, slightly **sweet rice vinegar** made from fermented rice, and the exquisite **balsamic vinegar**, an aged reduction of white Trebbiano grape juice. There's also a dazzling array of **fruit-** and **herb-flavored vinegars**, many of which you can make at home.

▶ Many balsamic vinegars contain sulfites, which are usually added to prevent unfavorable bacteria from affecting the flavor. Most people aren't adversely affected by sulfites, but those who are sulfite-sensitive can be adversely affected.

▶ Store vinegar in a cool, dark place. Unopened, it will keep almost indefinitely; once opened, store at room temperature for up to 6 months.

▶ When making your own flavored vinegar, the first step is to be sure the bottle is scrupulously clean. Use a screw-top bottle that can be tightly sealed.

- To make herb vinegar, immerse clean, fresh herbs in cider or wine vinegar. Seal and refrigerate for 2 weeks. To speed the steeping process, heat the vinegar before pouring over the herbs. Strain finished vinegar into another bottle; refrigerate for up to 6 months.

- For homemade fruit vinegar, combine fresh or frozen (loose-packed, not syrup-packed) fruit like raspberries, blueberries or cranberries with white wine vinegar in a wide-mouth quart jar. If desired, add whole spices like cloves or allspice berries. For a sweet-tart vinegar, stir in a little honey. Seal tightly, then refrigerate for 2 weeks, shaking the bottle every other day. Strain vinegar; refrigerate for up to 6 months.

- Because of vinegar's volatility, it loses much of its pungency when heated. If that's what you want, then add vinegar at the beginning of the cooking time. However, if you want that jolt of acidity, stir vinegar into a mixture after the dish is removed from the heat source.

- If a dish lacks pizzazz and tastes "flat," try stirring in 1 or 2 teaspoons of full-flavored vinegar such as balsamic.

- If you somehow oversweeten a savory dish (vegetables, salad dressings, etc.), try stirring in ½ to 1 teaspoon vinegar to balance the sweet.

W

WAFFLES

▶ Always follow the manufacturer's instructions for seasoning a waffle iron. If you have an iron that hasn't been used in a long time, reseason it by brushing the heated grids with vegetable oil. Turn off the iron and cool completely. Lightly wipe off excess oil, then reheat iron a second time. Unplug the iron and cool, thoroughly wiping off any excess oil. The first time you use it after seasoning, throw the first waffle away.

▶ If you haven't used your waffle iron for a while, use a pastry brush to lightly coat the grids with vegetable oil; use a paper towel to wipe off any excess oil. Or spray the grids with nonstick vegetable spray.

▶ Many waffle irons have nonstick grids, which cuts down on the use of oil to grease the grids.

▶ For lighter waffles, separate the eggs and mix the yolks in with the rest of the liquid. Combine the wet and dry ingredients as usual. Then beat the egg whites until stiff and fold into the batter at the last minute.

▶ Adding 1 to 2 tablespoons sugar to the batter will produce waffles that are tender yet crisp.

▶ For extra-crisp waffles, add 1 to 2 tablespoons of additional vegetable oil to the batter. Extra oil in the batter will also help keep waffles from sticking.

▶ Substituting buttermilk for regular milk will give you delicate, tender waffles. If using buttermilk, add ¼ teaspoon baking soda to the dry ingredients.

▶ For a regular, four-square waffle iron, use about 1 cup batter.

▶ Using less batter will produce a thinner, crisper waffle.

▶ Never open a waffle iron during the first minute of baking or the waffle is likely to break apart.

▶ Waffles are done when the lid rises slightly, the steaming has completely stopped and the sides are golden brown. If the top resists when you try to lift it, the waffle's not done.

▶ Use a fork to lift the waffle from the iron.

▶ To keep waffles warm until serving time, place them on a rack set on a baking sheet and heat in a 350°F oven.

▶ Stacking warm waffles will make them sweat and turn soggy.

▶ Make a double batch of waffles and freeze the leftovers for future breakfasts. Cool the waffles completely before packaging and freezing for up to 6 months.

▶ Slightly underbake waffles that you plan to reheat. That way, they won't dry out when reheated.

▶ The best way to reheat waffles is in a toaster or toaster oven. They can also be heated in a 350°F oven for about 5 minutes. You can reheat them in a microwave oven at HIGH (100 percent power) for about 7 seconds, but they usually won't be as crisp.

▶ A well-seasoned waffle iron should not be washed; simply brush off any remnants with a toothbrush.

▶ When through baking waffles and brushing off the grid, unplug the iron, cover the bottom grid with a sheet of waxed paper, close the iron and let it cool.

▶ *See also* MAPLE SYRUP; PANCAKES

WALNUTS

▶ The two most popular varieties of walnut are the English walnut and the black walnut. The so-called white walnut is more commonly known as the butternut.

▶ Walnuts will be easier to crack if you cover them with water, then bring to a boil. Remove from heat, cover and set aside for at least 15 minutes, or until cool. Blot the nuts dry, then crack end to end.

▶ *See also* NUTS, GENERAL *for general purchase, storage and usage information*

WATERMELONS

▶ Watermelon varieties range in size from giant thirty-five-pounders to those the size of a medium cantaloupe. Their flesh can range from red, to pink to yellow to creamy white; the speckled or solid-colored seeds can be black, brown, green, red or white.

▶ Seedless watermelons actually do, more often than not, have a few scattered seeds, though they're generally small, soft and edible—much like the seeds in a cucumber.

▶ Choose symmetrically shaped watermelons without any flat sides. Depending on the variety, the shape can be round or oblong-oval. Slap the side of a watermelon—if it resounds with a hollow thump, that's a good indicator that it's *probably* ripe. But also check the rind, which should be evenly colored, dull (not shiny) and just barely yield to pressure. Avoid watermelons with soft spots, gashes or other blemishes on the rind.

▶ When buying a cut melon, look for one with firm, juicy, brightly colored flesh; avoid those that look grainy or dry. An abundance of small, white seeds in all but "seedless" watermelons indicates an immature melon. Make sure a cut melon is tightly wrapped.

▶ Store whole watermelon in the refrigerator (if possible) and keep no more than 1 week. If it's too large for the fridge, keep the melon in a cool, dark place for up to 4 days.

- Store cut watermelon, tightly wrapped, in the refrigerator; use within a day or so.
- Unlike most melons, watermelon should be served cold.
- Add watermelon balls or chunks to a fruit salad at the last minute or their exceedingly juicy flesh will make the mixture watery.
- If you don't want to pick up a watermelon wedge and bury your face in it, do this: Make a horizontal cut from end to end about 1 inch down from the surface of the flesh. Then make lengthwise cuts about 1 inch apart, followed by crosswise cuts. This will give you 1-inch chunks which you can eat with a fork. When that layer's gone, repeat the process until you almost reach the rind.
- For a "spirited" watermelon, cut a plug out of a whole melon, insert a funnel and pour in rum until the melon won't accept any more. Reinsert the plug in the opening and refrigerate for 24 hours. The rum will disperse throughout the melon, producing a sweet, exotically flavored flesh that tastes delicious, but not particularly like rum.
- *See also* MELONS

WAX BEANS *see* BEANS, FRESH

WAXED PAPER

- Before freezing a loaf of sliced bread, place a piece of waxed paper between the bread slices. That way, they'll be much easier to separate while frozen.
- Place a sheet of waxed paper between layers of stored candy.
- Keep bottles and jars (such as maple syrup and honey) from dripping by rubbing the rim with a crumpled piece of waxed paper.
- If a pan lid is too loose, place a double layer of waxed paper between the pan and lid; press the lid down firmly.
- After cleaning a wooden salad bowl, rub it with a crumbled piece of waxed paper to seal the surface.
- Keep your waffle iron in good shape by unplugging the iron and brushing off the grids as soon as you remove the last waffle. Place a sheet of waxed paper on the bottom grid and close the iron. Remove the paper when the iron is cool.
- Whenever sifting or scooping cocoa powder or confectioners' sugar into a measuring cup, set the cup on a sheet of waxed paper. That way, you can easily transfer any cocoa or sugar spills back into the container.
- Grating foods like chocolate and lemon zest over a sheet of waxed paper saves on cleanup.
- Cleanup's easy when you roll out pastry or cookie dough on a waxed-paper-covered countertop. Keep the waxed paper from slipping by sprinkling a few drops of water on the countertop before arranging the paper.

▶ Separate layers of decorated, moist or sticky cookies with waxed paper to prevent them from sticking together.

▶ Before freezing cookies, place a sheet of waxed paper between cookie layers.

▶ Your cakes and breads won't stick to the pan if you grease the pan, line the bottom with waxed paper, then grease the waxed paper's surface. Turn the baked cake or bread out of the pan and peel off the waxed paper while it's still warm.

▶ If a cake or loaf of bread has cooled so long that the waxed paper sticks to the bottom, lightly brush the paper with warm water, let stand 1 minute, then remove the paper.

▶ To keep the plate clean while frosting a cake, first place several strips of waxed paper around the edges of the plate, then position the cake on top. Once the cake's frosted, carefully pull out the waxed paper strips and discard.

▶ When frosting a cake on a cooling rack, first place a sheet of waxed paper under the rack to catch any drips. The frosting on the paper can either be returned to the frosting bowl (providing it's crumb-free) or given to your favorite frosting licker. In either case, the countertop's clean.

▶ Make an instant, disposable pastry bag by folding a square of waxed paper in half diagonally to form a triangle. Shape the triangle into a cone, securing the top edge with Scotch tape or a paper clip. Fill two-thirds full with frosting, melted chocolate, etc., fold down the top of the bag, then snip off the pointed end so the hole is the desired diameter.

▶ When piping a decorative design out of melted chocolate, do so on a waxed-paper-lined baking sheet. Refrigerate until the chocolate is set, then peel off the waxed paper and transfer the chocolate decoration to the dessert.

▶ Protect yourself and your kitchen from spatters when whipping cream by laying a sheet of waxed paper (with a hole cut for the beater stems) on top of the bowl.

▶ Lining the bottom of your microwave oven with waxed paper will keep cleanup to a minimum.

▶ Waxed paper is a good cover for microwaved food when you want much of the steam to escape.

▶ When cooking or reheating thick mixtures like oatmeal or pea soup in a microwave oven, cover the container with waxed paper to protect against spatters.

▶ Heat tortillas quickly in the microwave oven by wrapping them loosely in waxed paper.

▶ When melting butter in the microwave oven always cover the container with waxed paper to protect against spattered oven walls.

▶ Waxed paper is the perfect wrap for microwaved corn on the cob. Start by rinsing each ear off with water, then immediately wrap in waxed paper.

► After cooking soup, lay a double sheet of waxed paper on the surface, then refrigerate until cold. When you remove the waxed paper, the solidified fat will lift right off with it.

► *See also* ALUMINUM FOIL; PLASTIC WRAP

WHITE CHOCOLATE *see* CHOCOLATE

WILD RICE

► Did you know that wild rice isn't really a rice at all, but a long-grain marsh grass?

► Wild rice can be found in supermarkets either packaged alone or with other, less expensive rices. Natural food stores also sell it in bulk.

► Store wild rice in an airtight container in a cool, dark place. Stored properly, it can be kept almost indefinitely.

► *Wild rice yields:* 1 cup = 3 cups cooked.

► Wild rice needs to be thoroughly cleaned before cooking. The best method is to place the rice in a medium bowl and fill it with cold water. Give it a couple of stirs and set it aside for a few minutes. Any debris will float to the surface and the water can then be poured off.

► Wild rice can be cooked by either boiling or baking. Its distinctive, nutty flavor and chewy texture makes it an ideal accompaniment for duck and other game birds and meats.

► Make the relatively expensive wild rice go farther by combining it with brown or white rice, or bulghur wheat. Cook the grains separately (they'll all have slightly different cooking times), then combine.

► Grind wild rice to a powder in a blender and use it in baked goods like breads, muffins and pancakes. Substitute up to a quarter of the all-purpose flour with wild-rice "flour."

► Wild rice can be used in all kinds of soups and stews. Or make a wild-rice soup by pureeing cooked brown rice with enough broth to make a nice soup base, then stir in cooked wild rice and some sautéed garlic and onions.

► Cooked wild rice is great in salads, stuffings for poultry or acorn squash, and pilafs. Combine it with other ingredients—a little of this flavorful food goes a long way.

► Puffed wild rice makes a delicious garnish for everything from salads to soups to vegetables. In a large skillet over medium heat, sauté about ⅔ cup cleaned (rinsed and blotted dry) wild rice in 1 tablespoon olive oil. Cook, stirring often, until most of the grains have cracked open and puffed slightly. Turn out onto paper towels; salt and pepper to taste.

WINE

▶ Don't take offense if someone calls you an oenophile [EE-nuh-fyl]. It simply describes someone who enjoys wine, and often is used to refer to a connoisseur.

▶ **Vintage wine:** A wine made from grapes harvested in a specific year (1992, for example), which is indicated on the wine label. **Nonvintage wine** is made from the juice of grapes harvested from several years—there's no year noted on the label of a nonvintage wine.

▶ **Blush wines** are generally made with red grapes (some producers mix red and white grapes), but the juice has had a very brief contact with the grape skins. This produces wines that can range in color from shell pink to pale orange to barely red. Blush wines can range from dry to sweet and may be light-to medium-bodied. They should be served chilled, but not icy. The term blush wine has all but replaced the more dated term "rosé."

▶ **Fortified wine** is one to which brandy or other spirit has been added in order to increase the alcohol content. Such wines include Madeira, Marsala, port and sherry.

▶ Storing wine bottles on their sides prevents the cork from drying and shrinking, which would allow air to enter the bottle and negatively affect the wine's flavor.

▶ Wine storage: The three basic parameters for a wine-storage location are that it be dark, vibration free and at an even temperature. The ideal temperature for wine storage is 55°F. However, it can be kept anywhere from 45° to 70°F, providing the temperature is consistent. The higher the temperature, the faster a wine will age; white wines are more susceptible to heat than are reds.

▶ White wine should be served at temperatures somewhere between 50° and 55°F. Since cold mutes flavors, the cheaper the wine, the colder you want it.

▶ White wine should be refrigerated for only about 2 hours before serving. Refrigerating it for more than a few hours can dull both flavor and aroma.

▶ You can "speed-chill" white wine at the last minute by completely submerging the bottle in a bucket or large pot filled with half ice and half water for about 20 minutes. This will chill the wine much faster than ice alone. If the container is shallow, invert the bottle for the last 5 minutes to make sure all the wine is chilled.

▶ If you're serving several wines at a meal remember these guidelines: Serve a young wine before an older one; a white wine before a red one; a light-bodied wine before a robust wine; and a dry wine before a sweet one.

▶ Buy a red wine at least 2 days before you're planning to serve it and let it rest in a cool, dark place.

▶ Red wine should be served at around 65°F. The term "room temperature" is now outdated—it's based on the chillier room temperatures of days gone by, not the 72°F average of today's home.

▸ To open a bottle of wine, cut through the foil all the way around, about ¼ inch below the lip of the bottle. There are special foil-cutter tools available in wine shops, or you can simply use a sharp knife. Remove the foil at the point you cut it. Use a damp cloth or heavy-duty paper towel to wipe any mold or other residue off the cork; also wipe the rim of the bottle. Position the corkscrew in the cork's center, turn the screw as far as it will go, then gently ease the cork out of the bottle. Wipe the rim of the bottle again, making sure to remove any bits of cork. During the entire uncorking process, handle the bottle gently so as not to unnecessarily disturb the wine.

▸ Red wines more than 8 years old often have a natural, harmless sediment in the bottle. Hold the bottle up to a strong light to check it. If you see sediment, decant the wine so no one gets the gritty residue in his or her mouth.

▸ Decanting is done either to separate the wine from any sediment deposited during the aging process, or to allow a wine to "breathe" in order to enhance its flavor. When decanting an older wine, care should be taken not to disturb the sediment. A wine basket (also called *cradle* or *Burgundy* basket) can be used to move the bottle in a horizontal position (so as not to disturb the sediment) from where it was stored to where it will be decanted. This keeps the sediment from disseminating throughout the wine. If you don't have a basket, stand the bottle upright for an hour so the sediment can settle to the bottom of the bottle. Once the foil and cork are removed, gently wipe the mouth of the bottle. Then begin slowly pouring the wine into the decanter, placing a strong light (a candle is charming, but a flashlight is more practical) behind or below the neck of the bottle. The light lets you see the first signs of sediment, at which point you stop pouring.

▸ If tiny pieces of cork break off and fall into the wine, strain the wine through a fine sieve into a decanter. If you don't have a fine sieve, strain the wine through a double thickness of cheesecloth.

▸ Avoid drips when pouring wine by giving the bottle a slight twist just as you finish pouring and are returning the bottle to the upright position.

▸ Use wineglasses made of clear glass, with a rim that curves in slightly (the exception being the champagne flute). The clear glass allows you to see the true color of the wine, and the inwardly curving rim makes it possible to swirl the wine in order to release its bouquet.

▸ Wineglasses should be filled only half to two-thirds full so the wine has room to be swirled, thereby releasing more of its aroma.

▸ In some states (California, for example) it's not uncommon for people to bring a special bottle of wine to a restaurant. A quick call to the establishment will confirm if this is possible, as well as the amount of the corkage fee—a charge for opening and serving a patron's bottle of wine. Some restaurants charge a lower fee if the wine you bring is not on their wine list, such as might be the case with an older wine or a particularly distinctive vintage.

▶ Contact with air over a prolonged period can absolutely ruin the flavor of most wines. If you don't finish a bottle of wine, transfer the contents to a smaller bottle (thereby minimizing airspace) and seal it tightly. Try to drink the wine the next day. It's a good idea to keep a clean, empty half bottle (*see* WINE BOTTLES) on hand for just this purpose.

▶ Another way to keep air out of an opened bottle of wine is to "gas it." There are harmless canned gasses (a combination of nitrogen—N_2—and carbon dioxide—CO_2) on the market today that can simply be squirted into a partially full wine bottle. This blankets the wine's surface with gas, thereby blocking out the flavor-destructive oxygen. This wine-preserving gas is available in cans at most wine stores and specialty markets. Don't worry if the can feels empty—remember, gases are weightless.

▶ Cut down on calories and wine consumption by making wine spritzers. Pour about 4 ounces wine into a wineglass filled with ice cubes, fill the glass with carbonated water and stir gently. Top with a thin slice of lemon, if desired.

▶ *See also* BEER; CHAMPAGNE; LIQUORS, LIQUEURS AND MIXED DRINKS

WINE BOTTLES

▶ The *standard* wine bottle is 750 ml (milliliters), which is almost exactly equivalent to an American fifth (⅘ of a quart or 25.6 ounces). In answer to the stricter driving/alcohol limits in many states, the wine industry is introducing a new 500 ml bottle size. This new size—midway between a standard bottle and a *half bottle* (12.8 ounces)—is about 17 ounces, or two thirds of a standard bottle. Other wine-bottle sizes are: *split* (one quarter of a standard wine bottle); *magnum* (equivalent to 2 standard bottles in 1); *Jeroboam* (4 in 1); *gallon* (5 in 1); *Rehoboam* (6 in 1); *Methuselah* (8 in 1); *Salmanazar* (12 in 1); *Balthazar* (16 in 1); and *Nebuchadnezzar* (20 in 1).

▶ *See also* WINE

WINE IN FOOD

▶ Never cook with any wine or spirit you wouldn't drink. Cooking—and the process of reducing a sauce—will bring out the worst in an inferior potable.

▶ The "cooking wine" commonly found in supermarkets is generally an inferior product that would not be drunk on its own. It not only lacks distinction and flavor, but some of these potables have, at times, been adulterated with salt.

▶ Wine should never overpower the flavor of a dish. It should be a subtle and mysterious flavor that simply makes one want more of whatever dish it complements. Start by adding 1 to 2 tablespoons, cook the dish for a few minutes, then taste for flavor. You can always add more.

▶ In general, use dry, white wines for delicate seafood and poultry dishes; full-bodied wines are better partnered with hearty meat dishes, stews and dark sauces.

▶ If you're serving an expensive bottle of Cabernet or Bordeaux with dinner, there's no need to cook with the same wine (unless you're rich). Instead, choose a less expensive wine with compatible qualities.

W

▶ Unsure of which wine to cook with? Ask your local wine merchant for advice, telling him or her what you're preparing, as well as what wine you're serving with it.

▶ Fortified wines like Madeira, port and sherry have very strong flavors so caution is the byword when adding them to food.

▶ When preparing slow-cooking dishes like stew, add a splash of wine 20 minutes before the cooking time is finished. The flavor of wine dissipates during long cooking, and the final addition will give it more balance.

▶ Poaching fish in white wine (or part broth and part wine) gives it a delicious flavor.

▶ Wine makes a great marinade. Combine it with the other marinade ingredients, add the meat or poultry to be marinated, then cover and refrigerate overnight.

▶ Use wine mixed with a little oil or melted butter to baste meat and poultry.

▶ Wine is great for deglazing a pan. After food (usually meat) has been sautéed and removed from the pan, deglazing is done by adding a little wine (or other liquid) to the pan and stirring to loosen the browned bits of food on the bottom. After cooking a few minutes, this rich liquid can be drizzled over the cooked food, or used as a base for sauce.

▶ If you have a little wine left after dinner, recork and refrigerate it and use it the next day as part of a marinade for meat, chicken or fish (depending on the wine). It's also great added to soups, stews or sauces.

▶ Or add leftover wine (up to 1 cup per quart) to vinegar for instant wine vinegar.

▶ *See also* ALCOHOL; BEER; FLAMBÉING; WINE

WOKS *see* STIR-FRYING

YAMS

▶ Yams and sweet potatoes are often confused with one another, though they are from different plant species. In the southern United States, sweet potatoes are often called yams; to add to the confusion, canned sweet potatoes are frequently labeled yams.

▶ True yams are seldom grown in the United States. They're similar in size and shape to sweet potatoes, but have a higher moisture and sugar content. Yams can be found in most Latin-American markets.

▶ Look for unblemished specimens with tight, unwrinkled skins. They should be free of soft spots.

▶ Store yams in a cool, dry, well-ventilated place for up to 1 week. Under perfect temperature conditions (dry and around 55°F), they can be kept for up to 4 weeks. Do not refrigerate.

▶ Yams may be substituted for sweet potatoes in most recipes.

▶ *See also* SWEET POTATOES

YEAST

▶ Yeast is a living organism that thrives on the natural sugar in starch. When combined with moisture and warmth, yeast begins to ferment, converting the flour's starchy nutrients into alcohol and carbon dioxide gas. Gas bubbles trapped in the elastic gluten mesh of a dough or batter make it rise.

▶ **Active dry yeast** comes in ¼-ounce envelopes; it can also be purchased in jars, or in bulk at natural food stores. Active dry yeast comes in two forms—regular and quick-rising, which may be used interchangeably. All active dry yeast has been dehydrated; its cells are alive, but dormant.

▶ Quick-rising yeast is an active dry yeast that leavens breads in a third to half the time of regular dry yeast.

▶ Quick-rising yeast can be substituted for regular active dry yeast in most bread recipes, measure for measure.

▶ Store dry yeast in a cool, dry place; it can also be refrigerated or frozen. Properly stored, it's reliable when used by the expiration date stamped on the envelope or jar. Bulk dry yeast is often risky because you don't know how old it is or under what conditions it's been stored.

▶ **Compressed, fresh yeast**, which is sold in .6-ounce and 2-ounce cakes, is moist and extremely perishable. It should be used by the expiration date on the package.

▶ Store compressed, fresh yeast in a plastic bag in the refrigerator for 2 to

4 weeks. It can also be frozen for up to 6 months; defrost it at room temperature.

▸ Before using compressed yeast, bring it to room temperature.

▸ *Yeast yields:* 1 ¼-ounce package dry yeast = 1 scant tablespoon dry yeast, 1 .6-ounce cake compressed, fresh yeast.

▸ If you're not sure if yeast is still okay, all you need to do is "proof" it. Combine the yeast and 1 teaspoon sugar with the warm liquid called for in the recipe; let stand for about 5 minutes. If the mixture begins to swell and bubble, the yeast is alive and well. If there's no activity, discard the mixture and start over with new yeast. There's absolutely no way to revive dead yeast.

▸ The temperature of the liquid in which yeast is dissolved is very important. Too much heat will kill it, too little will slow its growth. Dissolve dry yeast in liquids at 105° to 115°F; compressed yeast at 95°F. Unless you're an experienced baker, use a thermometer for accurate temperature readings.

▸ Quick-mix method: Dry yeast doesn't have to be dissolved before it's used. It can be combined with part of the flour then mixed with very warm water with a temperature range of 120° to 130°F. The flour buffers the yeast from the higher water temperature.

▸ Generally, 1 package or cake of yeast will leaven 4 to 5 cups flour.

▸ Extra yeast may be used to speed leavening, but too much produces a porous texture and yeasty flavor.

▸ Too little yeast creates a heavy, dense loaf of bread.

▸ Doughs rich in butter, eggs, sweeteners, fruits or nuts often require double the amount of yeast.

▸ *See also* BREADS, GENERAL; BREADS, YEAST

Y

YOGURT

▸ Always check the pull-date on the bottom of a yogurt carton to be sure the yogurt you buy is the freshest possible.

▸ Store yogurt in the refrigerator for up to 10 days after the carton date.

▸ Stirring yogurt vigorously will cause it to become thin and runny.

▸ For extra-thick yogurt to use in sauces and desserts, turn yogurt into a sieve lined with a double layer of dampened cheesecloth; set over a bowl. Cover with plastic wrap and refrigerate for 1 hour to drain. Use a rubber spatula to gently stir the yogurt. Cover and refrigerate for 4 to 6 hours, or until yogurt reaches the desired thickness. Discard the liquid in the bowl, or save and use in baked goods. Cover and refrigerate thickened yogurt for up to 1 week.

▸ Bringing yogurt to room temperature before adding to a hot mixture will prevent the mixture from separating.

▸ When cooking with yogurt, heat it gently and only until the mixture is warmed through. Allowing the mixture to boil will cause it to separate.

▶ Yogurt won't separate as easily in hot preparations that are flour-based.

▶ Heating yogurt to temperatures higher than 120°F destroys the beneficial bacteria, though nutrients such as protein and calcium remain. To retain the friendly bacteria in mixtures such as soups and sauces, stir the yogurt into the hot mixture toward the end of the cooking time and heat only until warmed through.

▶ To reconstitute a cooked yogurt mixture that has separated, try this: For each cup yogurt, mix 1 teaspoon cornstarch or 2 teaspoons all-purpose flour with ½ tablespoon cold water and stir into the separated mixture. Heat slowly, stirring constantly, until mixture recombines and thickens.

▶ Make your own fruit-flavored yogurt by buying plain yogurt and adding crushed or chopped fruit, honey, vanilla extract, spices, etc. That way you know exactly what you're getting, and you get exactly what you want.

▶ Reduce calories in salad dressing and dips by substituting plain yogurt for mayonnaise or sour cream.

▶ Yogurt can also be substituted for sour cream in baked goods.

▶ Mix plain yogurt with chopped or crushed fruit, flavor with vanilla and spices, if desired, and sweeten to taste. Turn the mixture into a plastic-wrap-lined loaf pan, freeze until solid, then wrap airtight. Cut off slices of this frozen fruited yogurt as you want them. Let the slices stand at room temperature for about 10 minutes before serving.

▶ The benefits of yogurt have long been touted. It's a good source of B vitamins, protein and calcium and is much more digestible than fresh milk. It's said to keep the intestinal system populated with good bacteria and therefore healthy. Most of this last benefit, however, is lost when yogurt is frozen.

Z

ZEST, CITRUS *see* CITRUS FRUITS

ZESTER *see* CITRUS ZESTER

ZUCCHINI *see* SQUASH

ABOUT THE AUTHOR

Sharon Tyler Herbst is a nationally known culinary expert and media personality. She appears on ABC's *Good Morning America* as their "kitchen-tip" expert, and is the award-winning author of *Food Lover's Companion*, *The Joy of Cookies*, and *Simply Sensational Desserts* and *Breads*. Her 1992 book *Cooking Smart* was both a Julia Child Cookbook Award nominee and the winner of the Cook's Choice Award. She is a past president of the International Association of Culinary Professionals and served on its board of directors for eight years. She lives in the San Francisco Bay area.